BIRDS *of* FLORIDA

Bill Pranty
Kurt A. Radamaker
Gregory Kennedy

with contributions from
Krista Kagume, Chris Fisher & Andy Bezener

Lone Pine Publishing International

Distributed by Lone Pine Publishing
1808 B Street NW, Suite 140
Auburn, WA USA 98001

Website: www.lonepinepublishing.com

Library and Archives Canada Cataloguing in Publication

Pranty, Bill
 Birds of Florida / Bill Pranty, Kurt Radamaker, Gregory Kennedy.

Includes bibliographical references and index.
ISBN-13: 978-976-8200-06-8
ISBN-10: 976-8200-06-5

 1. Birds—Florida—Identification. I. Radamaker, Kurt, 1960–
II. Kennedy, Gregory, 1956– III. Title.

QL684.F6P73 2006   598'.09759   C2006-901650-X

Illustrations: Gary Ross, Ted Nordhagen, Ewa Pluciennik
Cover Illustration: Great Egret, by Gary Ross
Scanning & Digital Film: Elite Lithographers Co.

PC: P13

CONTENTS

NONPASSERINES

PASSERINES

ACKNOWLEDGMENTS

We thank our editors Nicholle Carrière and Wendy Pirk for their enthusiasm and assistance in producing this book. Bill Pranty thanks Holly Lovell and Darcy Stumbaugh for their support and Darcy for taking the author photograph. Kurt Radamaker thanks his wife Cindy for her support.

—*Bill Pranty and Kurt Radamaker*

Thanks are also extended to the growing family of ornithologists and dedicated birders who have offered their inspiration and expertise to help build Lone Pine's expanding library of field guides. Additional thanks go to John Acorn, Chris Fisher, Andy Bezener and Eloise Pulos for their contributions to previous books in this series. Furthermore, thank you to Gary Ross, Ted Nordhagen and Ewa Pluciennik, whose skilled illustrations have brought each page to life.

Monk Parakeet

Black-bellied Whistling-Duck
size 21 in • p. 36

Fulvous Whistling-Duck
size 20 in • p. 37

Snow Goose
size 31 in • p. 38

Canada Goose
size 35 in • p. 39

Muscovy Duck
size 31 in • p. 40

Wood Duck
size 17 in • p. 41

Gadwall
size 20 in • p. 42

American Wigeon
size 20 in • p. 43

American Black Duck
size 22 in • p. 44

Mallard
size 24 in • p. 45

Mottled Duck
size 21 in • p. 46

Blue-winged Teal
size 15 in • p. 47

Northern Shoveler
size 19 in • p. 48

Northern Pintail
size 23 in • p. 49

Green-winged Teal
size 14 in • p. 50

Canvasback
size 21 in • p. 51

Redhead
size 20 in • p. 52

Ring-necked Duck
size 16 in • p. 53

Greater Scaup
size 18 in • p. 54

Lesser Scaup
size 17 in • p. 55

Black Scoter
size 19 in • p. 56

Bufflehead
size 14 in • p. 57

Common Goldeneye
size 18 in • p. 58

Hooded Merganser
size 17 in • p. 59

Red-breasted Merganser
size 23 in • p. 60

Ruddy Duck
size 16 in • p. 61

Wild Turkey
size 36 in • p. 62

Northern Bobwhite
size 12 in • p. 63

Red-throated Loon
size 25 in • p. 64

Common Loon
size 32 in • p. 65

Pied-billed Grebe
size 13 in • p. 66

Horned Grebe
size 13 in • p. 67

Cory's Shearwater
size 20 in • p. 68

Audubon's Shearwater
size 12 in • p. 69

Wilson's Storm-Petrel
size 7 in • p. 70

Masked Booby
size 30 in • p. 71

Brown Booby
size 30 in • p. 72

Northern Gannet
size 36 in • p. 73

American White Pelican
size 60 in • p. 74

Brown Pelican
size 48 in • p. 75

Double-crested Cormorant
size 29 in • p. 76

Anhinga
size 36 in • p. 77

Magnificent Frigatebird
size 36 in • p. 78

American Bittern
size 25 in • p. 79

Least Bittern
size 13 in • p. 80

Great Blue Heron
size 48 in • p. 81

Great Egret
size 36 in • p. 82

Snowy Egret
size 24 in • p. 83

Little Blue Heron
size 24 in • p. 84

Tricolored Heron
size 26 in • p. 85

Reddish Egret
size 30 in • p. 86

Cattle Egret
size 21 in • p. 87

Green Heron
size 19 in • p. 88

Black-crowned Night-Heron
size 25 in • p. 89

Yellow-crowned Night-Heron
size 24 in • p. 90

White Ibis
size 22 in • p. 91

Glossy Ibis
size 24 in • p. 92

Roseate Spoonbill
size 32 in • p. 93

Wood Stork
size 36 in • p. 94

Black Vulture
size 25 in • p. 95

Turkey Vulture
size 29 in • p. 96

Greater Flamingo
size 48 in • p. 97

Osprey
size 24 in • p. 98

Swallow-tailed Kite
size 23 in • p. 99

White-tailed Kite
size 16 in • p. 100

Snail Kite
size 17 in • p. 101

Mississippi Kite
size 15 in • p. 102

Bald Eagle
size 40 in • p. 103

Northern Harrier
size 20 in • p. 104

Sharp-shinned Hawk
size 12 in • p. 105

Cooper's Hawk
size 17 in • p. 106

Red-shouldered Hawk
size 19 in • p. 107

Broad-winged Hawk
size 17 in • p. 108

Short-tailed Hawk
size 16 in • p. 109

Red-tailed Hawk
size 23 in • p. 110

Crested Caracara
size 23 in • p. 111

American Kestrel
size 8 in • p. 112

Merlin
size 11 in • p. 113

Peregrine Falcon
size 17 in • p. 114

REFERENCE GUIDE

RAILS, LIMPKINS & CRANES

Black Rail
size 6 in • p. 115

Clapper Rail
size 14 in • p. 116

King Rail
size 15 in • p. 117

Virginia Rail
size 10 in • p. 118

Sora
size 9 in • p. 119

Purple Swamphen
size 16 in • p. 120

Purple Gallinule
size 13 in • p. 121

Common Moorhen
size 14 in • p. 122

American Coot
size 15 in • p. 123

Limpkin
size 27 in • p. 124

Sandhill Crane
size 48 in • p. 125

Whooping Crane
size 60 in • p. 126

SHOREBIRDS

Black-bellied Plover
size 12 in • p. 127

American Golden-Plover
size 11 in • p. 128

Snowy Plover
size 7 in • p. 129

Wilson's Plover
size 7 in • p. 130

Semipalmated Plover
size 7 in • p. 131

Piping Plover
size 7 in • p. 132

Killdeer
size 10 in • p. 133

American Oystercatcher
size 18 in • p. 134

Black-necked Stilt
size 15 in • p. 135

American Avocet
size 18 in • p. 136

Greater Yellowlegs
size 14 in • p. 137

Lesser Yellowlegs
size 11 in • p. 138

Solitary Sandpiper
size 8 in • p. 139

Willet
size 15 in • p. 140

Spotted Sandpiper
size 8 in • p. 141

Upland Sandpiper
size 12 in • p. 142

Whimbrel
size 18 in • p. 143

Long-billed Curlew
size 23 in • p. 144

Marbled Godwit
size 18 in • p. 145

Ruddy Turnstone
size 10 in • p. 146

Red Knot
size 11 in • p. 147

Sanderling
size 8 in • p. 148

Semipalmated Sandpiper
size 6 in • p. 149

Western Sandpiper
size 7 in • p. 150

Least Sandpiper
size 6 in • p. 151

White-rumped Sandpiper
size 8 in • p. 152

Pectoral Sandpiper
size 9 in • p. 153

Purple Sandpiper
size 9 in • p. 154

Dunlin
size 9 in • p. 155

Stilt Sandpiper
size 9 in • p. 156

Buff-breasted Sandpiper
size 8 in • p. 157

Short-billed Dowitcher
size 12 in • p. 158

Long-billed Dowicher
size 12 in • p. 159

Wilson's Snipe
size 11 in • p. 160

American Woodcock
size 11 in • p. 161

Wilson's Phalarope
size 9 in • p. 162

Pomarine Jaeger
size 22 in • p. 163

Parasitic Jaeger
size 18 in • p. 164

Laughing Gull
size 16 in • p. 165

Bonaparte's Gull
size 13 in • p. 166

Ring-billed Gull
size 19 in • p. 167

Herring Gull
size 25 in • p. 168

GULLS & ALLIES

Lesser Black-backed Gull
size 21 in • p. 169

Great Black-backed Gull
size 30 in • p. 170

Gull-billed Tern
size 14 in • p. 171

Caspian Tern
size 21 in • p. 172

Royal Tern
size 20 in • p. 173

Sandwich Tern
size 15 in • p. 174

Roseate Tern
size 14 in • p. 175

Common Tern
size 15 in • p. 176

Forster's Tern
size 15 in • p. 177

Least Tern
size 9 in • p. 178

Bridled Tern
size 15 in • p. 179

Sooty Tern
size 16 in • p. 180

Black Tern
size 10 in • p. 181

Brown Noddy
size 16 in • p. 182

Black Noddy
size 14 in • p. 183

Black Skimmer
size 18 in • p. 184

DOVES, PARROTS & CUCKOOS

Rock Pigeon
size 13 in • p. 185

White-crowned Pigeon
size 14 in • p. 186

Eurasian Collared-Dove
size 14 in • p. 187

White-winged Dove
size 12 in • p. 188

Mourning Dove
size 12 in • p. 189

Common Ground-Dove
size 7 in • p. 190

Budgerigar
size 7 in • p. 191

Monk Parakeet
size 12 in • p. 192

Black-hooded Parakeet
size 12 in • p. 193

White-winged Parakeet
size 9 in • p. 194

Yellow-chevroned Parakeet
size 9 in • p. 194

DOVES, PARROTS & CUCKOOS

Mitred Parakeet
size 15 in • p. 195

Red-masked Parakeet
size 14 in • p. 195

Rose-ringed Parakeet
size 16 in • p. 196

Red-crowned Parrot
size 12 in • p. 197

Orange-winged Parrot
size 12 in • p. 197

Yellow-billed Cuckoo
size 12 in • p. 198

Mangrove Cuckoo
size 13 in • p. 199

Smooth-billed Ani
size 14 in • p. 200

OWLS

Barn Owl
size 16 in • p. 201

Eastern Screech-Owl
size 9 in • p. 202

Great Horned Owl
size 22 in • p. 203

Burrowing Owl
size 9 in • p. 204

NIGHTJARS, SWIFTS & HUMMINGBIRDS

Barred Owl
size 21 in • p. 205

Short-eared Owl
size 15 in • p. 206

Lesser Nighthawk
size 9 in • p. 207

Common Nighthawk
size 9 in • p. 208

Antillean Nighthawk
size 8 in • p. 209

Chuck-will's-widow
size 12 in • p. 210

Whip-poor-will
size 10 in • p. 211

Chimney Swift
size 5 in • p. 212

Ruby-throated Hummingbird
size 4 in • p. 213

Black-chinned Hummingbird
size 3 in • p. 214

Rufous Hummingbird
size 4 in • p. 215

WOODPECKERS

Belted Kingfisher
size 13 in • p. 216

Red-headed Woodpecker
size 9 in • p. 217

Red-bellied Woodpecker
size 10 in • p. 218

Yellow-bellied Sapsucker
size 8 in • p. 219

WOODPECKERS

Downy Woodpecker
size 6 in • p. 220

Hairy Woodpecker
size 9 in • p. 221

Red-cockaded Woodpecker
size 8 in • p. 222

Northern Flicker
size 13 in • p. 223

Pileated Woodpecker
size 18 in • p. 224

Eastern Wood-Pewee
size 6 in • p. 226

Acadian Flycatcher
size 6 in • p. 227

Least Flycatcher
size 5 in • p. 228

FLYCATCHERS

Eastern Phoebe
size 7 in • p. 229

Vermilion Flycatcher
size 6 in • p. 230

Great Crested Flycatcher
size 9 in • p. 231

La Sagra's Flycatcher
size 7 in • p. 232

Western Kingbird
size 9 in • p. 233

Eastern Kingbird
size 8 in • p. 234

Gray Kingbird
size 9 in • p. 235

Scissor-tailed Flycatcher
size 10 in • p. 236

SHRIKES & VIREOS

Loggerhead Shrike
size 9 in • p. 237

White-eyed Vireo
size 5 in • p. 238

Yellow-throated Vireo
size 5 in • p. 239

Blue-headed Vireo
size 6 in • p. 240

Philadelphia Vireo
size 5 in • p. 241

Red-eyed Vireo
size 6 in • p. 242

Black-whiskered Vireo
size 6 in • p. 243

JAYS & CROWS

Blue Jay
size 12 in • p. 244

Florida Scrub-Jay
size 11 in • p. 245

American Crow
size 19 in • p. 246

Fish Crow
size 15 in • p. 247

SWALLOWS

Purple Martin
size 8 in • p. 248

Tree Swallow
size 5 in • p. 249

Northern Rough-winged Swallow
size 5 in • p. 250

Bank Swallow
size 5 in • p. 251

Cliff Swallow
size 5 in • p. 252

Cave Swallow
size 5 in • p. 253

Barn Swallow
size 7 in • p. 254

CHICKADEES, NUTHATCHES & WRENS

Carolina Chickadee
size 4 in • p. 255

Tufted Titmouse
size 6 in • p. 256

Red-breasted Nuthatch
size 4 in • p. 257

White-breasted Nuthatch
size 6 in • p. 258

Brown-headed Nuthatch
size 4 in • p. 259

Brown Creeper
size 5 in • p. 260

Carolina Wren
size 5 in • p. 261

House Wren
size 5 in • p. 262

KINGLETS, GNATCATCHERS & THRUSHES

Winter Wren
size 4 in • p. 263

Sedge Wren
size 4 in • p. 264

Marsh Wren
size 5 in • p. 265

Red-whiskered Bulbul
size 8 in • p. 266

Golden-crowned Kinglet
size 4 in • p. 267

Ruby-crowned Kinglet
size 4 in • p. 268

Blue-gray Gnatcatcher
size 4 in • p. 269

Eastern Bluebird
size 7 in • p. 270

Veery
size 7 in • p. 271

Gray-cheeked Thrush
size 8 in • p. 272

Swainson's Thrush
size 7 in • p. 273

Hermit Thrush
size 7 in • p. 274

Wood Thrush
size 8 in • p. 275

American Robin
size 10 in • p. 276

Gray Catbird
size 9 in • p. 277

Northern Mockingbird
size 10 in • p. 278

Brown Thrasher
size 11 in • p. 279

European Starling
size 8 in • p. 280

Common Myna
size 9 in • p. 281

Hill Myna
size 10 in • p. 282

American Pipit
size 7 in • p. 283

Cedar Waxwing
size 7 in • p. 284

Blue-winged Warbler
size 5 in • p. 285

Golden-winged Warbler
size 5 in • p. 286

Tennessee Warbler
size 5 in • p. 287

Orange-crowned Warbler
size 5 in • p. 288

Northern Parula
size 4 in • p. 289

Yellow Warbler
size 5 in • p. 290

Chestnut-sided Warbler
size 5 in • p. 291

Magnolia Warbler
size 5 in • p. 292

Cape May Warbler
size 5 in • p. 293

Black-throated Blue Warbler
size 5 in • p. 294

Yellow-rumped Warbler
size 6 in • p. 295

Black-throated Green Warbler
size 5 in • p. 296

Blackburnian Warbler
size 5 in • p. 297

Yellow-throated Warbler
size 5 in • p. 298

Pine Warbler
size 5 in • p. 299

Prairie Warbler
size 5 in • p. 300

Palm Warbler
size 5 in • p. 301

Bay-breasted Warbler
size 6 in • p. 302

Blackpoll Warbler	Cerulean Warbler	Black-and-white Warbler	American Redstart
size 5 in • p. 303	size 5 in • p. 304	size 5 in • p. 305	size 5 in • p. 306

Prothonotary Warbler	Worm-eating Warbler	Swainson's Warbler	Ovenbird
size 5 in • p. 307	size 5 in • p. 308	size 5 in • p. 309	size 6 in • p. 310

Northern Waterthrush	Louisiana Waterthrush	Kentucky Warbler	Common Yellowthroat
size 6 in • p. 311	size 6 in • p. 312	size 5 in • p. 313	size 5 in • p. 314

Hooded Warbler	Yellow-breasted Chat	Summer Tanager	Scarlet Tanager
size 5 in • p. 315	size 7 in • p. 316	size 8 in • p. 317	size 7 in • p. 318

Eastern Towhee	Bachman's Sparrow	Chipping Sparrow	Field Sparrow
size 8 in • p. 319	size 6 in • p. 320	size 6 in • p. 321	size 6 in • p. 322

Vesper Sparrow	Savannah Sparrow	Grasshopper Sparrow	Henslow's Sparrow
size 6 in • p. 323	size 6 in • p. 324	size 5 in • p. 325	size 5 in • p. 326

Nelson's Sharp-tailed Sparrow	Saltmarsh Sharp-tailed Sparrow	Seaside Sparrow	Song Sparrow
size 5 in • p. 327	size 5 in • p. 328	size 6 in • p. 329	size 7 in • p. 330

Swamp Sparrow
size 6 in • p. 331

White-throated Sparrow
size 7 in • p. 332

White-crowned Sparrow
size 6 in • p. 333

Dark-eyed Junco
size 6 in • p. 334

Northern Cardinal
size 8 in • p. 335

Rose-breasted Grosbeak
size 8 in • p. 336

Blue Grosbeak
size 7 in • p. 337

Indigo Bunting
size 5 in • p. 338

Painted Bunting
size 5 in • p. 339

Dickcissel
size 7 in • p. 340

Bobolink
size 7 in • p. 341

Red-winged Blackbird
size 9 in • p. 342

Eastern Meadowlark
size 9 in • p. 343

Yellow-headed Blackbird
size 10 in • p. 344

Brewer's Blackbird
size 9 in • p. 345

Common Grackle
size 12 in • p. 346

Boat-tailed Grackle
size 15 in • p. 347

Shiny Cowbird
size 8 in • p. 348

Bronzed Cowbird
size 9 in • p. 349

Brown-headed Cowbird
size 7 in • p. 350

Orchard Oriole
size 7 in • p. 351

Spot-breasted Oriole
size 9 in • p. 352

Baltimore Oriole
size 8 in • p. 353

House Finch
size 6 in • p. 354

Pine Siskin
size 5 in • p. 355

American Goldfinch
size 5 in • p. 356

House Sparrow
size 6 in • p. 357

INTRODUCTION

BIRDING IN FLORIDA

In recent decades, birding has evolved from an eccentric pursuit practiced by a few elderly folks to a continent-wide activity that boasts tens of thousands of professional and dedicated amateur participants, as well as literally millions of feeder-watchers and other interested observers. There are plenty of good reasons why birding has become so popular. Many people find it simple and relaxing, while others enjoy the outdoor exercise that it affords. Some see it as a rewarding learning experience, an opportunity to socialize with like-minded people and a way to monitor the health of the local environment. Most of us watch birds to connect with nature—*birds are beautiful!* A visit to any of our region's premier birding locations, such as Apalachicola National Forest, Everglades National Park, Fort De Soto Park or Merritt Island National Wildlife Refuge, would undoubtedly uncover still more reasons why people go birding.

We are fortunate to live in Florida, a state known for its great biological diversity and its conservation ethic (more than 25% of the state is in public ownership). In addition to supporting about 150 breeding species of birds, a large majority of which are year-round residents, we have more than 50 migratory species that move through during spring and/or fall, and nearly 130 species that winter here after migrating from their breeding grounds north of the state. An additional 135 species visit the state irregularly (i.e., less than annually) or no longer occur (i.e., are extirpated or extinct). Finally, Florida harbors breeding populations of about 30 exotic species—those whose ranges do not naturally include Florida but that were brought here as pets or for ornamental or hunting purposes. Florida contains more exotic birds than any other state (more than 100 exotic species have been documented!), most of which fortunately do not impact native species or habitats. In all, 494 species are on the official Florida bird list maintained by the Florida Ornithological Society Records Committee. The bird list increases by 3 or 4 species each year, as birds stray from their native ranges or as their populations and ranges expand.

From Florida's nearly 600 documented bird species, we have selected for the main part of this book 325 that occur annually. An additional 39 species are found in the appendix (pp. 358–67); these species are either less common, occur less frequently or unpredictably or require great effort to see (e.g., taking a boat trip many miles offshore). Space restrictions prevent us from including dozens of other species that may be seen in Florida, especially by tenacious birders or by those who "chase" rarities that show up throughout our state.

Snowy Egret

BEGINNING TO LEARN THE BIRDS

The Challenge of Birding

Birding can be extremely challenging, and learning to identify most of the birds that may be seen in Florida is a long process. But fear not! The species pictured in this guide will help you get started. Although any standard North American field guide will help you identify birds, such guides can be daunting because they cover the entire continent and present an overwhelming number of species. By focusing specifically on the regularly occurring bird life of Florida, we hope to make the introduction to the world of birding a little less intimidating.

Do not expect to become an expert quickly. It takes years of careful study to become knowledgeable on the status and distribution of Florida's birds, and to recognize the more than 1500 different plumages that may be seen in our state. And remember that not even the most expert birder or ornithologist has seen every species that has occurred in Florida, or can identify all the birds that he or she encounters. Nevertheless, all birders enjoy—and are thrilled by—the continual learning process that birding provides. As your interest grows, your experience and competence will increase. Christmas Bird Counts, Breeding Bird Surveys, birding festivals, banding stations, hawk watches and biannual meetings of the Florida Ornithological Society all provide a chance for novice, intermediate and expert birders to share enthusiasm for birds and birding. Whatever your interest and skill levels, there are ample opportunities to get involved.

Classification: The Order of Things

To biologists, the fundamental unit of classification of plants and animals is the species (this word is singular as well as plural—"specie" is not a word). Members of a species look alike and typically breed solely among themselves, although species may hybridize on rare occasions. Each species has a scientific name—usually derived from Latin or Greek—that designates genus and species (and which is always italicized) and a single accredited English name. (Many species have several local or vernacular names that may cause confusion or have had their English names changed over the years. To avoid confusion, birders should always use the currently accepted English name.) A bird has been properly identified only when it has been identified "to species," and most birders use the accredited English name. For example, "Common Moorhen" is the accredited English name for a common and widespread wetland bird in Florida, even though some people still call it by previous English names of "Florida Gallinule" or "Common Gallinule." *Gallinula chloropus* is its scientific name (*Gallinula*, always capitalized, is the genus or general name, and

Wood Duck

chloropus, always in lower-case, is the species or specific name). Some species with cosmopolitan distributions have different English names in various parts of the world. In the Old World, for instance, *Gallinula chloropus* is known simply as "Moorhen." Efforts to standardize the English names of birds worldwide are under way.

Many species are composed of races or subspecies (the two words are synonymous) that differ in appearance (sometimes considerably so) but are genetically similar. The human species is a good example—we differ in language, body proportions and skin, hair and eye color but we all belong to the same species. Subspecies may interbreed if their ranges overlap, or they may be geographically separate. In addition to race and species, ornithologists further group species into larger units. In increasing scope, these primary groups are genus, family, order, class, phylum and kingdom. The American Coot (*Fulica americana*) and Common Moorhen (*Gallinula chloropus*) are different species in different genera (plural of the word genus) in the family Rallidae (rails and allies). The rail, limpkin and crane families in turn are grouped within the order Gruiformes. All orders of birds are in the class Aves (birds), the phylum Vertebrata (animals with backbones) and the kingdom Animalia (animals).

Ornithologists arrange bird families according to their perceived evolutionary sequence, beginning with those thought to be most like the ancestors of modern birds and ending with those thought to have evolved most from ancestral birds. This taxonomic sequence changes as ornithologists, paleontologists and other scientists learn more about the relationships of birds. We have organized this book according to the current taxonomic sequence adopted by the American Ornithologists' Union, beginning with waterfowl and ending with finches. Some books group birds by color, by similarity of structure or even alphabetically by English name, but such guides quickly become obsolete once birders learn the proper taxonomic sequence.

Bald Eagle

TECHNIQUES OF BIRDING

Being in the right place at the right time to see birds involves both skill and luck. The more you know about a bird—its geographic and seasonal distributions in Florida, its preferred habitats, food preferences and hours of activity—the better your chances will be of finding it. It is much easier to find a Barred Owl in a swamp or oak hammock, or an Eastern Meadowlark in a prairie or grassy field than in habitats seldom or never used by these species. Winter, spring and fall are the busiest birding seasons in Florida. Temperatures may be moderate, and many birds are on the move. Male songbirds are easy to identify during spring and summer as they sing their courtship songs.

Throughout much of the year, diurnal birds are most visible in the first few hours after dawn and before dusk when they are foraging. But during winter, birds are often seen throughout the day, especially groups such as waterfowl, wading birds and hawks.

Binoculars

The small size, fine details and wary behavior of many birds make binoculars essential equipment for birding—even for backyard birding. Binoculars cost anywhere from $50 to $1500, and there is a large selection to choose from. Most beginners pay less than $200 for their first binoculars and then upgrade after a few years to more expensive ones once they decide that birding is a hobby that they want to pursue. The highest-quality binoculars cost more than $1000, but they have superb optics, are usually waterproof and fogproof, stand up to years of use and may have no-fault, lifetime guarantees.

The optical power of binoculars is designated by two numbers separated by an "x." For example, compact binoculars might be "8 x 21," while larger binoculars might have "10 x 40" stamped on them. In each case, the first number (always between 7 and 10 for a birding binocular) refers to the magnification, while the second number (between 20 and 45) indicates the diameter of the objective lens in millimeters. Larger lenses gather more light during low-light conditions than do smaller lenses but result in a heavier binocular. Most birders have 8x or 10x binoculars; beginners may want to start with an 8x glass. Field of view (the amount of area visible when looking through binoculars, expressed as the number of yards visible when viewing an image 1000 feet away) is another consideration. We recommend that beginners choose binoculars with a wide field of view to facilitate finding the bird in the binocular field.

Look through several binoculars before making a purchase. Talk to other birders, visit a birding store or attend a birding festival where major optics companies have booths at which you may compare several binoculars side-by-side and choose a model suitable for your needs and budget. Once you have made your purchase, get in the habit of keeping your eyes on the bird while raising your binocular up to your eyes, to avoid losing sight of it. You can also note an obvious landmark near the bird (a flower or a dead branch, for example) and then use that as a reference point to find the bird in your binocular field.

*Yellow-throated
Vireo*

Rufous Hummingbird

Spotting Scopes and Cameras

Birding in Florida, with its extensive shorelines and large lakes, requires the eventual purchase of a spotting scope. Most spotting scopes have interchangeable eyepieces that allow one to upgrade the scope rather than having to replace it with a more expensive model. Scopes generally come equipped with a 20x eyepiece, and eyepieces of up to 60x may be purchased. Most convenient is a zoom eyepiece that offers a range of magnification. A recent feature of spotting scopes is an angled eyepiece, which is more convenient for group viewing (with a straight eyepiece, the height of the scope must often be reset for birders of different heights. With an angled eyepiece, birders look *down* to use the scope, so the height needs to be adjusted less). As with binoculars, the price of spotting scopes varies considerably, ranging from $200 to nearly $2000. Because most scopes weigh several pounds, don't forget a sturdy tripod—those with many plastic components, used for lightweight camcorders or cameras, should be avoided. A sturdy tripod costs at least $100.

Birding by Ear

Identifying birds by their vocalizations greatly enhances your birding experiences. There are numerous commercial CDs or DVDs on the market that can help you learn the vocalizations of birds. There are two primary types of vocalizations. *Calls* are uttered year-round, often when the bird is alarmed or nervous, and are often simple chips or squawks. *Songs* are usually reserved for the breeding season (or the weeks leading up to it), are usually restricted to males (although females of some species sing) and are often composed of many notes strung together, often in variable arrangements. Songs often are beautiful renderings that, along with the birds' flashy breeding plumages, provide many observers with the impetus to start birding.

One way to remember bird songs is to make up words for them. Some bird calls—onomatopoeic renderings by the Willet or Chuck-will's-widow or the classic "*Who cooks for you? Who cooks for you all?*" call of the Barred Owl—are easily remembered and understood. But the calls and songs of most species are less easily rendered; some songs can be quite complicated and cannot easily be converted to words. And like people, birds have regional dialects that make some songs or calls differ from what may be found in field guides or disks. Most of the Eastern Towhees in Florida, for instance, sing songs very different from the "*Drink your tea*" rendering listed in most guides.

BIRDING BY HABITAT

Florida can be separated into 11 biophysical regions or "bioregions": Southern Pine Plains and Hills, Dougherty Plain, Tallahassee Hills–Tifton Upland, Flatwoods, Central Florida Ridges and Uplands, Okefenokee Swamp and Plains, Coastal Marsh, Everglades, Big Cypress, Miami Ridge–Atlantic Coastal Strip and the Southern Coast and Islands. Each bioregion is composed of a number of different habitats. Each habitat is a community of plants and animals that is regulated by topography, climate, rainfall and other factors. There are more than 80 habitat communities in Florida and each supports a different bird community.

Red-winged Blackbird

Learning to identify Florida's plant communities will help you become a better birder. Even novices quickly learn that Eastern Meadowlarks and most sparrows are found in grassy or shrubby fields, while woodpeckers and most warblers are found in wooded areas. As your experience increases, you will learn the subtle differences in habitats and how these affect the distribution of birds. As another example, Yellow-throated Vireos breed in oak hammocks and mixed oak-pine sandhills, but you will not find them in pine flatwoods, whereas Summer Tanagers breed in all three habitats.

During migration and winter, when literally tens of millions of birds that breed north of Florida move into or through our state to winter locally or in the tropics, Florida's habitats host dozens of species that are not found here year-round. During migration, many songbirds are less choosy about particular habitat types so long as their basic needs are met. Northern Waterthrushes, for example, can be found in many different habitats so long as shallow water is present.

BIRDING LISTING

Many birders list the species they have seen during excursions or at home. It is up to you to decide what kind of list—systematic or casual—you will keep, and you may choose not to make lists at all. However, lists may prove rewarding in unexpected ways. For example, after you visit a new area, your list becomes a souvenir of your experiences there. By reviewing the list, you can recall memories and details that you might otherwise have forgotten. Keeping regular, accurate lists of birds in your neighborhood can also be useful for local researchers. It can be interesting to compare the arrival dates and last sightings of hummingbirds and other seasonal visitors, or to note the first sighting of a new visitor to your area.

BIRDING ACTIVITIES
Birding Groups and Organizations

Birding is much more enjoyable when you join others, and beginners can learn from experienced birders. Those wishing to go birding with others have several options. One is to join one of the several Internet lists that serve Florida and to contact birders who live near you (see list below). Another is to join a local Audubon chapter (there are 42 in Florida currently; see http://www.audubonofflorida.org/main/chapters.htm), all of which sponsor birding trips in which the public is always welcome. Additionally, some state or national parks in Florida schedule birding trips for beginners. Other opportunities for joining birding trips would be to assist with a local Christmas Bird Count (http://www.audubon.org/bird/cbc or http://www.fosbirds.org/cbc) or attend a birding festival (http://americanbirding.org/festivals).

Finally, we recommend that all birders join two organizations that support birding activities in Florida and nationally. The American Birding Association (http://www.americanbirding.org) publishes *Birding*, one of the best birding magazines in the world, and *North American Birds*, which chronicles the seasonal occurrence of birds for every state and Canadian province as well as several Middle American countries. Locally, the Florida Ornithological Society (http://www.fosbirds.org) is worthy of support. FOS publishes an excellent quarterly birding and ornithological journal, *Florida Field Naturalist.* FOS also convenes twice yearly around the state, allowing birders of all skill levels to meet, go birding, listen to bird-related talks, and participate in bird identification quizzes.

The primary Internet birding websites in Florida:

BirdBrain: http://listserv.admin.usf.edu/archives/brdbrain.html
Florida Rare Bird Alert: http://listserv.admin.usf.edu/archives/flrba.html
Floridabirds-L: http://www.lists.ufl.edu/archives/floridabirds-l.html
Miami Bird Board: http://www.tropicalaudubon.org/tasboard/index.html

American Robin

Bird Feeding

Many people set up backyard bird feeders or plant native berry- or seed-producing plants in their garden to attract birds to their yard. The kinds of food available will determine which birds visit your yard. Staff at birding stores can suggest which foods will attract specific birds. Sugarwater feeders are popular in summer to attract hummingbirds and are filled with a simple sugar solution made from one part sugar and three to four parts water.

Contrary to popular opinion, birds do not become dependent on feeders, nor do they subsequently forget to forage naturally. Winter is when birds use feeders the most, but it is also difficult to find food in spring before flowers bloom, seeds develop and insects hatch. Birdbaths will also entice birds to your yard at any time of year, and heated birdbaths are particularly useful in the colder months. Avoid birdbaths that have exposed metal parts because wet birds can accidentally freeze to them in winter. There are many good books written about feeding birds and landscaping your yard to provide natural foods and nest sites.

Nest Boxes

Another popular way to attract birds is to set out nest boxes, especially for Carolina Wrens, Eastern Bluebirds, Tufted Titmice and Purple Martins. Not all birds will use nest boxes: only species that normally use cavities in trees are comfortable in such confined spaces. Larger nest boxes can attract kestrels, owls and cavity-nesting ducks.

Cleaning Feeders and Nest Boxes

Nest boxes and feeding stations must be kept clean to prevent birds from becoming ill or spreading disease. Old nesting material may harbor a number of parasites, as well as their eggs. Once the birds have left for the season, remove the old nesting material and wash and scrub the nest box with detergent or a 10 percent bleach solution (1 part bleach to 9 parts water). You can also scald the nest box with boiling water. Rinse it well and let it dry thoroughly before you remount it.

Orange-winged Parrot

Feeding stations should be cleaned monthly. Feeders can become moldy and any seed, fruit or suet that is moldy or spoiled must be removed. Unclean bird feeders can also be contaminated with salmonellosis and possibly other avian diseases. Clean and disinfect feeding stations with a 10 percent bleach solution, scrubbing thoroughly. Rinse the feeder well and allow it to dry completely before refilling it. Discarded seed and feces on the ground under the feeding station should also be removed.

We advise that you wear rubber gloves and a mask when cleaning nest boxes or feeders.

West Nile Virus

Since its discovery in North America in 1999, West Nile Virus has caused widespread fear and misunderstanding. Some people fear contracting the disease from proximity to birds, and some health departments have advised residents to eliminate bird feeders or birdbaths. To date, the virus has affected 138 species of birds. The virus is transmitted to birds and to humans (as well as some other mammals) by mosquitoes that have bitten infected birds. Humans cannot contract the disease from casual contact with infected birds, and birds do not get the disease from other birds. Furthermore, not all mosquito species carry the disease. According to the Centers for Disease Control and Prevention, only about 20 percent of people who are bitten and become infected will develop any symptoms at all, and less than one percent will become severely ill. The effects of West Nile Virus in Florida seem to be less serious compared to other states. One possible explanation for this moderated impact may be that Florida's birds and other animals have built up some resistence to other mosquito-borne diseases, and are therefore less susceptible to contracting West Nile Virus.

Crested Caracara

TOP BIRDING SITES IN FLORIDA

Some sites are better for finding birds than are others, and some sites support many more species of birds than do others. For these and other reasons, birders select particular sites to visit over and over while ignoring sites that may be closer to home. From literally millions of birding sites in Florida—even suburban backyards or small urban parks may be visited by a few dozen species of birds each year—we have chosen 80 sites distributed throughout our state that provide some of the best birding opportunities during one or more seasons. Nearly all of these sites are protected parks, refuges or forests that offer easy access to those in standard passenger vehicles. For 10 of these locations, which are truly exemplary birding sites, we provide additional information. For detailed information on more than 325 birding sites throughout our state, consult *A Birder's Guide to Florida*, written by Bill Pranty and published in 2005 by the American Birding Association.

Dry Tortugas National Park

Some of the most spectacular scenery in Florida can be found in this park, which is composed of five tiny keys in the Gulf of Mexico about 70 miles west of Key West. Massive Fort Jefferson—three stories tall, with walls eight feet thick and built of more than 16 million bricks—occupies most of Garden Key, one of only two keys open year-round to the public. Access to the park is via private boat or seaplane from Key West. The keys support the only regular breeding grounds in North America for the Magnificent Frigatebird, Sooty Tern and Brown Noddy, the latter two species in the thousands of individuals. The Tortugas is also a well-known migrant trap during spring (less is known about fall migration, since few birders visit the park during this season). In addition, several first-for-Florida records have been established from the park, including the Black Noddy, White-tipped Dove, Bahama Mockingbird, and Piratic Flycatcher.

Eglin Air Force Base

At 463,448 acres, this active military reservation in the western Panhandle represents one of the most significant conservation lands in Florida and is the largest forested military installation in the United States. Most of its acreage is composed of longleaf pine flatwoods or sandhills, but Eglin also contains numerous creeks and extensive undeveloped coastline along the Gulf of Mexico. Although birders have access to only a small part of the site, the Base supports more than 325 species of birds, including the fourth-largest population of Red-cockaded Woodpeckers remaining in the world (more than 300 families), about 25% of the Florida's population of Snowy Plovers, and an extremely isolated population of Burrowing Owls.

Bay-breasted Warbler

Everglades National Park

One of the most famous and instantly recognizable natural areas in the world, Everglades National Park contains 1,550,865 acres at the southern tip of the peninsula and dozens of small mangrove keys lying in Florida Bay. The park is the largest single conservation area in Florida. Perhaps not surprisingly, given its size, location in the subtropics and the millions of visitors it receives annually, the bird list for Everglades National Park is the largest of any site in Florida, exceeding 350 species. The park hosts huge numbers of wintering shorebirds and landbirds, thousands of wading birds year-round and the only flock of Greater Flamingos found in North America. Anhinga Trail, Snake Bight Trail and Eco Pond are among the most well-known birding spots in Florida. Note that the use of tape recordings to attract birds is prohibited in the park.

Common Loon

Fort De Soto Park

This 1136-acre park at the mouth of Tampa Bay is justly known as a migrant trap, primarily during spring, but it also offers excellent birding during fall and winter. In addition to its draw for migrant landbirds, it supports a great diversity of wintering and migrant shorebirds. Shorebirding along North Beach is best during early morning, before the arrival of most sunbathers and their dogs. During spring, a grove of mulberry trees hosts a great diversity of hungry migrant landbirds, and a bird fountain built to honor a local birder adds further attraction. There is also a diversity of rarities, including Heermann's Gull, Sulphur-bellied Flycatcher, Kirtland's Warbler and Bananaquit. Overall, more than 300 species have birds have been sighted in the park.

Honeymoon Island State Park

This 2808-acre island park off Clearwater supports significant populations of resident Snowy Plovers and wintering Piping Plovers, as well as large numbers of other shorebirds. During migration, large numbers of Common Terns and migrant landbirds can be found; 800 Hooded Warblers were estimated one day in April 1994! Many rarities have been found here as well, including the Long-billed Murrelet, Elegant Tern and Green-tailed Towhee. More than 275 species of birds have been reported.

Lake Apopka North Shore Restoration Area

For decades, this 20,00-acre former farming area northwest of Orlando had been one of the best-known shorebirding sites in Florida during fall. By 1999, all of the farms were purchased by the state and discontinued as part of the effort to restore Lake Apopka, Florida's most polluted wetland. Since its public acquisition and management, this site has shown its birding potential during other seasons of the year for diverse groups of birds such as waterfowl, wading birds, raptors and sparrows. In the past six years, more than 335 species of birds have been found here, including such rarities as Florida's first Rough-legged Hawks and Eurasian Kestrel, and its first breeding Dickcissels. Regrettably, pesticide residues in the soil caused a die-off of fish-eating birds in 1998–99. The tainted soil was removed from the site and the site is believed to now be clean. Entry into Lake Apopka North Shore Restoration Area is closely controlled at present, but it is hoped that the site will be much more accessible in the future.

J.N. "Ding" Darling National Wildlife Refuge

This well-known site on Sanibel Island along the southern Gulf Coast is named for J.N. Darling (1876–1962), a Pulitzer Prize–winning editorial cartoonist, creator of the highly successful "Duck Stamp" program and the head (under President Franklin Roosevelt's administration) of what is now called the U.S. Fish and Wildlife Service. The Wildlife Drive on the refuge is one of the most famous birding spots in Florida, well-known for being a reliable spot to see the Roseate Spoonbill. Among its 6310 acres, it hosts significant populations of wading birds year-round and of shorebirds during migration and winter. In all, the area has a total diversity of more than 230 species. The use of tape recordings to attract birds is prohibited in the refuge.

Merritt Island National Wildlife Refuge

Although a very popular birding area, this vast refuge (139,155 acres), part of NASA's John F. Kennedy Space Center, has a tragic history. Originally composed of thousands of acres of salt marshes—and uncountable millions of mosquitoes—much of Merritt Island was altered once NASA acquired the property in the 1960s. The marshes were diked and flooded for long periods to control mosquito populations, but this severe alteration of the habitat helped to cause the extinction of the Dusky Seaside Sparrow, a small songbird endemic to the area. Today, some of the marshes have been restored but most remain flooded, and they support large populations of wintering waterfowl and American Coots as well as wintering and migratory shorebirds. The bird list exceeds 315 species. Parts of the refuge are closed prior to space shuttle launches.

Painted Bunting

Paynes Prairie Preserve State Park

More than 270 species of birds have been reported in this extensive wetland and associated habitats (20,945 acres) along the south edge of Gainesville. Currently a marsh system, Paynes Prairie has at times been a large lake and a wet prairie, with conditions dependent on local water levels. Large flocks of Greater Sandhill Cranes winter here, and numerous pairs of Florida Sandhill Cranes are resident. Extensive oak hammocks surrounding the prairie to the west often contain a great diversity of migrant landbirds during fall, primarily thrushes and warblers. During winter, dike trails in the prairie are good for Marsh and Sedge wrens and several species of sparrows.

Purple Sandpiper

St. Marks National Wildlife Refuge

This gem along the Big Bend—the region where the Panhandle and the peninsula coast meet—is perhaps the most visited birding site in north Florida. Among its 67,623 acres are more than 20 miles of coastline, composed primarily of extensive salt marshes. The main road through the refuge, which ends at the St. Marks Lighthouse, passes by several freshwater impounds that are favored by numerous species of wintering waterfowl, as well as wading birds year-round and shorebirds during migration and winter. Nearly every year, these impounds are enlivened by the appearance of one or more Vermilion Flycatchers. More than 325 species of birds have been reported on the refuge, including such rarities as the Tundra Swan, Yellow-nosed Albatross, Lesser Sand-Plover and Groove-billed Ani.

INTRODUCTION

1. Fort Pickens, Gulf Island National Seashore
2. Eglin Air Force Base
3. Florida Caverns SP
4. Apalachicola NF
5. T.H. Stone Memorial St. Joseph Peninsula SP
6. Dr. Julian D. Bruce St. George Island SP
7. Bald Point SP
8. St. Marks NWR
9. Edward Ball Wakulla Springs SP
10. Tall Timbers Research Station
11. Suwannee River SP
12. Osceola NF
13. Fort Clinch SP
14. Talbot Islands SP
15. Huguenot Memorial Park
16. Guana River Reserve
17. Hagen's Cove
18. San Felasco Hammock Preserve SP
19. Paynes Prairie Preserve SP
20. Ocala NF
21. Lake Woodruff NWR
22. Washington Oaks Gardens SP
23. Smyrna Dunes Park/ Ponce de Leon Inlet
24. Cedar Key
25. Withlacoochee SF
26. Emeralda Marsh Conservation Area
27. Wekiwa Springs SP
28. Lake Apopka North Shore Restoration Area
29. Orlando Wetlands Park
30. Canaveral National Seashore
31. Merritt Island NWR
32. South Central Regional Wastewater Treatment Facility ("Viera Wetlands")
33. Turkey Creek Sanctuary
34. Alfred McKethan Pine Island Park
35. Green Key Road
36. J.B. Starkey Wilderness Park
37. Honeymoon Island SP
38. Dunedin Hammock Park
39. Fort De Soto Park
40. Wilderness Park
41. Saddle Creek Park
42. Lake Wales Ridge SF
43. Three Lakes WMA
44. Highlands Hammock SP
45. Kissimmee Prairie Preserve SP
46. St. Sebastian River Preserve SP
47. Pelican Island NWR
48. Savannas Preserve SP
49. Jonathan Dickinson SP
50. Oscar Scherer SP
51. Sarasota "Celery Fields"
52. Myakka River SP
53. Fred C. Babcock–Cecil M. Webb WMA
54. J.N. "Ding" Darling NWR
55. Little Estero Lagoon
56. Okaloacoochee Slough SF
57. Stormwater Treatment Area 5
58. Everglades Agricultural Area
59. Arthur R. Marshall Loxahatchee NWR
60. Wakodahatchee Wetlands
61. Spanish River Park
62. Eagle Lakes Mitigation Site
63. Tigertail Beach
64. Fakahatchee Strand Preserve SP
65. Collier–Seminole SP
66. Big Cypress National Preserve
67. Everglades NP
68. Markham County Park/ Water Conservation Area 2B
69. Hugh Taylor Birch SP
70. Miami Springs
71. Matheson Hammock County Park
72. Bill Baggs Cape Florida SP
73. Frog Pond WMA
74. Biscayne NP
75. Dagny Johnson Key Largo Hammock Botanical SP
76. John Pennekamp Coral Reef SP
77. Curry Hammock SP
78. Boot Key
79. Key West city parks
80. Dry Tortugas NP

BEST SITES ABBREVIATIONS

NF = National Forest
NP = National Park
NWR = National Wildlife Refuge
SF = State Forest
SP = State Park
WMA = Wildlife Management Area

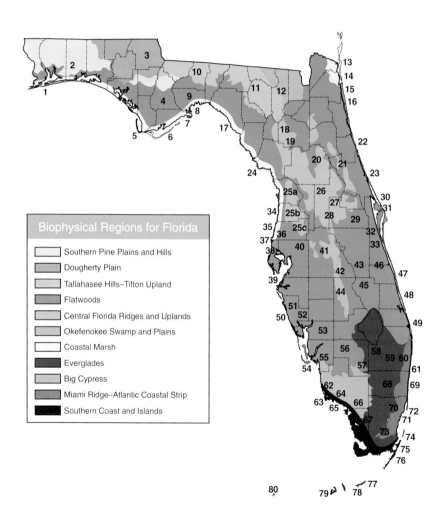

Biophysical Regions for Florida

- Southern Pine Plains and Hills
- Dougherty Plain
- Tallahasee Hills–Tifton Upland
- Flatwoods
- Central Florida Ridges and Uplands
- Okefenokee Swamp and Plains
- Coastal Marsh
- Everglades
- Big Cypress
- Miami Ridge–Atlantic Coastal Strip
- Southern Coast and Islands

ABOUT THE SPECIES ACCOUNTS

The main section of this book contains 325 species of birds that are found annually in Florida, in fair to huge numbers. Another 39 species listed in the appendix (pp. 358–67) occur less commonly and/or less numerously. The accounts follow a standardized format composed of the following headings:

ID: One of the challenges of birding is that many species look different in spring and summer ("alternate" or breeding plumage) than they do in fall and winter ("basic," nonbreeding or winter plumage) or the males differ greatly from the females. Many subadult plumages differ considerably from adults, and some species (such as eagles and large gulls) go through a juvenal and then several immature plumages before attaining adult plumage) Because we cannot describe or illustrate every possible plumage that may be seen in Florida, we focus on most adult and juvenal or immature plumages that are likely to be seen here. (Juveniles are birds in their first calendar year of life, whereas immatures are in their second, third or fourth calendar years of life).

Size: We present the average length of the bird's body from its bill to its tail. Often a range of sizes is given for some species because of racial or sexual variation; female hawks and eagles, for instance, are noticeably larger than males. We also present the wingspan length, measured from wingtip to wingtip.

Status: A general comment such "common," "uncommon" or "rare" is usually sufficient to describe the relative abundance of a species. We provide the seasonal status in Florida for all birds. Note that some winter residents or spring migrants may linger into summer, or some breeding residents may winter in small numbers in the state, especially the extreme southern peninsula and the Keys. *Local* birds occur spottily in suitable habitat, while *irruptive* species occur commonly in some years and rarely in others. Geographically, we divide Florida into easily understood regions such as the western Panhandle or southern peninsula.

Habitat: We present the habitats in which each species is most typically found. Some birds may be found in several different habitats, while others are restricted to one or two. Most birds are specific in their choice of habitat when they are breeding, but tend to be less choosy during winter or, especially, migration.

Pileated Woodpecker

Nesting: The reproductive strategies used by birds vary greatly. In each species account, we discuss the nest location and structure, clutch size, incubation period, parental duties and other breeding behaviors for each species. We do not provide nesting information for birds that do not breed in Florida.

Feeding: We list the most common foraging styles and food items of birds while in Florida. Food items consumed in our state often differ greatly from other areas.

Voice: Vocalizations are provided for all species, whether calls and/or songs (primarily for species that breed in Florida). We use memorable paraphrases of distinctive songs or calls but do not "translate" many vocalizations.

Similar Species: All birders misidentify—they confuse one species for another. Reasons for misidentifying birds vary, but inexperience with one or more species is often a primary factor. Beginners are therefore most likely to misidentify birds, but even experienced birders can mistake one species for another; some birds simply cannot be conclusively identified in the field. We recommend that great caution be used when reporting rare birds—especially extremely rare birds—and that effort be taken to obtain photographs or video. For each species, we list one to four other species that may be mistaken for it, but we cannot list every species that may be mistaken for another.

Purple Gallinule

33

Range Maps: The range map for each species represents its generalized expected range; small areas from which a species is absent are not shown. Note that the abundance of a species may vary greatly within its mapped range. We use cross-hatching to denote where birds occur rarely; in these areas, you should not expect to see more than a few individuals of a species in any year—and you may go several years without seeing any individuals.

Range Map Legend

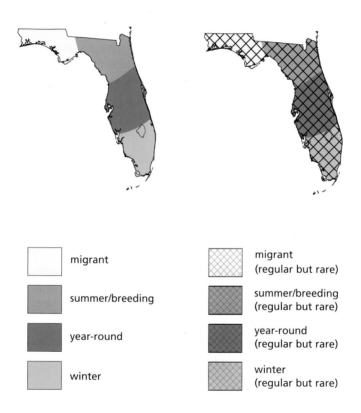

migrant

summer/breeding

year-round

winter

migrant
(regular but rare)

summer/breeding
(regular but rare)

year-round
(regular but rare)

winter
(regular but rare)

Waterfowl

Grouse & Allies

Diving Birds

Heronlike Birds

Birds of Prey

Rails, Coots
& Cranes

Shorebirds

Gulls & Allies

Doves

Owls

Nightjars, Swifts
& Hummingbirds

Woodpeckers

NONPASSERINES

Nonpasserine birds represent 19 of the 20 orders of birds found in Florida and about 59 percent of the species seen here. They are grouped together and called "nonpasserines" because, with few exceptions, they are easily distinguished from the "passerines," or "perching birds," which make up the 20th order. Being from 19 different orders, however, means that nonpasserines vary considerably in their appearance and habits—they include everything from the 5-foot-tall Great Blue Heron to the 4-inch-long Ruby-throated Hummingbird.

Generally speaking, nonpasserines do not "sing." Instead, their vocalizations are usually limited to "calls." There are also other differences in form and structure. For example, whereas the muscles and tendons in the legs of passerines are adapted to grip a perch, and the toes of passerines are never webbed, nonpasserines have feet adapted to a variety of uses.

Many nonpasserines are large, so they include some of our most notable birds. Waterfowl, raptors, gulls, shorebirds and woodpeckers are easily identified by most people. However, novice birders may mistake small nonpasserines such as doves, swifts and hummingbirds for passerines, thus complicating their identification. With a little practice, it will become easy to recognize the nonpasserines. By learning to distinguish the nonpasserines from the passerines at a glance, birders effectively reduce by about half the number of possible species for an unidentified bird.

BLACK-BELLIED WHISTLING-DUCK
Dendrocygna autumnalis

With its long legs and long neck, the whistling-duck looks like a colorful cross between a duck and a swan or goose. Of the two species found in Florida, the Black-bellied is much more widespread, even though its presence here is recent. In the early 1980s, a Black-bellied flock was found near Sarasota; it was thought to have arrived in Florida naturally, perhaps from the Yucatan Peninsula. Since that time, the Black-bellied Whistling-Duck has colonized much of the central peninsula, and its range continues to expand, primarily northward. • With their rusty bodies, bold white wing stripes, black bellies and bright red bills, Black-bellied Whistling-Ducks cannot be mistaken for any other species. These gregarious ducks are active day and night and can often be located by their high-pitched whistling calls. They are often seen in flocks, loafing in freshwater marshes or along the edges of ponds. • Black-bellied Whistling-Ducks are said to nest in tree cavities or nest boxes, but the sole nest found in Florida was built on the ground.

ID: long-legged, long-necked duck of freshwater habitats; often seen standing on ground; brown upperparts and breast; remainder of underparts black; gray head with white eye ring; red bill; pink legs and feet. *Juvenile:* paler overall; gray bill and legs; dingy underparts. *In flight:* bold white wing stripe.
Size: *L* 21 in; *W* 30 in.
Status: locally common and increasingly permanent resident of the peninsula; very rare in the Panhandle and Keys.

Habitat: freshwater marshes, lakes and ponds; flooded agricultural fields.
Nesting: on the ground or in a tree cavity or nest box; nest is a platform of trampled vegetation; pair incubates 12–16 white eggs for 25–30 days.
Feeding: on the ground or in water; eats grass seeds, waste grain, insects and aquatic vegetation.
Voice: 4–5 syllable, nasally wheezing whistle, sounds like a squeezed "rubber ducky."
Similar Species: *Fulvous Whistling-Duck* (p. 37): pale orange body; bands of orange on dark back; dark bill and legs; white tail band.
Best Sites: Emeralda Marsh CA; Sarasota "celery fields"; Viera Wetlands.

FULVOUS WHISTLING-DUCK

Dendrocygna bicolor

The Fulvous Whistling-Duck, like the Black-bellied, is a fairly recent colonizer of Florida: the first Fulvous was documented in the state in the 1960s. This species quickly increased its numbers to thousands of individuals, mostly in the extensive agricultural area southeast of Lake Okeechobee and in freshwater marshes farther north. However, the Fulvous Whistling-Duck remains very localized in the peninsula and has not shown the rapid range expansion of its close cousin. • Small roving flocks of either whistling-duck species may travel hundreds of miles north of their breeding range, on very rare occasions north even to southern Canada. • Whistling-ducks were previously known as "tree-ducks," but the name was changed because these ducks always feed and often nest on the ground. • Fulvous hens have been known to "dump" their eggs in other Fulvous Whistling-Ducks' nests, or in the nests of other species; according to one report, over 100 eggs were found in a single nest!

ID: long-legged, long-necked duck of fresh-water habitats; rich tawny overall; brown back; bold white stripes on flanks; black rump; black tail with broad, white band; blackish wings; white undertail coverts; gray bill, legs and feet. *Juvenile:* somewhat duller overall.
Size: *L* 18–21 in; *W* 26 in.
Status: uncommon to common but very local permanent resident of the central and southern peninsula.
Habitat: freshwater marshes, ponds or lakes; flooded agricultural fields.

Nesting: on the ground; nest consists of trampled vegetation; pair incubates 12–17 white to creamy white eggs for 24–26 days.
Feeding: eats mainly plant material, including aquatic vegetation, grains and seeds; forages in water by gleaning from the surface, tipping or, occasionally, diving; prefers to forage in damp fields; feeds mostly at night.
Voice: loud, rising whistle given in flight.
Similar Species: *Black-bellied Whistling-Duck* (p. 36): brown upperparts; black underparts; gray face; red bill; broad, white wing stripe visible in flight.
Best Sites: Emeralda Marsh CA; Everglades Agricultural Area; Lake Apopka North Shore Restoration Area.

SNOW GOOSE

Chen caerulescens

Snow Geese breed in the High Arctic from Alaska to Greenland, and they winter in the southern U.S. and Mexico. In recent years, Snow Goose populations have increased dramatically in North America as the birds take advantage of human-induced changes in the landscape and food supply. In Florida, Snow Geese are generally uncommon winter residents, but flocks of several dozen or even 100 or more may be observed at times. • Snow Geese are mostly vegetarian, often targeting the underground parts of plants. Their strong, serrated bills are well designed for pulling up the rootstocks of marsh plants and gripping slippery grasses. • Unlike Canada Geese, which fly in V-formations, migrating Snow Geese usually form oscillating, wavy lines. • Snow Geese occur in two color morphs —white and blue; both are seen with roughly equal frequency in Florida. Until 1983, each morph was considered a separate species—the Snow Goose and the Blue Goose, respectively.

blue morph

white morph

ID: large, stocky goose found in fields or wetlands; pink legs; pink bill with dark "grinning patch." *White morph:* all white except for black primaries. *Blue morph:* white head and upper neck; dark bluish gray body. *Immature:* gray or dusty white plumage; dark bill and feet.
Size: *L* 28–33 in; *W* 4½–5 ft.
Status: generally rare to uncommon resident in the Panhandle and northern third of the peninsula from November to February; rare and irregular farther south.
Habitat: shallow freshwater or saltwater marshes, lakes, agricultural fields and suburban areas.

Nesting: does not breed in Florida.
Feeding: grazes on aquatic vegetation, grasses, sedges and roots; also takes grain in agricultural fields; occasionally eats insects.
Voice: loud, nasal, constant *houk-houk* in flight.
Similar Species: *Domestic (Graylag) Goose:* larger; white wing tips; usually in city parks or farm or ranch ponds. *Pekin Duck* (white domesticated form of Mallard): much larger bill and body; limited to city parks and residential areas. *Ross's Goose:* rare; smaller; rounder head; lacks dark "grinning patch"; shorter neck.
Best Sites: Fort Walton Beach Spray Fields; St. Marks NWR.

CANADA GOOSE

Branta canadensis

Thousands of Canada Geese of the *B. c. canadensis* and *B. c. interior* races once wintered in the salt and brackish marshes around St. Marks in the eastern Panhandle. These large flocks now overwinter farther north, having cut short their migration to feed in the fields of corn and other grain that cover the Midwest. To offset the loss of these natural wintering flocks, state game officials began releasing a western race—*B. c. maxima*, the Giant Canada Goose—into Florida beginning in the 1960s. These exotic geese are found in a semi-feral state throughout the peninsula, but are common only around Tallahassee. Even though wild Canada Geese likely migrate to Florida each winter, their presence is usually masked by the increasingly common populations of Giant Canada Geese. • Few people realize that at one time Canada Geese were hunted almost to extinction. Populations have since been reestablished and, in recent decades, these large, bold geese have become pests in some northern states, inundating urban waterfronts, picnic sites, golf courses and city parks.

ID: large goose with brown body; paler underparts; long, black neck; white chin strap; black bill, legs and feet; white undertail coverts. **Size:** *L* 21–48 in; *W* 3½–5 ft.

Status: *B. c. canadensis* and *B. c. interior:* formerly abundant winter residents in the St. Marks area but now rare. *B. c. maxima:* uncommon to locally common and increasingly permanent resident of farmlands and urban and suburban areas almost statewide. **Habitat:** ponds, lakes, farmland, residential areas and city parks; originally wintered in salt and brackish marshes and bays.

Nesting: on the ground near water; hen builds nest of plant materials lined with down and incubates 4–5 white eggs for 28–30 days while the male stands guard. **Feeding:** grazes on new sprouts, aquatic vegetation, grass and roots; tips up for aquatic roots and tubers. **Voice:** loud, familiar *ah-honk.* **Similar Species:** *Brant:* rare; much smaller; lacks white chin strap; has white "necklace" on upper neck; black upper breast. **Best Sites:** most common in parts of the Tallahassee area but found sparsely south to the Miami area.

MUSCOVY DUCK

Cairina moschata

Native from Mexico to central South America, the Muscovy Duck has been introduced widely into Florida. Although some wild-caught individuals were released in an attempt to establish a population available to hunters, the Muscovy Ducks now seen in the state probably originate from domesticated stock; most are tame and run or fly toward people who approach them. Muscovies were released into thousands of ponds and lakes in residential areas to provide a natural feel to what would otherwise be sterile water bodies surrounded by expanses of mowed grass and houses or apartments. • Wild Muscovy Ducks are all black with white wing linings, a greenish sheen to the secondary flight feathers and bare, black "warty" skin on the face. Few, if any, of Florida's Muscovy Ducks look like this; rather, they range from all white to various black and white pied plumages. All adults have bright red facial skin, but it is most extensive in males. A few Muscovy Ducks in Florida apparently hybridize with feral Mallards.

ID: large duck found in freshwater habitats; dark, glossy white, black or pied plumage; bare, red "warty" face; pale bill; orange or pink legs and feet. *In flight:* rarely seen in sustained flight; large white patch on leading edge of wings of black or pied birds; short, thick neck.
Size: *Drake: L* 31 in; *W* 4 ft. *Hen: L* 25 in; *W* 3–3½ ft.
Status: uncommon to locally common permanent resident of urban and suburban areas virtually throughout the state.

Habitat: urban and suburban parks and residential areas; rarely seen in natural wetlands away from human influence.
Nesting: on the ground near water, usually under shrub or at base of tree; heavily lined with feathers; hen incubates 8–9 white eggs for 35 days, then tends young; 2 or more broods annually.
Feeding: primarily vegetarian; readily accepts handouts of bread and other foods from humans.
Voice: *Drake:* hisses. *Hen:* quacks weakly.
Similar Species: red, "warty" face is unique. *American Coot* (p. 123): found in marshes, ponds and lakes; white frontal shield and chickenlike bill.
Best Sites: ubiquitous in most suburban and urban areas.

WOOD DUCK

Aix sponsa

The drake Wood Duck is one of the most colorful waterbirds in North America; books, magazines, postcards and calendars routinely celebrate his beauty. The hen is much subtler in plumage but shares the drake's crest and sports a large teardrop-shaped white patch around her eyes. • Pairs or small flocks of Wood Ducks are often seen around dawn or dusk flying to or from night-roosting areas. • Birds of the forest, Wood Ducks nest in tree cavities that may be as much as a mile from the nearest body of water. Newly hatched ducklings may have to jump 20 feet or more out of their nest to follow their mother to the nearest body of water. The little bundles of down bounce well and seldom sustain injury when they hit the ground. • Landowners with swamps, marshes, tree-lined ponds or bayheads close at hand may attract Wood Ducks by erecting nest boxes above or near the water.

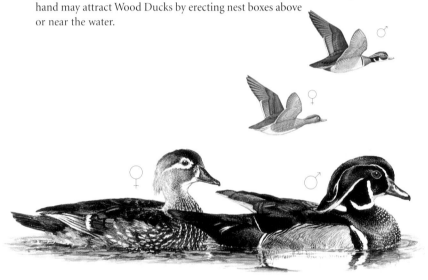

ID: rather large duck of freshwater habitats; stocky head; short, thin neck. *Drake:* extremely colorful; multicolored head; long, slicked-back greenish crest edged with white; red eyes; white throat extends into neck ring and facial "spur"; mostly reddish bill; rusty breast with small, white spots; black and white shoulder slashes; golden sides. *Hen:* mostly grayish brown above; brown face with white, teardrop-shaped eye patch; mottled brown breast streaked with white.
Size: *L* 15–20 in; *W* 30 in.
Status: uncommon permanent resident throughout the peninsula.

Habitat: swamps, ponds, marshes and lakeshores with wooded edges; some birds in city parks may be semi-feral.
Nesting: in a tree cavity or box lined with down; may be as high as 30 ft above the ground; sometimes far from water; hen incubates 9–14 white to buff eggs for 25–35 days.
Feeding: gleans the water's surface and tips up for aquatic vegetation, especially duckweed, aquatic sedges and grasses; picks acorns and other nuts from the ground.
Voice: *Drake:* ascending whistle. *Hen:* slurred, squeaky note.
Similar Species: *Hooded Merganser* (p. 59): slim, black bill; black and white breast; male has black head with white crest patch.
Best Sites: widespread.

GADWALL

Anas strepera

D rake Gadwalls lack the striking plumage of most other male ducks, but they nevertheless have a dignified appearance and subtle beauty. Once you learn their field marks—a black rump and white wing patches on mostly gray plumage—Gadwalls are easy to identify. The hens resemble female teals and other ducks, but they may be identified by their orange and black bills and white wing patches. • Gadwalls are one of the rarest wintering ducks in Florida; only in a few favored areas can one see more than 10 or 15 Gadwalls in a day. They are usually found in small flocks with other ducks. • An attempt to introduce a breeding population of Gadwalls along the central Florida Gulf Coast in the 1960s was not successful. • Ducks in the genus *Anas*, the dabbling ducks, are most often observed tipping up their hindquarters and submerging their heads to feed, but Gadwalls dive more often than others of this group.

ID: nondescript, gray or brown duck generally of freshwater habitats; white belly. *Drake:* dark above; grayish brown head; dark eyes and bill; yellow legs; black breast patch; gray flanks; black upper- and undertail coverts and tail. *Hen:* mottled brown body; brown bill with orange sides. *In flight:* white speculum.
Size: *L* 18–22 in; *W* 33 in.
Status: generally rare to uncommon resident in the Panhandle and northern half of the peninsula from November to March;

rare and perhaps irregular south of Lake Okeechobee.
Habitat: freshwater lakes or ponds; less common in brackish or saline ponds or estuaries.
Nesting: does not breed in Florida.
Feeding: dabbles for aquatic plants; also grazes on grass and waste grain.
Voice: Mallard-like quack.
Similar Species: drake's gray plumage and black hindquarters are unique. *Mallard* (p. 45): hen has blue speculum bordered with white, orange legs and feet and lacks black hindquarters.
Best Sites: Merritt Island NWR; St. Marks NWR.

AMERICAN WIGEON

Anas americana

The American Wigeon breeds throughout Alaska and Canada; it winters along the Atlantic, Gulf and Pacific coasts and from the West Indies to Central America. In Florida, it occurs rather commonly in brackish or freshwater habitats throughout the mainland and is abundant at favored wintering spots. This duck is found in large flocks with other dabbling ducks. • American Wigeons favor the succulent stems and leaves of pond-bottom plants. These plants grow far too deep for a dabbling duck to reach, so wigeons often pirate them from accomplished divers such as Canvasbacks, Redheads, Lesser Scaup or American Coots. • In contrast to other ducks, the American Wigeon walks well on land and commonly grazes on shore. • Years ago, the American Wigeon was called "baldpate" because of the drake's white crown and forehead. The word "wigeon" is thought to be derived from the Old French *vipio*, an onomatopoeic rendering of the high-pitched, piping calls of the drake Eurasian Wigeon, a close relative of the American Wigeon.

ID: large, rufous brown duck with rounded head; pale bluish gray bill with black tip; large, white upperwing patches. *Drake:* rusty breast and sides; gray head; white forehead and crown; wide, iridescent, green swipe extends back from eye; white belly; black undertail coverts. *Hen:* grayish head; brown underparts; dusky undertail coverts.
Size: *L* 18–22½ in; *W* 32 in.
Status: uncommon to common winter resident statewide from October to March, decreasing in abundance southward.
Habitat: shallow wetlands, lakes, ponds and estuaries.

Nesting: does not breed in Florida.
Feeding: dabbles for leaves and stems of pondweeds and other aquatic plants or pirates them from diving ducks; also grazes on land; may eat some invertebrates.
Voice: *Drake:* nasal, frequently repeated whistle. *Hen:* soft, seldom-heard quack.
Similar Species: drake's head pattern is distinctive. *Gadwall* (p. 42): white speculum; brown or dusky brown patches on leading edges of wings; drake lacks green face patch; hen has orange and black bill. *Eurasian Wigeon* (p. 358): gray "wing pits"; drake has rufous head with pale forehead; lacks green face patch; rosy breast; hen usually has browner head.
Best Sites: Merritt Island NWR; St. Marks NWR; Edward Ball Wakulla Springs SP.

43

AMERICAN BLACK DUCK
Anas rubripes

The American Black Duck breeds in eastern Canada and the northeastern U.S., and it winters in much of eastern North America, from New Brunswick, Canada, to Florida. In Florida, the American Black Duck is a generally rare winter resident of the eastern Panhandle and extreme northern peninsula. It is quite rare, with maybe one or two sightings each winter, south to the central peninsula, usually at Lake Apopka or Merritt Island National Wildlife Refuge. Many reports south of Gainesville are probably misidentified Mottled Ducks or hen Mallards, species that are very similar in plumage and habits. • Like other puddle ducks, American Black Ducks forage by "tipping up" to reach prey along the bottom of marshes. • Populations of American Black Ducks are declining, partially as a result of hybridization with Mallards, whose range is expanding and now overlaps much the Black Duck's breeding range. • Drake and hen American Black Ducks are remarkably similar in appearance, which is unusual for waterfowl.

ID: large duck with blackish body; paler head and neck; streaked throat; orange legs and feet; violet speculum lacks white borders. *Drake:* dull yellowish bill. *Hen:* olive bill. *In flight:* whitish underwings contrast with very dark body.
Size: *L* 20–24 in; *W* 35 in.
Status: rare to uncommon resident of the eastern Panhandle and adjacent northern peninsula from November to March; rare farther south.

Habitat: marshes, lakes, flooded agricultural fields.
Nesting: does not breed in Florida.
Feeding: tips up in shallows to reach eelgrass and other plants; also takes mollusks, crustaceans and other small prey.
Voice: *Drake:* croaks. *Hen:* loud quacks.
Similar Species: *Mottled Duck* (p. 46): paler overall with buffy head and unstreaked throat; speculum bordered by narrow white lines. *Mallard* (p. 45): hen is paler overall with unstreaked throat, orange and black bill and speculum bordered with narrow white lines.
Best Site: St. Marks NWR.

MALLARD
Anas platyrhynchos

In Florida, Mallards occur as two distinct populations, but distinguishing the two is often difficult. Wild Mallards are winter residents through at least the northern half of the peninsula. Feral Mallards are found throughout Florida in all months of the year. Along with Muscovy Ducks, Mallards are commonly released into city parks and residential areas. Also like Muscovies, feral Mallards frequently become inbred, resulting in a wide variety of strange plumages; males often lack the white neck ring, or they may have dark heads with white throats and necks. Also seen in Florida is the Pekin Duck (not Peking), which is the domesticated descendant of the Mallard and is all white, with an orange bill, legs and feet.

breeding

breeding

ID: large, well-known duck generally of freshwater habitats. *Breeding Drake:* "dirty white" upperparts and paler underparts; glossy, green head separated from chestnut breast by bold white ring; yellow bill; black central tail feathers curl upward. *Hen:* mottled brown overall; finely streaked, grayish brown head; orange bill spattered with black. *In flight:* dark blue speculum bordered with white.
Size: *L* 20–27 in; *W* 35 in.
Status: uncommon to common permanent resident of urban and suburban areas statewide; uncommon resident of the Panhandle and northern peninsula from October to March.
Habitat: ponds, lakes and marshes; residential areas and city parks.

Nesting: under a bush near water; nest of plant material is lined with down; hen incubates 7–10 light green to white eggs for 26–30 days.
Feeding: dabbles in shallows for the seeds of aquatic vegetation; may take some aquatic invertebrates; commonly accepts handouts of bread.
Voice: *Drake:* deep, quiet quacks. *Hen:* loud quacks; very vocal.
Similar Species: *Mottled Duck* (p. 46): very similar to hen Mallard, but with yellow or yellow-orange bill, unstreaked throat and speculum bordered by narrow white borders. *Mallard* x *Mottled Duck hybrids:* increasingly common; variable plumage. *Northern Shoveler* (p. 48): much larger bill; drake has white breast. *American Black Duck* (p. 44): very rare in the peninsula; darker than hen Mallard; olive or greenish yellow bill; purple speculum lacks white borders.
Best Sites: widespread.

MOTTLED DUCK

Anas fulvigula

Mottled Ducks are breeding residents from coastal South Carolina through the Florida peninsula and from Louisiana to northeastern Mexico. Because they persist in developed areas, nesting on golf courses and in parks and residential areas, they are increasingly threatened by hybridization with feral Mallards, which are locally common permanent residents throughout suburban and urban areas. As a result, "pure" Mottled Ducks may eventually disappear from Florida. Today, many apparent Mottled Ducks are probably Mallard x Mottled Duck hybrids. Some ducks show clear signs of hybridization: "Mottled-type" ducks have green on the head or curled central tail feathers. • Banding studies show that Mottled Ducks readily move around the Florida peninsula, with rare observations in the Panhandle. They are commonly seen in pairs or loose flocks.

ID: large, stocky duck generally of freshwater habitats; mottled brown overall; green speculum bordered with black; yellow or yellow-orange bill; dark tail; buffy, unstreaked, throat.

Size: *L* 20–22 in; *W* 30 in.

Status: uncommon to locally common permanent resident of the central and southern peninsula; absent from the Keys.

Habitat: primarily freshwater marshes, ponds, lakes or flooded agricultural fields; also in brackish estuaries.

Nesting: on dry ground, usually close to water; shallow bowl of grass or aquatic vegetation concealed by surrounding vegetation; hen incubates 8–12 whitish to buffy olive eggs for 24–28 days.

Feeding: dabbles just below the water's surface or tips up for aquatic vegetation and invertebrates; also grazes on land.

Voice: loud quack similar to that of hen Mallard.

Similar Species: *Mallard* (p. 45): hen is paler with black markings on orange bill; eclipse drake has contrasting rusty breast, white tail and blue speculum bordered with white. *American Black Duck* (p. 44): little or no range overlap; darker overall with more contrasting white underwings; streaked throat; purple speculum.

Best Sites: widespread.

BLUE-WINGED TEAL

Anas discors

Found throughout the state in a variety of habitats, the Blue-winged Teal is probably Florida's most abundant, widespread wintering waterfowl. The first fall arrivals appear in August, and small numbers remain into May or even throughout the entire summer. There have even been several observations of adults with young; the adults may have been injured and left disabled during hunting season. • Blue-winged Teals are quick and evasive fliers; they can be identified in the air by their quick, precise twists and turns. • Despite the similarity of their names, the Green-winged Teal is not the Blue-winged Teal's closest relative. The Blue-winged Teal is more closely related to the Northern Shoveler and the Cinnamon Teal, two other species that share the pale blue forewing patch. • Two races of Blue-winged Teal are found in Florida: *A. d. discors* is common, and the Atlantic Coast race *A. d. orphna* is probably rare.

ID: smallish duck generally in freshwater habitats; bold, pale blue patch on leading edge of upperwing; blackish bill; yellow legs. *Drake:* blue-gray head with bold, white crescent on face; black-spotted, rusty breast and sides. *Hen:* mottled brown overall; fairly bold, dark eye line; white throat. *In flight:* blue forewing patch.
Size: *L* 14–16 in; *W* 23 in.
Status: common resident statewide from September to April; rare breeder.
Habitat: ponds, lakes, shallow marshes and estuaries; favors areas with short, dense emergent vegetation.

Nesting: in grass close to water; nest is built with grass and down; hen incubates 8–13 white or olive-tinged eggs for 23–27 days.
Feeding: gleans the water's surface for sedge and grass seeds, pondweeds, duckweeds and aquatic invertebrates.
Voice: *Drake:* soft *keck-keck-keck. Hen:* soft quacks.
Similar Species: *Green-winged Teal* (p. 50): hen is smaller with smaller bill, black and green speculum and no blue forewing patch. *Northern Shoveler* (p. 48): much larger bill; drake has yellow eyes, green head and white breast. *Cinnamon Teal* (p. 358): very rare; hen closely resembles Blue-winged hen, but with larger, more spatulate bill.
Best Sites: widespread.

NORTHERN SHOVELER

Anas clypeata

The Northern Shoveler drake's large, green head may recall a Mallard drake, but the resemblance ends there. The shoveler's large bill allows for immediate identification; no other duck has a bill so proportionately large. Both the common name and the former scientific name *Spatula* refer to this feature. • Like most other ducks in Florida, Northern Shovelers are winter residents, arriving during fall and departing in spring. • Shovelers are found primarily in freshwater wetlands, but they will use brackish marshes or estuaries. They are usually found in flocks with other dabbling ducks. • The Northern Shoveler does not tip up to feed like other dabbling ducks; rather, it stirs up shallow water with its feet, then submerges its bill—or sometimes its entire head. Using its tongue, it pumps water into and out of its bill; long comblike structures called lamellae that line the sides of the bill filter out food before the water is expelled.

ID: large duck with large, spatulate bill; blue forewing patch; green speculum. *Drake:* yellow eyes; green head; black bill; white breast; chestnut flanks. *Hen:* mottled brown overall; orange-tinged bill.

Size: *L* 18–20 in; *W* 30 in.

Status: uncommon to locally common resident statewide from September to April; least common in the south.

Habitat: ponds, lakes, shallow marshes and estuaries.

Nesting: does not breed in Florida.

Feeding: dabbles in shallow water; strains out plant and animal matter, especially aquatic crustaceans, insect larvae and seeds; also takes small fish.

Voice: generally silent in Florida, although courtship begins on the wintering grounds; occasional raspy call or quack.

Similar Species: spatulate bill is distinctive in all plumages. *Mallard* (p. 45): blue speculum bordered by white; lacks pale blue forewing patch; drake has chestnut breast and white flanks. *Blue-winged Teal* (p. 47): smaller overall; much smaller bill; drake has white crescent on face and spotted breast and sides.

Best Sites: fairly widespread.

NORTHERN PINTAIL

Anas acuta

The trademark of the elegant Northern Pintail is the drake's long, tapering tail feathers, which make up one-quarter of his body length. These feathers are easily seen in flight and point skyward when this duck dabbles. Only the rare Long-tailed Duck has a similar tail, but it is usually found in salt water, whereas the pintail is often in freshwater habitats. • Pintails are locally common winter residents at favored areas where they may be seen in flocks of dozens or hundreds among numerous other dabbling ducks. • Although Northern Pintails were once one of the most numerous ducks in North America, populations have declined in recent decades. Drought, wetland drainage and loss of grassland habitat are serious threats for many waterfowl species, but Northern Pintails have suffered more than most. These ducks are especially susceptible to lead poisoning as well, often mistaking the lead shot left behind by hunters for edible seeds. One ingested pellet contains enough lead to poison a bird.

ID: large duck with long, slender neck and slender gray bill. *Drake:* grayish above and below; white neck e   s onto nape as   w wedge; brown   ; long, tapering black tail feathers. *Hen:* mottled light brown overall; paler, plain head. *In flight:* slender body; brownish speculum with white trailing edge.
Size: *L* 21–25 in; *W* 34 in.
Status: uncommon resident throughout the mainland from October to March; rare in the Keys.

Habitat: estuaries, impoundments, marshes, lakes and ponds.
Nesting: does not breed in Florida.
Feeding: dabbles in shallows for the seeds of grasses and sedges; also eats aquatic invertebrates.
Voice: generally silent in Florida. *Drake:* soft, whistling call. *Hen:* rough quack.
Similar Species: drake is distinctive. *Mottled Duck* (p. 46) and *Mallard* (p. 45): females are chunkier, with orange and black or yellow-orange bills and without tapering tail or long, slender neck. *Blue-winged Teal* (p. 47): green speculum; blue forewing patch; hen is smaller.
Best Sites: Merritt Island NWR; St. Marks NWR.

GREEN-WINGED TEAL
Anas crecca

The Green-winged Teal is our smallest dabbling duck and one of the speediest and most maneuverable of waterfowl. When disturbed, this species flies up from the water's surface, circles overhead in a tight, fast-flying flock, then returns to the water after the threat has passed. A predator's only chance of catching a healthy teal is to snatch it from the water. • Most birds molt their flight feathers gradually, but ducks generally lose all their flight feathers at once, rendering them flightless for a few weeks. During this vulnerable time, ducks hide in thick vegetation or roost in open water, where they can scan for predators. Unique to ducks, males molt into a duller plumage—termed eclipse plumage—after breeding; during this time, males resemble females. • The name "teal" possibly originated from the medieval English word *tele* or the old Dutch word *teling*, each of which means "small." • The Eurasian race of the Green-winged Teal, which is a very rare visitor to Florida, has a white horizontal stripe on the scapular rather than the white vertical bar on the shoulder.

ID: smallest duck in Florida; small, dark bill; green and black speculum. *Drake:* chestnut head with green face stripe outlined in white; creamy breast spotted with black; gray flanks with white vertical shoulder slash; pale gray sides; yellow undertail coverts; black tail. *Hen:* mottled brown overall; dark eye line.
Size: *L* 12–16 in; *W* 23 in.

Status: uncommon to common resident statewide from October to April, decreasing in abundance southward.
Habitat: marshes, ponds and shallow lakes.
Nesting: does not breed in Florida.
Feeding: dabbles in shallows for seeds of sedges, grasses and other aquatic plants; also feeds on mollusks and aquatic invertebrates.
Voice: *Drake:* crisp whistle. *Hen:* soft quack.
Similar Species: drake unmistakable. *Blue-winged Teal* (p. 47): hen has larger bill, blue forewing patch and heavily spotted undertail coverts.
Best Sites: widespread.

CANVASBACK

Aythya valisineria

Ducks of the genus *Aythya* are generally diving ducks that are found in large flocks off the coast; five species occur along Florida's coasts. Canvasbacks breed in much of Alaska, western Canada and the northwestern U.S., and they winter along the Atlantic, Gulf and Pacific coasts to southern Mexico. In Florida, Canvasbacks are uncommon in the northern part of the state and are generally rare farther south. The very rare summer occurrences in Florida are probably birds that were injured during hunting season. • In profile, the Canvasback casts a noble image—the long bill meets the forecrown with no apparent break in angle, allowing birds of either sex to be distinguished at long range. The drake's back appears to be wrapped in bright white canvas. Both the unique profile and back are unmistakable field marks. • Like other diving ducks, Canvasbacks are typically found on bays and other deep salt or brackish water.

ID: large duck of coastal habitats; usually found in flocks; unique shaped head, with forehead sloping into large, black bill. *Drake:* very pale body; chestnut head; red eyes; black breast and hindquarters. *Hen:* pale body; light brown head and neck; dark eyes.
Size: *L* 19–22 in; *W* 29 in.
Status: uncommon coastal resident of northern Florida from November to March; generally rare farther south and inland; not known from the Keys.

Habitat: bays, estuaries, coastal salt marshes and occasionally inland marshes and lakes.
Nesting: does not breed in Florida.
Feeding: dives to depths of 10–15 ft to feed on seeds, roots, tubers and other plant material; favors wild celery and tape grass; occasionally eats aquatic invertebrates.
Voice: generally silent in Florida.
Similar Species: *Redhead* (p. 52): rounded rather than sloped forehead; drake has gray back and bluish bill with black tip.
Best Sites: widespread.

51

REDHEAD

Aythya americana

The Redhead breeds in Alaska and from southwestern Canada to the southwestern U.S. It winters from the southern states to Guatemala. In Florida, the Redhead winters off the Panhandle coast in vast numbers; rafts of tens of thousands may amass at favored sites, often among flocks of scaup. Elsewhere in our state, this bird is local in the peninsula but has never been observed in the Keys. • Redheads seem to be entirely vegetarian when in Florida, diving for plants such as tape grass. • The Redhead and the Canvasback have very similar plumage and habitat preferences. The best way to distinguish the two species is by head shape. The Redhead has a round head that meets the bill at an angle, whereas its close cousin has a sloping head that seems to merge with the bill. In drakes, back color is another reliable mark—the Redhead's is gray and the Canvasback's is white.

ID: large duck of coastal habitats; often found in flocks, frequently with scaup; rounded head with black-tipped, blue-gray bill. *Drake:* red head; yellow eyes; black breast and hindquarters; gray back and sides. *Hen:* dark brown overall; lighter chin and cheek patches.
Size: *L* 18–22 in; *W* 29 in.
Status: uncommon to locally common coastal winter resident of the northern half of Florida; less common farther south and inland.
Habitat: bays, estuaries, salt marshes and occasionally inland marshes and lakes.

Nesting: does not breed in Florida.
Feeding: dives to depths of 10 ft; primarily eats aquatic vegetation, especially ditchgrass, sedges and water lilies; occasionally eats aquatic invertebrates.
Voice: generally silent in Florida.
Similar Species: *Canvasback* (p. 51): clean, white back; bill slopes onto forehead. *Ringnecked Duck* (p. 53): little habitat overlap; hen has more prominent white eye ring, white ring on bill and peaked head. *Lesser Scaup* (p. 55) and *Greater Scaup* (p. 54): drake has dark head and whiter sides; hen has white patch at base of bill.
Best Sites: fairly widespread along the coast.

RING-NECKED DUCK
Aythya collaris

Although its distinctive tricolored bill and black back should be obvious to an observer, the Ring-necked Duck is often misidentified as a scaup. Habitat is another clue to help distinguish a Ring-necked from a scaup: the Ring-necked Duck is limited to freshwater ponds and lakes, whereas scaup are found mostly in salt or brackish water. The Ring-necked is the only *Aythya* duck that is consistently found on fresh water in Florida. • The common name of the Ring-necked Duck is derived from its scientific name *collaris,* which is Latin for collar. Close-up, the drake Ring-necked Duck does have a narrow, indistinct, cinnamon collar, but it is easy to overlook. After seeing the Ring-necked Duck in the field, you may wonder why it was not named "Ring-billed Duck" instead. • Ring-necked Ducks normally nest no closer to Florida than Michigan and New York, but there are several undocumented Florida reports, which, if the species was correctly identified, probably represented birds injured during hunting.

ID: large duck exclusively of freshwater marshes and lakes; distinctive tricolored bill; distinctive peaked crown. *Drake:* black upperparts; dark purple head; yellow eyes; black breast and hindquarters separated by gray sides; white shoulder slash. *Hen:* brown overall; paler head; whitish face; white eye ring extends behind eye as a narrow line.
Size: *L* 14–18 in; *W* 25 in.
Status: common resident throughout the mainland from November to March; rare in the Keys.
Habitat: ponds with lily pads and other surface vegetation, swamps, marshes and lakes.

Nesting: does not breed in Florida.
Feeding: dives for aquatic vegetation, including seeds and tubers of smartweed, water lilies and other plants; rarely eats aquatic invertebrates and mollusks.
Voice: generally silent in Florida.
Similar Species: *Lesser Scaup* (p. 55): rare on fresh water but may use large, deep lakes where Ring-necked Ducks are unlikely; gray back; white sides; lacks peaked crown and tricolored bill; hen has white patch at base of bill. *Greater Scaup* (p. 54): very rare on fresh water; same field marks as Lesser Scaup.
Best Sites: widespread.

GREATER SCAUP

Aythya marila

Scaup are common wintering sea ducks along the coasts of the Panhandle and in favored areas in the peninsula. Both the Greater Scaup and the Lesser Scaup are found in Florida, but the species of sighted birds can often not be accurately determined. The primary field mark to distinguish scaup species can be seen when the birds are in flight or when they are stretching their wings while resting on the water. The white wing stripe of the secondary flight feathers extends onto the primaries on the Greater Scaup, but it is dull gray on the primaries of the Lesser Scaup. Some field guides state that an additional field mark is the drake's head color—green for Greater Scaup and purple for Lesser Scaup. However, scaup head color is the result of iridescence not pigment, and scaup of one species can show iridescence supposedly diagnostic of the other species.

ID: large diving duck of the coasts; usually found in tight flocks; rounded head; yellow eyes; bluish bill with black tip. *Drake:* iridescent head usually appears greenish; pale back; white sides; black breast; dark hindquarters. *Hen:* brown overall; white patch at base of bill. *In flight:* white wing stripe extends onto primary feathers.
Size: *L* 16–19 in; *W* 28 in.
Status: fairly common resident off the Panhandle from November to March; rare to uncommon south to Tampa Bay and Merritt Island NWR; very rare farther south and inland.

Habitat: ocean, bays and estuaries; less common in coastal impoundments.
Nesting: does not breed in Florida.
Feeding: dives for crustaceans and other aquatic invertebrates and seeds of glasswort and other plants.
Voice: generally silent in Florida.
Similar Species: *Lesser Scaup* (p. 55): best identified in flight by white wing stripe limited to secondaries. *Ring-necked Duck* (p. 53): virtually no habitat overlap; black back; peaked crown; white shoulder slash; tricolored bill. *Redhead* (p. 52): drake has red head and darker back and sides; hen has dark eyes and lacks white patch at base of bill.
Best Sites: Alligator Pt.; St. George I.; St. Marks NWR.

LESSER SCAUP

Aythya affinis

esser Scaup used to be Florida's most abundant ducks, with more than a half-million individuals estimated as recently as 50 years ago. However, scaup numbers have declined severely in the past few decades, presumably owing to loss of habitat on the breeding grounds. Nonetheless, flocks of Lesser Scaup remain a common sight during winter off our northern coasts. Although far less common inland, they are regularly found on some of Florida's larger lakes. • Lesser Scaup are rarely seen on the small, thickly vegetated ponds that are the preferred habitat of the Ring-necked Duck, with which they are often confused. • The word "scaup" might refer to a preferred winter food of these ducks—shellfish beds are called *skalps* in Scotland—or it might be a phonetic rendering of one of their calls.

ID: large diving duck; mostly limited to coastal habitats; usually found in flocks; yellow eyes; bluish bill with black tip. *Drake:* iridescent head usually appears purplish; grayish back; white sides; black breast and hindquarters. *Hen:* dark eyes; white patch at base of bill. *In flight:* white wing stripe limited to secondary feathers.
Size: *L* 15–18 in; *W* 25 in.
Status: common to locally abundant coastal resident south to Tampa Bay and Merritt Island NWR from November to April; rare to uncommon farther south.
Habitat: coastal areas; rarely inland on large lakes.

Nesting: does not breed in Florida.
Feeding: dives for seeds and fibers of grasses and other plants and for mollusks, crustaceans and other aquatic invertebrates.
Voice: generally silent in Florida; alarm call is a deep *scaup*.
Similar Species: *Greater Scaup* (p. 54): best identified in flight by white wing stripe extending onto primaries; field marks such as head color and shape are unreliable. *Ring-necked Duck* (p. 53): little habitat overlap; black back; peaked crown; tricolored bill. *Redhead* (p. 52): drake has red head and darker back and sides; hen has dark eyes and no white patch at base of bill.
Best Sites: widespread.

BLACK SCOTER
Melanitta nigra

Scoters are dark sea ducks that feed primarily on shellfish and barnacles. Males have "swollen" bills that are brightly colored. Three species occur in North America, and all are found in small numbers off Florida's northern coasts. Black Scoters are the most numerous scoter in our state, although numbers fluctuate annually. • They are often seen migrating south of the northern part of Florida's Atlantic Coast during fall, when flocks fly in tight groups, usually just above the water. • Except for the conspicuous yellow knob on his bill, the Black Scoter drake is entirely black, and he is one of the only North American ducks that is all black in plumage. • While resting on the water's surface, Black Scoters tend to hold their bills parallel to the water, whereas Surf Scoters and White-winged Scoters tend to hold their bills downward. • Scoters use their sturdy bills to wrench shellfish off underwater rocks or the sea floor. They swallow mollusks whole and grind the shells in their muscular gizzards.

ID: dark sea duck. *Drake:* black overall; large, yellow-orange knob on bill. *Hen:* dark brown overall; large, pale patch on face, cheeks and upper neck; dark bill.
Size: *L* 17–20 in; *W* 28 in.
Status: rare to uncommon, sometimes locally common coastal winter resident off the Panhandle and northern Atlantic coasts from November to March; irregular farther south.
Habitat: ocean, estuaries and sometimes bays.

Nesting: does not breed in Florida.
Feeding: dives for mollusks, crustaceans and other aquatic invertebrates; rarely takes aquatic vegetation.
Voice: silent in Florida; wings whistle in flight.
Similar Species: *White-winged Scoter:* white wing patch; drake has white slash below eye; hen has pale, indistinct patches in front of and behind eye. *Surf Scoter* (p. 359): drake has white on head; hen has white patches in front of and behind eye.
Best Sites: Alligator Pt.; often seen in flight off Florida's northern Atlantic Coast.

BUFFLEHEAD

Bucephala albeola

Buffleheads are small sea ducks that breed across most of Canada and winter throughout the U.S., except in the northern Great Plains. In Florida, they are most conspicuous off our northern coasts, where they often are seen bobbing among the waves just offshore. • The male Bufflehead is strikingly marked in black and white, his most characteristic features being a large white patch on the back of his head and white underparts. The female is somber but appealing, her sooty head ornamented with a white "cheek" patch. • Although Buffleheads are most at home off Florida's coasts and in adjacent bays and estuaries, small numbers winter on large inland lakes. • The scientific name *Bucephala*, meaning "ox-headed" in Greek, refers to the shape of this bird's head; *albeola* is Latin for "white," obviously referring to the drake's plumage.

ID: small, chunky duck mostly of coastal areas; rounded head; short, thick neck; short, gray bill. *Drake:* black upperparts, with large amount of white in wings; blackish head with large white patch; white below. *Hen:* dark brown upperparts; paler underparts; oval, white cheek patch. *In flight:* white speculum.
Size: *L* 13–15 in; *W* 21 in.
Status: uncommon to locally common resident, primarily of Gulf Coast areas south to about Tampa Bay from November to March; less common farther south, along the Atlantic Coast and inland.

Habitat: ocean, bays and estuaries; also on large inland lakes.
Nesting: does not breed in Florida.
Feeding: dives for aquatic crustaceans, insects and other aquatic invertebrates; also eats seeds of glasswort and other plants.
Voice: generally silent in Florida.
Similar Species: *Hooded Merganser* (p. 59): larger; longer, slender bill; yellow eyes; male has brown flanks and white crest outlined in black; hen has shaggy crest on dark head. *Common Goldeneye* (p. 58): less common and less widespread; larger; yellow eyes; male has greenish head with round, white face patch; female has mostly yellow bill.
Best Sites: fairly widespread along the northern Gulf Coast.

57

COMMON GOLDENEYE

Bucephala clangula

Goldeneyes are named for their yellowish eyes. Of the two species that occur in North America, only Common Goldeneyes are found in Florida. They are generally rare wintering sea ducks of Florida's northern coasts, where small flocks may be seen feeding offshore or in protected bays and estuaries. • The Common Goldeneye drake is easily identified by the round white facial patch on his dark green head and by his mostly white body. The hen is less noticeable but perhaps equally distinctive, having a rounded, rust-colored head and gray body separated by a wide, white neck ring. • The courtship display of the drake begins in spring, soon after the birds leave Florida. One display features the drake arching his head backward until his nape touches his back, then uttering a *peent* call and catapulting his head forward.

ID: large duck virtually limited to coastal areas; steep forehead; peaked crown; black wings with large white patches; yellow eyes. *Drake:* black back with extensive white areas; iridescent green head; round, white face patch; short, dark bill; white below except for black hindquarters. *Hen:* mostly gray body separated from rusty head by white neck; mostly yellow bill.
Size: *L* 16–20 in; *W* 26 in.
Status: uncommon resident along the Panhandle coast from November to March,

usually found in small flocks; rare and irregular elsewhere.
Habitat: ocean, bays and estuaries; rare on large inland lakes.
Nesting: does not breed in Florida.
Feeding: dives for crustaceans, mollusks and aquatic insects; may also eat seeds, tubers and other plant material.
Voice: generally silent in Florida.
Similar Species: *Bufflehead* (p. 57): much smaller; short, gray bill; drake has white patch on back of head, hen has oval, white cheek patch. *Hooded Merganser* (p. 59): drake has white crest outlined in black, slender bill and brown flanks; hen has bushy crest and brownish neck.
Best Sites: Alligator Pt.; St. Marks NWR.

HOODED MERGANSER

Lophodytes cucullatus

Mergansers are fish-eating ducks that are easily identified by their very narrow, sawtooth bills that are used to capture and hold their slippery prey. • Because of the drake's beautiful plumage, the Hooded Merganser is one of the most sought after and appreciated of Florida's waterfowl. The drake's rounded crest is usually lowered, but it is raised when he is courting or wary. • Hooded Mergansers are fairly common winter residents throughout Florida's mainland and are usually seen in small flocks. They are rare breeders in the northern half of the state, and several breeding reports indicate that they have nested in nest boxes intended for Wood Ducks. • In most areas, Hooded Mergansers are found in freshwater ponds and marshes, but they commonly winter in shallow salt water in Florida, primarily along the Gulf Coast. They are also seen on stormwater retention ponds and other small wetlands. • Hooded Mergansers are the smallest mergansers and have a more diverse diet than their larger relatives.

ID: small duck with crested head; thin, blackish bill. *Drake:* fan-shaped head; black back and wings; bold, white crest is outlined in black; white breast with 2 vertical black slashes; rusty sides. *Hen:* dusky brown back, wings and head; shaggy, reddish brown crest; white belly. *In flight:* small, white wing patches on black (drake) or brown (hen) wings.
Size: *L* 16–18 in; *W* 24 in.
Status: fairly common resident occurring coastally and inland throughout the mainland from October to March; rare in the Keys; rarely nests in Florida.

Habitat: bays, estuaries, lakes, ponds and marshes.
Nesting: in a tree cavity or nest box lined with down or feathers; hen incubates 10–12 glossy white eggs for about 31 days.
Feeding: dives for small fish, aquatic insects, crustaceans and the seeds and roots of aquatic plants.
Voice: usually silent in Florida but utters occasional low grunts and croaks. *Drake:* froglike *crrrrooo* during courtship display.
Similar Species: *Bufflehead* (p. 57): drake has white underparts and no black outline at back of white head patch; white underparts. *Red-breasted Merganser* (p. 60): rare on fresh water; larger; female has orange eyes, grayer body and longer, reddish bill.
Best Sites: widespread.

59

RED-BREASTED MERGANSER

Mergus serrator

The Red-breasted Merganser breeds throughout Alaska and much of Canada, and it winters on the Great Lakes and from Alaska and Newfoundland along the Pacific, Atlantic and Gulf coasts to northern Mexico. It is the most common and perhaps the most widespread merganser in Florida. • Unlike Hooded Mergansers, Red-breasted Mergansers are mostly restricted to salt water, although small numbers are found inland on larger lakes. They are usually seen in loose flocks just offshore, diving for small fish and crustaceans. Flocks will occasionally swim in a line to "herd" fish into shallower water for easy capture. • Most Red-breasted Mergansers in Florida are females or nonbreeding males; the bright, distinctive plumage of breeding males is rarely seen in our state. • Unlike Hooded or Common Mergansers, which nest in tree cavities or boxes, Red-breasted Mergansers prefer to build nests on the ground.

breeding

breeding

ID: large duck with slender body and conspicuous shaggy crest; thin, serrated, reddish bill; red eyes. *Breeding drake:* black and white back; green head; white collar; rusty breast spotted with black; black and white shoulders; gray flanks; white belly and undertail coverts. *Hen, nonbreeding drake and juvenile:* gray-brown back and wings; rusty head with white chin; whitish or pale gray throat and breast; white belly and undertail coverts. *In flight:* conspicuous white patch on inner wing.
Size: *L* 19–26 in; *W* 30 in.

Status: generally common coastal resident statewide from November to April, becoming rare inland.
Habitat: coastal waters and estuaries; large inland lakes.
Nesting: does not breed in Florida.
Feeding: dives underwater for small fish; also eats aquatic invertebrates.
Voice: generally silent in Florida.
Similar Species: *Hooded Merganser* (p. 59): hen is smaller, with darker body and yellow eyes. *Common Merganser:* exceedingly rare in Florida; drake has white breast, red bill with much thicker base and no crest; hen's rusty foreneck contrasts sharply with white chin and breast.
Best Sites: widespread.

RUDDY DUCK
Oxyura jamaicensis

Ruddy Ducks are small bay ducks that winter along Florida's northern coasts or on large lakes or mine impoundments in the central interior, often in large flocks. • The Ruddy has a flattened and somewhat elongated head, short neck and short tail, which is often held upraised at an angle. The drake has gleaming white cheek patches that contrast with the black crown and grayish brown body of his nonbreeding plumage. The hen looks similar, but her cheek is marked with a wide, dark line. • On rare occasions, Ruddy Ducks have bred in Florida, sometimes on small, protected stormwater retention ponds. When the drake molts into his resplendent breeding plumage, he develops a bright rusty body and bright azure bill. As part of his courtship display, he inflates sacs in his neck with air, tilts his head backward and emits a series of notes.

nonbreeding

ID: small, pudgy sea duck; large head; short neck; short tail, often held upraised. *Breeding drake:* rarely seen in Florida; bright, rusty body; black crown and nape; bright azure bill. *Nonbreeding drake:* dull brownish body, darker above; blackish crown and nape; large white cheek patch; grayish bill. *Hen:* similar to nonbreeding drake, but with wide, dark horizontal stripe across cheek.
Size: *L* 15–16 in; *W* 18½ in.
Status: local and declining resident throughout the mainland from November to April; rare in the Keys.
Habitat: bays, estuaries and ocean; also large inland lakes.

Nesting: rare in Florida: in cattails, bulrushes or other emergent vegetation; hen suspends woven platform nest over water and incubates 5–10 rough, whitish eggs for 23–26 days.
Feeding: dives for aquatic vegetation and lesser amounts of crustaceans and insects.
Voice: generally silent in Florida.
Similar Species: *Masked Duck:* exceedingly rare in Florida; drake has black face and rusty upperparts strongly marked with black streaking; hen has buffy body marked with blackish spots and stippling, buffy nape and eyebrow and conspicuous black eye line giving appearance of double-striped cheek.
Best Sites: Lake Apopka; Merritt Island NWR; Tampa Bay.

61

WILD TURKEY
Meleagris gallopavo

Wild Turkeys were once common throughout most of central and eastern North America, but habitat loss and overhunting during the 20th century took a toll on their populations. Florida remained a vital refuge during this time, and many of the state's turkeys were captured and transported to other states as part of restoration programs. Despite the state's rampant development, Wild Turkeys are still found in each of Florida's 67 counties, and they were recently reestablished at Everglades National Park. • Although turkeys forage on the ground and travel mostly by foot, they can fly strongly for short distances. As surprising as it may seem, turkeys avoid predation by bobcats and other terrestrial predators by roosting in trees at night! • Wild Turkeys are wary, but flocks become fairly tame where they are not molested. It remains a common sight to see flocks of dozens of turkeys feeding in early morning or late afternoon in pastures near oak hammocks or cypress swamps.

ID: large terrestrial fowl; usually found in flocks; unfeathered head; dark, glossy, iridescent body; barred, copper-colored tail. *Male:* long central breast tassel; colorful head and body. *Female:* smaller; lacks breast tassel; blue-gray head; less iridescent body.
Size: *Male: L* 3–3½ ft; *W* 5½ ft. *Female: L* 3 ft; *W* 4 ft.
Status: surprisingly common permanent resident of the mainland south to Everglades NP.
Habitat: open deciduous or mixed woodlands or cypress swamps adjacent to pastures and other open fields.

Nesting: in a depression on the ground under thick cover; nest is lined with grass and leaves; female incubates 10–12 brown-speckled, pale buff eggs for about 28 days.
Feeding: in open woodlands or fields near protective cover; forages on the ground for acorns, seeds and fruits; also eats insects, especially beetles and grasshoppers; may take small amphibians.
Voice: wide array of sounds, including loud *pert* alarm call, cluck gathering call and loud *keouk-keouk-keouk* contact call. *Male:* gobbles loudly during courting.
Similar Species: none except domestic fowl.
Best Sites: widespread.

NORTHERN BOBWHITE

Colinus virginianus

The Northern Bobwhite is the only quail species found in the East, and many people refer to the bird as simply "quail." • Throughout fall and winter, several families of bobwhites form a flock, known as a covey, in which the birds forage and roost together. At night, bobwhites roost in a circle with each bird facing outward to better detect predators. When disturbed, bobwhites "explode" from underfoot with whirring wings. By late winter, the covey breaks up as males leave to search for mates. • The male's characteristic, whistled *oh-bob-white* call, issued in spring, is often the only evidence of this bird's presence among the dense grass and palmettos. The bobwhite is mostly terrestrial, but the male may sing from a fence post, tree or the roof of a house. • Northern Bobwhites may benefit from some forms of habitat disturbance, but they cannot survive in urban or suburban areas where dense nesting cover is removed and where cats and other nonnative predators are found.

ID: small, chunky terrestrial bird; found in family groups or small flocks; brown or brownish black upperparts, mottled with buff; slightly peaked crown; chestnut flanks marked with black and white stripes; short tail. *Male:* broad white eyebrow; white throat. *Female:* buffy throat and eyebrow.

Size: *L* 10 in; *W* 13 in.

Status: fairly common but declining permanent resident nearly statewide; most common where understory is burned frequently; generally rare in the southern peninsula; absent from the Keys.

Habitat: open woodlands and woodland edges, grassy or brushy fields and prairies.

Nesting: in a shallow depression on the ground, often concealed by surrounding vegetation or a woven dome; nest is lined with grass and leaves; pair incubates 12–16 white to pale buff eggs for 22–24 days.

Feeding: eats seeds, fruit, leaves and acorns; also takes insects and other invertebrates.

Voice: year-round whistled *hoy-hee*. *Male:* whistled, rising *bob-white* or *oh-bob-white* in spring and summer.

Similar Species: none.

Best Sites: widespread.

RED-THROATED LOON
Gavia stellata

Loons are medium- to large-sized, fish-eating birds that breed on freshwater lakes in northern North America but winter primarily on salt water. Of the five species that occur in North America, three have been found in Florida. • The Red-throated Loon breeds in the Arctic and winters along the Atlantic and Pacific coasts. In Florida, it is mainly a rare wintering species off our northern coasts. Sometimes a flock along the eastern Panhandle coast will contain more than a dozen individuals, and many dozens have been seen migrating off the Atlantic Coast during late fall or early winter. • The scientific name *stellata* refers to the white, starlike speckles on this bird's back during its nonbreeding plumage, which is the plumage observed in Florida.

nonbreeding

nonbreeding

ID: medium-sized diving bird found in salt water; slim bill held upward. *Nonbreeding:* white face and underparts; white-speckled back; dark gray on crown and back of head. *In flight:* hunched back; legs trail behind tail; rapid wingbeats.
Size: *L* 23–27 in; *W* 3½ ft.
Status: generally rare, very local resident of the Panhandle and northeastern coasts from November to March; irregular farther south and inland.

Habitat: coastal waters including estuaries; very rare on large inland lakes.
Nesting: does not breed in Florida.
Feeding: captures fish by diving.
Voice: silent in Florida.
Similar Species: *Common Loon* (p. 65): larger overall; nonbreeding bird has more extensive dark markings on head and neck, white "indentation" on lower neck, heavier bill, and unspeckled back.
Best Sites: Alligator Pt.; small numbers often offshore at Jacksonville during migration.

COMMON LOON

Gavia immer

The quavering wail of the Common Loon—a characteristic sound of ponds and lakes on this bird's breeding grounds in New England, Canada and Alaska—is almost never heard in Florida. Similarly, the Common Loon is rarely in its resplendent black and white breeding plumage while it resides in our state. • Common Loons are well adapted to their aquatic lifestyle. They float low on the water in between bouts of diving for food. These divers have nearly solid bones that make them less buoyant, and their feet are placed well back on their bodies for more effective underwater propulsion. On land, however, their rear-placed legs make walking difficult, and their heavy bodies and small wing size mean that they require a lengthy sprint over water before taking off. • It is thought that the word "loon" is derived from the Scandinavian word *lom,* meaning "clumsy person," in reference to this bird's clumsiness on land. • The Common Loon also occurs in the Old World, where it is known as "Great Northern Diver."

nonbreeding

nonbreeding

ID: large diving bird of coasts and large lakes; thick, stout bill. *Nonbreeding:* brown back, nape and back of head; white "indentation" where neck meets body; white underparts. *In flight:* long wings beat constantly; hunchbacked appearance; legs trail behind tail.
Size: *L* 28–35 in; *W* 4–5 ft.
Status: fairly common coastal resident from the Panhandle to the central peninsula from November to April; generally rare farther south; uncommon on large lakes inland.
Habitat: coastal waters, estuaries and bays; also on large inland lakes.
Nesting: does not breed in Florida.
Feeding: dives to great depths for fish.
Voice: usually silent in Florida.
Similar Species: *Red-throated Loon* (p. 64): smaller; slender bill; sharply defined white face and white-spotted back in nonbreeding plumage. *Double-crested Cormorant* (p. 76): juvenile has strongly hooked, yellow bill.
Best Sites: widespread.

PIED-BILLED GREBE
Podilymbus podiceps

G rebes are like smaller varieties of loons, which they resemble in their plain plumage and diving habits. • The odd, exuberant chuckling of the Pied-billed Grebe is one of the most frequently heard and distinctive avian sounds of Florida's freshwater wetlands. As a breeder, the Pied-billed Grebe is most numerous in the central peninsula. Heard more frequently than it is seen, the Pied-billed Grebe nests inconspicuously among the abundant grasses and sedges of marshes and the cattail clumps of lakes. But during winter, when it is found throughout the state, this grebe is conspicuous in the open water of Florida's deep lakes and coastal waters. • A grebe frightened off its nest will quickly cover its eggs with vegetation and slide underwater until only its eyes and nostrils are above the surface.

breeding

nonbreeding

ID: small, stocky diving bird; short neck; stocky, pale bill. *Breeding:* brown body; black ring on bill; black throat; pale belly. *Nonbreeding:* bill lacks black ring; white chin and throat; brownish crown.
Size: *L* 12–15 in; *W* 16 in.
Status: fairly common but somewhat local permanent resident throughout the mainland; rare in the Keys; most common during winter.
Habitat: ponds, marshes, impoundments and lakes with emergent vegetation; also uses flooded agricultural lands; rare on salt water.

Nesting: in a pond or marsh; floating platform of plant material is anchored to or placed among emergent vegetation; pair incubates 4–5 white to buff eggs for about 23 days.
Feeding: dives shallowly and gleans the water's surface for aquatic invertebrates, small fish and amphibians; occasionally eats aquatic plants.
Voice: loud, variable whooping call begins quickly then slows down: *kuk-kuk-kuk cow cow cow cowp cowp cowp.*
Similar Species: *Horned Grebe* (p. 67): prefers salt water; short, thin bill; red eyes; nonbreeding has black and white plumage. *Eared Grebe* (p. 359): rare; short, thin bill; red eyes; nonbreeding has black and white plumage. *American Coot* (p. 123): black body; white bill extends onto forehead.
Best Sites: widespread.

HORNED GREBE

Podiceps auritus

The Horned Grebe breeds across Alaska, Canada and parts of Montana, North Dakota and Minnesota. It winters along the coast from Alaska and New Brunswick to northern Mexico and Florida. The Horned Grebe is found throughout Florida during winter, occurring off both the Gulf and Atlantic coasts and on large inland lakes. It rides high in the water and has a rounded head outline with slightly puffed cheeks. • Grebes catch their food in long dives that may last up to two minutes, and they can dive to depths of almost 20 feet. • Unlike the fully webbed front toes of most swimming birds, the grebes toes are individually webbed, or "lobed." • This bird's common name and its scientific name *auritus*, meaning "eared," both refer to the golden feather tufts that this grebe acquires in breeding plumage—a plumage that is seldom seen in Florida.

nonbreeding

ID: small diving bird; mostly of coastal habitats. *Nonbreeding:* lacks "ear" tufts; black upperparts; white cheek, foreneck and underparts. *In flight:* wings beat constantly; large white patch at rear of inner wing.
Size: *L* 12–15 in; *W* 18 in.
Status: fairly common to locally common coastal resident of the Panhandle and northern half of the peninsula from

November to March; less common farther south and inland.
Habitat: mainly coastal waters; also uses large inland lakes.
Nesting: does not breed in Florida.
Feeding: dives shallowly and gleans the water's surface for invertebrates and small fish.
Voice: silent in Florida.
Similar Species: *Pied-billed Grebe* (p. 66): mostly brown body; short, thick neck; thick bill. *Eared Grebe* (p. 359): rare; mostly black head with white crescent behind cheek; dark foreneck.
Best Sites: widespread.

CORY'S SHEARWATER

Calonectris diomedea

Shearwaters introduce one of the most pelagic families of birds, the Procellariiformes, which includes albatrosses, shearwaters and petrels. Except when driven to shore by tropical storms, procellariids are not usually found in Florida. To see them, a birder would usually have to board a boat and travel to the deep waters over which these seabirds dwell. • Shearwaters and petrels spend most of their lives at sea. They use ocean breezes and uplifts from waves to soar or glide great distances, and they forage by plucking marine prey from the ocean's surface. • The Cory's Shearwater is the only shearwater that breeds and winters in the Northern Hemisphere. It breeds in burrows dug into rocky cliffs on islands in the Mediterranean. After breeding, this species disperses hundreds of miles into the Atlantic Ocean, including the seas off Florida, where it is the most numerous large shearwater. • This shearwater is named after Charles B. Cory (1857–1921), who was one of the most important ornithologists in North America in his day.

ID: large seabird with yellowish bill; gray-brown upperparts; white underparts; dark wing tips and tail tip; white neck and cheek blend with pale brown head; small, white rump patch. *In flight:* wings slightly bent while gliding.
Size: *L* 18–21 in; *W* 3½ ft.

Status: fairly common nonbreeding visitor offshore in the Atlantic from May to October; less numerous in the Gulf.
Habitat: open ocean; favors warm waters.
Nesting: does not breed in Florida.
Feeding: picks fish, squid and crustaceans from the ocean's surface or just below.
Voice: usually silent at sea.
Similar Species: *Greater Shearwater:* white collar extends around nape; blackish upperparts and white underparts have greater contrast; dark smudge on belly; dark bill.
Best Sites: Atlantic Ocean; Gulf of Mexico.

AUDUBON'S SHEARWATER

Puffinus lherminieri

While visiting the Dry Tortugas National Park by boat or when fishing on a vessel in the Atlantic, you are likely to come across a few Audubon's Shearwaters during spring or summer. Unlike some other seabirds that are notorious ship-followers, such as Albatross, these small shearwaters do not follow vessels. Birders usually catch only glimpses of these small, black and white seabirds as they cross the bow or are startled off the surface of the water. • While pursuing small fish or squid, Audubon's Shearwaters skim the water's surface, alternately flapping, gliding and diving. • These seabirds nest on tropical islands around the world, including in the Atlantic, Pacific and Indian oceans. Their closest breeding grounds to Florida are in the Bahamas. During the nesting season, these birds leave their nesting burrows at night to feed and then return by day. • Audubon's Shearwaters are named after the great American ornithologist John James Audubon.

ID: small seabird with blackish upperparts and pale underparts with black undertail coverts. *In flight:* quick wingbeats and short glides.

Size: *L* 12 in; *W* 27 in.
Status: uncommon to fairly common non-breeding offshore resident of the Atlantic Ocean and Caribbean Sea from April to October but surprisingly rare in the Gulf.
Habitat: open ocean.
Nesting: does not breed in Florida.

Feeding: picks fish, squid and other small marine animals from the ocean's surface.
Voice: generally silent at sea.
Similar Species: *Greater Shearwater:* much larger; brown upperparts; black cap and tail; brown smudge on belly. *Manx Shearwater:* very rare; white undertail coverts.
Best Sites: Straits of Florida; Atlantic Ocean.

69

WILSON'S STORM-PETREL
Oceanites oceanicus

Storm-petrels are swallow-sized seabirds that breed in rocky burrows and spend the rest of the year on the ocean. Eight species are found off the coasts of North America and three—the Wilson's, the Leach's and the Band-rumped—have been observed off Florida. The Wilson's Storm-Petrel is encountered fairly commonly during spring and summer off Florida's Atlantic Coast and less commonly in the Gulf of Mexico. • Wilson's Storm-Petrels are long-distance migrants that travel from their Antarctic and sub-Antarctic nesting grounds to their nonbreeding grounds, which cover much of the world's oceans. • This seabird flies with shallow wingbeats just above the water's surface. While foraging, it may hover or patter its feet on the water. • Some ornithologists believe that the Wilson's Storm-Petrel is the most abundant bird in the world.

Size: *L* 7 in; *W* 18 in.
Status: probably rare but regular visitor offshore from April to October; most numerous in the Atlantic.
Habitat: open ocean.
Nesting: does not breed in Florida.

ID: small blackish-brown seabird; white rump and undertail coverts. *In flight:* shallow, stiff, swallow-like wingbeats; toes extend beyond end of square tail.

Feeding: feeds on plankton and other small aquatic prey plucked from the ocean's surface; often "patters" feet on the surface, more so than other storm-petrels.
Voice: usually silent at sea.
Similar Species: *Band-rumped Storm-Petrel* (p. 360): narrower white rump patch; less extensive white on undertail coverts; shearwater-like flight with shallow wing beats and stiff-winged glides; does not dangle feet. *Leach's Storm-Petrel:* distinct and diagnostic forked tail; white rump often divided by narrow brown line, but may be hard to see.
Best Sites: Atlantic Ocean.

MASKED BOOBY

Sula dactylatra

Boobies are tropical seabirds that feed by plunge-diving into the sea, often from heights of 30 feet or more. They are never seen from the Florida mainland except after tropical storms, when they may be driven to shore. Four species occur in North America, and three of them—the Masked, the Brown and the Red-footed—are found in Florida. • The Masked Booby is the largest of the boobies, with a wingspan of over 5 feet. • This seabird was previously a regular nonbreeding visitor to Dry Tortugas National Park, about 70 miles west of Key West. However, in 1984 a pair of boobies bred at Hospital Key, and nesting has occurred there in most years subsequently. This was the first breeding colony of Masked Boobies in North America. • To attract a mate, the male booby selects a nest site, lures females to view his "sky pointing" performances and offers feathers and stones as gifts. • Unlike Brown Boobies or Red-footed Boobies, which commonly roost in trees or on buoys or channel markers, Masked Boobies roost on land or on the water.

ID: large seabird; mostly white with black mask, flight feathers and tail; long, pinkish bill. **Size:** *L* 27–33 in. *W* 5½ ft.
Status: rare breeding resident at Dry Tortugas NP; otherwise rare to uncommon offshore.
Habitat: *Breeding:* barren shores of tropical or subtropical islands. *Nonbreeding:* open ocean.

Nesting: nest is a depression in sand surrounded by debris; female incubates 1–2 bluish white eggs for 38–49 days.
Feeding: tucks wings back and dives head-first into the ocean to feed on fish and squid.
Voice: *Male:* hoarse whistles. *Female:* deep honks.
Similar Species: *Northern Gannet* (p. 73): white tail; black in wings restricted to primaries; yellow wash on head and neck. *Red-footed Booby* (p. 360): white morph is smaller and has bluish bill and red feet.
Best Sites: Dry Tortugas NP; offshore.

BROWN BOOBY

Sula leucogaster

Brown Boobies are most often seen resting on buoys and channel markers at Dry Tortugas National Park. These elevated perches give the birds an extra boost during takeoff. • Although common at the Tortugas—on some days more than 100 may be seen—Brown Boobies are rarely seen elsewhere in Florida. John James Audubon claimed that Brown Boobies bred at the Tortugas in 1832, but his account contained inconsistencies and has since been discounted by ornithologists; there has been no subsequent report of Brown Boobies breeding in our state. • Like other gannets and boobies, Brown Boobies feed by diving headlong into the water, often from great heights. • The genus name *Sula* is derived from an Icelandic word meaning "an awkward fellow" and probably refers to the clumsy walk of the birds. The species name comes from two Greek words: *leuko*, which means "white" and *gaster*, which means "belly."

ID: large seabird with brown head, neck and back; yellow bill; white underparts; large, yellow feet. *Juvenile:* dark brown overall. *In flight:* short, pointed wings with black primaries and secondaries; long, pointed tail.

Size: *L* 30 in; *W* 4½–5 ft.

Status: uncommon to occasionally common nonbreeding year-round resident at the Tortugas; generally rare elsewhere offshore.

Habitat: open ocean.

Nesting: does not breed in Florida.

Feeding: plunge dives to catch fish and squid.

Voice: generally silent in Florida; females honk when disturbed.

Similar Species: *Masked Booby* (p. 71): mostly white with black flight feathers; does not perch on buoys or channel markers; immature has white rump, collar and underwings. *Northern Gannet* (p. 73): much larger, with longer wings; mostly white with black wing tips; does not perch on buoys or channel markers; immature has white uppertail coverts.

Best Site: Dry Tortugas NP.

NORTHERN GANNET

Morus bassanus

The Northern Gannet is the only pelagic species in Florida that can often be seen from shore. From fall through spring, small to occasionally large numbers can be seen feeding just offshore, especially along the Atlantic and Panhandle coasts. • Northern Gannets fly along slowly, scanning the surface of the water from heights of 50 feet or more. When a school of fish is sighted, gannets suddenly fold back their wings and plunge headfirst into the ocean. Their skull is reinforced to cushion the brain from the impact of diving. • Northern Gannets nest in large colonies, called ganneries, on the cliff faces of islands in eastern Canada and in the Old World. They often mate for life, reestablishing pair bonds each year at their nest sites by indulging in elaborate face-to-face nest-duty exchange sequences that involve wing raising, tail spreading, bowing, sky-pointing and preening. • The word "gannet" is derived from the Anglo-Saxon word *ganot*, meaning "little goose." This bird was once classified taxonomically and popularly with the geese.

juvenile

ID: large white seabird; black wing tips; buffy wash on nape; thick, tapered bill; long, narrow wings; pointed tail. *Immature:* various stages of mottled gray, black and white.
Size: *L* 3 ft; *W* 6 ft.
Status: uncommon to sometimes-abundant nonbreeding migrant and resident offshore from November to March; often seen from shore along the Panhandle and Atlantic coasts.
Habitat: open ocean.
Nesting: does not breed in Florida.
Feeding: dives for fish or squid; also forages by submerging its head while floating on the ocean's surface.
Voice: generally silent at sea.
Similar Species: *Masked Booby* (p. 71): smaller; adult has black mask and tail; immature has white collar and more white on underwings.
Best Sites: Atlantic and Panhandle coasts.

AMERICAN WHITE PELICAN

Pelecanus erythrorhynchos

The American White Pelican is not nearly as well known and loved in Florida as its relative the Brown Pelican, nor is it resident in our state. However, it is perhaps the more majestic and awe-inspiring of the two species, especially when seen in large, soaring flocks. • American White Pelicans breed in colonies in southwestern Canada and the western U.S., and they winter from California and Florida to Central America, traveling between breeding and wintering areas in flocks of dozens of individuals. • Unlike the Brown Pelican, which dives singly for fish, the American White Pelican feeds by swimming in flocks and "herding" fish into shallow water. Each bird then dips its bill into the water, scooping the prey into its flexible pouch. As the pelican lifts its head, the water drains from its pouch through the sides of the bill, leaving behind the fish, which are then swallowed whole. A pelican's pouch can hold more than 3 gallons of water!

nonbreeding

ID: huge, stocky, white bird; often seen in large, soaring flocks; long, orange bill and pouch; black flight feathers; short tail. *Breeding:* plate develops on upper mandible.

Size: *L* 4½–6 ft; *W* 9 ft.

Status: uncommon to locally abundant migrant and winter resident throughout the mainland from October to April; less common summer nonbreeder in the Keys and the peninsula.

Habitat: estuaries, bays and freshwater lakes; also uses flooded agricultural fields.

In migration: flocks may be seen over any habitat.

Nesting: does not breed in Florida.

Feeding: work cooperatively to herd fish into shallow water, then forages by dipping its bill into the water while floating on the ocean's surface.

Voice: generally silent in Florida.

Similar Species: no other large, white bird has long bill with pouch. *Wood Stork* (p. 94) and *Whooping Crane* (p. 126): fly with necks extended and long legs trailing beyond tail.

Best Sites: fairly widespread.

BROWN PELICAN

Pelecanus occidentalis

Brown Pelicans are among the most conspicuous and familiar birds in our state, known even to tourists and nonbirders. They are commonly seen perched on mangroves or pilings, or flying single file just inches above the ocean. Brown Pelicans are primarily a coastal species but are increasingly seen inland in the peninsula; a few pairs even bred at Lake Okeechobee in 1991–92. • Among the world's six species of pelicans, the Brown Pelican has a unique foraging method: it flies slowly over the water at heights of perhaps 10–20 feet, then folds back its wings, pulls back its head and dives headfirst into the water. All other pelicans scoop up their prey while swimming in shallow water. • In the 1950s and 1960s, poisoning from the now-banned pesticide DDT resulted in the near-extirpation of Brown Pelicans from many areas, including Louisiana, which calls itself the "Pelican State." Fortunately, the effects of DDT had less of an impact in Florida than elsewhere, and our birds were used to reestablish pelican populations in other states.

breeding

ID: large, familiar seabird; grayish brown body; very large, pouched bill. *Breeding:* yellow head; white foreneck; dark brown nape. *Nonbreeding:* white neck; head washed with yellow. *Immature:* uniformly dusky; buff-tipped head and neck contrast with pale underparts.
Size: *L* 4 ft; *W* 7 ft.
Status: species of special concern (FWC); common permanent resident of most coastal areas; nonbreeders becoming regular inland.

Habitat: bays, estuaries and shorelines; rare inland on large lakes.
Nesting: on the ground or in a mangrove; nest may be a scrape or an elaborate platform built of sticks and lined with vegetation; both parents incubate 2–3 white eggs for 29–32 days.
Feeding: forages almost exclusively for fish, which are caught by diving headfirst into the water; fish are held in the flexible pouch until water is drained.
Voice: generally silent away from colonies.
Similar Species: *American White Pelican* (p. 74): white body with extensive black in wings.
Best Sites: widespread.

DOUBLE-CRESTED CORMORANT

Phalacrocorax auritus

The Double-crested Cormorant is one of the most abundant and widespread waterbirds in Florida. Although rare in the Panhandle, it is ubiquitous in the peninsula, occurring commonly along both Gulf and Atlantic coasts as well as inland around lakes and springs. The Double-crested Cormorant is easily spotted when flying in large, V-shaped or single-file flocks between foraging and roosting areas. • Double-crested Cormorants are often seen perched on oyster bars, channel markers or piers, with their wings partially spread to dry their feathers after foraging. The cormorant's feathers are "wettable" rather than water repellant, making the bird less buoyant so it can more easily pursue fish underwater. • Japanese fishermen once commonly used other species of cormorants to catch fish—a ring was placed around the bird's throat to prevent it from swallowing the fish, and a leash was attached to the ring. The cormorant was released into the water to fish, then reeled in back to the boat once it made a catch.

juvenile

ID: rather large, black seabird; stocky neck; orange gular patch; hook-tipped, dark bill; blue eyes. *Juvenile:* brown upperparts; pale throat and breast; yellowish gular patch. *In flight:* strong, direct flight with rapid wingbeats; kinked neck.
Size: *L* 26–32 in; *W* 4½ ft.
Status: common to abundant permanent resident throughout Florida; mostly coastal during winter in the Panhandle.
Habitat: open water, ranging from salt to fresh; avoids small ponds; roosts and nests in trees or shrubs.
Nesting: colonial; in a shrub or tree, usually on an island or in a swamp; nest is built of sticks; pair incubates 3–4 bluish white eggs for 25–29 days; young are fed by regurgitation.
Feeding: long underwater dives to depths of 30 ft or more to capture fish; surfaces to swallow prey.
Voice: generally quiet away from breeding colonies; deep, guttural grunts at nest.
Similar Species: *Anhinga* (p. 77): restricted to fresh water; black body streaked with silver and white; longer, thinner neck, usually held outstretched; fanlike tail; red eyes; female has brown head and neck. *Great Cormorant:* very rare in Florida; larger; white throat borders yellow gular patch; larger head and body; shorter, thicker neck.
Best Sites: widespread.

ANHINGA
Anhinga anhinga

The name "Anhinga" comes to us from the Tupi-speaking natives of the Amazon; it means "evil spirit of the woods" in their language. The Anhinga, which ranges from the southeastern U.S. to northern South America and the West Indies, is the sole New World member of the Darters (Anhingidae), a family of birds related to cormorants but restricted to fresh water. • The Anhinga's ability to control its buoyancy gives it a stealthy hunting technique and makes it an ominous presence in Florida's freshwater ponds and canals. Possessing dense bones and easily waterlogged feathers, it swims almost completely submerged, holding its curved neck just above the water, often appearing snakelike. With a quick lunge and a stab of the Anhinga's long, sharp bill, it captures its prey. Serrations on the top of the bill keep the prey from flopping off until the Anhinga flips its catch in the air and swallows it headfirst. • Following a foraging bout, Anhingas must dry out their feathers before they can fly.

breeding

ID: rather large waterbird with long, curved neck; black body with silver and white streaking; long, fanlike tail; red eyes. *Breeding:* blue-green orbital ring. *Female* and *juvenile:* buffy head and neck.
Size: *L* 2½–3 ft; *W* 4 ft.
Status: generally common permanent resident in the peninsula; less common and local in the Panhandle; very rare in the Keys.

Habitat: quiet, sheltered, slowly moving or still fresh water.
Nesting: colonial; in a tree above the water; male brings sticks for the female to build the nest; pair incubates 2–5 whitish eggs for 25–29 days.
Feeding: swims submerged or perches motionless, then stabs prey; feeds primarily on fish; may also take frogs and snakes.
Voice: descending metallic clicks while perched.
Similar Species: *Double-crested Cormorant* (p. 76): heavier body without silver streaking; heavy, hooked bill; blue eyes; yellow gular pouch; often feeds in salt water.
Best Sites: widespread.

MAGNIFICENT FRIGATEBIRD

Fregata magnificens

Piracy of food from other birds, known as kleptoparasitism, is a strategy often employed by the Magnificent Frigatebird. Gulls, terns and other birds carrying food are harassed in flight until they drop or regurgitate their meal, which is then snatched up by the frigatebird. • The only Magnificent Frigatebird breeding colony in the U.S. is found on Long Key at Dry Tortugas National Park and includes about 100 pairs. Other breeding sites are found in the West Indies, Central America and South America. • During courtship, groups of male Magnificent Frigatebirds put on a spectacular performance for onlooking females. The males inflate their red gular sacs, which look like large balloons, and shake their wings and heads while clacking their bills and uttering hoarse, cackling calls. • Based on body weight, frigatebirds have the largest wing surface area of any bird. With great wings and a deeply forked tail, they are virtually unsurpassed at both soaring and overall aerial ability.

ID: very large aerial seabird with long, narrow wings; long, deeply forked tail; long, hooked bill. *Male:* glossy black overall, with inflatable red throat patch. *Female:* blackish brown plumage with white breast. *Juvenile:* varying amount of white on head and breast.

Size: L 3–3½ ft; W 7–8 ft.

Status: breeding resident at Dry Tortugas NP; otherwise local but sometimes abundant nonbreeding resident of the southern half of the peninsula and Keys; rare farther north and inland, usually after tropical storms.

Habitat: roosts and nests among mangroves on coastal islands; feeds along coastal waters or offshore.

Nesting: colonial; in a mangrove; builds flimsy stick platform; pair incubates 1 white egg for about 40 days; both adults feed the young.

Feeding: swoops down to snatch prey off the water's surface or steals prey from other birds; eats mostly fish but occasionally takes jellyfish, crustaceans and even small birds.

Voice: silent except at nesting colonies, where it utters hoarse, cackling notes.

Similar Species: usually unmistakable. *Swallow-tailed Kite* (p. 99): may be mistaken for juvenile frigatebird but is smaller, with all-white underparts and shorter bill, and prefers terrestrial habitats.

Best Sites: Dry Tortugas NP; Fort De Soto Park; the Keys.

AMERICAN BITTERN
Botaurus lentiginosus

The American Bittern breeds over much of southern Canada and the northern U.S., and it winters in the southern U.S. and along the Pacific Coast north to British Columbia. • At the approach of an intruder, an American Bittern's first reaction is to freeze with its bill pointed skyward—its vertically streaked, brown plumage blends in well with its typical surroundings. Intruders usually simply pass by without noticing the bird. This defensive reaction can sometimes place the bittern in a humorous situation—it will try to mimic reeds in an open field or while standing in the middle of a road. The American Bittern prefers to hunt at dawn or dusk, when its camouflage is most effective. • American Bitterns are seldom seen in Florida because of their retiring habits and usually inaccessible wetland habitats, but they are uncommon winter residents throughout the mainland. There are several unverified reports of breeding. • The American Bittern's distinctive call is rarely heard in Florida.

ID: large, elusive wading bird with brown upperparts; streaking on neck and breast; straight, stout bill; yellow legs and feet; black "mustache." *In flight:* distinctive pointed wings and blackish flight feathers.
Size: *L* 23–27 in; *W* 3½ ft.
Status: fairly common, although inconspicuous, migrant and resident throughout the mainland from October to April; rare in the Keys.
Habitat: shallow freshwater wetlands.

Nesting: not confirmed to breed in Florida.
Feeding: patient stand-and-wait predator; strikes at small fish, crayfish, frogs and snakes.
Voice: generally silent in Florida; deep, slow, resonant, "pumping" *pomp-er-lunk* given around dawn or dusk.
Similar Species: *Black-crowned Night-Heron* (p. 89) and *Yellow-crowned Night-Heron* (p. 90): juveniles have darker brown upperparts flecked with white and no "mustache."
Best Sites: widespread.

LEAST BITTERN

Ixobrychus exilis

The Least Bittern is the smallest of the herons and is one of the most reclusive marsh birds in North America. It inhabits marshes where tall, impenetrable stands of cattails conceal its movements. This bird moves about with ease, its slender body passing freely and usually unnoticed through dense marshland habitat. An expert climber, the Least Bittern can often be seen perched three or more feet above water, clinging to vertical stems. • Least Bitterns are fairly common permanent residents in Florida, breeding throughout the mainland, on the Keys and sometimes in the mangroves of Florida Bay. Most of the birds that breed in the Panhandle and northern peninsula winter farther south. Although they occur commonly in Florida—virtually every stand of cattails contains this species—Least Bitterns are seldom seen because of their secretive behavior, solitary lifestyle and inaccessible habitats. However, knowledge of the Least Bittern's vocalizations will help birders find this elusive species.

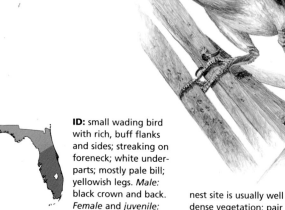

ID: small wading bird with rich, buff flanks and sides; streaking on foreneck; white underparts; mostly pale bill; yellowish legs. *Male:* black crown and back. *Female* and *juvenile:* chestnut head and back; juvenile has darker streaking on breast and back. *In flight:* large, buffy wing patches.

Size: *L* 11–14½ in; *W* 17 in.

Status: fairly common breeding resident virtually statewide; largely resident from the central peninsula southward.

Habitat: freshwater marshes with cattails and other dense emergent vegetation.

Nesting: the male constructs a platform of dry plant stalks on top of marsh vegetation; nest site is usually well concealed within dense vegetation; pair incubates 4–5 pale green or blue eggs for 17–20 days; young are fed by regurgitation.

Feeding: stabs prey with bill; eats mostly small fish; also takes large insects, tadpoles, frogs and crayfish.

Voice: staccato *kuk-kuk-kuk-kuk-kuk* call; *Male:* rapid 3-syllable cooing.

Similar Species: *Green Heron* (p. 88): longer neck; entirely dark wings.

Best Sites: widespread; common in the Everglades.

GREAT BLUE HERON

Ardea herodias

Great Blue Herons are arguably the best-known wading birds in Florida. In our state, they are often mistakenly called cranes. But unlike cranes, which hold their necks outstretched in flight, herons fly with their long necks tucked toward their bodies. • Like most other wading birds, Great Blue Herons nest in colonies known as rookeries. These rookeries can contain dozens to thousands of pairs, usually among other species of waterbirds. They are usually located on isolated islands or in wooded swamps to avoid terrestrial predators such as raccoons. • Everglades National Park and the Florida Keys are home to the "Great White Heron," a spectacular white morph of the Great Blue Heron that some ornithologists believe is actually a separate species.

breeding

breeding

ID: large, blue-gray wading bird; long, dark legs; curved neck; blue-gray back and wing coverts; large, straight, yellow bill; chestnut thighs. *Breeding:* richer colors; plumes on crown and breast. *In flight:* slow, steady wingbeats. *White morph:* white plumage overall, yellow legs.
Size: *L* 4–4½ ft; *W* 6 ft.
Status: common permanent resident statewide, with numbers augmented during fall.
Habitat: forages along the edges of various types of wetlands, from saline to fresh water; also stalks fields or yards.
Nesting: colonial; stick platform up to 4 ft in diameter is built in a tree or shrub; pair incubates 3–5 pale blue-green eggs for 22–24 days.
Feeding: patient stand-and-wait predator; spears fish, snakes, amphibians and even rodents, then swallows prey whole.
Voice: deep *frahnk-frahnk-frahnk* when startled.
Similar Species: *Sandhill Crane* (p. 125): unfeathered, red crown; flies with neck outstretched. *Tricolored Heron* (p. 85): smaller; slimmer neck and bill; darker upperparts; white underparts. *Little Blue Heron* (p. 84): much smaller; dark overall; dark, bicolored bill; juvenile is similar to white morph, but lacks yellow bill and legs. *Great* (p. 82), *Snowy* (p. 83) and *Cattle* (p. 87) *egrets:* juveniles resemble white morph, but smaller, without yellow bill and yellow legs.
Best Sites: widespread.

GREAT EGRET

Ardea alba

Great Egret and Snowy Egret plumes were widely used to decorate women's hats during the early 20th century. An ounce of egret feathers cost as much as $32—more than an ounce of gold at the time! As a result, egret populations rapidly plummeted toward extirpation. Some of the most successful conservation legislation in North America was enacted to outlaw the killing of the Great Egret and other birds for their plumes. Great Egret populations have since recovered, and the birds now breed farther north than they did historically. • Egrets are named after their silky breeding plumes, called aigrettes, which most species produce during courtship. The aigrettes of a Great Egret can grow up to 4½ feet long! • Great Egrets are widespread permanent residents throughout Florida. Because of their long legs and long neck, they can forage in deeper water than other egrets.

nonbreeding

breeding

ID: large, white wading bird; black legs; yellow bill. *Breeding:* white plumes trail from lower back; green lores. *In flight:* slow wingbeats; neck folds back over shoulders; legs extend backward.
Size: *L* 3–3½ ft; *W* 4 ft.
Status: common permanent resident statewide.
Habitat: edges of marshes, lakes and ponds; flooded agricultural fields.

Nesting: colonial; in a tree or tall shrub; pair builds a platform of sticks and incubates 3–5 pale blue-green eggs for 23–26 days.
Feeding: patient stand-and-wait predator; occasionally stalks slowly; feeds primarily on fish and aquatic invertebrates.
Voice: generally silent.
Similar Species: *Great Blue Heron* (p. 81): white morph is larger, with yellow bill and dull yellow legs. *Snowy Egret* (p. 83): much smaller; black bill; yellow feet. *Little Blue Heron* (p. 84): much smaller; white phase has greenish legs and dark, bicolored bill.
Best Sites: widespread.

SNOWY EGRET

Egretta thula

The dainty Snowy Egret is distinguished by its small size, white plumage and famously yellow feet on black legs. It was perhaps the most sought-after target for the plume trade because of the abundance of its fine aigrettes. Like other wading birds, the Snowy Egret teetered on the brink of extirpation in Florida by the early 1900s. Its population has recovered dramatically, however, and it now occurs beyond its historical range limits in North America. • Herons and egrets, particularly Snowy Egrets, use a variety of feeding techniques. By poking their bright yellow feet in the muck of shallow wetlands, Snowy Egrets flush prey from hiding places, then actively pursue the fish in shallow waters. They also "canopy feed" by extending their wings over open water and waiting for a fish to be attracted to the shaded spot, so that it can be quickly seized and eaten. • Snowy Egrets are found in virtually any wetland habitat in Florida, and they occur statewide.

breeding

nonbreeding

ID: medium-sized, white wading bird; yellow lores; black bill and legs; bright yellow feet. *Breeding:* long plumes on throat and lower back.
Size: *L* 22–26 in; *W* 3½ ft.
Status: species of special concern (FWC); common and widespread permanent resident statewide.
Habitat: edges of marshes, rivers, lakes and ponds; flooded agricultural fields.

Nesting: colonial; in a tree or tall shrub; pair builds a platform of sticks and incubates 3–5 pale blue-green eggs for 23–26 days.
Feeding: stand-and-wait predator; also actively chases after fish in shallows.
Voice: generally silent away from colonies; occasionally utters hoarse, raspy squawks.
Similar Species: *Great Egret* (p. 82): much larger; yellow bill; black feet. *Cattle Egret* (p. 87): yellow-orange legs and bill; favors fields and pastures. *Little Blue Heron* (p. 84): juvenile has bicolored bill and greenish legs.
Best Sites: widespread.

LITTLE BLUE HERON

Egretta caerulea

With its dark plumage and less attractive aigrettes, the Little Blue Heron was not as sought after by plume hunters as the white-feathered egrets, but it suffered nonetheless at the rookeries; because many wading birds breed in mixed colonies, persecution of one species affected them all. Like most other wading birds, the Little Blue Heron has made a dramatic recovery in the past century. It is once again a fairly common permanent resident throughout Florida, although it is somewhat rare in parts of the Panhandle. • Little Blue Herons are unique among North America's herons and egrets in having a true white phase: the juveniles are white, whereas birds in their second calendar year and older have no white at all in their plumage. The transitional immature plumage, in which the slate blue feathers of the adult plumage are molted in gradually, is known as "pied" or "calico." • When foraging, Little Blue Herons stand in or next to shallow water and wait for prey to pass by, or they slowly walk through water with their necks and bills held outstretched at a 45-degree angle.

breeding

immature

ID: medium-sized, slate-blue heron. *Breeding:* shaggy, maroon head and neck. *Nonbreeding:* purplish head and neck. *Immature:* white overall, usually with dusky tipped primaries, developing slate blue spots while molting to adult plumage; yellowish green legs; blue-gray bill with black tip.
Size: *L* 24 in; *W* 3½ ft.
Status: species of special concern (FWC); fairly common to common and widespread permanent resident across most of the state; somewhat rare in parts of the Panhandle.

Habitat: edges of marshes, lakes and ponds; flooded agricultural fields.
Nesting: nests in a shrub or tree above water; female uses sticks collected by male to build a bulky platform nest; pair incubates 3–5 pale greenish blue eggs for 22–24 days.
Feeding: patient stand-and-wait predator; also wades slowly to stalk prey; primarily eats fish, amphibians and aquatic invertebrates.
Voice: generally silent.
Similar Species: *Snowy Egret* (p. 83): yellow lores; black legs; bright yellow feet; black bill. *Cattle Egret* (p. 87): stocky, yellow bill; yellow legs and feet; not found in water; juvenile has black feet.
Best Sites: widespread.

TRICOLORED HERON

Egretta tricolor

Tricolored Herons are so named because they have three colors in their plumage: blue, white and chestnut. Juveniles have a rather different plumage than adults, but it consists of the same three colors. • The Tricolored Heron is easily identified by its extremely long, thin neck and bill, as well as by its unique plumage, which is dark above and white below • It is a fairly common permanent resident in most of Florida but generally rare in the western Panhandle. Some sources claim that it is the most abundant heron in the state—or at least the second most common, behind the Cattle Egret. • Although they are most partial to coastal habitats such as estuaries, Tricolored Herons are found in many types of wetlands, including those inland. When foraging, they are one of the most active wading birds, often pursuing fish in shallow water, or "canopy feeding."

breeding

nonbreeding

ID: rather large, dark heron with long, slender neck and bill. *Breeding:* purplish to grayish blue plumage with white underparts and foreneck; chestnut-tinged wing feathers; pale rump; long plumes on head and back. *Juvenile:* chestnut nape and wing coverts.
Size: *L* 26 in; *W* 3 ft.
Status: species of special concern (FWC); fairly common to common permanent resident across most of the state; generally rare in the western Panhandle.
Habitat: edges of marshes, mangrove swamps, estuaries, lakes and ponds; flooded agricultural fields.

Nesting: colonial; female uses sticks and vegetation collected by the male to build a bulky platform in a tree or shrub; pair incubates 3–4 greenish blue eggs for 21–25 days.
Feeding: feeds primarily on small fish caught by active pursuit or standing and waiting.
Voice: generally silent.
Similar Species: *Reddish Egret* (p. 86): mostly restricted to coasts; shaggy, reddish head and neck; dark underparts; black-tipped, pinkish (breeding) or all-dark (nonbreeding) bill. *Little Blue Heron* (p. 84): nonbreeding bird has slate blue plumage; breeding bird has shaggy, maroon head and neck, bicolored bill and dark underparts.
Best Sites: widespread.

REDDISH EGRET

Egretta rufescens

The Reddish Egret is Florida's rarest and most range-restricted wading bird, although it is fairly common in suitable areas. • When foraging for fish among Florida's bays and estuaries, the Reddish Egret reveals itself to be a most entertaining bird. It characteristically feeds by lurching through shallow water in a weaving half-run while stabbing its bill in all directions. At other times, it takes a more calculated approach to feeding by standing motionless with outstretched wings as it "canopy feeds." The shade produced provides better visibility by reducing the sun's glare and likely also attracts fish seeking shelter from the sun. • The Reddish Egret occurs in two color morphs: red and white. The red morph is by far more common throughout Florida. Occasionally, a red-morph egret will be seen with scattered white feathers in its wings.

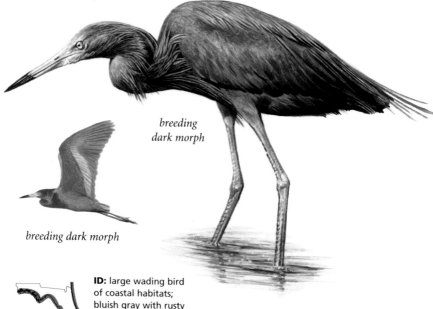

breeding
dark morph

breeding dark morph

ID: large wading bird of coastal habitats; bluish gray with rusty neck and head; dark bluish legs and feet; dark bill; pale eyes. *Breeding:* shaggy neck plumes; pinkish bill with black tip. *Juvenile:* gray with cinnamon head, neck and inner wing; dark bill. *White morph:* white plumage.
Size: L 27–32 in; W 3½–4 ft.
Status: species of special concern (FWC); fairly common permanent resident of the southern half of the mainland and the Keys; generally rare but potentially increasing farther north; rare inland.
Habitat: coastal lagoons, tidal flats, estuaries and mangrove swamps.

Nesting: colonial; often in mangroves; pair builds a platform of sticks; pair incubates 3–4 pale, bluish green eggs for about 26 days.
Feeding: various foraging methods, some quite active; feeds mainly on small fish.
Voice: generally silent.
Similar Species: *Tricolored* (p. 85), *Little Blue* (p. 84) and *Great Blue* (p. 81) *herons:* breeding birds do not have rusty necks or pink bills with dark tips. *Snowy Egret* (p. 83) and *Little Blue Heron, white phase* (p. 84): lack dark bluish legs and feet of adult white-morph Reddish Egret.
Best Sites: fairly widespread.

CATTLE EGRET

Bubulcus ibis

Arguably Florida's most common member of the wading bird group, even though it is not associated with wetlands, the Cattle Egret is ubiquitous in fields and pastures throughout the state. It is equally at home following behind tractors as it is behind cattle, feeding on the insects and other prey they both stir up. • The Cattle Egret is a recent colonizer of the New World. Originally found in Africa, this species flew across the Atlantic Ocean to South America, then moved northward and spread throughout North and Central America. The first reported Cattle Egret in the U.S. was found in Florida in 1941 or 1942. Since that time, the Cattle Egret has colonized the entire state—there now are hundreds of thousands of individuals in Florida—and beyond. • Cattle Egrets normally feed on small invertebrates, but egrets that land at the Dry Tortugas quickly discover that such prey is unavailable. Instead, Cattle Egrets stalk warblers and other small birds that are attracted to a small fountain built on Garden Key. They soak the bodies of dead or dying birds in the water to aid in swallowing them!

breeding

breeding

ID: medium-sized, stocky wading bird of upland habitats; white plumage; yellow-orange bill. *Breeding:* long plumes on throat and lower back; buff orange throat, rump and crown; orange-red legs and bill. *Nonbreeding:* dark legs and feet. *Juvenile:* dark bill; black feet.
Size: *L* 19–21 in; *W* 3 ft.
Status: common to abundant permanent resident, withdrawing from the Panhandle and northern peninsula during fall.
Habitat: primarily uses fields and pastures; also visits backyards.
Nesting: colonial; in a tree or tall shrub; male supplies sticks for the female to build a platform; pair incubates 3–4 pale blue eggs for 21–26 days.
Feeding: picks grasshoppers and other invertebrates from fields; often associated with livestock; also stalks anoles (lizards) in yards.
Voice: generally silent.
Similar Species: *Great Egret* (p. 82): much larger; black legs and feet. *Snowy Egret* (p. 83): black legs; yellow feet; black bill. *Little Blue Heron* (p. 84): juvenile has blue-gray bicolored bill and yellowish green legs.
Best Sites: widespread.

GREEN HERON
Butorides virescens

Sentinel of mangrove or marsh, the ever-vigilant Green Heron sits hunched on a shaded branch at the water's edge. It often perches just above the water's surface along wooded streams, waiting to stab small fish or other prey with its sturdy, daggerlike bill. This heron has been observed to drop feathers, leaves or other small debris into the water to attract fish, which are then captured and eaten. The Green Heron is therefore one of the few birds in North America known to use tools. • In good light, you can see a glimmer of green on the back and outer wings of adults, but the Green Heron is poorly named. • Unlike most herons, this one usually nests singly rather than communally, although it sometimes is found in loose colonies. Similarly, it tends to forage alone. • When disturbed, a Green Heron characteristically raises its crest and flicks its tail.

nonbreeding

nonbreeding

ID: small, stocky wading bird; slight crest; greenish black crown; chestnut face and neck; white foreneck and belly; blue-gray back and wings with greenish iridescence; yellow-green legs; short tail. *Breeding:* bright orange legs. *Juvenile:* heavy streaking along neck and underparts; dark brown upperparts.
Size: *L* 15–22 in; *W* 26 in.
Status: fairly common but solitary permanent resident statewide, largely withdrawing from the north during fall.
Habitat: marshes, lakes and canals; mangroves.

Nesting: usually close to water; in a tree or shrub; male begins and female completes a stick platform; pair incubates 3–5 pale blue-green to green eggs for 19–21 days; young are fed by regurgitation.
Feeding: stabs prey with bill after slowly stalking or standing and waiting; eats mostly small fish.
Voice: generally silent; alarm call is a loud *skow*.
Similar Species: *Black-crowned Night-Heron* (p. 89) and *Yellow-crowned Night-Heron* (p. 90): juveniles are much larger and have brownish plumage with white streaks or spots on upperparts. *Least Bittern* (p. 80): rich buff shoulder patches, sides and flanks.
Best Sites: widespread.

BLACK-CROWNED NIGHT-HERON
Nycticorax nycticorax

As their name suggests, night-herons are active at night, but they are not entirely nocturnal; Florida's two species of night-herons also forage during daylight hours, especially when nesting. Both species are medium-sized herons with streaked juvenal plumages reminiscent of the American Bittern. The Black-crowned Night-Heron is the stockier species, with a short, thick neck, short legs and a hunched posture. • One of the most cosmopolitan herons in the world, the Black-crowned Night-Heron occurs virtually worldwide. In Florida, it is widespread in the peninsula but surprisingly rare in much of the Panhandle, where it occurs primarily as a migrant and winter resident. Black-crowned Night-Herons are usually most common in freshwater habitats. • The Black-crowned Night-Heron's loud call, often heard as it flies to and from roosting or feeding areas, is a single *quock!*

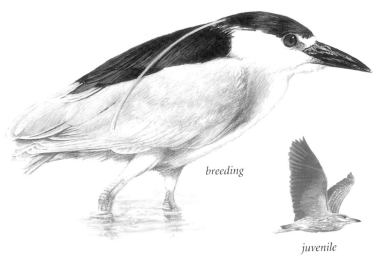

breeding

juvenile

ID: medium-sized, stocky wading bird; black crown and back; white cheek, forehead, foreneck and underparts; gray neck and wings; stout, black bill; red eyes. *Breeding:* 2 white plumes from crown. *Juvenile:* lightly brown-streaked underparts; brown upperparts with white flecking; yellowish bill. *In flight:* only tips of feet project beyond tail.
Size: *L* 23–26 in; *W* 3½ ft.
Status: uncommon permanent resident throughout the peninsula; rare migrant and winter resident in the Panhandle.
Habitat: a variety of wetlands, but more common in fresh water.

Nesting: colonial; in a tree or shrub; male gathers nest material; female builds a platform of twigs lined with finer materials; pair incubates 3–4 pale green eggs for 21–26 days.
Feeding: often at dusk; patient stand-and-wait predator; stabs for fish, crustaceans, amphibians and other aquatic prey.
Voice: deep, guttural *quock!*
Similar Species: *Yellow-crowned Night-Heron* (p. 90): rare inland; juvenile resembles juvenile Black-crowned but with small white spots on back, black bill and legs that extend farther beyond tail in flight. *American Bittern* (p. 79): similar to juvenile Black-crowned, but larger with black "mustache"; rarely seen in open; never in flocks.
Best Sites: widespread.

YELLOW-CROWNED NIGHT-HERON
Nyctanassa violacea

The Yellow-crowned Night-Heron is more diurnal than its black-crowned relative, and it is much more likely to be seen along coastal shorelines than inland. It also differs in being restricted to the New World. In North America, it is found in the Southeast, especially during winter. In Florida, it is a fairly common permanent resident in the peninsula but is only a spring and summer resident in parts of the Panhandle. • Although large numbers are occasionally seen roosting together, the Yellow-crowned tends to be the more solitary of the two night-herons. It is often seen standing quietly along a beach or among mangrove roots waiting for a ghost crab or fiddler crab to pass by. When this wading bird captures a crab, it removes the legs before swallowing the body whole. • Interestingly, Yellow-crowned juveniles winter farther north in Florida than do the adults, which are found primarily from the central peninsula southward.

breeding

juvenile

ID: medium-sized wading bird with entirely blue-gray body; black head with white cheeks, white crown and yellowish forehead; stout, black bill; red eyes. *Breeding:* long, white head plumes extend down back of neck. *Juvenile:* brown plumage with white spotting; greenish legs. *In flight:* legs extend well beyond tail.
Size: *L* 24 in; *W* 3½ ft.
Status: fairly common permanent resident nearly statewide, withdrawing from the western Panhandle during fall; local inland.

Habitat: beaches, mudflats and mangroves; less common inland at swamps and springs.
Nesting: nests singly or in colonies, occasionally with other wading bird species; in a shrub or tree; builds a platform above the ground or water; pair incubates 2–4 pale bluish green eggs for 21–25 days.
Feeding: forages by standing and waiting or slow, methodical walking or wading; primarily eats crabs, crayfish and fish.
Voice: call is a high, short *woc*.
Similar Species: *Black-crowned Night-Heron* (p. 89): juvenile is similar to juvenile Yellow-crowned, but with more white streaking on back and wing coverts, legs that barely project beyond tail in flight and mostly yellow bill.
Best Sites: widespread.

WHITE IBIS

Eudocimus albus

Despite severe declines in numbers in recent decades, the White Ibis remains one of the most abundant and conspicuous wading birds in Florida. It is found in virtually all wetland habitats and even commonly forages in fields and on lawns. • Breeding occurs in large colonies that are located along the coast or inland. However, nesting White Ibises typically forage inland, because their chicks cannot tolerate a high intake of salt in their diets. • The sharply plumaged adults take on an even more impressive look during the courtship season, when their faces, legs and bills become bright red, contrasting with their brilliant blue eyes. • White Ibises commute between nesting or roosting sites and foraging areas in long, cohesive lines or V-formations. • As shocking as it may seem today, as recently as the early 20th century, White Ibises were routinely shot for the cooking pot and were known as "Chokoloskee Chickens"! This activity is perhaps still practiced by a few Floridians today.

ID: largish wading bird with white body; black tips on outer primaries; long, red, downcurved bill; red face and legs. *Immature:* gradual transition to adult plumage; has more white than juvenile. *Juvenile:* brown upperparts with white rump; orange face and bill; dull orange legs; white belly; streaked neck and breast.
Size: L 22 in; W 3 ft.
Status: species of special concern (FWC); common to abundant permanent resident nearly statewide, but rare overall in the western Panhandle.

Habitat: estuaries, mangroves and swamps; flooded agricultural fields and roadsides.
Nesting: colonial; in mangroves, thickets or swamps; nest is a platform of sticks; pair incubates 2–4 brown-splotched, buff or bluish eggs for 21–22 days.
Feeding: probes for fish, crustaceans or worms; also scans for insects in fields.
Voice: mostly silent; muffled *hunk-hunk-hunk* call in alarm or flight.
Similar Species: *Glossy Ibis* (p. 92): resembles subadult White Ibis, but entirely black, with iridescent colored areas and thinner, black bill. *Long-billed Curlew* (p. 144): resembles subadult White Ibis, but with streaked, brown body, blackish bill and dark legs; restricted to saline habitats; never in flocks.
Best Sites: widespread.

GLOSSY IBIS

Plegadis falcinellus

Originally restricted to the Old World, the Glossy Ibis is thought to have colonized North America in the early 1800s. Rare until the 1930s, it is still expanding its range on the continent. Like the Cattle Egret several decades later, the Glossy Ibis probably used the trade winds to fly westward from Africa and colonize the West Indies and then the southeastern coast of North America. • In Florida, the Glossy Ibis is a local and increasingly permanent resident in the peninsula, where it can be abundant in favored areas. The Glossy Ibis reaches its abundance in the southern half of the peninsula, where it can be seen in flocks of several hundred or more birds foraging in rice fields southeast of Lake Okeechobee or in freshwater marshes in the prairie region to the west.

breeding

breeding

ID: largish wading bird with dark plumage; thin, downcurved bill; dark facial skin bordered by 2 bluish stripes. *Breeding:* chestnut head, neck and sides; green and purple iridescence on upperparts. *Nonbreeding:* grayish brown head and neck streaked with white. *In flight:* neck fully extended; hunchbacked appearance; flocks fly in lines or V-formation.
Size: *L* 22–25 in; *W* 3 ft.
Status: uncommon to locally abundant and increasingly permanent resident of the southern half of the peninsula; rare or very rare farther north and west and in the Keys.

Habitat: primarily freshwater marshes, swamps and lakes and flooded agricultural fields; less common in estuaries.
Nesting: in mixed colonies; over water, in a shrub or tree; bulky platform built of sticks; pair incubates 3–4 pale blue or green eggs for about 21 days.
Feeding: probes bill into mud or sand; feeds on crayfish, fish, reptiles, amphibians and insects.
Voice: generally silent away from colonies; sheeplike *huu-huu-huu* call.
Similar Species: *White Ibis* (p. 91): white plumage; orange or red bill; juvenile is mainly brown, with some white markings. *Limpkin* (p. 124): brown body boldly streaked with white; bill is thicker, paler and mostly straight.
Best Sites: Everglades Agricultural Area; Lake Apopka; Merritt Island NWR; Myakka River SP.

ROSEATE SPOONBILL

Platalea ajaja

Unquestionably the most flamboyant of Florida's diverse assemblage of wading birds, the adult Roseate Spoonbill is a shocking combination of pink body, scarlet shoulders, orange tail and featherless, greenish head. Of the world's six species of spoonbills, the Roseate is unique in having colored plumage—all other spoonbills are white. Another peculiarity is its unfeathered head in adult plumage. Roseate Spoonbills also engage in a unique behavior called "sky-gazing," in which spoonbills on the ground extend their necks and bills upward toward other spoonbills flying overhead. • Roseate Spoonbills breed from Tampa Bay and Merritt Island National Wildlife Refuge south through Florida Bay. Most colonies are on islands along the coast, but a few spoonbills breed inland. They are fairly common residents, with about 1000 pairs in the state. After breeding, Roseate Spoonbills, especially juveniles, disperse widely northward, and many move inland to feed at flooded agricultural fields, mine impoundments and other wetlands.

ID: large wading bird with pink plumage; long, spoon-shaped bill; white neck and back; greenish, unfeathered head; red shoulders; orange tail. *Juvenile:* mostly white, with pale pink wings; white-feathered head.
Size: *L* 32 in; *W* 4–4½ ft.
Status: species of special concern (FWC); locally fairly common permanent resident of the southern half of the peninsula and the Keys; less common inland and farther north.

Habitat: estuaries, bays, mangrove swamps, coastal islands and flooded agricultural fields.
Nesting: in mixed colonies; in a mangrove or other tree; male brings sticks and female builds bulky platform; pair incubates 2–3 whitish eggs for 23–24 days.
Feeding: sweeps bill back and forth in shallow water to capture fish, crustaceans, mollusks and other aquatic animals.
Voice: generally silent.
Similar Species: *Greater Flamingo* (p. 97): limited to Florida Bay; pink overall; extremely long neck and legs; unique bill shape and foraging posture.
Best Sites: "Ding" Darling NWR; Everglades NP; Fort De Soto Park; Merritt Island NWR.

WOOD STORK

Mycteria americana

The sole stork found regularly in North America, the impressive Wood Stork is characteristic of the Southeast's cypress and tupelo swamps. In Florida, it breeds in colonies from the eastern Panhandle to the southernmost tip of the peninsula. • The Wood Stork is endangered because of its sensitivity to water levels during the nesting season, but its numbers are stable. • In order to feed their large young over the protracted nestling period, Wood Storks need receding water levels 6 to 10 inches deep to concentrate prey in pools and other easily accessible areas. In southern Florida, the foraging areas may be as far as 80 miles from the breeding colony. A large wing surface allows Wood Storks to soar to great heights—often in large swirling flocks—which aids in efficient travel between feeding and nesting areas.

ID: large wading bird with large, dark, slightly downcurved bill; white plumage with black flight feathers and tail; unfeathered, blackish head and neck. *Juvenile:* yellow bill; grayish feathered head and neck. *In flight:* often soars in flocks.
Size: *L* 3–3½ ft; *W* 5–5½ ft.
Status: endangered (FWC, USFWS); an uncommon to locally abundant permanent resident of the peninsula and eastern Panhandle; rare farther west and in the Keys.
Habitat: freshwater ponds and marshes, cypress swamps, ponds, mangroves and flooded agricultural fields.

Nesting: colonial; high in a cypress, or lower in mangroves; male brings materials; female builds a stick platform lined with leaves and twigs; pair incubates 2–5 white eggs for 28–32 days; young are fed by regurgitation.
Feeding: wades in shallow water, sweeping partly open bill back and forth, quickly shutting it upon contact with prey; also forages visually; feeds on fish, reptiles, amphibians and crustaceans.
Voice: generally silent.
Similar Species: *American White Pelican* (p.74): larger; large, yellow bill evident even in flight, but short legs inconspicuous. *Whooping Crane* (p. 126): much rarer; red crown on white-feathered head; less extensive black on wings; white tail; often forages in uplands.
Best Sites: widespread.

BLACK VULTURE

Coragyps atratus

American vultures were previously thought to be related to hawks and other raptors, but recent examinations of the genetic structure, anatomical features and behaviors of vultures show that they are more closely related to storks. The two species of vultures found in North America are common to abundant permanent residents virtually throughout Florida. The Black Vulture is arguably the less abundant species, especially in the Keys. • Both species feed primarily on carrion, which usually consists of armadillos and other animals killed on Florida's roads and highways. • Unlike Turkey Vultures, Black Vultures do not have a well-developed sense of smell. Instead, Black Vultures rely on their eyesight to spot carrion, and they will also resort to following Turkey Vultures to a meal. • Despite the abundance of vultures in Florida and their wide range, few birders have been fortunate to find a nest. Although communal and conspicuous otherwise, vultures become secretive and hide in dense swamps or under clumps of palmettos when nesting.

ID: large, black soaring bird; black body with white outer feathers; short, broad tail; unfeathered, grayish head.
Size: *L* 25 in; *W* 4½ ft.
Status: common to abundant permanent resident of the mainland; very rare in the Keys.
Habitat: forages over open country but roosts and nests in forested areas.
Nesting: on the ground, often under saw palmettos; no nest is built; pair incubates 1–3 pale green, creamy white or faintly buff eggs for 28–32 days.
Feeding: carrion forms bulk of diet, supplemented with garbage and other offal.
Voice: generally silent.
Similar Species: *Turkey Vulture* (p. 96): red head; 2-tone wings with dark linings and light flight feathers; longer, narrower wings and tail; wings usually held in shallow "V."
Best Sites: widespread.

95

TURKEY VULTURE

Cathartes aura

Turkey Vultures are widespread permanent residents throughout Florida, although they are very local breeders in the Keys. Their long wings are well suited for soaring on thermals, allowing the birds to cover considerable distances without expending much energy. One or more Turkey Vultures at a time soaring on thermals above highways and pastures is a common sight in our state. Flocks of vultures with spread wings are also commonly seen perched in trees, warming up and waiting for thermals to develop. • The Turkey Vulture feeds mostly on carrion, which it locates with its extraordinarily refined sense of smell. The featherless, red head of a Turkey Vulture may appear grotesque, but it allows the vulture to remain relatively clean while feeding on messy carcasses. • Vultures have mastered the art of regurgitation. This ability allows parents to transport food over long distances to their young. Regurgitation also enables engorged vultures to "lighten up" for a quick takeoff and works as a defense mechanism—a trapped vulture will vomit up its stomach contents at a would-be attacker.

ID: large, soaring bird; black body with paler flight feathers; unfeathered, red head; longish, slender tail. *Juvenile:* gray head. *In flight:* head appears small; wings held in shallow "V"; rocks from side to side when soaring.
Size: *L* 26–32 in; *W* 5½–6 ft.
Status: common to abundant migrant and permanent resident statewide; less common in the Keys except during fall migration.
Habitat: forages over open country; roosts and nests in forested areas.

Nesting: on the ground, often under saw palmettos; no nest is built; pair incubates 2 white eggs blotched with reddish brown for 38–41 days; young are fed by regurgitation.
Feeding: eats carrion, often road-killed mammals, especially nine-banded armadillos.
Voice: generally silent.
Similar Species: *Black Vulture* (p. 95): shorter, rounded wings with bold white tips; short, rounded tail; gray head. *Bald Eagle* (p.103): larger; larger head; always shows white in plumage, even if only splotchy on subadults; wings held flat when soaring.
Best Sites: widespread.

GREATER FLAMINGO

Phoenicopterus ruber

Flamingos are one of the most instantly recognizable families of birds. North America's sole species in this family, the Greater Flamingo, is a rare and extremely local nonbreeding resident of Florida Bay, primarily around Snake Bight. Except for a few individuals brought to our country by tropical storms, the Snake Bight population represents the only wild flamingos found in the U.S. However, flamingos of several species are held captive in many zoos and other animal exhibits, and a semi-feral flock of Greater Flamingos has been resident at Hialeah Race Track in Miami since the 1930s. Thus, it is often difficult to determine if a flamingo seen "in the wild" is an escapee or a genuine vagrant. The source of the Snake Bight flock was debated for decades, until a flamingo color-banded as a nestling in Mexico was photographed at Snake Bight in 2002. This sighting finally established that at least some of Florida's flamingos occur naturally.

ID: instantly recognizable, large, pink wading bird with extremely long legs and neck; unique tricolored bill is white, orangy pink and black. *In flight:* black flight feathers.

Juvenile: mostly grayish body. *Immature:* pale pink body; adult plumage acquired after 3–4 years.

Size: *L* 3½–4 ft; *W* 5 ft.

Status: flock of about 30–40 nonbreeding residents around Snake Bight, Everglades NP.
Habitat: coastal mudflats; estuaries.
Nesting: not known to breed in Florida, but undocumented historical reports exist.
Feeding: holds bill inverted and swings it from side to side to strain algae and tiny aquatic animals from shallow water or mud.
Voice: deep honks in flight.
Similar Species: *Roseate Spoonbill* (p. 93): shorter, stouter, white neck; longer, spoon-shaped bill; different foraging method.
Best Sites: Snake Bight Trail (Everglades NP.)

OSPREY

Pandion haliaetus

The Osprey is one of the most cosmopolitan of birds, occurring on all continents except Antarctica. It feeds almost exclusively on fish and is often called "Fish Hawk." • The Osprey suffered considerably during the mid-20th century. The effects of DDT contamination caused its eggs to have very thin shells that broke under the weight of the incubating adult, causing nesting failure As a result, Osprey numbers dropped precariously in much of North America. Since the banning of DDT in the 1970s, populations of this magnificent bird have recovered. • The sole member of its own subfamily (Pandioninae), the Osprey has evolved several interesting anatomical features that distinguish it from other birds of prey. For instance, it has a reversible fourth toe and very long and strongly curved talons. It also has spines, called "spicules," on its feet. All these adaptations aid the Osprey in holding on to its slippery prey. • When flying with prey, Ospreys usually position the fish to face forward for better aerodynamics.

ID: large, pale hawk; dark brown upperparts; white face with brown crown, nape and eye line; yellow eyes. *Female:* indistinct "necklace" across upper breast. *In flight:* white underparts; underwings have dark "wrist" marks; wings held in shallow "M" shape.
Size: *L* 22–25 in; *W* 4½–6 ft.
Status: species of special concern (FWC; Keys only); common and conspicuous permanent resident of the coasts and common inland in much of the peninsula.
Habitat: forages in all open-water habitats except shallow marshes.

Nesting: in a tree, usually a snag, atop a telephone pole or on some other human-made structure; massive stick nest, reused over many years; pair incubates 2–4 yellowish eggs blotched with reddish brown for 32–33 days.
Feeding: dramatic, feetfirst dives into water; feeds almost solely on fish.
Voice: series of melodious ascending whistles, often uttered while performing aerial courtship displays.
Similar Species: *Bald Eagle* (p. 103): larger; immature always has some dark brown on its underparts, holds its wings flatter in flight and has larger bill with yellow base and yellow legs.
Best Sites: widespread.

SWALLOW-TAILED KITE

Elanoides forficatus

The favorite species of many Florida birders, the Swallow-tailed Kite is a breathtaking sight as it glides and swoops gracefully above the treetops. Its striking black and white plumage accentuates its long, narrow, bent-back wings and long, forked tail, which allow great maneuverability in flight.
• Swallow-tailed Kites breed in the Deep South and from Mexico through central South America. In Florida, they breed throughout the mainland and the Upper Keys. • Prior to departing for their wintering grounds, Swallow-tailed Kites stage at spectacular communal roosts that can include 2000 birds at peak periods! On leaving, the kites head south through the southern peninsula, "island hop" through the Keys and western Cuba to the Yucatan peninsula, then fly overland to their wintering grounds in central South America.

ID: medium-sized, graceful raptor with long, slender wings and tail; white body; black back and wings; long, black, deeply forked tail. *In flight:* extremely graceful; white underwing linings with black flight feathers.
Size: *L* 23 in; *W* 4 ft.
Status: fairly common but somewhat local migrant and breeding resident of the mainland from February to August; rare breeder in the Keys; may be common during fall migration, especially near communal roosts.
Habitat: open woodlands, cypress swamps and riparian forests; forages over most habitats.
Nesting: in a tall tree, often a pine or cypress; platform of sticks is lined with lichens and moss; pair incubate 3–4 brown-blotched, white eggs for 28–31 days.
Feeding: forages aerially, plucking large insects, especially dragonflies, and small vertebrates such as tree frogs, small snakes and nestling birds out of the air or off foliage; often eats prey in flight; drinks by skimming the water's surface.
Voice: generally silent except around nest or roost; shrill *klee-klee-klee* call.
Similar Species: bold black and white plumage and long swallowtail are generally unmistakable. *Magnificent Frigatebird* (p. 78): prefers coastal and offshore habitats; juvenile is larger, with long bill and partially black underparts.
Best Sites: widespread; roosts are located along Fisheating Creek, Lake Woodruff NWR and near Corkscrew Swamp.

WHITE-TAILED KITE

Elanus leucurus

Kites are a subfamily of hawks that have very long, narrow wings and tails that allow the birds to soar or glide for great distances with little effort. All of Florida's four species of kites are spectacular birds. The rarest, most local and least known of our kites is the White-tailed Kite, until recently known as the Black-shouldered Kite. It is a rare but increasingly common permanent resident of the southern half of the peninsula, and it is virtually unknown farther north and absent from the Keys. • White-tailed Kite populations throughout North America declined severely in the early 20th century but rebounded beginning in the 1960s. Florida observations mirror this recent recovery, and, in 1986, White-tailed Kites resumed breeding in the state after a 56-year absence. • White-tailed Kites forage for small mammals such as cotton rats, shrews and small rabbits.

ID: medium-sized raptor that often hovers; gray back and wings with black shoulders; white head with gray crown and nape; red eyes; white underparts; gray uppertail with white outer feathers. *Juvenile:* "scaly" brown back, nape and crown; brown-streaked breast. *In flight:* white underwings with black "wrist" marks; white undertail; buoyant flapping; hovers with body held at steep angle.
Size: *L* 15–17 in; *W* 3–3½ ft.
Status: rare to locally uncommon and increasing permanent resident of the southern half of the peninsula; very rare elsewhere.

Habitat: pastures with scattered trees, wet prairie and dry Everglades marshland.
Nesting: in a shrub or tree; pair builds a bulky stick platform lined with grasses; female incubates 3–4 brown-blotched, creamy white eggs for 26–32 days.
Feeding: flies slowly over grasslands, often hovering; drops to ground feetfirst to capture prey; this small-mammal specialist rarely takes other prey.
Voice: generally silent away from nest; shrill *keep-keep-keep* call.
Similar Species: *Mississippi Kite* (p. 102): little regional or habitat overlap; lacks black shoulders; gray underparts; black tail. *Northern Harrier* (p. 104): conspicuous white rump; lacks black shoulders; does not hover.
Best Sites: Everglades NP; Kissimmee Prairie Preserve SP.

SNAIL KITE

Rostrhamus sociabilis

The Snail Kite is one of Florida's conservation success stories. By the early 1960s, probably fewer than 25 individuals remained in the state as a result of widespread drainage of the Everglades for agriculture and development. But the population has recovered dramatically, and by 1994 it had grown to nearly 1000. • Formerly known as "Everglades Kite," the Snail Kite is a tropical species that is limited in North America to central and southern Florida, but it also occurs in the West Indies and Central and South America. • As is suggested by its common name, the Snail Kite feeds almost exclusively on snails, especially apple snails (*Pomacea* species). During drought years, when snails may be scarce, this kite is nomadic, scouring the peninsula for suitable marshes.

ID: large raptor of shallow, freshwater wetlands; slow, hovering flight; broad wings; black tail with conspicuous white base; short, strongly downcurved bill. *Male:* blackish gray body; orange-red eyes, bill and legs. *Female:* brownish black upperparts; dark head with whitish eyebrow, cheek patch and throat; white underparts heavily streaked with dark brown. *Juvenile:* similar to female, but with brown upperparts; less streaking on underparts; yellow bill and feet.
Size: *L* 16–18 in; *W* 3½–4 ft.
Status: endangered (FWC); fairly common but very local permanent resident of freshwater marshes in the southern half of the peninsula.

Habitat: freshwater marshes; large lakes.
Nesting: over water; in a low shrub or tree; large platform of sticks is lined with marsh vegetation; pair incubates 2–4 brown-blotched, white eggs for 23–28 days.
Feeding: flies slowly over marshes looking for snails; drops down feetfirst to grab snail and flies to favored perch to extract it from shell.
Voice: silent except when nesting; sharp *ka-ka-ka-ka-ka* call.
Similar Species: *Northern Harrier* (p. 104): owl-like face; brown or blue-gray body; white rump; low-flying hunting pattern and white rump may confuse birders, but Snail Kite has white uppertail not rump.
Best Sites: Lake Kissimmee; Tamiami Trail; water conservation areas.

MISSISSIPPI KITE

Ictinia mississippiensis

The Mississippi Kite is a circum-Gulf migrant: it follows the western Gulf Coast and the Central American peninsula while migrating between its breeding grounds in the southeastern U.S. and its wintering grounds in southern South America. Because the Mississippi Kite breeds no farther south in Florida than Cedar Key and Gainesville, birders in the southern half of the peninsula and the Keys have little opportunity to view this bird. On the breeding grounds, though, the Mississippi Kite is a fairly common spring and summer resident of the Panhandle and northwestern peninsula. • Mississippi Kites were traditionally restricted to the southern states, but their breeding range seems to be expanding northward, with spring or summer sightings now occurring up to southern New England. • This raptor feeds on flying insects such as dragonflies, cicadas, beetles and grasshoppers, which are plucked out of the air with its feet and eaten while in flight.

ID: largish raptor with long wings and tail; dark gray back and wings; pale head; dark gray underparts; black tail; chestnut at base of primaries is often inconspicuous. *Juvenile:* dark brownish upperparts; underparts heavily marked with rufous; banded tail.
Size: *L* 14½ in; *W* 3 ft.
Status: fairly common breeding resident of the Panhandle and northwestern peninsula from April to September; very rare migrant elsewhere.
Habitat: deciduous or mixed woodlands and riparian areas.

Nesting: in a tall tree; pair constructs flimsy stick platform lined with leaves; pair incubates 2 bluish white eggs for 30–32 days.
Feeding: plucks flying insects from the air and takes small vertebrates from foliage.
Voice: generally silent; *kee-kew, kew-kew* alarm call; fledgling produces emphatic *three-beers* call.
Similar Species: *White-tailed Kite* (p. 100): pale gray wings with black shoulders; white underparts, including undertail; black "wrist" patches on underwings; little habitat or regional overlap. *Northern Harrier* (p. 104): male has banded tail and white on rump, with little seasonal or habitat overlap and does not hover.
Best Sites: widespread.

BALD EAGLE

Haliaeetus leucocephalus

One of the most magnificent and majestic birds in Florida is the Bald Eagle, a species that no birder ever tires of seeing. • Bald Eagles in Florida begin their nesting activities in October or November, and most eggs hatch in December. By March or April, the young fledge, and most of Florida's eagles then migrate northward out of the state. Chesapeake Bay is a favored summering area for Florida's eagles. • Beginning in the late 1940s, populations of eagles and other fish-eating species suffered dramatic declines, which were linked to DDT poisoning. The banning of DDT in the 1970s allowed eagle popula-tions to recover. • Although the Bald Eagle is con-sidered a Species of Special Concern in Florida, its population in the state is about 1200 nesting pairs, the largest population in the world outside of Alaska and British Columbia. • Bald Eagles do not molt into adult plumage until their fourth year, only then acquiring their char-acteristic white head and tail.

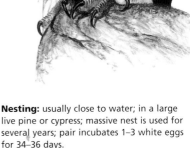

immature

ID: huge, bird that soars on broad, flat wings; white head and tail; dark brown body; yellow bill and feet. *Immature:* acquires adult plumage in fourth year; juvenile and immatures have variable amounts of white mottling on upperparts, underwings and undertail; mostly dark bill with yellow at base.
Size: *L* 30–43 in; *W* 5½–8 ft. Female typi-cally larger than male.
Status: federally endangered (USFWS); species of special concern (FWC); fairly common to locally common resident nearly statewide, but less common in the western Panhandle; generally rare during summer after breeding.
Habitat: forages over large bodies of water.

Nesting: usually close to water; in a large live pine or cypress; massive nest is used for several years; pair incubates 1–3 white eggs for 34–36 days.
Feeding: feeds primarily on fish and waterbirds such as American Coots; fre-quently pirates fish from Ospreys.
Voice: thin, weak squeal or gull-like cackle.
Similar Species: adult is distinctive. *Golden Eagle:* rare in northern Florida; dark overall, except for golden nape; immature has prominent white patches on wings and base of tail.
Best Sites: widespread.

NORTHERN HARRIER

Circus cyaneus

The Northern Harrier is one of the easiest raptors to identify on the wing, because no other large hawk flies so close to the ground with its wings raised in a very wide "V." This raptor's conspicuous white rump patch is also diagnostic; only the Snail Kite, which has a much more limited range in Florida, has a similar patch, but it is on the base of the kite's tail, not its rump. • The Northern Harrier cruises low over fields, marshes and prairies, often just above the vegetation, relying on sudden surprise attacks to capture its prey. Its owl-like facial disc allows it to hunt by sound instead of sight when it cannot see its prey. • Northern Harriers are widespread migrants and winter residents in Florida. There were a few early 20th-century breeding reports from the peninsula, but they were undocumented and are often discounted. • The Northern Harrier was previously known as "Marsh Hawk." It also occurs in the Old World, where it is known as "Hen Harrier."

Size: *L* 16–24 in; *W* 3½–4 ft. Female typically larger than male.
Status: fairly common migrant and winter resident from September to April throughout the mainland; rare in the Keys.
ID: large raptor with long wings and tail; flies low over marshes; conspicuous white rump; black wing tips. *Male:* gray upperparts; white underparts with faint rusty streaking; black-banded tail. *Female:* dark brown upperparts; buff underparts streaked with dark brown. *Juvenile:* rich brown upperparts; orangy buff underparts; brown-streaked head and upper breast.
Habitat: open habitats such as fields, pastures and marshes.
Nesting: does not breed in Florida.
Feeding: flies low, often skimming the top of vegetation; feeds on rats, small rabbits, snakes and birds such as Red-winged Blackbirds.
Voice: generally silent in Florida.
Similar Species: *Snail Kite* (p. 101): has dark rump with white on base of tail; little habitat overlap.
Best Sites: widespread.

SHARP-SHINNED HAWK

Accipiter striatus

Accipiters are small to medium-sized woodland hawks that prey mostly on birds. They have short, rounded wings and long, rudderlike tails to help maneuver quickly to chase and capture their feathered quarry. All three of North America's accipiters have been reported in Florida, but only two of them are found regularly. • The Sharp-shinned Hawk breeds over much of North America and winters across the continental U.S., the West Indies and Central America. It is a fairly common and widespread winter resident throughout our state, often "staking out" backyard bird feeders to prey on the doves and other birds that gather there. • Sharp-shinned Hawks have recently been discovered to breed at Conecuh National Forest in Alabama within 10 miles of the Florida border, so we may soon see a new breeding species documented for our state. • Most raptors are an example of reverse sexual dimorphism, with the females being larger than the males.

juvenile

ID: small raptor with short, rounded wings; long, square-tipped tail; blue-gray upperparts; pale face with dark crown and nape; red eyes; white underparts heavily barred with orange. *Juvenile:* brown upperparts; yellow eyes; white underparts heavily streaked with brown. *In flight:* flap-and-glide.
Size: *Male: L* 10–12 in; *W* 20–24 in. *Female: L* 12–14 in; *W* 24–28 in.
Status: uncommon to fairly common migrant and resident statewide from September to April.
Habitat: forages over any wooded or semi-wooded habitats, even suburban yards.
Nesting: does not breed in Florida, but may eventually be discovered nesting in our state.

Feeding: chases or dives to capture small to medium-sized birds.
Voice: generally silent in Florida.
Similar Species: *Cooper's Hawk* (p. 106): larger; more rounded tail tip has broader terminal band; crown is darker than nape and back. *American Kestrel* (p. 112): long, pointed wings; two black facial stripes; typically seen in open country, often perched on power lines. *Merlin* (p. 113): rapid wing-beats; pointed wings; single, dark facial stripe; brown streaking on buff underparts; dark eyes.
Best Sites: widespread.

COOPER'S HAWK
Accipiter cooperii

Unlike its close cousin the Sharp-shinned Hawk, the Cooper's Hawk is a permanent resident of Florida. It breeds from extreme southern Canada to Mexico and winters in most of its breeding range southward through Central America. In Florida the Cooper Hawk is an increasing resident virtually throughout the peninsula. • Distinguishing the Cooper's Hawk from the Sharp-shinned Hawk can be challenging. In flight, the Sharpie has a squared-off tail, whereas the tail of the Cooper's is rounded. The head of a Cooper's Hawk projects farther beyond its body than the head of a Sharpie does. In addition, the Cooper's Hawk often perches on the tops of telephone poles or on power lines, whereas the Sharpie usually perches only in trees. • Cooper's Hawks feed mostly on birds up to the size of large doves, which typically are captured via a short, ambushing flight.

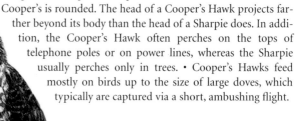

juvenile

Status: uncommon to fairly common (and increasing) permanent resident of the mainland; rare to uncommon migrant in the Keys.
Habitat: forages over any wooded or semi-wooded habitats, even suburban yards.
Nesting: in the fork of a tree; builds nest of sticks and twigs or may reuse an abandoned squirrel nest; female incubates 4–5 bluish white eggs for 30–36 days.
Feeding: chases or dives at medium-sized birds.
Voice: silent except around nest; fast *cac-cac-cac-cac* call.
Similar Species: *Sharp-shinned Hawk* (p. 105): not found during summer; smaller; square tail tip; dark nape. *American Kestrel* (p. 112): long, pointed wings; 2 black facial stripes; typically seen in open country, often perched on power lines. *Merlin* (p. 113): rapid wingbeats; pointed wings; 1 dark facial stripe; brown streaking on buff underparts; dark eyes.
Best Sites: widespread.

ID: medium-sized raptor with short, rounded wings; long, round-tipped tail; blue-gray upperparts; pale face with dark crown; pale nape; red eyes; white underparts heavily barred with orange. *Juvenile:* brown upperparts; yellow eyes; white underparts streaked with brown. *In flight:* flap-and-glide.
Size: *Male: L* 15–17 in; *W* 27–32 in.
Female: L 17–19 in; *W* 32–37 in.

RED-SHOULDERED HAWK
Buteo lineatus

The Red-shouldered Hawk is arguably the most widespread and conspicuous hawk in Florida, occurring even in suburban areas. It is commonly seen perched on power lines along roads, scanning for prey. No other raptor makes such frequent use of power lines as perches; indeed, many species, such as the Red-tailed Hawk and the Short-tailed Hawk, never perch on lines. • Red-shouldered Hawks are equally noticeable repeating their loud, piercing *kee-yah* calls—a call perfectly mastered by Blue Jays—as they soar above swamps or hammocks. • Two Red-shouldered races breed in Florida: *B. l. alleni* throughout the mainland and *B. l. extimus* in the Keys; the latter race appears particularly "washed out," with a pale grayish head. A third race, *B. l. lineatus*, which breeds farther north, reaches Florida during winter. • Red-shouldered Hawks are mostly sit-and-wait hunters that drop down from a perch to capture prey.

ID: medium-sized raptor often seen perched on power lines; bold black and white barring on back and wings; rusty or pale grayish head; whitish underparts with bold orange or buffy barring; prominent rusty shoulder patch; banded tail with wider black bars. *Juvenile:* brown upperparts; wide, brown, teardrop-shaped streaks on white underparts; shoulder may have faint rusty patch. *In flight:* light and dark barring on underside of flight feathers and tail; white crescent or "window" at base of primaries.
Size: *L* 19 in; *W* 3½ ft. Female typically larger than male.
Status: common permanent resident statewide; breeders from farther north winter in Florida.

Habitat: virtually any wooded or semi-wooded habitat that contains oaks or cypresses.
Nesting: in a tree; pair builds bulky nest of sticks and twigs or reuses an old nest; female incubates 2–4 darkly blotched, bluish white eggs for about 33 days.
Feeding: drops down on prey from perch; feeds on variety of animal prey, including insects, snakes, frogs, small mammals and, rarely, birds.
Voice: *kee-yah*, often uttered as a series.
Similar Species: *Broad-winged Hawk* (p. 108): rare in the southern peninsula; entirely brown wings; wide, white tail bands.
Best Sites: widespread.

107

BROAD-WINGED HAWK
Buteo platypterus

The Broad-winged Hawk is misnamed, as its wings are no broader than those of other buteos. It is an uncommon breeding resident in the Panhandle, a rare breeder in the northwestern peninsula and a rare to uncommon winter resident in the extreme southern peninsula and the Keys. It is not nearly as conspicuous as the Red-shouldered Hawk, preferring the deciduous woodlands of the interior. • Broad-winged Hawks migrate between their breeding and wintering grounds in flocks called "kettles" that can contain hundreds of birds at times. Although hundreds of Broad-wingeds are sometimes seen in the Keys, on the mainland large flocks are usually limited to the Panhandle. Their primary migratory route is along the western Gulf Coast through Mexico to their wintering grounds, which extend from Mexico to central South America. • Broad-winged Hawks hunt from a perch, sometimes a power line, and drop down on prey.

light morph

*juvenile
light morph*

ID: medium-sized raptor with brown upperparts; white underparts with heavy rusty barring; broad, black and white tail bands; broad wings with pointed tips. *Juvenile:* white underparts with dark brown, teardrop-shaped streaking; buff and dark brown tail bands. *In flight:* pale underwings outlined with dark brown.

Size: *L* 14–19 in; *W* 32–39 in. Female typically larger than male.

Status: uncommon breeding resident of the Panhandle and the northwestern peninsula; rare to fairly common migrant statewide; rare to uncommon winter resident of the southern third of the peninsula and the Keys.

Habitat: *Breeding:* dense mixed and deciduous woodlands. *Winter:* variety of woodlands.

Nesting: in a deciduous tree; bulky stick nest is built in a crotch next to the trunk; mostly the female incubates 2–4 brown-spotted, whitish eggs for 28–31 days.

Feeding: swoops down on prey from a perch; feeds on small vertebrates, especially rodents.

Voice: high-pitched, whistled *peeeo-wee-ee* on breeding grounds,.

Similar Species: *Red-shouldered Hawk* (p. 107): barred upperparts; obvious rusty shoulders; juvenile has underparts heavily streaked with brown; white "window" at base of primaries in flight.

Best Sites: fairly widespread.

SHORT-TAILED HAWK

Buteo brachyurus

Short-tailed Hawks are one of the rarest and most range-restricted raptors in North America; about 500 birds are thought to exist. They are virtually limited to Florida, where they may breed throughout the peninsula, but they winter nearly exclusively south of Lake Okeechobee. • Short-tailed Hawks are often seen catching the first thermals in mid-morning with Black Vultures or Turkey Vultures. From up to several hundred feet in altitude, they scan treetops for prey, then drop earthward in dramatic, bulletlike dives. They feed almost exclusively on birds ranging in size from sparrows to doves and meadowlarks. • These small hawks occur in two color morphs; the dark morph is more common in Florida. Mixed pairs breed, but intermediate plumages are not produced—offspring are either white or black.

dark morph

light morph

ID: smallish buteo rarely seen perched except inside forest canopy near nest; relatively short, broad wings with trailing edge "pinched" at body; tail may appear pinkish in flight in some light. *Dark morph:* all-black body. *In Flight:* underparts look entirely black from a distance, but white bands on flight feathers visible at close range. *Light morph:* dark upperparts contrast with white underparts. *In flight:* conspicuous dark hood; white wing linings contrast with black-banded flight feathers.
Size: *L* 16 in; *W* 37 in. Female typically larger than male.
Status: locally uncommon resident of the peninsula, moving north into breeding areas from February to March and returning to wintering areas by October.

Habitat: found over any upland habitat, sometimes over mangroves.
Nesting: in a sturdy tree; male gathers material; female builds a sturdy nest of sticks; female incubates 2 bluish white to dull white eggs for 34 days; male brings food and female feeds young.
Feeding: soars high and dives to capture avian prey.
Voice: silent away from nest.
Similar Species: *Red-tailed Hawk* (p. 110): larger; distinct brown belly band; bright rufous tail; immature has streaked underparts. *Red-shouldered Hawk* (p. 107): longer wing with prominent "window" at base of primaries; banded or streaked breast; often vocal in flight.
Best Sites: Everglades NP from October to February; Lake Wales Ridge SF from March to July.

RED-TAILED HAWK

Buteo jamaicensis

Red-tailed Hawks are the most common hawks in many parts of North America, but not in Florida. They are widespread but uncommon residents throughout the mainland and are surprisingly rare nonbreeding visitors in the Keys. Unlike Red-shouldered or Broad-winged Hawks, they never perch on power lines, but they are frequently seen scanning for prey from the tops of telephone poles or power line towers. • The Red-tailed Hawk is one of the most variably plumaged raptors, with numerous races found in North America. Of Florida's two breeding races, *B. j. borealis* is found in the Panhandle and northern peninsula, and *B. j. umbrinus* nests from about Gainesville southward. Several other races have been observed in the state during winter. • The Red-tailed Hawk's impressive drawn-out, piercing call is often combined with the image of a Bald Eagle in television commercials and movies.

during winter from northern or western breeders; rare migrant in the Keys.

Habitat: open country with scattered trees.

Nesting: in open pinewoods or at a woodland edge; often in a pine; bulky stick nest is usually added to each year; pair incubates 2–4 brown-blotched, whitish eggs for 28–35 days; male brings food to female and nestlings.

Feeding: forages by scanning the ground from a tall perch; captures prey after a short flight; feeds primarily on rodents but takes a variety of animal prey.

Voice: powerful, descending *keeearrr!* scream year-round.

Similar Species: *Short-tailed Hawk* (p. 109): white morph has similar shape in flight, but with conspicuous dark hood, pure white underwing linings and no brown "belly band"; note that banded tail may appear pinkish in some light.

Best Sites: widespread.

ID: large hawk of open country; mottled brown wings and back; white throat; brown head; white or pale buff underparts with brown "belly band;" reddish orange tail. *Juvenile:* brown tail with dark bands. *In flight:* white or buffy underwing linings; pale underwings have faint barring and dark leading edge.

Size: *Male: L* 18–23 in; *W* 3½–4½ ft. *Female: L* 20–25 in; *W* 4–5 ft.

Status: uncommon permanent resident of the mainland, with numbers augmented

CRESTED CARACARA

Caracara cheriway

The Crested Caracara is a tropical species that occurs in the U.S. at its extreme southern borders in Arizona, Florida and Texas. Although it is predominantly terrestrial and feeds largely on carrion, similar to vultures, the Crested Caracara is most closely related to the falcons. • Thousands of years ago, caracaras were probably continuously distributed along the then-current Gulf Coast, but, as sea levels rose with the end of the last ice age, the caracaras in present-day Florida became isolated. • Today, the Crested Caracara is a threatened species in our state, with about 500 birds remaining. It is at risk largely because the citrus industry has been destroying large amounts of its habitat. • Crested Caracaras are often seen feeding on carrion in the presence of vultures. They also walk around pastures and flip over cow patties, apparently in search of insects and other animals hiding underneath. • The caracara's unusual name is an onomatopoeic rendering of its grating call.

ID: large, terrestrial, carrion-eating raptor; long, yellow legs; black body; white head; black crest and crown; unfeathered, pinkish facial skin; black-and-white barred neck. *Juvenile:* brown body; brown-and-white-streaked neck. *In flight:* all ages show white wing tips and white tail with wide, black subterminal band.
Size: *L* 23 in; *W* 4 ft. Female typically larger than male.
Status: threatened (FWC); fairly common, presumably declining permanent resident in the interior central peninsula.

Habitat: prairies, pastures and other upland grasslands.
Nesting: typically at the top of a cabbage palm; bulky stick nest may be used over successive years; pair incubates 2–3 heavily blotched, whitish eggs for about 28 days.
Feeding: terrestrial forager; primarily eats carrion along roadsides but also takes insects, other invertebrates and small vertebrates.
Voice: seldom heard harsh, cackling call.
Similar Species: none; plumage and terrestrial habits are unique.
Best Sites: wet prairie regions north and west of Lake Okeechobee.

111

AMERICAN KESTREL

Falco sparverius

F alcons are small to medium-sized hawks with narrow, pointed wings and long tails. Three species of falcons occur in Florida annually, and a fourth species has been observed only once. The American Kestrel is the smallest and most common of our falcons. • In Florida, the American Kestrel is represented by two or three races. The resident breeding race is *F. s. paulus*, the so-called "Southeastern American Kestrel." The race that breeds north of Florida, *F. s. sparverius*, is a fairly common winter resident statewide and a common fall migrant along the Atlantic Coast. A third race, *F. s. sparverioides*, the so-called "Cuban Kestrel," may occur in the Keys occasionally, but it has yet to be documented with photographs. • American Kestrels hunt from a perch—often a power line—and pounce on prey after a short flight, or they hover over prey and then drop down to capture it.

ID: small falcon often perched on power lines; rufous back barred with black; multi-colored head; gray crown; white face; buffy nape with black patch; 2 black facial stripes; whitish underparts; rufous tail. *Male:* blue wings; underparts spotted with black; bold black subterminal tail band. *Female:* rufous wings; underparts streaked with rufous; rufous-and-black-banded tail. *In flight:* frequently hovers.
Size: *L* 7½–8 in; *W* 20–24 in. Female typically larger than male.
Status: *F. s. paulus*: rare to uncommon locally permanent resident of the Panhandle and northern two-thirds of the peninsula.

F. s. sparverius: fairly common resident statewide from September to April.
Habitat: virtually any open or semi-wooded habitat.
Nesting: in a tree cavity or nest box; mostly the female incubates 4–6 finely speckled, white to pale brown eggs for 29–30 days.
Feeding: swoops from perch or hovers overhead; eats primarily insects and small vertebrates.
Voice: shrill *killy-killy-killy*.
Similar Species: *Merlin* (p. 113): larger; lacks rufous on back, wings and tail; only 1 facial stripe; does not hover. *Sharp-shinned Hawk* (p. 105): lacks rufous on back, wings and tail; lacks facial stripes; does not hover; flap-and-glide flight.
Best Sites: widespread during winter.

MERLIN
Falco columbarius

The Merlin breeds in Alaska, most of Canada and parts of the northwestern continental U.S. Its winter range, which extends to northern South America, includes the West Indies, the Great Plains and the U.S. Pacific, Gulf and Atlantic Coasts. The Merlin is also found in the Old World. It is generally rare throughout Florida, but can be fairly common along the Atlantic coast during fall migration. Even when migrating, the Merlin is a solitary species. During winter, it tends to occur along the coasts to take advantage of the large flocks of shorebirds that winter along Florida's shores. • Merlins feed almost exclusively on birds as large as doves that they capture in steep dives or in short chases originating from a perch. Unlike American Kestrels, Merlins seldom perch on power lines, usually preferring to hunt from a snag or other conspicuous perch. • North America's three Merlin populations differ in plumage coloration, with the Pacific birds being the darkest and the prairie birds the lightest. Florida's Merlins are from the eastern-breeding taiga population, which are intermediate in color.

ID: small to medium-sized falcon generally of open country; dark crown and nape; pale narrow eyebrow; pale face with 1 dark "sideburn"; white throat; white underparts heavily streaked with brown; black tail with white bands. *Male:* dark gray back and wings. *Female:* brown back and wings. *In flight:* very rapid, shallow wingbeats.
Size: *L* 10–12 in; *W* 23–26 in. Female typically larger than male.
Status: rare to uncommon spring migrant and winter resident, mostly along the coasts; locally fairly common migrant along the Atlantic Coast from September to April.
Habitat: virtually any open habitat, usually near water.
Nesting: does not breed in Florida.
Feeding: swoops down on prey from a perch or overtakes prey in flight; primarily eats birds.
Voice: generally silent in Florida.
Similar Species: *American Kestrel* (p. 112): smaller; more colorful; 2 facial stripes; often hovers. *Peregrine Falcon* (p. 114): larger; well-marked dark "helmet"; pale, unmarked upper breast.
Best Sites: fairly widespread; Boot Key; Curry Hammock SP; Guana River SP.

PEREGRINE FALCON

Falco peregrinus

Peregrine Falcons are magnificent raptors that breed on every continent except Antarctica. However, in North America in the mid-1900s, Peregrine populations were decimated throughout much of their range. The effects of DDT caused the birds to lay eggs with thin shells that broke during incubation, resulting in widespread breeding failure. After DDT was banned in the 1970s, a recovery program succeeded in reestablishing Peregrine Falcons in the eastern U.S. • In Florida, Peregrines are rare winter residents statewide, occurring as two races: *F. p. anatum* and the paler *F. p. tundrius*. During fall migration, they can be literally common along the Atlantic Coast or in the Keys—about 2000 Peregrines migrate through the Keys each year!

ID: large, powerful falcon with black-banded tail; blue-gray back and wings; prominent black "helmet"; white face with bold black "sideburn"; pale underparts with fine, black barring; blue-gray tail. *Juvenile:* brown where adult is blue-gray; pale crown; narrower "sideburn"; breast streaked with brown. *In flight:* wide, pointed wings; often soars.
Size: *Male: L* 15–17 in; *W* 3–3½ ft. *Female: L* 17–19 in; *W* 3½–4 ft.
Status: endangered (FWC; Arctic race); rare winter resident and spring migrant statewide, more common coastally; uncommon to locally common fall migrant along the Atlantic Coast, especially in the Keys.
Habitat: various open habitats, mainly coastal.
Nesting: does not breed in Florida.
Feeding: high-speed, diving stoops; strikes birds in midair with clenched feet; wide variety of prey includes ducks, shorebirds and gulls.
Voice: generally silent in Florida.
Similar Species: *Merlin* (p. 113): much smaller and much less powerful in flight; dark crown, not "helmet"; mostly dark face has 1 stripe and no bold "sideburn"; heavily streaked breast and belly.
Best Sites: fairly widespread; Boot Key; Curry Hammock SP; Guana River SP.

BLACK RAIL

Laterallus jamaicensis

Rails are narrow-bodied marsh birds that are seldom seen because of the thick vegetation and generally inaccessible nature of their habitat. The sparrow-sized Black Rail is one of Florida's most elusive and seldom-seen birds. Its diminutive size and secretive, partly nocturnal habits challenge birders to find it, and its calls are typically the only clues to its presence. • Much remains to be learned about the natural history and population dynamics of the Black Rail in our state. An apparently large population of rails was recently found along the central Gulf Coast, and additional populations probably await discovery. Black Rails are found primarily in the highest parts of salt marshes, where the ground is wet from rain but is not affected by tides; populations are also found inland.

ID: very small, mouse-like rail; black back and wings densely peppered with white spots; plain brown upper back; sooty head, breast and belly; red eyes; black undertail coverts densely spotted with white; pale legs.
Size: *L* 6 in; *W* 9 in.
Status: fairly common but extremely local permanent resident of the mainland, both coastally and inland; rare migrant statewide.
Habitat: nontidal portions of coastal marshes, often in open sawgrass; also inland in freshwater marshes that are moist but not flooded.
Nesting: very local; builds cup-shaped nest of vegetation, sometimes with a woven, domed canopy, among dense vegetation; pair incubates 4–10 creamy white eggs for 16–20 days.
Feeding: not well known; probably forages visually for invertebrates and some seeds.
Voice: drawn-out growl call when agitated. *Male:* repeated *ki-kee-der* call. *Female:* utters single *churt*.
Similar Species: none; may be mistaken for a mouse as it runs through vegetation.
Best Sites: St. Johns NWR; St. Marks NWR; south of Steinhatchee.

CLAPPER RAIL
Rallus longirostris

Found in saline or brackish habitats, the Clapper Rail is largely resident from the coasts of California and Connecticut through the West Indies and Central America to Peru and Brazil. Throughout Florida, it is a common permanent resident of mangrove forests and salt marshes. • Like all rails, the Clapper is heard much more frequently than it is seen, uttering its rapid series of loud *kek* calls even during the middle of the day. • The Clapper Rail characteristically flicks its tail as it forages. • Three races of the Clapper Rail breed in Florida: *R. l. waynei* on the northern Atlantic Coast, *R. l. scottii* along the southern Atlantic Coast and entire Gulf Coast and *R. l. insularum* in the Keys. Other races are found in our state during winter. • Some ornithologists suggest that the Clapper Rail and the King Rail should be combined into a single species.

ID: large rail, quite variable in color depending on race; generally grayish brown streaked upperparts; brownish nape and crown; generally grayish cheeks; long, mostly orangy bill; breast and belly vary from grayish brown to rusty; thin, vertical, white stripes on blackish lower belly and undertail coverts.
Size: *L* 14 in; *W* 19 in.
Status: fairly common to common permanent resident of coastal wetlands; very rare inland.
Habitat: salt or brackish marshes and mangrove forests; forages along marshy tidal channels during low tide.

Nesting: in dense cover above or near water; pair builds a cup nest of vegetation; nest usually has domed canopy and entrance ramp; pair incubates 7 brown-blotched, olive brown eggs for 20–23 days.
Feeding: probes mud or gleans mud or vegetation for crabs, crayfish and other crustaceans; also eats small fish, plant seeds and tubers.
Voice: loud, harsh series of *kek* notes, accelerating at first and slowing toward end.
Similar Species: *King Rail* (p. 117): rufous neck, breast and belly; stronger black and white barring on flanks; little habitat overlap. *Virginia Rail* (p. 118): smaller; gray face; mostly reddish bill.
Best Sites: widespread.

KING RAIL

Rallus elegans

The King Rail is the largest rail in North America. It is largely resident along the Atlantic and Gulf coasts and is locally resident in the interior of the continental U.S., with another race resident in Mexico. In Florida, the King Rail is a fairly common but rarely seen permanent resident of freshwater habitat throughout the mainland. • Unlike the Clapper Rail, the King Rail tends to vocalize chiefly at night and during dusk and dawn. • King Rails are very similar in plumage to some races of the Clapper Rail, but the two species can usually be distinguished by habitat type. When the birds overlap—Clapper Rails can occur inland and King Rails can be found in brackish marshes—conclusive identification of some individuals is probably not possible.

ID: large rail of freshwater habitats; upperparts, including wings, streaked with brown and black; rather inconspicuous gray face; dusky nape and crown; long, mostly orangy bill; boldly barred, black and white underparts with rusty throat, neck, breast and belly.
Size: *L* 15 in; *W* 20 in.
Status: generally uncommon to fairly common permanent resident of much of the peninsula but surprisingly rare or absent in much of the Panhandle; rare or very rare in the Keys.

Habitat: freshwater marshes, flooded fields or prairies and edges of shallow ponds or lakes; rare in brackish marshes.
Nesting: among clumps of vegetation, often with the base resting in water; mostly the male builds a nest of marsh vegetation; pair incubates 6–15 lightly spotted, pale buff eggs for 21–23 days.
Feeding: probes mud or gleans mud or vegetation for crayfish, crabs, small fish and various other aquatic prey.
Voice: series of *kek* notes may be indistinguishable from call of Clapper Rail but are uttered chiefly at night, dusk and dawn.
Similar Species: *Virginia Rail* (p. 118): smaller; more distinct gray face; mostly reddish bill. *Clapper Rail* (p. 116): plumage may be extensively grayish or grayish brown, depending on race; less strongly barred flanks; little habitat overlap.
Best Sites: widespread.

117

VIRGINIA RAIL
Rallus limicola

The Virginia Rail breeds in extreme southern Canada and over most of the continental U.S. except the Southeast, and it winters from British Columbia and southern New England to southern Mexico and Guatemala. It is a fairly common winter resident throughout Florida, with one surprising breeding record from the northwestern peninsula in June 1984. • The Virginia Rail seems rare in our state because it vocalizes less than other species and is perhaps less likely to feed out in the open. It is secretive and easily overlooked, and it may be somewhat more numerous than generally believed. • This rail will use any wetland type and can be identified by its medium size and its calls. When seen, the Virginia Rail resembles a King Rail but is much smaller and has distinctive gray cheeks, perhaps its most distinctive field mark.

ID: medium-sized rail; dark upperparts with rusty streaking; dark crown; gray cheeks; mostly reddish bill; boldly barred, black and white underparts with rufous throat, breast and upper belly.

Size: *L* 9–11 in; *W* 13 in.

Status: generally uncommon migrant and resident throughout the mainland from September to April; rare to very rare in the Keys; only 1 breeding record in Florida.

Habitat: fresh, brackish or salt marshes and pond or lake edges.

Nesting: in a freshwater marsh; builds a loose basket nest of vegetation; pair incubates 5–13 spotted, pale buff eggs for about 20 days.

Feeding: probes into mud or gleans vegetation for insects, earthworms, crustaceans, mollusks and seeds.

Voice: various calls, including a series of *kid-ick* notes and a descending, Mallard-like series of quacking notes.

Similar Species: *King Rail* (p. 117): much larger; less distinct gray cheek; paler, mostly orange bill; mostly restricted to fresh water. *Clapper Rail* (p. 116): often much grayer, with no rusty tones; less distinct gray cheek; muted black and white barring on underparts; restricted to salt water.

Best Sites: widespread.

SORA

Porzana carolina

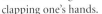

The Sora is the most common and widespread rail in North America. It is a charming little bird with a black face and a chickenlike, short, yellow bill. The Sora breeds over much of Canada and the northern and western U.S., and it winters from Oregon and Maryland south through the West Indies to northern South America. In Florida, the Sora is a common winter resident throughout the mainland but is rare in the Keys. It is found in any type of marsh. Like other rails, it is much more likely to be heard than seen, although the Sora seems less wary than its relatives. • Even though its feet are not webbed or lobed, the Sora swims quite well over short distances. And although it is rarely seen flying, its long migrations—potentially over thousands of miles—prove that it is quite capable of sustained flight. • Soras can often be induced to call by loudly clapping one's hands.

ID: smallish rail with short, yellow bill; black upperparts with brown and white streaking; brown nape and crown; black facial area ahead of eyes; gray head, neck and breast with remainder of underparts barred black, brown and white; yellow legs and feet.
Size: L 8–10 in; W 14 in.
Status: fairly common to locally very common migrant and resident throughout the mainland from September to April; rare in the Keys, usually as a migrant.

Habitat: fresh, brackish or salt marshes and pond or lake edges.
Nesting: does not breed in Florida.
Feeding: gleans or probes shallow water or mud for aquatic insects, mollusks and seeds.
Voice: several calls, including a simple *peep*, a *kerwee* and a 3-second "whinny" consisting of a rolling, descending jumble of notes.
Similar Species: *Yellow Rail:* seen very rarely, often in fields or prairies; black upperparts with yellow streaking; plain yellowish throat, breast and belly; yellow bill; lacks black face; bold white wing patches in flight.
Best Sites: widespread.

119

PURPLE SWAMPHEN
Porphyrio porphyrio

This large Old World rail is proof that almost any bird kept in zoos in Florida may be found outside of captivity. The Purple Swamphen was first noticed in late 1996 on the eastern edge of the Everglades. By 1999, the population numbered at least 135 individuals. Since that time, the swamphen has been colonizing native wetlands in the central and southern peninsula. It has already been found in several areas including Big Cypress Swamp, Lake Okeechobee and Loxahatchee National Wildlife Refuge. • Although it closely resembles the Purple Gallinule, the Purple Swamphen has different foraging habits. It spends more time wading in shallow water and avoids walking on the tops of lily pads. The swamphen is primarily vegetarian. • The Purple Swamphen is a highly variable species with distinctive plumages. Most or all of the individuals found in Florida are of the gray-headed race that inhabits the Indian subcontinent and southeast Asia.

Habitat: shallow freshwater marshes.
Nesting: over shallow water in dense marsh vegetation; builds a platform of plant material; pair incubates 3–5 cream-colored eggs with irregular purplish brown markings for 23–27 days.
Feeding: pulls up vegetation with bill and holds it with foot while biting off pieces; also digs in soil for earthworms; may glean other animal prey from the surface of the ground or vegetation.
Voice: most common call, often doubled, is a loud, piercing *creek!*
Similar Species: *Purple Gallinule* (p. 121): smaller; much slimmer; yellow-tipped, red bill; pale blue frontal shield; yellow legs; commonly walks on top of lily pads.
Best Sites: artificial wetlands in Pembroke Pines; Everglades Agricultural Area; water conservation areas.

ID: large rail, blue overall, with a grayish white head; white undertail coverts; orange eyes; large, red bill and frontal shield; reddish legs with blackish heel and toe joints.
Juvenile: muted blue plumage; brownish head; dusky bill and frontal shield.
Size: *L* 16 in; *W* 35 in.
Status: locally uncommon permanent resident of 1 suburban area southwest of Fort Lauderdale; dispersing into, and colonizing, native wetlands in the central and southern peninsula; may become widespread and well established.

PURPLE GALLINULE

Porphyrio martinica

The Purple Gallinule is closely related to the Purple Swamphen, Common Moorhen and American Coot. All four species have similar body shapes and prominent frontal shields, and all of them flick their conspicuous white undertail coverts when they walk. • The Purple Gallinule is largely resident, with some northern withdrawal in winter, from North Carolina through Central America to Chile and Argentina, as well as in the West Indies. It breeds throughout Florida, even locally in the Keys, and winters primarily from the central peninsula southward. • The Purple Gallinule's richly varied adult plumage is quite colorful. Although quite different, the juvenile's rich buff coloration, with azure highlights on the wings, is also attractive. • Purple Gallinules prefer quiet freshwater marshes heavily grown with lily pads, alligator flag and other plants, which they nimbly navigate with their large feet and long toes. • In the southern half of the Florida peninsula, these birds have two broods per year, with the young of the first brood helping to feed and defend their younger siblings.

ID: slender marsh bird with yellow legs and very long toes; greenish upperparts; dark blue head and underparts; yellow-tipped, red bill with pale blue frontal shield; white undertail coverts. *Juvenile:* bronzy upperparts; white underparts with buffy brown breast and head; dusky bill and frontal shield.

Size: *L* 12–14 in; *W* 22 in.

Status: uncommon migrant and breeding resident of freshwater wetlands statewide from April to October; mostly resident from the central peninsula southward.

Habitat: freshwater marshes, ponds and lakes with floating vegetation and dense cover.

Nesting: over water; pair builds a platform of marsh vegetation; pair incubates 5–10 finely spotted, creamy buff eggs for 22–25 days; 2 broods per year.

Feeding: forages for snails, aquatic insects and spiders, seeds and other plant material; often uses toes to turn over lily pads to search for prey hiding underneath.

Voice: various henlike clucks, cackles and high-pitched notes.

Similar Species: *Purple Swamphen* (p. 120): much larger; longer, reddish legs with blackish heel and toe joints; grayish white head; larger, red bill.

Best Sites: fairly widespread.

121

COMMON MOORHEN

Gallinula chloropus

Found throughout the peninsula and locally in the Panhandle and the Keys, the Common Moorhen is one of Florida's most common, widespread and conspicuous waterbirds. It inhabits a variety of freshwater habitats, even those in city parks or residential areas, but avoids deep open water. • The Common Moorhen is largely resident throughout the eastern U.S., with some northern withdrawal during fall. It is locally resident in the Southwest, through the West Indies and Central America to southern South America. • Although its feet are not webbed, the Common Moorhen swims well, and it comically bobs its head and neck with each stroke. Moorhens are also at ease on land and can run if necessary to escape danger. • Like Purple Gallinules, young moorhens from the first brood of the year assist with feeding and defending the young of the second brood. • This species was previously known in North America as "Common Gallinule," but its name was changed to conform to usage in the Old World, where this species is widespread and is known as "Moorhen."

ID: fairly large, chunky waterbird of shallow freshwater habitats; generally blackish, with brownish black back and wings; red frontal shield; yellow-tipped, red bill; wide, white stripe along each flank; white undertail coverts; yellow legs and feet. *Juvenile:* dusky bill; whitish throat; paler underparts; less distinct flank stripe.

Size: *L* 12–15 in; *W* 21 in.

Status: fairly common to abundant permanent resident statewide; less numerous in the Keys.

Habitat: freshwater marshes and edges of ponds or lakes.

Nesting: in or just above water; pair builds a platform nest of marsh vegetation; pair incubates 8–11 spotted or blotched, buff-colored eggs for 19–22 days; typically has 2 broods per year.

Feeding: gleans food from the water's surface or grazes on land; feeds on aquatic plants, with some insects, snails and worms also taken.

Voice: various chickenlike clucks, screams, squeaks and pips.

Similar Species: *American Coot* (p. 123): white bill; less conspicuous white undertail coverts; lacks white flank stripe.

Best Sites: widespread.

AMERICAN COOT
Fulica americana

The American Coot breeds from southern Canada through much of the western and central U.S. and the West Indies to Nicaragua and Costa Rica. During fall, it withdraws from most of Canada and the north-central U.S. In Florida, it is a common to abundant winter resident but a rare and unpredictable breeder. • American Coots are commonly seen in tight rafts of hundreds of individuals at favored wintering areas, but are found singly when breeding. Most recent breeding reports are from the central peninsula, where natural and artificial wetlands are abundant. • Coots are strong swimmers and use their lobed toes and their wings to paddle quickly through the water. They are capable of completely submerging to avoid the attacks of predators. Bald Eagles frequently prey on American Coots in Florida, and coots are a game bird in our state.

ID: fairly large, chunky waterbird with blackish body; white frontal shield; white, chicken-like bill with dark band near tip; red eyes; pale yellow legs; lobed toes. *Juvenile:* paler underparts; lacks frontal shield.
Size: *L* 13–16 in; *W* 24 in.
Status: fairly common to abundant migrant and winter resident statewide from October to April; less common in the Keys; rare, irregular and unpredictable breeder statewide.
Habitat: shallow marshes, ponds and lakes; also uses brackish impoundments and marshes.

Nesting: in a freshwater marsh; pair builds a floating nest of aquatic vegetation; pair incubates 6–11 brown-spotted, buffy white eggs for 21–25 days.
Feeding: grazes on land, gleans the water's surface or dives to depths of up to 25 ft to obtain primarily plant material.
Voice: various cackles, grunts and whistles.
Similar Species: *Common Moorhen* (p. 122): red frontal shield and bill; white flank stripe; not found in flocks. *Ducks* (p. 36, 37, 40–61): all lack white, chickenlike bill and uniformly black body.
Best Sites: widespread. *Winter:* especially abundant at Merritt Island NWR and St. Marks NWR.

123

LIMPKIN

Aramus guarauna

The Limpkin is the sole member of its family, Aramidae, and it resembles a wading bird, has the gait of a rail and flies like a crane. • In North America, the Limpkin is limited to Florida, but it is also resident from the West Indies to northern South America. In Florida, it is a fairly common but somewhat local permanent resident of the peninsula and extreme eastern Panhandle. • Limpkins are active throughout the day, and at night they can be heard uttering their loud, screaming or wailing calls. • Limpkins were once hunted extensively in Florida, nearly to extirpation. However, decades of protection have allowed them to recolonize their earlier range. • The Limpkin's name is derived from its gait—as it walks, the Limpkin lifts its feet high and twitches its tail—but the name is a misnomer, as it does not actually limp.

ID: large, heronlike bird of freshwater habitats; brown body with variable white streaks, especially heavy on head and neck and absent on flight feathers, belly and tail; long, slightly downcurved, mostly yellow bill; long, blackish legs; blackish feet.
Size: *L* 26–28 in; *W* 3½ ft.
Status: species of special concern (FWC); uncommon to fairly common local permanent resident of the peninsula; very rare to rare in the Panhandle and Keys.
Habitat: freshwater marshes, cypress swamps and along rivers and creeks.

Nesting: in a marsh or up to 40 feet high in a bush or tree; pair builds a nest of twigs and other vegetation; pair incubates 4–8 brown-marked, creamy buff eggs for about 27 days.
Feeding: walks in shallow water, scanning for snails and freshwater clams.
Voice: loud, eerily haunting calls, such as drawn-out *kreow* and *kow*, mostly by males.
Similar Species: *American Bittern* (p. 79): large, dark "mustache"; not found in the open. *Night-herons* (p. 89–90): juveniles are smaller, with much shorter bills, red eyes and shorter, yellow legs.
Best Sites: widespread; Lake Kissimmee (Kenansville); Saddle Creek Park; Shark Valley (Everglades NP).

SANDHILL CRANE

Grus canadensis

The Sandhill Crane breeds in much of Alaska and Canada and locally in the continental U.S. It winters in the southern U.S. and Mexico. In Florida, three races have been observed. The breeding race, the "Florida Sandhill Crane" *(G. c. pratensis)*, is a fairly common permanent resident of pastures and freshwater marshes of the northern two-thirds of the peninsula. The "Greater Sandhill Crane" *(G. c. tabida)* and "Lesser Sandhill Crane" *(G. c. canadensis)* have both been seen during winter. The latter race is quite rare in the state, but noisy flocks of "Greaters" are often observed as they head southward high overhead during November and December. The coiled tracheas of cranes allow their calls to be heard for perhaps a mile or more. • Sandhill Crane pairs typically mate for life, reinforcing pair bonds each spring with elaborate courtship dances. Successful pairs usually produce one or two young—called colts—each year, but continuing development increasingly threatens our Sandhill populations.

ID: very large, gray bird found in upland areas or shallow marshes; unfeathered, red crown bordered by "shaggy," whitish tail; blackish bill, legs and feet. *In flight:* flies with neck and legs extended; large migrant flocks often soar.
Size: *L* 3½–4 ft; *W* 6–7 ft.
Status: Florida Sandhill Crane is threatened (FWC); other races are fairly common permanent residents of the northern and central peninsulas; also fairly common to locally abundant migrants and winter residents, primarily of the northern and

central peninsulas; only one report from the Keys.
Habitat: pastures, shallow freshwater marshes and agricultural fields.
Nesting: in shallow water; pair builds a large mound of aquatic vegetation; pair incubates 2 brown-splotched, olive buff eggs for 29–32 days.
Feeding: probes and gleans the ground for plant tubers; occasionally takes invertebrates and small vertebrates.
Voice: loud, resonant, rattling call audible for great distances.
Similar Species: *Great Blue Heron* (p. 81): no red crown patch; neck is drawn to body during flight.
Best Sites: widespread.

WHOOPING CRANE

Grus americana

The magnificent Whooping Crane historically occurred in Florida, at least as a winter resident. The species wavered on the brink of extinction in the 1940s, when the total wild population dropped to only 16 birds. • One of the most intensive programs in the history of conservation has significantly increased the number of Whooping Cranes alive today to about 400 birds, including those in captivity. The wild population breeds in northern Canada and winters along the Texas coast. • To reduce the possibility of extinction through disease or perhaps a direct hit by a hurricane, ornithologists have created two new populations, both of which are found in Florida. Since 1993, a nonmigratory population that numbers about 90 cranes has been established south of Kissimmee. A second project that started in 2001 involves establishing a population that will breed in Wisconsin and winter along Florida's central Gulf Coast; this population already numbers over 50 individuals. • A major milestone was achieved in 2000, when a pair of Florida Whooping Cranes hatched the first two noncaptive chicks in the U.S. in over 60 years.

Habitat: pastures, coastal and freshwater marshes, shallow lakes and ponds.
Nesting: in a marsh; pair builds a large mound of aquatic vegetation; pair incubates 1–2 finely speckled, creamy buff to greenish eggs for 33–35 days.
Feeding: probes and gleans ground for aquatic invertebrates, amphibians and reptiles.
Voice: loud, resonant, rattling call, similar to that of Sandhill Cranes.
Similar Species: *Sandhill Crane* (p. 125): smaller; gray overall, with no red streak below eye. *Wood Stork* (p. 94): conspicuous unfeathered, dark head and upper neck; in flight, black on wing includes secondary flight feathers.
Best Sites: Chassahowitzka NWR (winter flock); south of St. Cloud (Canoe Creek Road).

ID: very large, white bird of pastures and shallow marshes; usually seen singly or in pairs; white feathering on body; unfeathered, red crown; red streak below eye; black primary flight feathers; black bill, legs and feet. *Juvenile:* extensive rusty feathering on upperparts.
Size: *L* 4½–5 ft; *W* 6½–8 ft.
Status: wild population endangered (USFWS); experimental Florida populations locally uncommon in central peninsula.

BLACK-BELLIED PLOVER

Pluvialis squatarola

Plovers are part of the shorebird family, a highly diverse and conspicuous—and increasingly threatened—order of birds. Plovers are small to medium-sized, chunky shorebirds with large rounded heads, large eyes, short thin bills and rather short legs. They typically feed by running a short distance on the beach or mudflat and then stopping to probe or scan for prey. • The plaintive, three-noted ascending whistle of the Black-bellied Plover is a common sound of Florida's beaches and coastal mudflats. This bird is the largest of North America's plovers and is found in a variety of habitats. Although restricted to coastal areas during winter, the Black-bellied is found inland during fall migration. As with most shorebirds, its sharp breeding plumage is seen only briefly in Florida prior to migrating northward in spring. • Black-bellied Plovers breed in the Alaskan and Canadian tundra and winter along much of the North and Central American coasts.

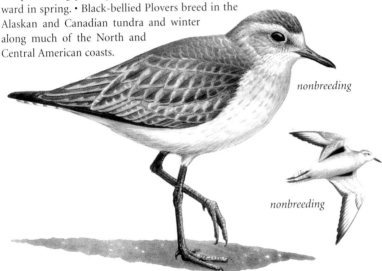

nonbreeding

nonbreeding

ID: medium-sized, chunky shorebird; rounded head; black legs and feet, short, black bill; white tail. *Breeding:* heavily mottled, black and white upperparts; black face, throat, foreneck, breast, belly and flanks; white stripe extends from crown to sides of breast; white undertail coverts. *Nonbreeding:* mottled, brown and white upperparts; pale nape and crown; bold, white eyebrow; white belly; lightly brown-streaked breast and flanks. *In flight:* black "wing pits"; bold white wing linings. **Size:** L 10½–13 in; W 29 in.

Status: fairly common to common migrant and resident from July to June, wintering coastally but migrating statewide.
Habitat: coastal mudflats and beaches; sod farms and shallowly flooded or recently plowed agricultural fields.
Nesting: does not breed in Florida.
Feeding: run-and-stop foraging technique; gleans or probes mudflats for marine worms, mollusks, crustaceans and other small prey.
Voice: loud, rich *pee-oo-ee* whistle.
Similar Species: *American Golden-Plover* (p. 128): gold-mottled upperparts; dark crown; all-black underparts in breeding plumage; in flight, black does not extend to "wing pits."
Best Sites: widespread.

AMERICAN GOLDEN-PLOVER

Pluvialis dominica

Few bird migrations in North America rival the route undertaken by American Golden-Plovers during fall. After breeding in the Alaskan or Canadian tundra, the birds feed almost continuously for weeks to accumulate extensive reserves of fat. They then depart eastern Canada and fly southeast over the Atlantic Ocean for a nonstop flight of over 2500 miles. At an average flight speed of 50 miles per hour, migrating American Golden-Plovers remain aloft for about 50 hours before landing in northern South America to rest and refuel. The birds winter in southern South America. During spring, American Golden-Plovers take a much more westerly route north, one that is largely overland through Central America. • Because their migration routes are mostly far from Florida, American Golden-Plovers are generally rare in our state. We see them primarily when their flight is affected by storms, particularly during spring, and usually when they are in their nonbreeding plumage.

nonbreeding

nonbreeding

Size: *L* 10–11 in; *W* 26 in.

Status: generally rare migrant statewide from March to April and from September to October; sometimes found in small or moderate-sized flocks along the Gulf Coast during spring.

Habitat: sod farms and other areas with short grass and recently plowed fields.

Nesting: does not breed in Florida.

Feeding: gleans grass or the ground for insects, especially grasshoppers and crickets.

Voice: soft, melodious, whistling *queedle* flight call.

Similar Species: *Black-bellied Plover* (p. 127): no gold speckling on upperparts; paler crown; white undertail coverts; conspicuous black "wing pits" in flight.

Best Sites: fairly widespread but somewhat unpredictable.

ID: medium-sized, chunky shorebird with rounded head; black legs and feet; short, black bill; dark rump. *Breeding:* heavily gold-mottled upperparts; black face, throat and underparts; wide, white stripe extends from crown to sides of breast. *Nonbreeding:* pale gold mottling on black and gray upperparts; rusty crown and dusky cheek patch contrast with white eyebrow; gray mottling on underparts, especially breast. *In flight:* dark underwing coverts with no contrasting "wing pits."

SNOWY PLOVER

Charadrius alexandrinus

The Snowy Plover is arguably Florida's most threatened bird. It nests on sandy beaches that are increasingly invaded by humans and their dogs, and its total population in the state is thought to be about 150 pairs, all of them nesting along the Gulf Coast. Snowy Plovers are named for their very pale, nearly white plumage; the birds look like snowballs running along Florida's sandy flats and shallow dunes. • Like most plovers, the Snowy forages by start-and-stop running. It feeds on a variety of small aquatic prey, such as mollusks, crustaceans, worms and insects. • Two races of the Snowy Plover have been recorded in Florida: the very pale breeding race, *C. a. tenuirostris,* and the darker, western-breeding *C. a. nivosus,* which visits the Panhandle at least occasionally. The two races often can not be distinguished in the field.

breeding

breeding

ID: small, whitish shorebird of sand flats and dunes; very pale grayish tan upperparts; short, thin, black bill; white underparts; darkish legs and feet. *Breeding:* black fore-crown, ear patch and incomplete breast band. *Nonbreeding* and *juvenile:* pale brown replaces black on head and breast.
Size: *L* 6–7 in; *W* 17 in.
Status: threatened (FWC); rare to locally uncommon permanent resident along the Gulf Coast; rare to very rare in the Keys and along the Atlantic Coast—perhaps strays from the Bahamas; not found inland.
Habitat: beaches, dunes and sand flats.

Nesting: on bare sand, usually near vegetation; lines shallow scrape with shells and other debris; pair incubates 3 black-dotted, pale buff eggs for 26–32 days; possibly 2 broods per year.
Feeding: run-and-stop foraging technique; gleans or probes surface of sand for small invertebrates and worms.
Voice: soft, whistled *chu-wee* flight call; also gives a low *krut.*
Similar Species: *Piping Plover* (p. 132): not found during summer; thicker bill; orangy legs and feet. *Semipalmated Plover* (p. 131): much darker back; complete breast band; bicolored bill; orangy legs.
Best Sites: Eglin AFB; Fort De Soto Park; Little Estero Lagoon (Lee Co.); Tigertail Beach (Marco I.).

129

WILSON'S PLOVER

Charadrius wilsonia

I n North America, the Wilson's Plover is restricted to the southeastern U.S. and Mexico, although it also occurs in the West Indies and in tropical America south to Peru. In Florida, the Wilson's Plover is restricted to the coasts, where it breeds fairly commonly along beaches and salt flats; it is very rare inland and does not occur in areas dominated by mudflats or mangrove forests. During winter, most birds leave the Panhandle and northern peninsula to winter farther south. • The Wilson's Plover is the largest plover with a single breast band in Florida; it is also the only one with a proportionately large bill. The female and juvenile of this species are the only plovers with dull pink legs and a pale breast band. • Along with the Wilson's Storm-Petrel, the Wilson's Phalarope and the Wilson's Warbler, this species was named after Alexander Wilson (1766–1813), the "father of American ornithology."

breeding

ID: small plover of beaches and dunes; brown upperparts; long, thick, black bill; white underparts; dull pink legs and feet. *Breeding male:* black forecrown; black breast band. *Breeding female, nonbreeding* and *juvenile:* brown replaces black on forecrown and breast band; breast band often incomplete.
Size: *L* 7½ in; *W* 19 in.
Status: fairly common but somewhat local breeding resident statewide; permanent resident in much of the peninsula; very rare inland.
Habitat: sandy beaches, dunes and sandflats.

Nesting: on the ground, near vegetation or debris; female chooses one of several sand scrapes excavated by the male; nest is sparsely lined with shell fragments or other debris; pair incubates 2–3 heavily marked, creamy buff eggs for 24–32 days; possibly 2 broods per year.
Feeding: run-and-stop foraging technique; gleans or probes surface of sand for fiddler crabs, shrimp, snails, insects and other small prey.
Voice: calls include a shrill *wheat!* and a lower *quit.*
Similar Species: *Semipalmated Plover* (p. 131): smaller; shorter, orange-based bill; black breast band in all plumages; orangy legs. *Killdeer* (p. 133): larger; 2 black breast bands; orange patch on rump and long tail; rarely seen on beaches and dunes.
Best Sites: fairly widespread.

SEMIPALMATED PLOVER
Charadrius semipalmatus

The Semipalmated Plover breeds throughout the Alaskan and Canadian tundra and winters coastally from Washington and South Carolina through to the West Indies and South America. In Florida, this plover is a common migrant and winter resident throughout all regions, but it is much more common coastally than inland. • The easiest way to distinguish the various small plovers in Florida—the Piping, the Semipalmated, the Snowy and the Wilson's—is by back and leg color. Because it is found throughout our coastal regions, the Semipalmated is the "template" to identify the others. It has a dark back and orange-yellow legs, whereas the Piping has a light back and yellowish legs, the Snowy has a light back and dark legs, and Wilson's has a dark back and dull pink legs. • Semipalmated Plovers feed on a variety of small aquatic prey such as crustaceans, mollusks, worms and insects. • The term "semipalmated"—used for this plover and a sandpiper—refers to the partial webbing present between the birds' toes. Most shorebirds have unwebbed toes.

ID: small shorebird, mostly of the coast; dark brown upperparts; white collar; brown crown; dark patch around eye; white eyebrow; short, orange-based bill, dusky toward tip; black breast band; white underparts; orange-yellow legs and feet.
Size: *L* 7 in; *W* 19 in.
Status: fairly common to very common migrant and resident throughout coastal areas; rare to uncommon inland during migration, primarily in fall.

Habitat: mudflats, sandflats and beaches. *In migration:* inland lakeshores and flooded agricultural fields.
Nesting: does not breed in Florida.
Feeding: run-and-stop foraging technique; gleans or probes the surface of the sand for small invertebrates and worms.
Voice: high-pitched, rising whistle: *tu-wee*.
Similar Species: *Piping Plover* (p. 132): much paler upperparts; yellowish legs; no dark patch around eye; all-black bill; paler breast band in nonbreeding plumage. *Wilson's Plover* (p. 130): larger; heavy, black bill; pink legs.
Best Sites: widespread.

PIPING PLOVER
Charadrius melodus

Piping Plovers are charming winter residents along Florida's quieter beaches and sandflats. They breed inland in north-central North America, locally around the Great Lakes and along the coast from New Brunswick to New England, and they winter along the Atlantic and Gulf coasts and in the West Indies. • Piping Plovers are a threatened species owing to disturbance, primarily on their breeding grounds, from beachgoers and their dogs. The Florida population is thought to number about 450 individuals, which are mostly distributed along the Gulf Coast, although a few sites along the Atlantic coast also support many birds. • The Piping Plover is easily distinguished from the Semipalmated Plover and the Wilson's Plover by its very pale back and from the Snowy Plover by its yellowish legs and orange-based bill. • This bird's common name and the word *melodus* both allude to the Piping Plover's musical, often-uttered call.

breeding

nonbreeding

ID: small, pale shorebird of the coast; yellowish legs and feet; pale gray upperparts; short bill. *Breeding:* orange-based bill with black tip; black breast band. *Nonbreeding:* all-black bill; pale breast band.
Size: *L* 7 in; *W* 19 in.
Status: threatened (FWC/USFWS); rare to locally common along the coasts; extremely rare inland during migration.
Habitat: coastal beaches and sandflats.

Nesting: does not breed in Florida.
Feeding: run-and-stop foraging technique; gleans or probes surface of the sand for small mollusks, crustaceans, worms and insects.
Voice: clear, whistled *peep* or *peep-lo*.
Similar Species: *Snowy Plover* (p. 129): thinner bill, always black; darkish legs and feet. *Semipalmated Plover* (p. 131): dark brown upperparts; orange-based bill year-round; breast band always black.
Best Sites: Bill Baggs Cape Florida SP; Fort De Soto Park; Honeymoon Island SP; Tigertail Beach (Marco I.).

KILLDEER

Charadrius vociferus

The ubiquitous Killdeer is the most common, widespread plover and is often the first shorebird that a birder learns to identify. Its loud *killdee* or *dee-dee-dee* calls and bright, distinctive plumage make it conspicuous, and its ability to adapt to human-made grassy or open habitats such as ball fields, golf courses and vacant lots allows urban and suburban birders to observe this species close to home. • The Killdeer is largely resident in the West Indies and from southern Canada through to South America, with some northern withdrawal during fall. It is a fairly common permanent resident throughout Florida. • When breeding, this shorebird puts on perhaps the most familiar "distraction display" of any bird in our state. If its nest or chicks are approached too closely, the Killdeer staggers along the ground, calling loudly and dragging a wing, as if broken. Once the would-be predator has been lured a safe distance away, the adult "recovers" and flies off to return discreetly to its eggs or chicks. • The scientific name *vociferus* aptly describes this vocal species.

ID: medium-sized shorebird of upland habitats; brown upperparts, often with rusty wings; brown crown, nape and ear patch; white eyebrow, throat and neck ring; 2 black breast bands; orange rump and tail; dull, pinkish legs and feet.
Size: *L* 9–11 in; *W* 24 in.
Status: fairly common permanent resident statewide, although less numerous in part of the Panhandle and the Keys; often locally abundant during winter, with the influx of breeders from farther north.

Habitat: most open or grassy habitats, except those directly along the coast; found even in urban and suburban areas.
Nesting: on open ground; in a shallow, unlined depression; pair incubates 4 darkly blotched, pale buff eggs for 24–28 days; sometimes raises 2 broods per year.
Feeding: run-and-stop forager; feeds on insects, spiders, worms, small crustaceans and some seeds.
Voice: distinctive onomatopoeic calls include *kill-dee*, *dee-dee-dee* and *deer-deer*.
Similar Species: *Semipalmated Plover* (p. 131): smaller; only 1 breast band.
Best Sites: widespread.

133

AMERICAN OYSTERCATCHER

Haematopus palliatus

Oystercatchers are large, boldly marked shorebirds that pry open the shells of oysters and other bivalves using their brightly colored, laterally compressed bills. Of the two species that breed in North America, the American Oystercatcher is the only one in the East. It is one of the most conspicuously marked and interesting shorebirds in Florida, occurring as a fairly common permanent resident of beaches in the eastern Panhandle and along both peninsular coasts. About 400 pairs are believed to breed in Florida, and during winter, this bird becomes locally abundant, with more than 1000 birds wintering around Cedar Key alone. • American Oystercatchers are easily disturbed when nesting, and their unattended eggs can quickly overheat under the hot summer sun. For this reason, oystercatchers need beaches free of humans and their dogs to breed successfully. Some American Oystercatchers now nest on the roofs of coastal buildings, perhaps an indication that state and federal agencies are not sufficiently protecting beach nest sites.

ID: large, boldly marked shorebird with long, red bill; black-tipped, white tail; brown back and wings; black head and upper breast; red orbital ring; yellow eyes; white underparts. *In flight:* bold white wing stripe on upperwing; white underwings.

Size: *L* 18½ in; *W* 32 in.

Status: species of special concern (FWC); fairly common breeding resident of much of the coast, but rare to very rare in the western Panhandle, along the southern Atlantic Coast, in the Keys and inland; much more common to locally abundant during winter.

Habitat: beaches, dunes, oyster bars and coastal mudflats.

Nesting: in sand; pair scrapes out a depression and lines it with shells; pair incubates 2–4 darkly marked, yellowish buff eggs for 24–27 days.

Feeding: visual forager; feeds on oysters and other bivalves, often pries individual shells off oyster bars; may also probe sand or mud for worms, crustaceans and other prey.

Voice: loud *wheet!* call, often given in series during flight.

Similar Species: none; bold plumage pattern and long, red bill are unique.

Best Sites: fairly widespread along the Gulf Coast.

BLACK-NECKED STILT

Himantopus mexicanus

Stilts are uniquely shaped shorebirds with long slender necks and—as is suggested by their name—extremely long legs. The sole species that occurs regularly in North America is the Black-necked Stilt; it is found from the U.S. through central South America and in the West Indies. In Florida, the Black-necked Stilt breeds throughout the peninsula—although just locally in the northern third—and in scattered locations in the Panhandle and the Keys. It may be seen anywhere during migration, and it winters from the central peninsula southward. • Black-necked Stilts are found in a variety of freshwater wetlands, such as impoundments, marshes and flooded agricultural fields; they also occur in brackish water. • When nesting, Black-necked Stilt parents are easily provoked; the birds circle low over their nest site while incessantly uttering loud *kip* notes.

ID: medium-sized shorebird with extremely long, red legs; black upperparts; white face; black eye patch merges with nape; white eyebrow; long, thin, black bill; white underparts. *Female:* back usually brownish toward center. *In flight:* black wings; white tail and rump form inverted "V" on back.
Size: *L* 14–15 in; *W* 29 in.
Status: rare to locally common migrant statewide and breeding resident, primarily of the central southern peninsula; rare or absent in the Panhandle, northern peninsula and Keys; local, possibly increasing permanent resident in the peninsula.
Habitat: primarily freshwater marshes and lakeshores; less numerous in brackish or saline marshes; flooded agricultural fields.
Nesting: in a shallow depression on dry land, or on a mound of sticks, shells or vegetation in water; pair incubates 4 darkly blotched, buff eggs for about 25 days.
Feeding: gleans prey from the water's surface or from the bottom substrate; feeds on small fish and invertebrates.
Voice: loud, sharp *kip* notes, repeated continuously, often while in flight.
Similar Species: none; black and white plumage and long, red legs are unique.
Best Sites: widespread. *Spring* and *summer:* common in Everglades Agricultural Area.

135

AMERICAN AVOCET

Recurvirostra americana

An avocet looks like a somewhat shorter-legged and bulkier version of a stilt, and indeed, avocets and stilts belong to the same family of shorebirds, the Recurvirostridae. All four of the world's species of avocets share the white underparts and bold black or black and white upperpart pattern, and one other species shares the American Avocet's reddish head and neck, but only the American Avocet has different breeding and nonbreeding plumages. • The American Avocet is a local winter resident of the southern half of the penin-sula and the Keys, but it may be seen anywhere—even inland—during migration. Although flocks in breed-ing plumage have been reported throughout spring and summer, there is no confirmed breeding record.

nonbreeding

ID: large shorebird with bold black and white wing pattern; long, slen-der, delicately upturned black bill; white under-parts; long, pale blue legs. *Breeding:* peachy head and neck. *Nonbreeding:* pale gray head and neck.
Size: *L* 17–18 in; *W* 31 in.
Status: rare migrant statewide; very local resident of the peninsula from September to April; has summered, but no definite breeding records exist.

Habitat: tidal mudflats, brackish marshes and estuaries; inland along lakeshores or in flooded agricultural fields during migration.
Nesting: does not breed in Florida.
Feeding: sweeps its bill from side to side along the water's surface, picking up minute crustaceans, aquatic insects and occasion-ally seeds; occasionally swims and tips up like a dabbling duck.
Voice: generally silent; alarm call is harsh, shrill *pleek*, often repeated.
Similar Species: none; bold black and white wing pattern and thin, upturned bill are unique.
Best Sites: Merritt Island NWR; Tampa Bay; Everglades NP.

GREATER YELLOWLEGS

Tringa melanoleuca

The two species of yellowlegs are medium-sized sandpipers with very similar plumages; they share the yellow legs and feet that give them their common name. Both species differ subtly, but a solitary yellowlegs is often difficult to identify until it flushes, when it typically utters its distinctive call. As its name suggests, the Greater Yellowlegs is the larger species. • Greater Yellowlegs breed in southern Alaska and across all of central Canada, and they winter from the U.S. coasts to southern South America. During winter, Greater Yellowlegs are fairly common throughout Florida's mainland, but they are rarer in the Panhandle, and they are locally abundant migrants statewide. • Other shorebirds use both yellowlegs as sentinels. At the first sign of danger, the Greater Yellowlegs utters its loud, distinctive *tew-tew-tew* call.

nonbreeding

nonbreeding

ID: medium-sized shorebird with plain plumage and long, yellow legs; white rump; speckled, black and white upperparts; finely streaked head and neck; narrow, white eye ring merges with eye line; slightly upturned bill is longer than length of head and may have gray base; finely barred tail. *Breeding:* streaked breast; black-barred flanks. *Nonbreeding:* less strongly marked upperparts; pale underparts with dusky breast.

Size: *L* 13–15 in; *W* 28 in.

Status: fairly common to locally abundant migrant and statewide resident; less numerous in the Panhandle during winter; usually much less numerous than Lesser Yellowlegs.

Habitat: any type of shallow wetland, whether freshwater, brackish or saltwater; flooded agricultural fields.

Nesting: does not breed in Florida.

Feeding: picks prey from the surface of the water or mud, or sweeps its bill back and forth avocet-like; feeds on small fish, crustaceans, tadpoles and aquatic insects.

Voice: loud, whistled *tew-tew-tew* call.

Similar Species: *Lesser Yellowlegs* (p. 138): smaller; straight bill is shorter, roughly equal to length of head; quieter call with 1–2 notes. *Stilt Sandpiper* (p. 156): smaller; nonbreeding bird has unbarred tail and downcurved bill.

Best Sites: widespread.

LESSER YELLOWLEGS
Tringa flavipes

The Lesser Yellowlegs breeds across subarctic Alaska and Canada, and it winters from the southern U.S. to southern South America. In Florida, it is the smaller but more common yellowlegs, being abundant during fall migration, when thousands may be seen in favored areas. Like its larger relative, the Lesser Yellowlegs can be found in any type of nonforested wetland, especially shallow ponds and marshes that offer foraging areas. • When silent, a yellowlegs is often difficult to identify to the species level. Pay attention to the bird's bill: if it is all dark, straight and equal to or less than the length of the head, the bird is probably a Lesser Yellowlegs. The bill of a Greater Yellowlegs is usually slightly upturned, often has a grayish basal third or half and is longer than the length of the bird's head.

nonbreeding

nonbreeding

ID: medium-sized shorebird with plain plumage and long, yellow legs; white rump; speckled, black and white upperparts; finely streaked head and neck; narrow, white eye ring merges with eye line; long bill is straight, black and equal to length of head; finely barred tail. *Breeding:* finely streaked breast; lightly black-barred flanks. *Nonbreeding:* less strongly marked upperparts; pale underparts with dusky breast.
Size: *L* 10–11 in; *W* 24 in.
Status: fairly common to locally abundant migrant and resident statewide; usually more numerous than Greater Yellowlegs.

Habitat: any type of shallow wetland, whether freshwater, brackish or saltwater; flooded agricultural fields.
Nesting: does not breed in Florida.
Feeding: picks prey from the surface of the water or mud; feeds on small fish, crustaceans, tadpoles and aquatic insects.
Voice: 1–2 *tew* note call, quieter than call of Greater Yellowlegs.
Similar Species: *Greater Yellowlegs* (p. 137): larger; slightly upturned bill, longer than length of head; 3 *tew* note call. *Solitary Sandpiper* (p.139): constantly bobs hind end; bolder eye ring; dark rump; greenish legs and feet. *Stilt Sandpiper* (p. 156): nonbreeding bird has unbarred tail and down-curved bill.
Best Sites: widespread.

SOLITARY SANDPIPER

Tringa solitaria

True to its name, the Solitary Sandpiper is usually seen alone, but it can sometimes be spotted in small, loosely grouped flocks. • It breeds across much of Alaska and Canada and winters from the extreme southern U.S. through central South America and in the West Indies. This bird occurs throughout Florida during migration, and it winters in small numbers from the central peninsula southward. • The Solitary Sandpiper favors freshwater ponds, marshes or flooded agricultural fields; it is not found along coastal beaches. • Solitary Sandpipers closely resemble both yellowlegs species. However, in addition to subtle differences in plumage and leg coloration, Solitary Sandpipers have a distinctive behavior that distinguishes them from yellowlegs: they slowly bob their hind end as they forage or rest. Their call, an explosive *peet-weet*, is also different.

ID: medium-sized shorebird of freshwater habitats; bobs hind end; dark upperparts are heavily spotted with white; mostly white underparts; fine, dark streaking on head, neck and breast; white eye ring; short, straight bill; olive legs and feet. *In flight:* dark wings; white tail with dark central tail feathers and heavy, dark barring.
Size: *L* 7½–9 in; *W* 22 in.
Status: rare to uncommon migrant; very rare to rare winter resident statewide.
Habitat: freshwater marshes, pond and lake edges, sewage treatment lagoons and flooded agricultural fields.

Nesting: does not breed in Florida.
Feeding: plucks prey from the surface of water or the ground; may also shake feet in shallow water to stir up or flush prey; feeds on small aquatic animals such as crustaceans, worms and insects.
Voice: high *peet-weet!* call.
Similar Species: *Lesser Yellowlegs* (p. 138) and *Greater Yellowlegs* (p. 137): larger; white rump; less obvious eye ring; yellow legs and feet; often in flocks. *Spotted Sandpiper* (p. 141): nonbreeding bird is more numerous in saltwater habitats; unspotted upperparts; incomplete eye ring; pale bill; white wing stripe in flight.
Best Sites: widespread.

WILLET

Catoptrophorus semipalmatus

Willets are one of the most typical shorebirds of Florida's coastal marshes and shorelines. Two races breed in North America: the eastern race, *C. s. semipalmatus*, is found along virtually the entire Atlantic and Gulf coasts, and the western race, *C. s. inornatus*, breeds in the Canadian Prairies and the Great Plains of the U.S. and winters along the Pacific and Gulf coasts. In Florida, the eastern race is a fairly common permanent resident of salt and brackish marshes and mangrove shorelines. The western race is found inland during migration, and it probably accounts for a good percentage of the Willets wintering along the Gulf Coast. • Although plain looking at rest, Willets are striking in flight—the bold black and white wing pattern is conspicuous—and they draw additional attention when they utter their loud *pill-will-willet* calls. They are commonly found in flocks of dozens of individuals, often towering over the other shorebirds.

nonbreeding

breeding

coastal winter resident. *C. s. inornatus:* rare inland during fall.

ID: large, dull-plumaged shorebird of coastal habitats; stocky, straight, black bill with gray base; gray legs and feet. *Breeding:* upperparts heavily mottled with black and white; short, white eyebrow; dark-mottled underparts with white belly. *Nonbreeding:* plain gray upperparts; whitish underparts. *In flight:* bold white wing stripe on mostly black wing.

Size: *L* 14–16 in; *W* 26 in.

Status: *C. s. semipalmatus:* fairly common permanent resident along the coasts; common to locally abundant migrant and

Habitat: brackish and saline marshes and beaches; flooded agricultural fields inland.

Nesting: scrapes out a depression in sand or mud; may line it with vegetation; female incubates 4 heavily spotted, olive or buff eggs for 22 days.

Feeding: picks prey from the ground or probes into mud or sand; feeds on mollusks, crabs, small fish, worms and insects.

Voice: loud, rolling *pill-will willet* call.

Similar Species: *Marbled Godwit* (p. 145): larger; buffy body; much longer, upturned, pink-based bill; lacks black and white wing pattern. *Greater Yellowlegs* (p. 137): longer, thinner bill; yellow legs and feet; lacks black and white wing pattern.

Best Sites: widespread.

SPOTTED SANDPIPER

Actitis macularius

The Spotted Sandpiper is a charming shorebird that bobs its hind end almost continuously. It flies on stiff, bowed wings, using rapid but shallow wingbeats followed by short glides. Its underparts are boldly marked with black spots in breeding plumage, which Florida birders often see in late spring. • Spotted Sandpipers breed throughout most of North America, but not in the Deep South. They winter from British Columbia and South Carolina through the West Indies to northern South America. In Florida, Spotted Sandpipers are uncommon winter residents throughout all coastal areas, but they are rare inland. During migration, they may be seen equally often inland or coastally. They are usually found singly during winter, but flocks of 20 or 30 may be seen during spring migration.

nonbreeding

nonbreeding

ID: small, short-legged shorebird that bobs hind end almost continuously; plain brown upperparts, including tail and rump; pale yellow or pink legs and feet. *Breeding:* white underparts with unique, bold, black spotting. *Nonbreeding:* brown head with short white eyebrow and black eye line; whitish throat; brown "spur" on side of breast. *In flight:* faint white wing stripe on upperwing.
Size: *L* 7–8 in; *W* 15 in.
Status: fairly common winter resident along our coasts from August to April; generally rare migrant statewide.
Habitat: estuaries, edges of salt or brackish marshes and oyster bars; also found inland along lake or pond edges and flooded agricultural fields during migration and, rarely, in winter.
Nesting: does not breed in Florida.
Feeding: gleans prey from the surface of water or the ground; feeds mostly on insects but also takes small fish, crustaceans, mollusks and worms.
Voice: sharp *peet-weet* call very similar to that of the Solitary Sandpiper.
Similar Species: *Solitary Sandpiper* (p. 139): spotted upperparts; dusky face with white eye ring; olive legs and feet; plain wings in flight; restricted to freshwater habitats. *"Peep" sandpipers* (pp. 149–52): usually in flocks; do not bob their hind end; lack combination of pale legs, feet and bill; lack spotted underparts in breeding plumage.
Best Sites: widespread.

141

UPLAND SANDPIPER
Bartramia longicauda

As is suggested by its name, the Upland Sandpiper is found in grassy upland habitats; it is not found in tidal marshes or on beaches. • The Upland Sandpiper breeds in eastern Alaska, western Canada, the Great Plains and the New England states. It winters in the northern half of South America. This sandpiper is generally a rare migrant throughout Florida, found singly or in small, loose flocks at sod farms, prairies, pastures and other grassy areas that are not flooded. It usually forages apart from other shorebirds, although Killdeers and perhaps Black-bellied Plovers or Buff-breasted Sandpipers may be nearby. • During the late 1800s, high market demand for the Upland Sandpiper's meat led to severe overhunting and catastrophic declines in its population over much of North America. Its numbers have since increased, but loss of grassland habitats in recent decades is a new threat. • The Upland Sandpiper gets its genus name from William Bartram (1739–1823), an early naturalist who spent four years cataloging the fauna of the southeastern U.S.

ID: medium-sized shorebird of upland habitats; upright posture; mottled upperparts; dusky face; large, black eyes; relatively short, mostly flesh-colored bill with black tip; lightly streaked neck, breast and flanks; pale yellow legs and feet.
Size: *L* 11–12½ in; *W* 26 in.
Status: rare to locally uncommon migrant statewide from April to May and from August to October.

Habitat: sod farms, pastures, agricultural fields and other grassy habitats that are not flooded.
Nesting: does not breed in Florida.
Feeding: forages visually for prey, which is gleaned from the ground; feeds on grasshoppers, crickets, other insects and snails.
Voice: nocturnal flight call is a soft *quip-ip-ip-ip*.
Similar Species: *Buff-breasted Sandpiper* (p. 157): smaller; shorter, thicker neck; short, blackish bill; buffy underparts. *Pectoral Sandpiper* (p. 153): usually more numerous; short, stocky body; strong contrast between finely streaked breast and white belly.
Best Sites: fairly widespread; sod farms during fall.

WHIMBREL

Numenius phaeopus

The Whimbrel introduces the shorebird genus *Numenius*, the curlews. Curlews are medium-sized to large shorebirds that have long, downcurved bills. Eight species of curlews occur in North America, a few of them solely as vagrants from the Old World. The Whimbrel is one of only two curlew species found in Florida. This shorebird breeds in the Alaskan and Canadian tundra, and it winters from the U.S. coasts through the West Indies to central South America. In Florida, the Whimbrel is a rare to locally uncommon migrant throughout coastal areas. During winter, it is found along the coasts north to the eastern Panhandle. Most or all of the birds seen in Florida are of the New World race *N. p. hudsonicus*. There have also been undocumented reports of *N. p. phaeopus*, an Old World race with a white rump. • In the Old World, the Whimbrel is known as "Hudsonian Curlew." *Numenius*, derived from the Greek word for "new moon," refers to the curved shape of the curlew's bill.

ID: large shorebird with long, downcurved bill; mottled, dark brown and white upperparts; black-and-white-striped crown; dark eye line; pale underparts with limited streaking. *In flight:* dark underwings.
Size: *L* 18 in; *W* 32 in.
Status: rare to uncommon migrant and resident of coastal areas from August to April, but has also summered; very rare inland during migration.
Habitat: coastal mudflats or sandflats; inland on flooded agricultural fields.
Nesting: does not breed in Florida.
Feeding: probes mudflats or sandflats for mollusks, crabs, worms or other aquatic prey.
Voice: generally silent in Florida; *pip-pip-pip* alarm call.
Similar Species: *Long-billed Curlew* (p. 144): less numerous; larger; longer bill; buffy body; unstreaked crown.
Best Sites: fairly widespread.

143

LONG-BILLED CURLEW
Numenius americanus

Although it is a rather nondescript tawny brown overall, the Long-billed Curlew is nonetheless one of our most impressive shorebirds. Not only is it our largest shorebird, but its remarkable bill, which on the female may be as much as 9 inches long, immediately calls attention to it. • Long-billed Curlews breed on the grasslands of the Great Plains, mostly in the U.S., and they winter along the coasts to Mexico. • They were common in Florida through the mid-19th century, but unregulated hunting and plowing of their prairie breeding grounds drove them to the brink of extinction. Their populations have recovered somewhat, and today, a few curlews winter at favored sites, mostly along the Gulf Coast. Recent studies indicate that individual Long-billed Curlews return to the same foraging territories each winter. • Long-billed Curlews use their long bills to probe deeply into mudflats or sandflats in search of marine prey; on the breeding grounds, they feed mostly on grasshoppers.

ID: large shorebird with very long, down-curved bill, orangy at base and gradually duskier toward tip; mottled, dark brown and buffy upperparts; unstreaked crown; buffy brown underparts with limited streaking. *In flight:* cinnamon underwing linings.
Size: *L* 20–26 in; *W* 3 ft.
Status: rare migrant and resident of a few coastal sites from August to April, but has also summered; very rare inland during migration.

Habitat: coastal mudflats or sandflats; also inland on flooded agricultural fields.
Nesting: does not breed in Florida.
Feeding: probes coastal flats for mollusks, crabs, worms or other aquatic prey.
Voice: loud, ascending *currleeeuuu* sometimes heard in Florida.
Similar Species: *Marbled Godwit* (p. 145): often indistinguishable plumage, but with diagnostic shorter, upturned, sharply bicolored bill. *Whimbrel* (p. 143): smaller; shorter bill; striped crown; darker upperparts.
Best Sites: Fort De Soto Park; Honeymoon Island SP; Little Estero Lagoon (Lee Co.).

MARBLED GODWIT

Limosa fedoa

There are four species of godwits in the world, and all have been observed in Florida. However, the Hudsonian Godwit is rare and probably does not occur annually in Florida, and the Bar-tailed Godwit and Black-tailed Godwit are extremely rare. Only the Marbled Godwit is found regularly. It breeds on the prairies of south-central Canada and north-central U.S., and it winters from Washington and South Carolina to Mexico. In Florida, the Marbled Godwit is found along the mainland coasts but is surprisingly rare in the Keys; a few are seen inland during migration. Flocks of dozens may be seen at favored wintering sites. • Interestingly, the plumages of Marbled Godwits and Long-billed Curlew are indistinguishable. However, whereas the bills of curlews are down-curved, those of godwits curve subtly upward. • Like curlews, godwits are named for their calls. The genus name *Limosa*, meaning "muddy," refers to the preferred foraging habitats of these birds.

ID: large shorebird with long, upturned, mostly pink bill with blackish tip; mottled, dark brown and buffy upperparts; dark crown and eye line; faintly barred under-parts. *In flight:* cinnamon underwing linings.
Size: *L* 16–20 in; *W* 30 in.
Status: rare to locally common migrant and resident of coastal areas in the eastern Panhandle and the entire peninsula from August to April, but has also summered; rare in the western Panhandle, the Keys and inland.
Habitat: coastal mudflats or sandflats; inland on flooded agricultural fields.
Nesting: does not breed in Florida.

Feeding: probes deeply in mud or sand for crustaceans, mollusks and worms.
Voice: usually silent in Florida; ascending *god-wit* call.
Similar Species: *Hudsonian Godwit:* rare in Florida; smaller; nonbreeding bird has grayish upperparts with black mottling, pale underparts and white tail with broad, black band, and shows dark upper- and under-wings with white stripe during flight. *Long-billed Curlew* (p. 144): often indistinguishable plumage, but with diagnostic longer, downcurved, gradually bicolored bill. *Whimbrel* (p. 143): downcurved, generally blacker bill; striped crown; less buff in plumage; darker upperparts.
Best Sites: fairly widespread.

RUDDY TURNSTONE
Arenaria interpres

Turnstones are small, boldly marked shorebirds that are named for their unusual foraging style. They walk along shorelines, flipping over rocks and other debris to search for prey hiding underneath. Two species are found in North America, and one of them, the Ruddy Turnstone, is common in Florida. • The Ruddy breeds in the High Arctic of Alaska and Canada, and it winters coastally from the U.S. all the way to Tierra del Fuego. This shorebird is also found in the Old World. In Florida, the Ruddy Turnstone is a common migrant and winter resident along both coasts, and it is also found in small numbers inland during fall migration. This bird is seen in small flocks actively walking along the beach, and it often roosts on washed-up vegetation, relying on its plumage for camouflage. Curiously, two specimens of the Old World race *(A. i. interpres)* are known from Florida in addition to the regularly occurring New World race *(A. i. morinella).*

nonbreeding

nonbreeding

ID: small shorebird that characteristically flips over items when foraging; short, black, slightly upturned bill; white belly and under-tail coverts; reddish or orange legs and feet. *Breeding:* black and rufous upperparts; white head with bold black markings; bold black bib. *Nonbreeding:* mottled, black, brown and white upperparts; brown head with blackish markings; dusky breast boldly outlined by blackish bib. *In flight:* conspicuous white wedge on back; white wing stripe; white tail with broad, black band.
Size: *L* 9½ in; *W* 21 in.
Status: fairly common to common migrant and resident of coastal areas statewide

from August to May, but has summered; rare to uncommon migrant inland.
Habitat: sandy or rocky beaches, estuaries and oyster bars. *In migration:* flooded agricultural fields.
Nesting: does not breed in Florida.
Feeding: varied methods: uses bill to flip rocks, shells and seaweed to expose small clams, other mollusks, crustaceans, worms and insects; also pierces tern eggs to feed on contents; may accept handouts from beachgoers—some individuals even ate the meat of a broken coconut!
Voice: low-pitched, rattling alarm call.
Similar Species: none; bold patterning on body and wings, short, upturned bill and stone-flipping behavior are unique.
Best Sites: widespread.

RED KNOT
Calidris canutus

Red Knots are well-known long-distance migrants. Some knots fly 19,000 miles in a year between their breeding grounds in the Alaskan and Canadian Arctic and their wintering grounds in southern South America. These birds also winter along the coasts of the continental U.S. and the West Indies, and they are also found in the Old World. • During spring, flocks of Red Knots that have just arrived from their southern wintering grounds amass at Chesapeake Bay to feed on the abundant horseshoe crab eggs. However, in recent years, large-scale harvesting of crabs for bait fishermen has dramatically lowered the crab population, and, with it, the population of Red Knots. Emergency legislation is pending before the U.S. Fish and Wildlife Service to declare the Red Knot an endangered species. In Florida, Red Knots were common coastal migrants and winter residents, but their numbers in our state have been declining owing to their overall population crash. • During spring, many Red Knots are in their bright, robinlike breeding plumage.

nonbreeding

nonbreeding

ID: medium-sized, chunky shorebird; short, thick, black bill; dark legs and feet; gray upperparts, including rump and tail. *Breeding:* rusty markings on upperparts; bright orange head; dusky crown and eye patch; bright orange underparts. *Nonbreeding:* gray head with white eyebrow and throat; white underparts with gray breast. *In flight:* faint white upperwing stripe; gray underwings.
Size: *L* 10½ in; *W* 23 in.

Status: rare to locally uncommon migrant and winter resident of coastal areas, especially the peninsular Gulf Coast, from August to May, but has summered; very rare inland during migration.
Habitat: beaches and estuaries.
Nesting: does not breed in Florida.
Feeding: probes sand or mud for prey; feeds on small invertebrates; may also take seeds of marine plants.
Voice: soft 1-note call.
Similar Species: *Short-billed Dowitcher* (p. 158): much longer bill; black-and-white-barred tail; white wedge on rump and back. *Dunlin* (p. 155): smaller; downcurved bill; white underwings.
Best Sites: fairly widespread.

SANDERLING
Calidris alba

The charming Sanderling is one of the most cosmopolitan shorebirds, being found in one or more seasons on every continent except Antarctica. It breeds in the Canadian Arctic and winters coastally from southern Alaska and Massachusetts to Tierra del Fuego. • In Florida, Sanderlings are one of the most conspicuous shorebirds on beaches, with flocks comically darting after a receding wave and then rapidly retreating from the next advancing wave, all while running so quickly that their legs are a blur. Sanderlings are common migrants and winter residents along beaches, but they are absent from areas with marshes or mangrove forests. • Although most small sandpipers have pale plumages, none is as pale as the nonbreeding Sanderling, with its light gray upperparts and white underparts. The distinctive breeding plumage, with a rusty head and upper breast, is seldom seen in Florida.

nonbreeding

nonbreeding

ID: small, pale shorebird that characteristically runs in and out of waves; straight, black bill; black legs and feet. *Nonbreeding:* very pale upperparts; conspicuous black eye; white underparts; black shoulder patch.
Size: *L* 7–8½ in; *W* 17 in.
Status: fairly common to locally abundant statewide migrant and winter resident on sandy coasts; rare inland during migration.

Habitat: primarily sandy beaches, where it darts in and out among waves; may roost on oyster bars or jetties.
Nesting: does not breed in Florida.
Feeding: probes for small clams, marine worms and crustaceans.
Voice: sharp *kip* call.
Similar Species: behavior of running in and out of waves is unique. *Snowy Plover* (p. 129): rare in Florida; no black shoulder patch; black or gray breast band; run-and-stop foraging technique.
Best Sites: widespread.

SEMIPALMATED SANDPIPER

Calidris pusilla

The Semipalmated Sandpiper introduces several species of small, similar sandpipers of the genus *Calidris*. Because all have high-pitched calls, the Semipalmated, Least, Western and White-rumped sandpipers are collectively known as "peeps." They are relatively nondescript birds, but many can be identified given good, close views. The most difficult species to distinguish are the Semipalmated Sandpiper and the Western Sandpiper in nonbreeding plumage. In fact, it was not proven until 1974 that Semipalmated Sandpipers were not an abundant wintering species in Florida and much of the Southeast—birders and ornithologists had been misidentifying Western Sandpipers for about 100 years! • The Semipalmated Sandpiper breeds in the Siberian, Alaskan and Canadian tundra, and it winters from extreme southern Florida and the West Indies through northern South America. It is a fairly common to abundant migrant throughout Florida and a rare or uncommon wintering species at Florida Bay and in the Keys.

nonbreeding

nonbreeding

ID: small shorebird with black legs and feet; short, black bill with slightly bulbous tip. *Breeding:* brown wash on upperparts; rufous-tinged crown and ear patch; boldly streaked breast. *Nonbreeding:* plain gray-brown upperparts; white eyebrow and throat; white underparts with faint streaking on upper breast. *In flight:* narrow, white wing stripe; white underwings; dark centerline through white tail.
Size: *L* 5½–7 in; *W* 14 in.
Status: uncommon to abundant migrant statewide from April to October; rare winter resident in the extreme south.

Habitat: mudflats, sandflats and estuaries; lakeshores and flooded agricultural fields inland.
Nesting: does not breed in Florida.
Feeding: probes or gleans prey from the surface of mud or sand; feeds on aquatic insects, small mollusks, crustaceans and worms.
Voice: *cherk* flight call.
Similar Species: *Least Sandpiper* (p. 151): nonbreeding bird has thinner bill, yellowish legs and feet and more conspicuously streaked breast. *Western Sandpiper* (p. 150): nearly identical nonbreeding plumage, but with longer, slightly downcurved bill without bulbous tip.
Best Sites: widespread.

WESTERN SANDPIPER

Calidris mauri

Although much more common along the Pacific Coast than in the East, Western Sandpipers are not confined to western North America. An estimated 6½ million Western Sandpipers migrate northward in spring to the Copper River Delta in Alaska. They breed in Alaska and Siberia, then fan out to winter from the coastal U.S. to central South America and the West Indies. In Florida, Western Sandpipers are common fall migrants statewide. They are generally rare in the western Panhandle during winter and spring, but they occur commonly throughout the remainder of the state during those seasons. Inland, Western Sandpipers are generally rare during winter but can be common during migration. • Conclusively distinguishing winter-plumaged Semipalmated and Western sandpipers is often not possible; some short-billed Westerns can have bill length and shape very similar to long-billed Semipalmateds.

nonbreeding

nonbreeding

ID: small shorebird with black legs and feet; short, black, slightly downcurved bill. *Breeding:* rufous wash on back, crown and cheek; faint eyebrow; bold streaking on breast and flanks. *Nonbreeding:* plain gray-brown upperparts; white eyebrow and throat; white underparts with faint streaking on upper breast. *In flight:* narrow, white wing stripe; white underwings; dark centerline through white tail.
Size: *L* 6–7 in; *W* 14 in.
Status: common to abundant migrant statewide from August to April; common to abundant coastally in winter and rare to uncommon inland; has summered.

Habitat: mudflats, sandflats and estuaries; lakeshores and flooded agricultural fields inland.
Nesting: does not breed in Florida.
Feeding: probes or gleans prey from the surface of mud or sand; often submerges head to feed on aquatic insects, small mollusks, crustaceans and worms.
Voice: *cheep* flight call.
Similar Species: *Semipalmated Sandpiper* (p. 149): rare to very rare during winter; nonbreeding bird is nearly identical but has slightly shorter bill with slightly bulbous tip. *Least Sandpiper* (p. 151): smaller; thinner bill; nonbreeding bird has more conspicuously streaked breast and yellowish legs and feet. *Dunlin* (p. 155): nonbreeding bird is larger, with longer, thicker bill.
Best Sites: widespread.

LEAST SANDPIPER

Calidris minutilla

Least Sandpipers are the smallest shorebirds in the world. They breed throughout the Alaskan and Canadian tundra, and they winter from Washington and North Carolina through to the West Indies and to northern South America. Least Sandpipers are generally common migrants and winter residents throughout Florida, although they are somewhat rare in the western Panhandle during winter. • Because of their small size and short legs, Least Sandpipers are found mostly along the edges of wetlands. They are often seen on sandflats and among seaweed on the coasts, or on mudflats and among grassy vegetation inland. They can even be found on sod farms far from water. • Of all the peeps, the Least Sandpiper is easiest to identify. In all plumages, it has a clearly streaked breast that contrasts sharply with its white underparts, and it is unique among the peeps in having yellow legs; the legs of other small sandpipers are blackish. • The Least Sandpiper's scientific name is aptly applied: *minutilla* is Latin for "very small."

nonbreeding

nonbreeding

ID: very small shorebird with yellow legs and feet; short, black, slightly downcurved bill; upperparts streaked with brown. *Breeding:* rusty wash to back and wings; finely streaked breast. *Nonbreeding:* faint, pale eyebrow; brown streaked breast contrasts with remainder of white underparts. *In flight:* narrow, white wing stripe; white underwings; black centerline through white tail.
Size: *L* 5–6½ in; *W* 13 in.

Status: common to abundant migrant statewide from July to May; common to abundant coastally during winter and rare to common inland; has summered.
Habitat: mudflats, sandflats and estuaries; also lakeshores and flooded agricultural fields inland.
Nesting: does not breed in Florida.
Feeding: probes or gleans prey from the surface of mud or sand; feeds on aquatic insects, small mollusks, crustaceans and worms.
Voice: high-pitched *kreee* call.
Similar Species: *Other peeps* (pp. 149, 150–52): larger; black legs.
Best Sites: widespread.

WHITE-RUMPED SANDPIPER
Calidris fuscicollis

The White-rumped Sandpiper is the least common of the four peeps that we typically see in Florida. Like other peeps, it breeds in the tundra of Alaska and Canada, but, unlike the other species, it winters exclusively in southeastern South America. Therefore, Florida birders see this species only during migration. • White-rumped Sandpipers use different migration routes during spring and fall, and the birds fly south well to the east of our state so they are seen mostly during spring. These sandpipers are late spring migrants, with individuals still passing through into early June. At this time, they are probably the easiest peeps to identify in Florida. Not only are they in their bright breeding plumage, but the birds are the only peeps with conspicuous white rumps, and their wings are longer, as would be expected for longer-distance migrants.

nonbreeding

nonbreeding

ID: smallish shorebird with black legs and feet; black bill with small reddish base to the lower mandible; wingtips extend beyond tail. *Breeding:* black-and-white-streaked upperparts with rufous feather edges; densely finely streaked head; rufous wash on crown and cheek; slightly downcurved bill of moderate length; white underparts with finely streaked breast and flanks. *Nonbreeding:* dull head and upperparts with no rufous wash; white eyebrow; light streaking on breast and flanks. *In flight:* narrow, white wing stripe; white underwings; conspicuous white rump diagnostic.

Size: *L* 7–8 in; *W* 17 in.

Status: migrant statewide from April to October; rare to uncommon during spring; very rare to rare during fall.

Habitat: beaches, mudflats, estuaries and lakeshores.

Nesting: does not breed in Florida.

Feeding: probes or gleans prey from the surface of mud or sand; eats mollusks, crustaceans, marine worms and insects.

Voice: high-pitched *tzeet* flight call.

Similar Species: *Peeps* (pp. 149–51): most are smaller; all have shorter wings that do not extend beyond tail and dark rumps.

Best Sites: fairly widespread.

PECTORAL SANDPIPER

Calidris melanotos

Another long-distance migrant shorebird, the Pectoral Sandpiper breeds in the Alaskan and Canadian tundra and winters in southern South America. It is found in Florida primarily during fall, when it is fairly common to abundant and widespread. During spring, it is generally rare and somewhat local. • Unlike most other calidrids, the Pectoral Sandpiper is easy to identify, thanks to its large size and boldly streaked breast that contrasts with its white belly. • The Pectoral Sandpiper is an upland species (or "grasspiper"), avoiding beaches and coastal mud-flats in favor of freshwater ponds or mudflats, sod farms and agricultural fields. It forages while walking, probing its bill into the muddy ground. • The male Pectoral Sandpiper has air sacs in his breast that he inflates on the breeding grounds during courtship. A hollow, hooting sound accompanies the visual display. • The Pectoral Sandpiper is named after the pectoral muscles, apparently referring to this species prominently streaked breast.

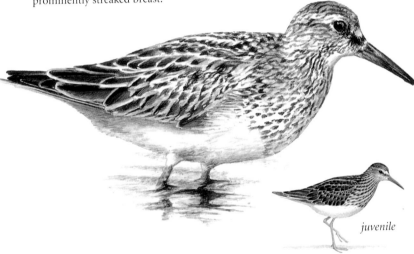

juvenile

ID: medium-sized shorebird of upland habitats; brown-streaked upperparts, usually with rufous wash; dark crown; finely streaked head with indistinct white eyebrow and throat; rather short bill with pale lower mandible; boldly streaked breast contrasts sharply with white belly and undertail coverts; yellow legs and feet. *In flight:* dark upperwings; white underwings; black line through white tail.
Size: *L* 9 in; *W* 18 in; female is noticeably smaller.
Status: uncommon to locally abundant migrant throughout the mainland from July to October and less numerous from March to May; rare in the Keys; 1 verified winter record.
Habitat: marshes and pond edges, sod farms and other agricultural fields with lit-tle or no water; rare in estuaries.
Nesting: does not breed in Florida.
Feeding: probes or gleans prey from the mud's surface; feeds on worms, insects, crustaceans and spiders.
Voice: sharp *krick* call.
Similar Species: *Peeps* (pp. 149–52): smaller; generally most numerous in coastal habitats; all lack the well-defined streaked breast; most have black legs and solidly black bill.
Best Sites: fairly widespread.

PURPLE SANDPIPER

Calidris maritima

The chunky Purple Sandpiper is an unusual shorebird in several respects. Firstly, it is limited to North America—it does not winter farther south in Central or South America. Secondly, it is found only in the eastern half of North America, whereas most shorebirds occur throughout the continent. Finally, it inhabits rocky shorelines, breakwaters and jetties, generally eschewing extensive beaches or mudflats. • Purple Sandpipers breed in the Canadian Arctic, and they winter from New Brunswick southward; they are one of our hardiest shorebirds. In Florida, Purple Sandpipers are virtually limited to the Atlantic Coast, and then to areas with natural outcroppings of coquina rock, limestone or rock jetties or breakwaters. They often associate with Ruddy Turnstones, and small mixed flocks can be seen braving the surf breaking against the rocks. Although they have been found as far south as the Keys, Purple Sandpipers mostly occur to about New Smyrna Beach.

nonbreeding

nonbreeding

ID: medium-sized, dark, stocky shorebird of rocky habitats along the Atlantic Coast; downcurved bill mostly yellow-orange with black tip; yellow or orange legs and feet. *Breeding:* pale upperparts with some rufous wash; streaked head and breast. *Nonbreeding:* dark gray upperparts, including head; white eye ring; white underparts with scattered dark streaking and dark gray breast.
Size: *L* 9 in; *W* 17 in.
Status: rare to locally uncommon resident along the Atlantic Coast south to about

New Smyrna Beach from November to March; very rare south to the Keys and along the Gulf Coast.
Habitat: rocky shorelines, jetties and breakwaters; less common on beaches.
Nesting: does not breed in Florida.
Feeding: probes bill into rock crevices or, less commonly, seaweed on beaches; feeds on small invertebrates; may also eat algae.
Voice: soft *prrt-prrt* call.
Similar Species: *Peeps* (pp. 149–52): all lack bicolored bill, yellow-orange legs and dusky upperparts and breast.
Best Sites: Fort Clinch SP; Matanzas Inlet (St. Johns Co.); Port Canaveral Jetty Park; Smyrna Dunes Park (Volusia Co.).

DUNLIN

Calidris alpina

The Dunlin breeds in the Alaskan and Canadian tundra and winters from Alaska and Massachusetts to Mexico and Panama. It also occurs widely in the Old World. The Dunlin is one of the most ubiquitous small shorebirds in Florida, occurring in flocks of hundreds—or even thousands—in favored areas away from human disturbance. It is a common winter resident along our coasts, and during migration it occurs inland as well. • The Dunlin is characteristically seen wading in water up to its belly and probing into the muddy or sandy soil with its down-curved bill. • Late spring migrants—or perhaps summering individuals—are occasionally seen in Florida in their full breeding plumage, which consists of a reddish back and a large black patch on the belly. • The name of the Dunlin comes from the Old English *dunn*, which means a "brownish gray color," referring to the bird's winter plumage. The suffix *lin* or *ling* refers to something small.

nonbreeding

nonbreeding

ID: medium-sized, chunky shorebird often seen in flocks; down-curved bill; black legs and feet. *Breeding:* distinctive rusty back and wings; pale head with pale rusty crown; faintly streaked breast; large black patch on belly; white undertail coverts. *Nonbreeding:* dull gray-brown upperparts, including head; pale eyebrow and throat; white underparts with dusky breast. *In flight:* white upperwing stripe; mostly white underwing.
Size: *L* 7½–9 in; *W* 17 in.

Status: fairly common to abundant resident of coastal habitats statewide from September to May; has summered; can be fairly common inland during fall migration but rare during other seasons.
Habitat: beaches, mudflats, estuaries and oyster bars; inland in shallow ponds or marshes and flooded agricultural fields.
Nesting: does not breed in Florida.
Feeding: active forager; probes bill into mud or sand; feeds on small mollusks, crustaceans, worms and insects.
Voice: harsh *kreep* call.
Similar Species: breeding plumage is distinctive. *Western Sandpiper* (p. 150): nonbreeding bird is smaller and lacks dark unstreaked breast.
Best Sites: widespread.

STILT SANDPIPER

Calidris himantopus

Although not nearly as long-legged as the Black-necked Stilt, the Stilt Sandpiper nonetheless has long legs for a sandpiper, hence its name. • These shorebirds breed in the Alaskan and Canadian tundra, and they winter from Florida, the West Indies and Texas to northern South America. In Florida, Stilt Sandpipers are fairly common to common migrants statewide, and they are rare to uncommon winter residents of the peninsula. They are typically found in flocks that often contain dozens or hundreds—sometimes thousands—of individuals. These sandpipers are much more likely to be found inland around freshwater ponds or flooded agricultural fields than along the coasts. • Stilt Sandpipers often associate with dowitchers, with which they are easily confused. Look for the sandpiper's subtly downcurved bill, longer legs and slimmer body. The sandpiper also has a habit of holding its body at more of an angle when foraging, the result of its having longer legs but a shorter bill than the dowitcher.

nonbreeding

nonbreeding

ID: medium-sized shorebird that often associates with dowitchers; slim head with conspicuous white eyebrow; long, slender, downcurved bill; long yellowish or yellow-green legs and feet. *Breeding:* upperparts including head blotched with black and white; rusty cheek patch; underparts heavily barred with black and white. *Nonbreeding:* pale gray upperparts and breast; remainder of underparts whitish. *In flight:* dark tail; white rump; plain upperwings; underwings are gray with white centers.

Size: *L* 8–9 in; *W* 18 in.

Status: fairly common to common migrant statewide; rare to locally uncommon winter resident of the peninsula, primarily the southern half.

Habitat: freshwater, brackish and salt marshes, estuaries, lakeshores and flooded agricultural fields.

Nesting: does not breed in Florida.

Feeding: wades into shallow water and probes mud or sand for crustaceans, worms, mollusks and aquatic insects.

Voice: infrequent in Florida; call is a whistled *too.*

Similar Species: *Short-billed Dowitcher* (p. 158) and *Long-billed Dowitcher* (p. 159): nonbreeding birds have white wedge on back, longer, straight bill, shorter legs and chunkier body. *Greater Yellowlegs* (p. 137) and *Lesser Yellowlegs* (p. 138): shorter bill, lack pale eyebrow and probe less often.

Best Sites: widespread.

BUFF-BREASTED SANDPIPER

Tryngites subruficollis

The Buff-breasted Sandpiper breeds in Alaska and the Canadian Arctic, and it winters in southern South America. It performs its long migrations down the center of North America, generally avoiding the eastern and western edges of the continent, then continues through Central America. • The Buff-breasted Sandpiper is an easily overlooked migrant throughout Florida and is usually seen only by skilled birders who make a concerted effort to find it. An upland sandpiper, or "grasspiper," it is found in pastures, sod farms, recently plowed fields and other habitats with low-growing grass. The Buff-breasted Sandpiper is usually found in Florida at inland sites during fall; rarely, flocks can be seen in spring after westerly winds have pushed them to our eastern Gulf Coast. • These birds appear dovelike with their somewhat bulbous heads, thin necks and short legs, and they are often partially obscured by grassy vegetation.

juvenile

ID: medium-sized, upland shorebird of grassy habitats; "scaly" patterned upperparts; pale head appears dovelike; dusky crown; prominent dark eyes; fairly short, thin, black bill; pale, buffy underparts; yellowish legs and feet. *In flight:* no wing stripe on upperwings; bright white underwings with dark edges.

Size: *L* 7½–8 in; *W* 18 in.

Status: generally rare migrant, probably statewide; sometimes less numerous during fall; few reports from the Panhandle, but may be the result of a scarcity of observers

Habitat: pastures, sod farms and other grassy fields with no standing water; not found on beaches or in estuaries.

Nesting: does not breed in Florida.

Feeding: gleans the ground and vegetation for insects and spiders.

Voice: usually silent in Florida.

Similar Species: *Upland Sandpiper* (p. 142): larger; more slender profile with longer neck; yellow bill; white underparts with black barring on flanks; dark underwings in flight. *Peeps* (pp. 149–52): smaller; usually dark legs and feet; often found in large flocks.

Best Sites: Everglades Agricultural Area. *Fall:* sod farms or agricultural fields.

157

SHORT-BILLED DOWITCHER

Limnodromus griseus

Dowitchers are large, plump shorebirds with long bills, barred tails and a unique white rump and wedge on the lower back. Distinguishing Short-billed Dowitchers from Long-billed Dowitchers is often a considerable, perhaps underappreciated challenge. • The Short-billed Dowitcher breeds in subarctic tundra in Alaska and Canada, and it winters from Washington and South Carolina through the West Indies to northern South America. In Florida, this shorebird is a fairly common to abundant migrant statewide and a common winter resident, primarily of the peninsula and the Keys. Two races are found in our state: *L. g. griseus* and *L. g. hendersoni*. • Short-billed Dowitchers are often reported inland during winter, but there is no documented evidence that they occur in freshwater habitats during that season; more information based on careful study is needed.

nonbreeding

nonbreeding

ID: medium-sized, chunky shorebird often seen feeding actively in shallow water; black-and-white-barred tail; white wedge extends from rump onto back; long, straight, blackish bill; long, pale yellow legs; pale yellow feet. *Breeding:* speckled, black and buffy upperparts. *L. g. hendersoni* is orangy below; *L. g. griseus* has whitish or buffy underparts and pale orange breast. *Nonbreeding:* mostly plain gray upperparts, including head; darker crown; white eyebrow; darkish eye line. *Juvenile:* buffy edges and internal markings on back and scapular feathers.
Size: L 11–12 in; W 19 in.

Status: generally common to abundant migrant statewide year-round; common to abundant winter coastal resident; least numerous in the western Panhandle.
Habitat: freshwater, brackish or saline mudflats or shallow water.
Nesting: does not breed in Florida.
Feeding: wades in shallow water and rapidly probes bill into mud in "sewing machine" fashion; feeds on worms, crustaceans, small mollusks and aquatic insects.
Voice: soft *too-too-too* call.
Similar Species: *Long-billed Dowitcher* (p. 159): often nearly identical; restricted to fresh water during winter; higher-pitched *keek* call. *Wilson's Snipe* (p. 160): median stripe on crown; no white wedge on rump and back; restricted to fresh water.
Best Sites: widespread.

LONG-BILLED DOWITCHER

Limnodromus scolopaceus

The Long-billed Dowitcher breeds in the High Arctic tundra of Alaska and western Canada, and it winters from British Columbia and Virginia south to Central America. • As with the Short-billed, the status of the Long-billed Dowitcher in Florida is somewhat muddled. It is known to be a fairly common to locally common migrant and winter resident of freshwater habitats throughout the mainland. Although often reported during July and August, specimen evidence suggests that Long-billed Dowitchers do not arrive until September. Again, additional data on the distribution of dowitchers in Florida is needed. • Vocalizations of the two dowitchers are distinctive and are the only conclusive way to distinguish the two species in the field year-round—bill length is not a field mark.

nonbreeding

nonbreeding

ID: medium-sized, chunky shorebird often seen feeding actively in shallow water; black-and-white-barred tail; white wedge extends from rump onto back; long, straight, blackish bill; long, pale yellow legs; pale yellow feet. *Breeding:* black and buffy speckled upperparts; orangy below, with black barring on flanks and undertail coverts. *Nonbreeding:* mostly plain gray upperparts, including head; darker crown; white eyebrow; darkish eye line. *Juvenile:* buffy edges and black interiors on back and scapular feathers.
Size: *L* 11–12½ in; *W* 19 in.
Status: uncommon to locally common migrant and resident of the mainland from September to May; no proven summer records; only 1 report from the Keys.
Habitat: freshwater mudflats and flooded agricultural fields.
Nesting: does not breed in Florida.
Feeding: wades in shallow water and rapidly probes bill into mud in "sewing machine" fashion; feeds on freshwater worms, crustaceans, mollusks and aquatic insects.
Voice: loud *keek* call, given singly or in a series.
Similar Species: *Short-billed Dowitcher* (p. 158): often found in salt or brackish habitats; little or no habitat overlap during winter; *too-too-too* call. *Wilson's Snipe* (p. 160): median stripe on crown; no white wedge on rump and back; very different call.
Best Sites: widespread inland.

WILSON'S SNIPE

Gallinago delicata

Known until very recently as the Common Snipe, a name now reserved for an Old World species rarely found in Alaska, the Wilson's Snipe breeds throughout Alaska, Canada and the northern third of the continental U.S. It winters from the southern part of North America through the West Indies to northern South America. The Wilson's Snipe is a fairly common to abundant winter resident in Florida but is less common in the southern peninsula and rare in the Keys, where fresh water is scarce. • Wilson's Snipes favor a variety of freshwater habitats and rarely visit salt marshes. Although never found in flocks when feeding, dozens of Wilson's Snipes may be flushed from small areas of ideal habitat. • The Snipe is well camouflaged, often concealed by vegetation. When an observer approaches too closely, a snipe utters a harsh *skape* note as it suddenly flushes, often unseen, and then flies in a low, rapid zigzag pattern to confuse would-be predators.

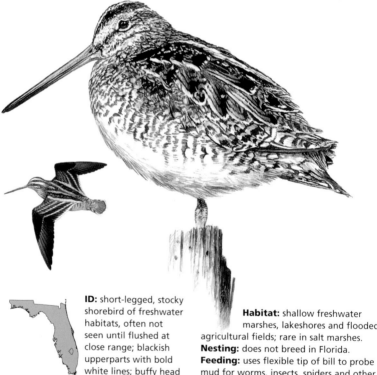

ID: short-legged, stocky shorebird of freshwater habitats, often not seen until flushed at close range; blackish upperparts with bold white lines; buffy head with dark stripes on crown and face; long, straight bill; white underparts barred with black; buffy breast streaked with black; orange tail.
Size: *L* 10½–11½ in; *W* 18 in.
Status: fairly common to locally abundant migrant and winter resident throughout the mainland but less common in the southern peninsula and rare in the Keys.

Habitat: shallow freshwater marshes, lakeshores and flooded agricultural fields; rare in salt marshes.
Nesting: does not breed in Florida.
Feeding: uses flexible tip of bill to probe mud for worms, insects, spiders and other prey; may also take seeds.
Voice: sharp, nasal alarm call: *skape!*
Similar Species: *Short-billed Dowitcher* (p. 158) and *Long-billed Dowitcher* (p. 159): nonbreeding birds usually feed in flocks in open water and have paler plumage, white wedge from rump onto back and no streaking on head.
Best Sites: widespread.

AMERICAN WOODCOCK

Scolopax minor

The American Woodcock is one of our most unusual shorebirds. It is a solitary upland species that never flocks, never visits saline habitats and never ventures out into the open during daylight hours. Consequently, few birders have seen it. • American Woodcocks breed throughout the entire eastern U.S. and extreme southeastern Canada, and they winter exclusively in the Southeast. In Florida, they are generally uncommon, and their nocturnal habits make them seem rarer than they are. • On the breeding grounds, the male American Woodcock performs a dazzling courtship display. Around dawn and dusk, the male struts around a woodland clearing or brushy field while uttering a series of loud *peent* notes. He then launches into the air, twittering upward in a circular flight until, with wings partly folded, he plummets to the ground in a zigzag pattern, chirping at every turn, until he lands in the same spot where he started. The twittering sounds are made by air rushing past his outer primary flight feathers.

ID: secretive, chunky, upland shorebird rarely seen during the day; boldly patterned upperparts; black nape and hindcrown with pale barring; buffy face; large, black eyes; long, straight, mostly pale bill; pale orange upperparts with grayish upper breast. *In flight:* flushes at close range; rounded wings make whistling sound.
Size: *L* 11 in; *W* 18 in.
Status: rare to uncommon winter breeder of the mainland south, at least occasionally, to the Everglades; summer status is less certain; very rare in the Keys.

Habitat: moist woodlands and hammocks adjacent to grassy clearings or fields.
Nesting: on the ground; female digs a scrape and lines it with dried leaves; female incubates 4 brown-blotched, pinkish buff eggs for 20–22 days; only the female tends the young.
Feeding: uses long bill to probe for earthworms, insects, spiders and other small invertebrates.
Voice: nasal *peent* call, very similar to that of Common Nighthawk.
Similar Species: *Wilson's Snipe* (p. 160): much more numerous; heavily striped upperparts and breast; black-barred, white underparts.
Best Sites: widespread.

WILSON'S PHALAROPE

Phalaropus tricolor

Phalaropes are interesting shorebirds. All three of the world's species are found in Florida. One species—the Wilson's Phalarope—is a landlubber year-round, whereas the Red Phalarope and the Red-necked Phalarope are pelagic for much of the year. All three phalaropes practice a mating strategy known as polyandry, in which a female mates with several males and may produce a clutch with each. The female then leaves the incubation and brooding responsibilities exclusively to the males. Other unusual features of phalaropes are that the female's breeding plumage is brighter than the male's, and that phalaropes forage by swimming rapidly in tight circles to stir up prey. One occasionally sees a phalarope "spin-walking" on dry land! • Wilson's Phalaropes breed in southwestern Canada and the northwestern U.S., and they winter in southern South America. In Florida, they are rare but regular fall migrants statewide and are irregular during spring. • The word "phalarope" is of Greek origin and means "coot-footed," referring to the birds' lobed feet.

nonbreeding

nonbreeding

ID: smallish shorebird with very long, thin bill. *Nonbreeding:* pale gray upperparts and upper breast; white underparts; gray crown, eye line and nape; dark eyes.
Size: *L* 9–9¹/₂ in; *W* 17 in.
Status: rare to locally uncommon fall migrant statewide; very rare during spring.
Habitat: flooded agricultural fields, freshwater marshes and lakeshores.
Nesting: does not breed in Florida.

Feeding: whirls in tight circles in shallow water to stir up prey, then picks from the surface; feeds on aquatic insects, worms and small crustaceans.
Voice: generally silent in Florida.
Similar Species: *Red-necked Phalarope* (p. 361) and *Red Phalarope* (p. 361): nonbreeding birds have black mark on crown and behind eye; little habitat overlap, being mostly pelagic, and more often seen during winter. *Other shorebirds* (pp. 127–61): do not forage by spinning in water.
Best Sites: Everglades Agricultural Area.

POMARINE JAEGER

Stercorarius pomarinus

Jaegers are "pirates" of the open ocean, robbing gulls or terns of their prey. Except when nesting, they spend their lives on the ocean. All three species of North American jaegers are found in Florida, and the Pomarine (pronounced pom-ar-INE) is the largest. It breeds in Alaska and Canada, as well as in the Old World, and it winters offshore from California and North Carolina to northern South America.
• In Florida, Pomarine Jaegers are uncommon winter residents and uncommon to occasionally abundant migrants offshore that are at times visible from land. The largest numbers are seen from key sites along the Atlantic Coast, especially at Canaveral National Seashore. Otherwise, birders in Florida need to board boats to observe jaegers. • The term "jaeger" is German for "hunter." • Adult jaegers have diagnostic tail patterns, but subadults are found in a variety of plumages and morphs, and many cannot be identified to species.

nonbreeding
light morph

subadult
light morph

ID: large, gull-like seabird of open oceans; white shafts on outer 4–6 primaries. *Light morph:* brown upperparts, crown and face; yellowish nape, cheek and throat; dusky or pale underparts with brown breast band; twisted, spoon-shaped central tail feathers. *Subadult:* many plumages, making identification difficult; generally larger and heavier than other subadult jaegers.
Size: *L* 20–23 in; *W* 4 ft.
Status: uncommon to locally abundant migrant and resident offshore from October to April; has summered; especially common off the Atlantic Coast during fall.

Habitat: open ocean; sometimes seen from shore.
Nesting: does not breed in Florida.
Feeding: chases after and steals food from other seabirds, usually gulls; also plucks prey off the water's surface; feeds on fish, crustaceans and human food items.
Voice: generally silent in Florida; may give sharp, chattering notes.
Similar Species: *Parasitic Jaeger* (p. 164): smaller; white shafts restricted to outer 3–5 primaries; adults have pointed central tail feathers; tends to chase after terns. *Long-tailed Jaeger:* very rare in Florida; smaller and buoyant in flight; white primary shafts usually restricted to outer 2 primaries; adults have long central tail feathers.
Best Sites: Canaveral NS; offshore, primarily in the Atlantic Ocean.

163

PARASITIC JAEGER

Stercorarius parasiticus

The Parasitic Jaeger often harasses other seabirds to rob them of their catch. But whereas its larger cousin the Pomarine Jaeger typically harasses gulls, the Parasitic Jaeger tends to chase terns. Like the other two jaegers, including the very rare Long-tailed Jaeger *(S. longicaudus)*, the Parasitic Jaeger breeds in Alaska and Canada, as well as in the Old World, where it is known as "Arctic Skua." The Parasitic Jaeger winters offshore from California and Maine to southern South America. It is a rare to uncommon migrant and winter resident off Florida's coasts, and it is seen much less frequently than is the Pomarine Jaeger.

• Most jaegers found in Florida are subadults; they lack the adults' conspicuous and distinctively shaped central tail feathers and therefore can be very difficult to identify to species.

*subadult
light morph*

ID: fairly large, gull-like seabird of open oceans; white shafts on outer 3–5 primaries. *Light morph:* brown upperparts, face and crown; yellowish nape, cheek and throat; pale or dusky underparts with brown breast band; long, pointed central tail feathers. *Subadult:* many plumages, making identification difficult.
Size: *L* 15–20 in; *W* 3 ft.
Status: rare to locally common migrant and resident statewide from September to May; has summered; especially common off the Atlantic Coast during fall.
Habitat: open ocean; sometimes seen from shore.

Nesting: does not breed in Florida.
Feeding: chases after and steals food from other seabirds, usually terns; also plucks prey off the water's surface; feeds on fish, crustaceans and human food items.
Voice: generally silent in Florida.
Similar Species *Pomarine Jaeger* (p. 163): larger; white shafts on outer 4–6 primaries; twisted, spoon-shaped central tail feathers; tends to chase after gulls. *Long-tailed Jaeger:* very rare in Florida; smaller and buoyant in flight; white primary shafts usually restricted to outer 2 primaries; adults have long central tail feathers.
Best Sites: Canaveral NS; offshore, primarily in the Atlantic Ocean.

LAUGHING GULL

Larus atricilla

Arguably the most ubiquitous gull in Florida, the Laughing Gull is also the only gull that breeds in our state. With its black "hood" in breeding plumage and "laughing" calls uttered frequently year-round, it is also one of our most familiar birds—even if known only as "seagull." • Laughing Gulls are mostly resident along the coasts from New Brunswick and Mexico south through the West Indies to northern South America. In Florida, they are locally abundant breeders along the coasts, and they occur elsewhere as nonbreeding residents. • Laughing Gulls nest in large colonies on coastal islands that are free of human disturbance and terrestrial predators such as raccoons. Some colonies contain more than 10,000 pairs. One-half or more of Florida's Laughing Gulls nest around Tampa Bay. • Aberrant Laughing Gulls with red bills and legs have been misidentified in Florida as Black-headed Gulls *(L. ridibundus).*

breeding

nonbreeding

ID: medium-sized gull of mostly coastal habitats; dark gray upperparts; white underparts, occasionally with pink flush; white tail; dark reddish legs and feet. *Breeding:* black head; white crescents above eyes; rather thick, reddish bill. *Nonbreeding:* white head with dark mottling on crown; black bill. *Juvenile:* upperparts mostly brown and "scaly"; dusky or whitish underparts; broad, black band on tail. *Immature:* intermediate plumage; acquires adult plumage gradually, completed in third year.
Size: *L* 15–17 in; *W* 3 ft.
Status: common to abundant permanent resident of coastal areas; nonbreeding population rare to locally common inland.

Habitat: any coastal habitat; also inland around landfills and large lakes.
Nesting: colonial nester; nests on the ground on coastal islands or beaches; pair builds cup-shaped nest of marsh vegetation; pair incubates 3 darkly splotched, buff to dark brown eggs for 22–27 days.
Feeding: plucks prey from the water's surface or the ground; feeds on a variety of prey, such as fish, small mollusks and crustaceans; scavenges garbage at landfills.
Voice: series of loud *ha-ha* call notes.
Similar Species: *Franklin's Gull (p. 362):* much rarer; smaller; thinner bill; nonbreeding and juvenile have extensive black hoods.
Best Sites: widespread.

165

BONAPARTE'S GULL

Larus philadelphia

The small, delicate Bonaparte's Gull breeds across Alaska and Canada and winters from British Columbia and Massachusetts through the West Indies to Mexico. In Florida, it is a fairly common migrant and winter resident statewide, occurring coastally and on larger lakes in the interior. • Bonaparte's Gulls are very buoyant, riding high on the water. In flight, they appear rather ternlike, not ponderous like most other gulls. • The white primary wedges on the wings of adults are conspicuous, and nonbreeding and juvenile plumages have a black spot behind each eye. Except for gulls that are very rarely found in Florida, these two field marks are diagnostic. • This gull was named after Charles Lucien Bonaparte (1803–1857), a French ornithologist who studied the North American avifauna in the early 1800s and who was a nephew of Napoleon I.

nonbreeding

nonbreeding

ID: small gull, buoyant in flight and when on the water; gray upperparts; short, thin, black bill; white underparts; pink legs and feet; white tail. *Breeding:* black hood. *Nonbreeding:* white head with black ear spot. *Juvenile:* resembles nonbreeding adult, but with dusky, dark "M" on wings in flight; black tail band. *In flight:* black edges on white primaries.
Size: *L* 11½–14 in; *W* 33 in.
Status: rare to locally abundant migrant and resident statewide from November to April but primarily coastal.

Habitat: beaches, estuaries and salt marshes; inland on lakes or flooded agricultural fields.
Nesting: does not breed in Florida.
Feeding: dives for food from short heights, plucks food from the water's surface or sometimes hawks insects over marshes; feeds on small fish, aquatic invertebrates and insects.
Voice: scratchy, soft *ear ear* while feeding.
Similar Species: *Black-headed Gull:* very rare in Florida; nonbreeding adult has red bill; juvenile has orange-red bill. *Laughing Gull* (p. 165): dark reddish bill, legs and feet.
Best Sites: widespread.

RING-BILLED GULL

Larus delawarensis

The Ring-billed Gull is the only competitor to the Laughing Gull's claim as the most widespread and familiar gull in Florida. Even though it does not breed here, it is found statewide in a wide variety of habitats, even during summer. Whereas the Laughing Gull is somewhat restricted to the coasts and inland areas around landfills, the Ring-billed Gull is commonly seen roosting in flocks in parking lots in our largest cities. • Ring-billed Gulls breed in southern Canada and the northern U.S., and they winter from British Columbia and Nova Scotia in Canada to southern Mexico. • The Ring-billed is a "three-year gull"—it first acquires adult plumage in its third calendar year of life, after going through a series of subadult molts.

nonbreeding

nonbreeding

ID: medium-sized gull found coastally and inland; medium gray upperparts; black wingtips with white spots; white underparts; yellow eyes; yellow bill with black ring near tip; yellow legs and feet. *Breeding:* entirely white nape, crown and cheek. *Nonbreeding:* dusky streaking on nape, crown and cheek. *Juvenile:* mostly brown, with blackish tail tip, wingtips, eyes and bill; pale pink legs and feet. *Immature:* resembles adult by second winter, except with heavily streaked head and breast.
Size: *L* 18–20 in; *W* 4 ft.
Status: common to abundant nonbreeding permanent resident statewide; less numerous during summer.

Habitat: virtually any type of open water habitat; landfills; often roosts in parking lots, especially inland.
Nesting: does not breed in Florida.
Feeding: plucks prey off the water's surface or the ground or plunge-dives for prey; feeds on crabs, small fish, shrimp and carrion; also eats garbage and begs for handouts from beachgoers.
Voice: high-pitched *splee* call.
Similar Species: *Herring Gull* (p. 168): less numerous; nonbreeding bird is larger, with red spot near tip of lower mandible and no black ring on bill, and usually has pink legs and feet. *Laughing Gull* (p. 165): nonbreeding bird is smaller, with dark gray upperparts, black bill, dark legs and feet and dusky markings on head.
Best Sites: widespread.

HERRING GULL
Larus argentatus

Herring Gulls breed throughout Alaska, Canada and the northeastern U.S., and they winter along the entire North American coast and much of the eastern U.S. south through the West Indies to Central America. They are also widespread in the Old World. In Florida, Herring Gulls are fairly common non-breeding permanent residents along the coasts. They can be locally abundant at landfills, ports or other areas with large amounts of prey or garbage. On their breeding grounds to the north, Herring Gulls can be great predators of nestling terns. • Like many gulls, the Herring Gull has a small red spot on its lower mandible that serves as a target for nestlings. When a chick pecks at the red spot, the parent recognizes the cue and regurgitates a meal.

nonbreeding

nonbreeding

ID: large gull with large bill; pink legs and feet; pale gray upperparts; black wing tips with white spots; white underparts; yellow eyes; yellow bill with red spot near tip of lower mandible. *Breeding:* entirely white head, neck and breast. *Nonbreeding:* brown streaking on most of head and breast. *Juvenile:* mostly brown with mostly black bill; subsequent plumages paler with bill turning yellow. *Immature:* molts into numerous plumages before attaining adult plumage in fourth calendar year.
Size: *L* 23–26 in; *W* 4 ft.
Status: fairly common to locally abundant nonbreeding permanent resident of coastal areas statewide; rare to absent inland.

Habitat: any coastal habitat; inland at landfills.
Nesting: does not breed in Florida.
Feeding: plucks prey from the water's surface or the ground or tips up in water; also scavenges; feeds on crabs, shellfish, fish, other marine invertebrates and carrion; also eats garbage.
Voice: calls include a loud *kyow-kyow-kyow*.
Similar Species: *Ring-billed Gull* (p. 167): nonbreeding bird is smaller, with black ring near tip of bill and no red spot on lower mandible and has yellow legs and feet. *Lesser Black-backed Gull* (p. 169): non-breeding bird has dark gray to blackish upperparts, extensive dark streaking on head and yellow legs and feet.
Best Sites: widespread.

LESSER BLACK-BACKED GULL

Larus fuscus

First recorded in Florida in 1971, the Lesser Black-backed Gull is a recent colonizer from the Old World that is now fairly widespread along the Atlantic Coast. Its numbers and range continue to increase in our state. • Lesser Black-backed Gulls breed from Greenland and Siberia to Britain and France, and they winter in much of their breeding range, as well as in eastern North America. • At least two races have been observed in Florida: *L. f. graellsii*, with dark gray upperparts, and *L. f. intermedius*, with black upperparts. The upperparts of *L. f. intermedius* are as dark as those of Great Black-backed Gulls, whereas the upperparts of *L. f. graellsii* are a shade paler.

nonbreeding

nonbreeding

ID: large gull observed increasingly in Florida; dark gray or black upperparts; black wing tips with white spots; white underparts; yellow bill with red spot near tip of lower mandible; yellow legs and feet. *Breeding:* entirely white head and neck. *Nonbreeding:* head and neck streaked with brown. *Juvenile:* mottled brown and white plumage; pale head; mostly black bill; pale pink legs and feet; subsequent plumages have gray on the upperparts, with bill, legs and feet turning yellow. *Immature:* various plumages; attains adult plumage in fourth calendar year.
Size: *L* 21 in; *W* 4½ ft.
Status: rare to locally common resident along the Atlantic Coast from September

to April and much less numerous along the Gulf Coast and inland; has summered.
Habitat: beaches and estuaries; also lakes and landfills inland.
Nesting: does not breed in Florida.
Feeding: plucks prey from the water's surface or the ground or scavenges; feeds on crabs, shellfish, fish, other marine invertebrates and carrion; also eats garbage.
Voice: call similar to that of Herring Gull, but lower pitched.
Similar Species: *Great Black-backed Gull* (p. 170): nonbreeding bird is much larger, with black upperparts, mostly unstreaked head and pale pinkish legs and feet. *Laughing Gull* (p. 165): nonbreeding bird is much smaller, with black bill, legs and feet and dark mottling on head.
Best Sites: fairly widespread along the Atlantic Coast.

169

GREAT BLACK-BACKED GULL

Larus marinus

The Great Black-backed Gull is the largest gull in North America, and its bold, aggressive disposition enables it to dominate other gulls and terns. Although nearly extirpated by egg collectors and plume hunters in the latter 1800s, the population has recovered with protection. Today, perhaps aided by the presence of abundant food found at landfills and fishing ports, the Great Black-backed Gull's range continues to expand beyond its historical limits. It breeds coastally from eastern Canada to the northeastern U.S., and it winters along the coast from Newfoundland to Florida; it is also found in the Old World. • In Florida, Great Black-backed Gulls are increasingly common winter residents along the Atlantic Coast, but they remain rare inland and along the Gulf Coast. • Like many large gulls, the Great Black-backed is a "four-year gull," which means that it attains its adult plumage in its fourth year, after molting through as many as eight subadult plumages.

nonbreeding

ID: huge gull with very large head; pale pink legs and feet; black back and wings; white body; huge yellow bill with red spot on lower mandible. *Breeding:* all-white head. *Nonbreeding:* dusky smudges above and behind eye. *Subadult:* variable plumage from years 1–3; white and black mottled back and wings; black bill with pale base.
Size: *L* 30 in; *W* 5½ ft.
Status: increasingly numerous and locally fairly common resident along the Atlantic Coast from September to April, rare to absent along the Gulf Coast and very rare inland; often summers.
Habitat: beaches, estuaries, around fishing fleets and at landfills.
Nesting: does not breed in Florida.
Feeding: gleans prey from land or the water's surface; feeds on fish, crustaceans and other aquatic animals; also scavenges carrion at beaches and garbage at landfills.
Voice: frequent harsh *kow* call, often repeated.
Similar Species: *Lesser Black-backed Gull* (p. 169): smaller; usually dark gray back and wings; yellow legs; nonbreeding bird has head streaked with brown.
Best Sites: fairly widespread.

GULL-BILLED TERN

Sterna nilotica

Terns are small to medium-sized seabirds, usually with white bodies, black caps and colored bills. All except the Gull-billed Tern plunge-dive for prey. • Gull-billed Terns breed in California and northwestern Mexico and from New York to Texas. They winter from northern Mexico and the Gulf Coast to northern South America; they also occur in the Old World. • In Florida, Gull-billed Terns breed extremely locally from the eastern Panhandle to the southern peninsula, both coastally and inland. They typically winter in the extreme southern peninsula, but recently they have also been observed in the northern Tampa Bay and Merritt Island regions during that season. Gull-billed Terns are found singly or in small flocks, often apart from other terns.

breeding

nonbreeding

ID: medium-sized tern that does not dive for prey; very pale gray upperparts; black eyes, legs and feet; thick, black bill; white underparts; short, moderately forked tail.
Breeding: black cap. *Nonbreeding:* white head with dusky markings.
Size: *L* 14 in; *W* 34 in.
Status: rare to locally uncommon and extremely local breeding resident of the eastern Panhandle and peninsula; rare winter resident in the southern half of the peninsula.
Habitat: beaches, coastal marshes and mudflats and estuaries; flooded agricultural fields.

Nesting: colony nester, often with other gulls and terns; on the ground; pair lines a shallow depression with vegetation or debris; pair incubates 2–3 variably marked, creamy to yellowish buff eggs for 22–23 days.
Feeding: drops down and gleans prey from the ground or the water's surface; also captures prey in flight; feeds on fiddler crabs, green anoles (lizards), mollusks, small fish and insects.
Voice: raspy *katy-did* call.
Similar Species: *Sandwich Tern* (p. 174): nonbreeding bird has slight black crest, yellow tip on long, thin bill and longer tail. *Forster's Tern* (p. 177): nonbreeding bird has black eye patch, thinner bill and longer tail.
Best Sites: fairly widespread but somewhat unpredictable; Everglades NP; Blue Heron Wastewater Treatment Facility (Titusville).

CASPIAN TERN

Sterna caspia

With its size and habits, the Caspian Tern bridges the gulf between the generally smaller terns and the generally larger gulls. It is the largest tern in North America, and its wingbeats are relatively slow and somewhat gull-like. • The Caspian Tern has an amazingly disjunct breeding range in North America; it includes southern Alaska, south-central Canada, the western U.S. and the Gulf Coast; it is also widespread in the Old World. It winters primarily coastally from California and North Carolina to Central America. In Florida, the Caspian Tern is a permanent resident of the peninsula but is rare in the Panhandle. The presence of dredged-material "spoil" islands along the coasts created breeding habitat for the species; it was first observed breeding in Florida in 1962. Although numbers are slowly increasing, barely 100 pairs of Caspian Terns nest in Florida, at a few coastal sites from the eastern Panhandle southward, with most at Tampa Bay. • This species was first described at the Caspian Sea, hence its name.

breeding

ID: large, gull-like tern with large, stocky, red or red-orange bill; very pale upperparts; white underparts; moderately forked tail; black legs and feet. *Breeding:* black cap extends over eyes and forehead. *Nonbreeding:* dusky crown and forehead.

Size: *L* 19–23 in; *W* 4–4½ ft.

Status: rare to uncommon nonbreeding permanent resident statewide, withdrawing from the western Panhandle during fall; very local breeding resident of the eastern Panhandle and peninsula south to Tampa Bay and Merritt Island NWR.

Habitat: beaches, mudflats, estuaries, lakes and flooded agricultural fields.

Nesting: colonial; on human-made coastal islands; on the ground; pair digs shallow scrape in a sand or shell beach and sparsely lines it with vegetation, rocks or other debris; pair incubates 2 darkly spotted, pale buff eggs for 20–22 days.

Feeding: plunge-dives or plucks prey from the water's surface; feeds primarily on fish.

Voice: low, harsh *kaaar* and *kowk* calls.

Similar Species: *Royal Tern* (p. 173): nonbreeding bird is much more numerous and has less bulky body, with white forehead and slimmer, orange or yellow-orange bill.

Best Sites: widespread.

ROYAL TERN

Sterna maxima

Despite the Royal Tern being named *Sterna maxima*, it is slightly smaller than the Caspian Tern. The Royal Tern is primarily restricted to coastlines, and it is largely resident from California and New Jersey south through the West Indies to northern South America; it also occurs in Africa. In Florida, the Royal Tern breeds in scattered colonies from the eastern Panhandle through the central peninsula and winter throughout coastal areas. About 2000 pairs now breed in Florida, mostly in Tampa Bay. In recent decades, Royal Tern has become a regular non-breeding inland visitor of mine impoundments and large lakes in the central peninsula. • Breeding is preceded by elegant courtship displays that include spiraling flights, strutting, bowing and offerings of fish. Colonies are densely packed, and the young hatch synchronously. The chicks form a flock, called a "creche," on the beach and are fed by their parents, which recognize their young by voice.

nonbreeding

ID: large tern with long, thin, orange or yellow-orange bill; pale gray upperparts; minor black crest; white underparts; black legs and feet; moderately forked tail. *Breeding:* black cap includes eyes and forehead. *Nonbreeding:* black band across back of head; white lores, forehead and forecrown. *Juvenile:* dusky markings on upperparts; yellow bill, legs and feet.
Size: *L* 20 in; *W* 3½ ft.
Status: fairly common to locally abundant permanent resident of coastal areas statewide, with winter numbers augmented by northern breeders; nonbreeders are rare to uncommon and very local inland in central peninsula.

Habitat: beaches, mudflats and estuaries; mine impoundments and lakes inland.
Nesting: colonial; on coastal islands; on the ground; pair digs shallow scrape in a sand or shell beach and sparsely lines it with vegetation, rocks or other debris; pair incubates 1–2 (rarely 3) darkly blotched, whitish eggs for 20–25 days.
Feeding: plunge-dives or plucks prey from the water's surface; feeds on fish, squid, shrimp and crabs.
Voice: high-pitched calls include *kee-er* and *turreee*.
Similar Species: *Caspian Tern* (p. 172): much less numerous; thick, red or orange-red bill; dusky crown and forehead in nonbreeding plumage; harsh calls.
Best Sites: widespread.

173

SANDWICH TERN

Sterna sandvicensis

The curiously named Sandwich Tern gets its name from the town in Kent County, England, in which it was discovered in 1787. In the New World, it breeds coastally from Virginia southward around the Gulf Coast to Central America and in the West Indies. It winters from Florida to northern South America. In Florida, the Sandwich Tern is an extremely local breeder, primarily at Tampa Bay. It winters along the coasts, mostly from the central peninsula southward, where it is fairly common. • Sandwich Terns are more common along the Gulf Coast than the Atlantic; nearly all of Florida's breeding colonies have been along the Gulf, typically among Royal Terns. As with Royal Terns, small to occasionally large numbers of Sandwich Terns are now found inland at mine impoundments in the central peninsula.

nonbreeding

ID: medium-sized tern; pale gray upperparts; short, black crest; long, thin, black bill with light yellow tip; white underparts; black legs and feet; moderately forked tail. *Breeding:* black cap includes forehead and eyes. *Nonbreeding:* black band across back of head; white forehead and forecrown. *Juvenile:* dusky markings on upperparts; shorter crest; black bill.
Size: *L* 14–16 in; *W* 34 in.
Status: rare to locally common permanent resident of coastal areas statewide; withdraws from the western Panhandle during fall; nonbreeders are local inland at mine impoundments in the central peninsula.

Habitat: beaches, mudflats and estuaries; mine impoundments inland.
Nesting: colonial; on coastal islands; on the ground; pair digs a shallow scrape in a sand or shell beach and may line it with debris; pair incubates 1–2 (rarely 3) variably marked yellowish-white eggs for 21–25 days.
Feeding: plunge-dives or plucks prey from the water's surface; eats small fish, squid and shrimp.
Voice: calls include a high-pitched *kee-rick*.
Similar Species: yellow-tipped, black bill is unique. *Gull-billed Tern* (p. 171): lacks crest; thicker, black bill; head mostly white in nonbreeding plumage. *Forster's Tern* (p. 177): nonbreeding bird has black bill and uncrested, white head with black eye patch.
Best Sites: widespread.

ROSEATE TERN

Sterna dougallii

Although the Roseate Tern is cosmopolitan in distribution, its populations in the Northern Hemisphere have shown severe declines in recent years. It breeds coastally from Quebec to North Carolina, as well as in southern Florida, the West Indies, Bermuda and Belize, and it winters from the West Indies to northern South America. This tern also occurs in Eurasia, Indochina, Africa and Australasia. • In Florida, Roseate Terns breed in the Keys, from Marathon to Key West, and 300–350 pairs have been recorded in the Lower Keys. Although found rather commonly at the Dry Tortugas, for unknown reasons they have not bred there since 1960, though the habitat remains seemingly suitable. Because the Keys are extensively developed and their beaches heavily used by humans for recreation, most of our Roseate Terns nest on rooftops. • The Roseate Tern is named for the pink blush that develops on its underparts during breeding plumage.

breeding

ID: medium-sized tern; pale gray upperparts; no crest; thin, black bill; white underparts; long, white, deeply forked tail; red legs and feet. *Breeding:* black cap and nape; faint pink wash on underparts. *Nonbreeding:* black hindcrown and nape; white lores, forehead and forecrown. *Juvenile:* "scaly" upperparts; dusky crown; black legs and feet.
Size: *L* 12–13 in; *W* 28 in.
Status: federally threatened (USFWS); species of special concern (FWC); uncommon to fairly common breeding resident of the Lower Keys from April to September; rare to very rare elsewhere along our coasts.
Habitat: sandy islands, coral keys and open ocean.
Nesting: colonially with other terns; on the ground; digs a shallow scrape in sand; may line it with shell or other debris; also uses rooftops; pair incubates 1–3 brown-blotched, creamy white eggs for 21–26 days.
Feeding: plunge-dives for small fish.
Voice: calls include a sharp *ack* and soft *chivy.*
Similar Species: *Least Tern* (p. 178): also breeds in the Keys, but smaller, with white forehead, mostly yellow bill and yellow legs and feet. *Common Tern* (p. 176): nonbreeding bird has distinctive black shoulder bar.
Best Sites: Dry Tortugas NP; Key West; Marathon Government Center (Islamorada Key).

COMMON TERN

Sterna hirundo

Although common during fall migration, the Common Tern is not our most numerous or widespread small tern—that title belongs to the Forster's Tern. The Common Tern breeds over much of southern Canada, around the Great Lakes, coastally along the northeastern U.S. to South Carolina and in Texas. It winters from Baja California and Florida through the West Indies to Peru and Argentina. This tern is also widespread in the Old World. • In Florida, Common Terns are fairly common migrants and may be locally abundant during fall; they are rare winter residents in the south. There were even a few breeding observations from the Panhandle in the 1960s and 1970s. • During winter, Common Terns are often reported in Florida, but most of these sightings are likely misidentified Forster's Terns—look for the Common Tern's bold blackish shoulder bars.

nonbreeding

nonbreeding

ID: medium-sized tern with long white tail with dark outer feathers; pale gray upperparts. *Breeding:* rare in Florida; black cap; orangy red bill; pale gray underparts; red legs and feet. *Nonbreeding:* black crown and nape reach to eyes; white forehead; thin, black bill; black shoulder bar; white underparts; black legs and feet.

Size: *L* 13–16 in; *W* 30 in.

Status: uncommon to locally abundant migrant of coastal areas statewide from July to April; has summered and bred; rare during winter in the southern half of the peninsula and Keys; rare inland during migration.

Habitat: beaches and estuaries.

Nesting: irregular in Florida; digs a small scrape in sand and may line it with shells or other debris; pair incubates 2–4 (usually 3) variably marked, white to greenish eggs for 20–23 days.

Feeding: plunge-dives for small fish or crustaceans; may pluck insects off the water's surface.

Voice: calls include a *kip*.

Similar Species: *Forster's Tern* (p. 177): nonbreeding bird has white head with black eye patch; gray tail with white outer feathers; lacks black shoulder patch. *Roseate Tern* (p. 175): little seasonal overlap; nonbreeding bird has white tail and no black shoulder bar.

Best Sites: widespread.

FORSTER'S TERN

Sterna forsteri

The Forster's Tern has a disjunct breeding range that includes scattered interior locations in southern Canada and the western U.S., as well as coastal areas from Massachusetts to South Carolina and along the Gulf Coast from Alabama to Mexico. It winters from California and Virginia south through the West Indies to Central America. Unlike most terns, the Forster's is restricted to the New World. • In Florida, the Forster's Tern is a common migrant and winter resident along the coasts and inland, except in the Keys, where it is surprisingly rare. It is found over most water bodies in our state, even small lakes far inland. This bird is probably the most common tern in Florida during winter, when individuals are often misidentified as Common Terns, despite the lack of a black nape and bold black shoulder bars. • The Forster's Tern is named after German naturalist Johann Reinhold Forster (1729–98), who was the first naturalist to attempt to catalog all American vertebrates.

nonbreeding

breeding

ID: medium-sized tern of coastal and inland areas; pale gray upperparts; long, gray tail with white outer feathers; white underparts; orange legs and feet. *Breeding:* rarely seen in Florida; black crown and nape extend ahead of eyes; orange bill with black tip. *Nonbreeding:* black bill; white head with black eye patch.
Size: *L* 14–16 in; *W* 31 in.
Status: fairly common to locally abundant migrant and resident throughout the mainland from August to April but has summered; rare in Keys.

Habitat: nearly any open water habitat, coastally and inland.
Nesting: does not breed in Florida.
Feeding: plunge-dives for small fish and aquatic invertebrates; may also pluck prey from water's surface.
Voice: calls include *za-a-ap* and *keer.*
Similar Species: *Common Tern* (p. 176): nonbreeding bird has black hindcrown and nape, black shoulder bar, white tail with dark outer feathers and black legs and feet. *Roseate Tern* (p. 175): little seasonal overlap; nonbreeding bird has black hindcrown and nape.
Best Sites: widespread.

LEAST TERN

Sterna antillarum

True to its name, the Least Tern is the smallest tern in North America. It breeds coastally from California and Maine to Mexico and inland along major rivers in the U.S., as well as in the West Indies. It winters along the coasts of South America. • In Florida, Least Terns breed primarily along the coasts, but they also breed inland locally around Tallahassee, in the central peninsula and around Lake Okeechobee. They are increasingly moving their breeding sites from beaches—where disturbance by humans and their dogs is severe—to rooftops, where breeding success is highly variable. To help ensure the future of Least Terns in Florida, state officials need to put much greater emphasis on protecting beach nest sites and enforcing no-entry restrictions for these colonies. • Least Terns do not winter in Florida—there are no verifiable records from November to March.

breeding

ID: small tern with shallowly forked, white tail; white forehead; pale gray upperparts; white underparts; yellow legs and feet. *Breeding:* black cap and nape; yellow bill with black tip. *Nonbreeding:* black hind-crown; white forecrown; black bill; black shoulder bar. *Juvenile:* like nonbreeding, but with "scaly" upperparts. *In flight:* dashing, rapid wingbeats.
Size: *L* 9 in; *W* 20 in.
Status: threatened species (FWC); uncommon to common breeding resident along the coasts from April to September and very local inland; absent statewide in winter.
Habitat: beaches, dunes, spoil islands and inland near large lakes.

Nesting: colonial; on the ground; pair digs a shallow scrape in sand and often lines it with pebbles, grass or other debris; pair incubates 1–3 (usually 2) variably marked, buff to pale olive eggs for 20–22 days.
Feeding: plunge-dives for small fish and shrimp.
Voice: calls include high-pitched, raspy *kip* and *kid-dick*.
Similar Species: small size and yellow bill are unique. *Common Tern* (p. 176): nonbreeding bird is larger and has longer tail with black outer feathers and black legs and feet. *Forster's Tern* (p. 177): nonbreeding bird is larger, with white head and black eye patch and without black shoulder bar. *Roseate Tern* (p. 175): little seasonal overlap; nonbreeding bird is larger, with red legs and feet.
Best Sites: widespread.

BRIDLED TERN

Sterna anaethetus

The Bridled Tern is a pelagic species that normally approaches land only to nest. It breeds on islands in tropical oceans around the world and spends the rest of its life over the open oceans. In Florida, the Bridled Tern was formerly found only offshore, mainly in the Atlantic Ocean, except when driven to shore by tropical storms. In 1987, a nest on Pelican Shoal, a tiny coral outcropping southeast of Key West, added a new breeding bird to the North American avifauna. The Bridled Tern continues to breed annually in small numbers at Pelican Shoal, which is now a posted Critical Wildlife Area, where human visitation is forbidden during the nesting season. • The only chance that most birders have to see Bridled Terns is to take a pelagic trip offshore from spring through fall. Even a boat trip to the Dry Tortugas should result in the sighting of one or more individuals.

ID: medium-sized, pelagic tern; dark gray upperparts; narrow, white partial collar on hindneck; black crown and nape; white forehead extends back to eyes; black bill; white underparts; gray tail with white outer feathers; black legs and feet. *Juvenile:* crown mottled with white; mostly white nape; "scaly" back and upperwings.
Size: *L* 15 in; *W* 30 in.

Status: uncommon to common visitor offshore from April to September; very rare breeder off Key West.
Habitat: open ocean. *Breeding:* coral keys.
Nesting: colonial; on the ground; pair digs shallow scrape or uses cranny in coral; pair incubates 1 variably marked, pinkish or creamy white egg for 28–30 days.
Feeding: plunge-dives or plucks prey from the ocean's surface; feeds on fish and squid.
Voice: usually silent in Florida.
Similar Species: *Sooty Tern* (p. 180): black upperparts; lacks white collar.
Best Sites: offshore.

SOOTY TERN

Sterna fuscata

Perhaps the most aerial of seabirds, Sooty Terns can remain at sea for several years, landing only occasionally on the back of a sea turtle or flotsam. Young terns fledge at eight or nine weeks and migrate to rich feeding areas off the western African coast, whereas adults winter in the Gulf of Mexico or the Florida Straits. At four to eight years of age, shortly before they first breed, Sooty Terns return to the nesting grounds. Colonies are extremely large; Christmas Island in the central Pacific Ocean supported 14 million terns into the 1980s. The Florida population, breeding exclusively on Bush Key at Dry Tortugas National Park, numbers about 20,000 pairs. • Researchers in Florida tested the Sooty Tern's homing ability by marking adults from the Dry Tortugas colony with dye, then releasing them in North Carolina and Texas. Within a week, all of the birds had returned to the Tortugas.

ID: medium sized, pelagic tern; white forehead; black crown and back; white underparts; deeply forked, black tail with narrow white outer edges. *Juvenile:* dark brown overall, with white stippling on back and upperwings.
Size: *L:* 16 in; *W:* 30 in.
Status: locally abundant breeding resident at Dry Tortugas NP from March to September; otherwise seen only offshore or when tropical storms drive birds to shore or even inland.
Habitat: open ocean. *Breeding:* only at Dry Tortugas NP.

Nesting: colonial; on offshore islands; on the ground; on bare sand, sometimes with a few pebbles added; pair incubates 1 white egg for 27-30 days.
Feeding: snatches fish or small invertebrates from the water's surface; follows schools of predatory fish that flush prey to the surface; does not dive but often plunges shallowly into the sea.
Voice: nasal chattering, uttered constantly day and night, resembles *wide-a-wake*.
Similar Species: *Bridled Tern* (p. 179): often distinctly gray upperparts; white partial collar on hindneck.
Best Sites: Dry Tortugas NP (March–September); often seen on pelagic trips off Keys.

BLACK TERN

Chlidonias niger

The Black Tern is unusual among the terns, being nearly solidly black in breeding plumage, but it acquires a more typical whitish plumage after breeding. • This tern breeds across the southern half of Canada and the northern half of the continental U.S., and it winters from Mexico to northern South America. The Black Tern is also found in the Old World. In Florida, it is a statewide migrant, more common during fall than spring, and can be found coastally as well as inland over lakes or flooded agricultural fields. • In past decades, Black Terns were occasionally found in flocks of thousands of individuals during August or September, but an overall population decline has led to fewer numbers presently appearing in Florida. • In order to spell this tern's generic name correctly, one must misspell *chelidonias*, the Greek word for "swallow."

nonbreeding

nonbreeding

ID: medium-sized tern often seen over freshwater wetlands; gray wings, rump and tail; white lower belly and undertail coverts; mix of breeding and nonbreeding plumages when molting. *Breeding:* black back and head; black breast and upper belly. *Nonbreeding* and *juvenile:* gray back ("scaly" in juvenile); white head with dusky nape and crown that extends downward behind eye; all-white underparts except for dusky "spur" on each side of breast.
Size: *L* 9–10 in; *W* 24 in.
Status: fairly common to locally abundant statewide migrant from August to November and rare to uncommon from April to May; found inland and coastally.
Habitat: any habitat with open fresh, brackish or salt water.
Nesting: does not breed in Florida.
Feeding: mostly while in flight; snatches flying insects from the air; also plunge-dives for small fish.
Voice: shrill, metallic *kik* call.
Similar Species: *Brown Noddy* (p. 182): larger; white undertail coverts. *Bonaparte's Gull* (p. 166): little or no seasonal overlap; nonbreeding bird resembles nonbreeding Black Tern, but larger, with paler upperparts and less black on head.
Best Sites: fairly widespread.

BROWN NODDY

Anous stolidus

With its white cap and dark body, the Brown Noddy resembles a photo negative of a typical tern. • Brown Noddies are tropical terns that are limited to a single island in North America when nesting; they and the far more numerous Sooty Terns breed abundantly on Bush Key in the Dry Tortugas. Although both birds display similar feeding habits, Brown Noddies usually feed closer to shore, often staying within sight of their breeding island. When not on land rearing their young, Brown Noddies winter in the West Indies and other tropical areas. • The origin of the name "noddy" is uncertain. The word "noddy" means "a stupid person" and may refer to this birds unwary behavior which allowed mariners to easily capture it off its nest. Or the name may be a reference to the bird's courtship movements of bowing and bobbing its head. • During the nesting season, these birds often remain active well into the night.

ID: medium-sized tern; brown body; gray nape fades to white forehead; black bill; bottom half of eye outlined in white; long, rounded tail.
Juvenile: smaller, pale forehead patch; paler wing coverts. *In flight:* strong, smooth wingbeats.
Size: *L* 15–16 in; *W* 30–36 in.
Status: abundant breeding spring and summer resident on Bush Key in Dry Tortugas NP; rare elsewhere offshore; may be driven inland after hurricanes and other tropical storms.
Habitat: oceanic; comes ashore only to nest or when blown inland by storms.
Nesting: colonial; low to the ground in a bay cedar or mangrove; pair constructs a platform nest of sticks, coral or seaweed and may reuse it every year; pair incubates 1 sparsely marked, white egg for 32–38 days.
Feeding: plucks fish and small squid from ocean's surface; may plunge-dive.
Voice: crowlike *caw;* quieter calls while nesting.
Similar Species: *Black Noddy* (p. 183): very rare; smaller body; darker plumage; thinner, proportionately longer bill.
Best Sites: regularly found off the Keys or lower Atlantic Coast. *Breeding:* Dry Tortugas NP.

BLACK NODDY

Anous minutus

Unlike its abundant cousin, the Black Noddy is a very rare bird in the U.S. In most years, a few individuals, mostly immatures, are found among the Brown Noddies at the Dry Tortugas. • The Black Noddies sit with the Brown Noddies on the old, rotting coaling docks east of Fort Jefferson, where side-by-side comparison allows the smaller size, darker plumage, more restricted white cap and longer, thinner bill of the Black Noddies to stand out. • Black Noddies occur in the Gulf of Mexico, the Caribbean Sea, off both coasts of Central and northern South America, around Hawaii and in the Indian Ocean. Their nearest breeding colony is off the Venezuelan coast. • The world population of Black Noddies is estimated at over 1 million breeding pairs and perhaps 4 million birds overall. At the Dry Tortugas, usually one to three—and rarely up to seven—birds can be found in most years.

ID: sooty black tern; sharply defined white forehead and cap; white crescent around the bottom half of eye; proportionately long, thin, black bill; dark legs and feet. *In flight*: wedge-shaped tail.
Size: *L* 13½ in; *W* 30 in.
Status: rare but usually annual nonbreeding spring and summer visitor to the Dry Tortugas; otherwise unknown in Florida except for one at Clearwater in June 2003.

Habitat: subtropical and tropical oceanic islands, ranging from sandy barrier islands to rocky islands; feeds over open ocean.
Nesting: does not breed in Florida.
Feeding: plucks prey off the ocean's surface or obtains it by shallow plunge-diving; eats primarily small fish, squid and crustaceans.
Voice: various rattling *kuk-kuk-kuk-kuk* or *krik-rik* calls; probably silent in Florida.
Similar Species: *Brown Noddy* (p. 182); slightly larger; somewhat browner overall; shorter, proportionately thicker bill; more extensive white cap contrasts less with body.
Best Site: Dry Tortugas NP.

183

BLACK SKIMMER

Rynchops niger

Skimmers belong to their own subfamily, the Rynchopinae, owing to their unique bill structure, in which the lower mandible is longer than the upper. Both mandibles are so laterally compressed that the bill almost disappears when a skimmer is seen straight on. • In Florida, the Black Skimmer population permanently resident along the mainland coasts is estimated at 1400 pairs, but this bird is absent from the Keys during the breeding season. It breeds in scattered colonies on beaches or "spoil" islands offshore, and some skimmers now nest on rooftops as a consequence of human and dog disturbance of ground colonies • The skimmer is a wonderful bird to observe as it flies on its long, swept-back wings. It forages in flight by plowing its lower mandible just under the water's surface. When a fish makes contact with the lower mandible, the upper mandible quickly closes down on it. • Black Skimmers often roost by lying almost flattened, with their entire body—from head to tail—in contact with the sand; at such times, they may appear to be dead.

breeding

ID: large, slender seabird; long, reddish bill with black tip; black upperparts; white underparts. *Breeding:* entirely black from crown onto back. *Nonbreeding:* white collar; dull black upperparts. *Juvenile:* mottled brown upperparts.
Size: *L* 18 in; *W* 3½ ft.
Status: species of special concern (FWC); locally common permanent resident of both coasts.
Habitat: coastal marine habitats, including estuaries, lagoons, sheltered bays and inlets; roosts on mudflats and beaches;

rare but has bred inland at lakes and on flooded farmland.
Nesting: colonial; on a beach, shell bank or, increasingly, on a gravel rooftop; nest is a shallow scrape; pair incubates 3–5 darkly blotched, creamy white to buff eggs for 23–25 days; pair feeds the young by regurgitation.
Feeding: catches small fish by skimming the water's surface with lower mandible submerged while in flight; may eat some crustaceans.
Voice: yapping or barking notes.
Similar Species: none; bill structure and foraging behavior are unique.
Best Sites: widespread along the coasts; large, nonbreeding flock often roosts along the northern shore of Lake Okeechobee.

ROCK PIGEON

Columba livia

The Rock Pigeon is the common city pigeon known to all; it is also the species of racing enthusiasts. Native to Eurasia and Africa, the Rock Pigeon has been domesticated for about 6500 years. It was first brought to North America in the early 1600s. When this pigeon first appeared in Florida is not known, but it now occupies all developed areas. The extremely variable plumage of the Rock Pigeon is the result of years of inbreeding and domestication. • As their name suggests, wild Rock Pigeons breed on cliffs. Their feral brethren have adapted to urban and suburban areas by nesting on building roofs and ledges or under bridges or highway overpasses. Rock Pigeons nest year-round in Florida. • All pigeons and doves—there is no real distinction between the two terms, although doves tend to be smaller than pigeons—feed "pigeon milk" to their young. It is not true milk, of course, but a nutritious liquid produced in the bird's crop. No other bird feeds its young in such a manner.

ID: large, stocky bird; highly variable color, but usually with white rump and red eyes; tail often has dark band. *In flight:* holds wings in deep "V" while gliding. **Size:** *L* 12–13 in; *W* 28 in.

Status: uncommon to locally permanent resident of developed areas; rare in natural areas.

Habitat: mainly cities and dairy farms or under road overpasses.

Nesting: on rooftop or ledge, often under roadway overpass; flimsy nest is built of sticks and grass; pair incubates 2 white eggs for 16–19 days; pair feeds the young "pigeon milk"; probably raises multiple broods per year.

Feeding: gleans the ground for waste grain and other seeds; occasionally eats insects.

Voice: soft cooing.

Similar Species: *White-winged Dove* (p. 188): pale grayish brown plumage; white leading edge on wing; mostly arboreal. *Eurasian Collared-Dove* (p. 187): pale brownish gray plumage; black partial collar on nape bordered with white. *White-crowned Pigeon* (p. 186): restricted range; blackish body with white crown; reddish bill with white tip.

Best Sites: widespread.

185

WHITE-CROWNED PIGEON

Patagioenas leucocephala

White-crowned Pigeons are one of the "specialties" that attract out-of-state birders to Florida. In North America, they are limited to the Florida Keys and the extreme southern peninsula; they also breed in the West Indies and on the Yucatan Peninsula, and they winter as far south as Panama. An estimated 5000 pairs of these pigeons inhabit Florida. Many of the pairs that breed here winter in the West Indies. • White-crowned Pigeons nest on raccoon-free mangrove keys in Florida Bay, and the adults regularly fly to the mainline Keys to feed on figs and other fruit growing in tropical hardwood hammocks. These hammocks are essential for the survival of the White-crowned Pigeon, which is protected in Florida. As a result, federal and state conservation agencies have purchased most of the remaining undeveloped hammocks in the Keys. • White-crowned Pigeons are a generally wary species—perhaps because they are extensively hunted in the West Indies. Often, the only indication of their presence is hearing their explosive flight as they take off from their dense hammock roosting and feeding areas.

ID: large, swift-flying bird; mostly slate-colored plumage appears black from distance; white crown; pale eyes; reddish bill with white tip; irides-cent green nape.
Juvenile: duller overall; indistinct pale forehead.
Size: *L* 13½ in; *W* 24 in.
Status: fairly common spring and summer resident of the extreme southern peninsula and the Keys; less common during winter.
Habitat: *Breeding:* mangrove keys.
Foraging: tropical hardwood hammocks.
Nesting: colonial; in a mangrove or other tree or shrub; cup nest of sticks is lined

with grass; pair incubates 2 white eggs for about 14 days; male incubates during day and female at night; both adults feed young "pigeon milk"; may raise 2 broods per year.
Feeding: plucks fruit, including figs, blolly and poisonwood; sometimes feeds on hammock floor in winter; rarely eats flowers and invertebrates.
Voice: song is a high-pitched series of descending coos.
Similar Species: *Rock Pigeon* (p. 185): only other dark-bodied dove; red eyes; not found in hammocks; mostly terrestrial and granivorous.
Best Sites: Everglades NP; mainline Keys.

EURASIAN COLLARED-DOVE

Streptopelia decaocto

The colonization of North America by the Eurasian Collared-Dove has been astonishing. From perhaps 50 doves released in the Bahamas in 1974, this bird probably reached the southeastern Florida peninsula and the Keys in the late 1970s, although it was misidentified as a similar species for years. Once a base was established in southern Florida, small flocks quickly spread throughout the peninsula in a leapfrogging pattern, eventually filling in areas between the formerly distant outposts. Since their formal "discovery" in Florida in 1986, Eurasian Collared-Doves have colonized much of the continent, and they have already reached California! Populations in North America continue to expand, and colonization of Central and South America can be expected. • Native originally from India to southeast Asia, Eurasian Collared-Doves greatly expanded their range to include other parts of Asia, Europe and Africa. • In Florida, Eurasian Collared-Doves may nest in any month. Like most doves, they feed on seeds and other grain and are frequent visitors to bird feeders. • *Streptopelia* is Greek for "twisted dove."

ID: large, chunky dove; pale brownish gray overall; black partial collar on nape outlined in white; square tail with white outer feathers.
Size: *L* 12–13 in; *W* 18–20 in.

Status: uncommon to abundant and increasing permanent resident nearly statewide.
Habitat: usually associated with humans; urban and suburban areas, especially along the coasts, and dairy farms.

Nesting: in a tree; female builds a platform of twigs and sticks; pair incubates 2 white eggs for about 14 days; both adults feed young "pigeon milk"; may raise 3 or more broods each year.
Feeding: eats mostly grains, from the ground or bird feeders.
Voice: a low *coo-coo, COOK*, repeated incessantly throughout the day.
Similar Species: *Mourning Dove* (p. 189): smaller, pointed tail; lacks collar. *White-winged Dove* (p. 188): similar in size and shape, but lacks collar; white leading edge on wing.
Best Sites: widespread.

WHITE-WINGED DOVE

Zenaida asiatica

The White-winged Dove breeds from the Desert Southwest and the West Indies to northern South America. It winters over most of its breeding range. Since the 1960s, the White-winged Dove has bred in Florida's southern peninsula, but there is disagreement about the provenance of the original breeding stock. Some claim that doves from Mexico were intentionally released, whereas others believe that the birds are natural colonizers from the West Indies. • Hundreds of White-winged Doves were transported to the peninsular interior as far north as Gainesville in the 1970s. The citrus region had few birds, and the former Florida Game and Fresh Water Fish Commission wanted to provide hunters in the area with a new avian target! Since these introductions, the White-winged Dove has dramatically increased its range and numbers in the peninsula. Some roosts now contain more than 1000 individuals, and the dove seems poised to colonize adjacent parts of Georgia.

ID: large, stocky dove; short, rounded tail; pale grayish brown plumage; blue orbital ring; red eyes. *In flight:* wing's white leading edge shows as upperwing patch.

Size: *L* 11–12 in; *W* 19 in.

Status: locally common permanent resident of the peninsula, increasing in range and numbers; fall migrant along the Gulf Coast from western-breeding populations.

Habitat: various semi-open habitats, including urban and suburban areas, citrus groves and farmland.

Nesting: on a horizontal limb or in a fork of a tree or shrub; pair builds a flimsy stick platform; pair alternates incubation of 1–4 (usually 2) white or pale buff eggs for 13–14 days; nestlings are fed "pigeon milk"; may raise 2 broods per year.

Feeding: mostly terrestrial; feeds on seeds, grain, insects and some fruit; visits bird feeders.

Voice: *who cooks for you?* and other cooing calls.

Similar Species: *Mourning Dove* (p. 189): slimmer; long, pointed tail; no white wing patches. *Eurasian Collared-Dove* (p. 187): no white wing patches; black partial collar on nape; incessant *coo-coo, COOK* call.

Best Sites: widespread.

MOURNING DOVE

Zenaida macroura

One of the most abundant and widespread native birds in North America, the Mourning Dove breeds from southern Canada more or less contiguously through Central America and in the West Indies. It winters throughout its breeding range except in the most northerly region. This species has benefited from human-induced changes to the landscape and has increased its numbers and widened its distribution over the past few centuries. • In Florida, Mourning Doves are common to abundant permanent residents, breeding throughout the state except in the Big Cypress–Everglades region. They are probably more numerous during winter, with the influx of northern breeders, but this is not readily noticeable. • It has been crudely estimated that Florida's population of Mourning Doves exceeds 50 million individuals, of which about 2 million supposedly are shot by hunters annually. To sustain such numbers, Mourning Doves must be prolific breeders. Because the average clutch is just two eggs, presumably each pair of doves raises multiple broods each breeding season, which is nearly year-round.

Size: *L* 11–13 in; *W* 18 in.
Status: common to abundant permanent resident of urban and suburban areas statewide; generally uncommon in natural areas.
Habitat: virtually any open or semi-open upland habitat.

ID: well-known, slender dove; long, pointed, white-trimmed tail; gray-brown plumage; small head; dull red legs; dark bill; pale underparts; black spots on upperwing.

Nesting: on the ground or in a tree, flower pot or gutter of a house; male supplies the materials; female builds fragile, shallow platform of grass (on the ground) or twigs (above ground); pair incubates 2 white eggs for 14 days; young are fed "pigeon milk"; multiple broods per year.
Feeding: gleans the ground and vegetation for seeds; visits feeders.
Voice: well-known, mournful, slow, 6-note song.
Similar Species: *Eurasian Collared-Dove* (p. 187): larger; stockier; short, rounded tail; black partial collar on nape. *White-winged Dove* (p. 188): larger; stockier; short, square tail; white stripe on leading edge of wing. *Zenaida Dove:* extremely rare in Florida; very similar, but chunkier; short, rounded tail.
Best Sites: ubiquitous.

189

COMMON GROUND-DOVE

Columbina passerina

The charming little Common Ground-Dove is a breeding resident from the southern U.S. and the West Indies through northern South America. It is a fairly common permanent resident of open sandy habitats throughout Florida, being absent only from the Everglades. • True to its name, the Common Ground-Dove is largely terrestrial, bobbing its head as it walks in search of food. It is usually seen in groups of two to four individuals that comprise pairs or families. When flushed, this dove flies a short distance on fluttering wingbeats and then quickly returns to the ground—often to be flushed repeatedly before fluttering off in a different direction. • The male Common Ground-Dove utters his soft and soothing two-syllable song during the lengthy breeding season. • *Columbina passerina* is Latin for "sparrowlike dove," referring to the small size of the Common Ground-Dove. This bird's size, short, rounded tail and short, rounded wings with bright rufous flashes make it distinctive among the other doves and pigeons.

ID: small, stocky dove; short, rounded wings and tail; brown upperparts; "scaly" head and breast; blackish marking on upperwing; small, red-based bill; pinkish brown underparts; blue and gray head. *Male:* bolder coloration on underparts and head. *In flight:* rufous primaries and underwing linings.
Size: *L* 6–7 in; *W* 10½ in.
Status: fairly common but declining permanent resident of open sandy habitats statewide.

Habitat: scrub, prairies, fields, citrus groves and coastal dunes; does not persist in developed areas.
Nesting: on the ground or in a tree; constructs a simple platform of grass (on the ground) or sticks (in a tree); pair incubates 2 white eggs for about 14 days; multiple broods per year.
Feeding: walks along the ground; feeds on grain and other seeds; may take insects.
Similar Species: all other doves are much larger. *Mourning Dove* (p. 189) juvenile has short tail and "scaly" head and breast, but wings not short and rounded and lack bright rufous flashes.
Best Sites: widespread.

BUDGERIGAR

Melopsittacus undulatus

The Budgerigar is one of the world's most-loved pet birds, and it may be seen nearly anywhere on rare occasions as the result of escaped captives. Originally from Australia, the only naturalized breeding population in the world resides in west-central Florida. First observed in the St. Petersburg area in the early 1960s, the Budgerigar population exploded to perhaps 20,000 individuals by the late 1970s. However, by the early 1980s, the population began a decline that continues to this day; there are now fewer than 50 Budgerigars remaining. Nesting competition with two other exotic birds, the European Starling and the House Sparrow, is believed to be the primary cause of the decline. • The wild population is mostly light green, whereas captive birds can also be blue, yellow or white. • The name "Budgerigar" is derived from the Aboriginal word *betcherrygah,* which means "good food"; the Australian Aborigines ate the birds! • Budgerigars are extremely gregarious, nesting, feeding and roosting together in flocks that, in the 1970s, often contained thousands of birds.

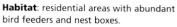

ID: small parakeet; yellow head; light green underparts; yellow back with black barring; long, blue tail; purple spotting on throat. *Juvenile:* barred forehead; less apparent spotting on throat.
Size: *L* 7 in; *W* 10 in.
Status: formerly locally abundant permanent resident along the central Gulf Coast, with numbers now declining and limited to residential areas at Bayonet Pt. and Hernando Beach.

Habitat: residential areas with abundant bird feeders and nest boxes.
Nesting: colonial; in a nest box, boat davit or other artificial or natural cavity; believed to be monogamous, at least through each breeding season; female incubates 4–8 white eggs for about 18 days while male feeds her; in Florida, typically produce 3–4 broods each year.
Feeding: normally on the ground, but also at feeders; feeds on birdseed, grass seeds and weed seeds.
Voice: mild screeches and clear warbles; chittering *chiirup* in flight.
Similar Species: none; tiny size, barred upperparts and pleasant calls are unique.
Best Sites: Hernando Beach (Hernando Co.); Bayonet Pt. (Pasco Co.).

MONK PARAKEET
Myiopsitta monachus

Native to South America, the Monk Parakeet is now the most abundant and widespread parrot in North America owing to accidental or intentional releases since the late 1960s. Unlike most parrots, the Monk Parakeet is native to temperate regions and can survive in cooler climates. • Monk Parakeets are considered agricultural pests in South America, but much of the blame placed on them is exaggerated. In the 1970s, the U.S. Fish and Wildlife Service started an eradication program, which was fairly successful, but it was discontinued after a few years. Since that time, populations have greatly expanded in much of the Florida peninsula and elsewhere in the U.S. • Whereas most parrots nest singly in cavities, Monk Parakeets nest communally in large, bulky stick nests built in trees, palms or on artificial structures. Each parakeet occupies its own "apartment."

ID: medium-sized parakeet; green crown, nape and upperparts; white face; gray forehead; pinkish-orange bill; neck and breast barred white and gray; yellow-green underparts with yellow belly; blue flight feathers. *Juvenile:* green-tinged forehead.
Size: *L* 11–12 in; *W* 19 in.
Status: locally common permanent resident of most coastal urban areas from Pasco Co. south through Lee Co. on the Gulf Coast and from Martin Co. south through Miami–Dade Co. along the Atlantic Coast; scattered "colonies" exist farther north, inland and in the Keys.
Habitat: suburban and urban areas; visits feeders year-round.
Nesting: colonial; on a light pole, power line tower or several other human-made structures, or in any of several species of trees or palms; group of parakeets builds a large, multi-compartment nest of twigs that may support 20 pairs; pair incubates 6–8 white eggs for 25–30 days; may produce 2 broods per year.
Feeding: eats a wide variety of flowers, fruits, seeds and other plant material; visits feeders for birdseed.
Voice: chattering and loud shrieking.
Similar Species: none; gray forehead and breast and nest-building habits are unique.
Best Sites: Ft. Lauderdale; Miami; St. Petersburg.

BLACK-HOODED PARAKEET
Nandayus nenday

This native of central South America is the second most common and wide-spread parrot in Florida. The Black-hooded Parakeet was first seen outside of captivity in 1969 at St. Petersburg, where its population continues to increase. Currently, perhaps 1000 individuals occur in the state, predominantly along the central Gulf Coast from Bayonet Pt. to Sarasota. Like many other exotics, this bird is confined to developed areas, where it nests and feeds in noisy flocks that can at times contain 100 or more birds. • Palm snags are favored nest sites, primarily Mexican fan palms in the St. Petersburg area and royal palms in Fort Lauderdale and Miami, but other nests have been built in telephone poles. • Black-hooded Parakeets feed on a variety of plant material, such as palm fruits, flowers and Australian-pine cones. Very little is known about the natural history of these birds in Florida.

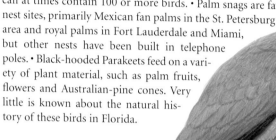

Size: L 12 in; W 23 in.
Status: locally common and increasingly permanent resident of coastal areas in the southern half of the peninsula and the Keys; rare in the northern peninsula.

ID: large, bright green parakeet; blackish face and bill; inconspicuous orbital ring; light blue breast; red thighs. *In flight:* dark blue flight feathers contrast with green coverts.

Habitat: suburban and urban areas planted with exotic palms and other vegetation.
Nesting: in a cavity in a palm snag or telephone pole; little information exists on nesting habits, even in South America; 3–4 white eggs are incubated for 21–23 days.
Feeding: not well known; often eats various flowers, fruits, seeds and acorns on the ground; visits feeders for birdseed.
Voice: grating screeches similar to those of Monk Parakeet.
Similar Species: none; dark hood and bill, light blue breast and red thighs are unique.
Best Sites: St. Petersburg metropolitan area; smaller numbers at Bradenton, Ft. Lauderdale, Miami, St. Augustine and Sarasota.

WHITE-WINGED PARAKEET
Brotogeris versicolurus

YELLOW-CHEVRONED PARAKEET
Brotogeris chiriri

The White-winged Parakeet and the Yellow-chevroned Parakeet were formerly grouped together as a single species, the Canary-winged Parakeet. But research in South America, where the birds occur naturally, indicated that the two forms are separate species. • The White-winged Parakeet was observed in Florida first, perhaps as early as the 1950s. Populations increased rapidly by the early 1970s, apparently as a result of birds escaping captivity. At least 1500 birds were found in Miami in 1972, and other White-winged Parakeets were found at West Palm Beach and Fort Lauderdale. However, White-winged Parakeet numbers have declined since the late 1970s. • Beginning in the early 1980s, a close relative, the Yellow-chevroned Parakeet, was imported in large numbers—about 75,000 birds before 1990. Not surprisingly, escapees were soon observed in Miami and, later, in Fort Lauderdale. • Today, there are perhaps 200 White-winged Parakeets and 400 Yellow-chevroned Parakeets in Florida. The two species appear to be hybridizing in the Fort Lauderdale area. The best field mark for distinguishing them, keeping in mind that apparent hybrids occur, is the face: unfeathered, gray lores for the White-winged Parakeet and green-feathered lores for the Yellow-chevroned Parakeet.

White-winged Parakeet

Yellow-chevroned Parakeet

ID: small parakeet; green overall, with yellow patches in the secondary flight feathers. *White-winged Parakeet:* large white patches in primary flight feathers, visible in flight; unfeathered, gray lores merge with gray orbital ring. *Yellow-chevroned Parakeet:* slightly paler green overall; feathered, green lores contrast with narrow, pale orbital ring.
Size: L 8–9 in; W 15 in.
Status: uncommon permanent residents of Miami and Ft. Lauderdale.

Habitat: parks and suburban neighborhoods with extensive landscaping of fruit- and nut-bearing trees and shrubs.
Nesting: both species burrow into dead fronds surrounding the trunk of a Canary Island date palm; female incubates 4–5 white eggs for about 26 days.
Feeding: fruit, berries, seeds and flower blossoms; visits feeders for birdseed.
Voice: shrill, rapid, repeated metallic note; high-pitched chatter.
Similar Species: none.
Best Sites: Miami; Ft. Lauderdale.

MITRED PARAKEET
Aratinga mitrata

RED-MASKED PARAKEET
Aratinga erythrogenys

The Mitred Parakeet and the Red-masked Parakeet introduce a confusing group of birds, the *Aratinga* parakeets from Central and South America. Both species, along with several others not included here, are characterized by green plumages with red markings. Together with juvenal plumages, which are largely undescribed, these birds create a serious identification challenge! • The Mitred Parakeet is native to Argentina, Bolivia, Chile and southern Peru, whereas the Red-masked Parakeet is found in Ecuador and northern Peru. • In Florida, both species occur primarily in Fort Lauderdale and Miami, but getting accurate population data is difficult. It seems that there are perhaps 300 Mitred Parakeets and 100 Red-masked Parakeets in these regions, and both species are breeding.

Mitred Parakeet

Red-masked Parakeet

ID: medium-sized parakeet; mostly green body; bold white orbital ring. *Red-masked Parakeet:* smaller; bright red face, often extending behind eyes and down to lower mandible; red along leading edge of wing. *Mitred Parakeet:* larger; less red on face, usually more splotchy; darker reddish brown forehead; little or no red on leading edge of wing.
Size: *Red-masked: L* 13½ in; *W* 22 in. *Mitred: L* 15 in; *W* 25 in.
Status: fairly common permanent residents of subtropical metropolitan areas.

Habitat: urban and suburban areas landscaped with native and exotic vegetation.
Nesting: in a cavity; specific information unknown. *Mitred Parakeet:* in a chimney or under the eaves of a building. *Red-masked Parakeet:* in any of various trees or palms.
Feeding: pluck fruit, nuts and flowers from various native and exotic plants.
Voice: typically loud, harsh squawks.
Similar Species: *Scarlet-fronted Parakeet* and *Crimson-fronted Parakeet:* rarer. *White-eyed Parakeet* and *Green Parakeet:* rarer.
Best Sites: Ft. Lauderdale; Miami.

195

ROSE-RINGED PARAKEET
Psittacula krameri

The Rose-ringed Parakeet is somewhat of an anomaly in Florida: like the Budgerigar, it is not native to the New World. The Rose-ringed Parakeet has one of the most broadly distributed ranges of any parrot, occurring widely in central Africa and southeast Asia. The birds found in Florida belong to the *P. k. manillensis* race, which is native to India. • There have been several populations of Rose-ringed Parakeets in Florida since at least the 1960s. Some of these populations have died out, such as the one previously found in Miami. Extant populations do still occur; there are perhaps 30 parakeets remaining at Fort Myers, more than 100 in Naples and a few in St. Augustine. • As is typical of exotic birds, little is known about the natural history of Rose-ringed Parakeets in Florida. They probably breed in cavities in palms or trees, but no Florida nest has been described in the literature. Rose-ringed Parakeets at Naples roost in Cuban royal palms, and the birds feed on royal palm fruits and birdseed.

ID: large, light green parakeet; extremely long tail; orange eyes; red bill. *Male:* black throat and chin; collar is black in front and pink and azure in back.
Size: *L* 16 in; *W* 18½ in.

Status: rare to locally uncommon permanent resident of Fort Myers, Naples and St. Augustine.
Habitat: parks and suburban neighborhoods with exotic fruit-bearing trees and shrubs.
Nesting: in a cavity in a palm or tree; breeding has not been studied in Florida.
Feeding: various fruits, nuts and blossoms; visits bird feeders.
Voice: high, shrill *kew* notes.
Similar Species: none; combination of red bill and neck ring is diagnostic.
Best Sites: Ft. Myers; Naples; St. Augustine.

RED-CROWNED PARROT
Amazona viridigenalis

ORANGE-WINGED PARROT
Amazona amazonica

Members of the genus *Amazona* are chunky parrots with large heads, broad wings and short, rounded tails. No species of this genus is native to North America, but, like many parakeets, several species have established naturalized populations. Amazingly, 14 species of *Amazona* have been reported in Florida, but only two of them, the Red-crowned Parrot and the Orange-winged Parrot, are found in any numbers. • The Red-crowned Parrot is native to northeastern Mexico, where it is endangered as a result of habitat destruction and excessive capture for the pet trade. In Florida, it is found from West Palm Beach to Miami and numbers perhaps 400 individuals. The Orange-winged Parrot is native to the northern half of South America. In Florida, it occurs in the Fort Lauderdale and Miami metropolitan areas and is thought to number about 100 individuals.

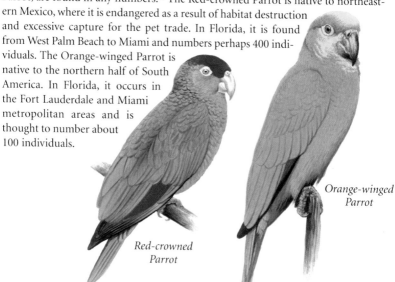

Orange-winged Parrot

Red-crowned Parrot

ID: medium-sized, chunky parrots; green bodies. *Red-crowned Parrot:* bright red forehead and forecrown; azure hindcrown; red wing patch on secondaries; green undertail. *Orange-winged Parrot:* yellow face and forecrown separated by a thick, blue eye line; orange wing patch on secondaries; yellowish green undertail with orange patches.
Size: *L* 12 in; *W* 25 in.
Status: *Red-crowned Parrot:* locally common resident in Palm Beach and Ft. Lauderdale; rare resident in Miami. *Orange-winged Parrot:* uncommon resident in Ft. Lauderdale and Miami.

Habitat: urban and suburban areas landscaped with native and exotic vegetation.
Nesting: in a cavity in a palm or tree; little specific breeding information exists.
Feeding: plucks fruit, nuts and flowers from various native and exotic plants.
Voice: various loud squawks and other calls.
Similar Species: *Lilac-crowned Parrot:* similar to Red-crowned Parrot, but with maroon forehead, lilac crown extending downward to behind eye, dark cere and longer tail. *Blue-fronted, Yellow-crowned* and *Yellow-headed parrots:* similar to Orange-winged Parrot, with blue or yellow face, but none have yellow face divided by thick, blue eyeline.
Best Sites: *Red-crowned Parrot:* Ft. Lauderdale; Palm Beach. *Orange-winged Parrot:* Ft. Lauderdale; Miami.

197

YELLOW-BILLED CUCKOO

Coccyzus americanus

Cuckoos are slender land birds with long, graduated tails. Old World cuckoos are brood parasites, and the voice of one of these species, the Common Cuckoo *(Cuculus canorus)*, was the inspiration for the cuckoo clock. North America's three species—all of which occur in Florida—are not brood parasites, nor do they utter *cuckoo, cuckoo* calls. • The Yellow-billed Cuckoo is by far the most widespread and numerous cuckoo in Florida. It breeds throughout the central and eastern U.S. south into Mexico and the West Indies, and it winters in the northern half of South America. In Florida, the Yellow-billed Cuckoo is a fairly common migrant and breeding resident statewide. When breeding, it is heard much more often than it is seen because it remains hidden in dense treetop vegetation. The male's song is a curious series of clicking or knocking notes followed by slower *kow* notes; it is superficially similar to the song of the Pied-billed Grebe.

ID: largish, slender-bodied land bird; olive brown upperparts; white underparts; downcurved, mostly yellow bill; yellow orbital ring; long tail has large white spots on underside; rufous primaries.

Size: *L* 11–13 in; *W* 18 in.

Status: fairly common migrant and breeder statewide and very rare during winter.

Habitat: hardwood hammocks, riparian forests, swamps and mangrove forests.

Nesting: on a horizontal branch in a deciduous shrub or small tree, within 20 ft of the ground; flimsy platform of twigs is lined with roots and grass; pair incubates 3–4 pale bluish green eggs for 9–11 days.

Feeding: gleans insect larvae, primarily caterpillars, from vegetation; also eats fruits and occasionally small vertebrates.

Voice: song a series of deep, "knocking" notes that ends with a series of slower *kow* notes.

Similar Species: *Mangrove Cuckoo* (p. 199): black mask; pale buffy underparts; restricted to coastal hammocks and mangroves. *Black-billed Cuckoo* (p. 363): rare migrant in Florida; red orbital ring; all-black bill; little or no rufous in primaries; mostly dark tail.

Best Sites: widespread.

MANGROVE CUCKOO

Coccyzus minor

The Mangrove Cuckoo is another "specialty" species that draws birders to Florida. It is largely resident from Florida and the West Indies to northern South America. In Florida, it occurs from Tampa Bay southward along the Gulf Coast through the Keys, but it is not found north of Miami along the Atlantic Coast. The Mangrove Cuckoo seems partially migratory in the state, appearing at Dry Tortugas National Park or Fort De Soto Park in spring, with perhaps some withdrawal out of the state during fall. • Mangrove Cuckoos are found in two primary habitats in Florida: coastal hardwood hammocks and mangrove forests, and they are most numerous in the Keys, which still support large amounts of both habitats. • Perhaps not surprisingly, because of their secretive habits and the mosquito-filled, difficult-to-access areas that they inhabit, little is known about the biology of the Mangrove Cuckoo in our state.

ID: largish, slender-bodied land bird; olive brown upperparts; black mask; down-curved, mostly yellow bill; yellow orbital ring; pale buffy underparts; long tail with large white spots on underside; rufous primaries.
Size: L 12–13 in; W 17 in.
Status: uncommon to fairly common breeding resident; less common during winter.
Habitat: coastal hardwood hammocks and mangrove forests.

Nesting: in a mangrove near or over water; nest of loose twigs sparsely padded with vegetation; pair incubates 2 pale bluish green eggs for 10–14 days.
Feeding: gleans insects and other invertebrates from vegetation; may also take small vertebrates.
Voice: song is similar to that of Yellow-billed Cuckoo, but shorter and quieter.
Similar Species: *Yellow-billed Cuckoo* (p. 198): no black "mask"; white underparts; rufous wing patches. *Black-billed Cuckoo* (p. 363): rare migrant in Florida; red orbital ring; all-black bill; little or no rufous in primaries; mostly dark tail.
Best Sites: Big Pine Key; "Ding" Darling NWR; Key Largo Hammocks; Sugarloaf Key.

199

SMOOTH-BILLED ANI
Crotophaga ani

R eadily distinguished from a grackle by its large, ridged bill and disheveled appearance, the Smooth-billed Ani is a sociable species that is another Florida "specialty." It is resident from Florida and the West Indies to central South America. It colonized Florida, probably from either the Bahamas or Cuba or both, and was first found breeding here in 1938. Afterward, the Smooth-billed Ani colonized much of the southern half of the peninsula and the Keys, becoming common in some areas. • Smooth-billed Ani populations began to decline beginning in the late 1970s. By 2005, only a few scattered groups of anis were known in Florida, and the species appears to be headed toward extirpation. The cause or causes of this decline are unknown. Some people have suggested that the ani's preferred habitat of brushy fields and road edges has largely been lost to increasing urbanization, but such habitat is still common in many areas of southern Florida. • The Smooth-billed Ani forages on the ground, where it hops or runs in search of prey.

ID: largish land bird of brushy habitats; disheveled appearance; long tail; black body with bronzy iridescence; thick, "puffinlike," black bill with ridge on upper mandible.
Size: *L* 13–14½ in; *W* 17 in.
Status: declining and unpredictable permanent resident, primarily restricted to the southeastern peninsula and the Keys.
Habitat: brushy fields or roadsides.
Nesting: rarely communal in Florida, but one male may have more than one mate; bowl-shaped nest of twigs and vegetation lined with leaves; Florida nests average 7 pale blue eggs; female incubates eggs for 12–15 days.
Feeding: primarily terrestrial; pursues insects or lizards on foot; may also eat fruit.

Voice: rising, whining *quee-eeek?* call.
Similar Species: *Groove-billed Ani* (p. 363): parallel grooves on upper mandible. *Boat-tailed Grackle* (p. 347), *American Crow* (p. 246) and *Fish Crow* (p. 247): found in open habitats; all lack black, puffin-shaped bill.
Best Sites: none.

BARN OWL
Tyto alba

The Barn Owl is a cosmopolitan species, occurring on all continents except Antarctica. It ranges from the continental U.S. to northern South America. Although it breeds spottily throughout the Florida mainland, it is solely a winter resident in the Keys. This owl roosts communally in abandoned buildings or groves of trees and may be found in loose flocks during winter. • True to their name, Barn Owls nest and roost in barns. They also nest in church steeples, silos, deer stands and other buildings, as well as in natural cavities such as in trees. They begin incubation as soon as the first egg is laid, resulting in considerable size differences between the first and last hatchlings. • Barn Owls forage at night, often from roadside perches such as telephone poles, which is why they frequently collide with vehicles.

ID: medium-sized owl; appears all white; golden brown upperparts spotted with black and gray; heart-shaped facial disc; dark eyes; white underparts with fine dark spots; long legs; white underwings.

Size: *L* 12½–18 in; *W* 3½ ft.

Status: rare to locally uncommon permanent resident of open habitats throughout the mainland; rare during winter in the Keys.

Habitat: roosts and nests in hollow trees, groves, barns and other buildings; forages over open habitats, especially agricultural fields.

Nesting: in a natural or artificial cavity, often in a sheltered, secluded hollow of a building; may dig a hole in a dirt bank or use a nest box; no actual nest is built; female incubates 5–7 whitish eggs for 29–34 days; young hatch asynchronously; male feeds incubating female.

Feeding: strictly nocturnal; forages more by sound than sight; eats mostly mammals, especially rodents, but also takes birds, such as grackles or even Black Skimmers, and perhaps other vertebrates.

Voice: harsh, raspy screeches and hisses; also makes metallic clicking sounds; often heard flying over cities and residential areas late at night.

Similar Species: *Short-eared Owl* (p. 206): less common; boldly streaked upperparts; yellow eyes; dark "wrist" patches.

Best Sites: widespread.

EASTERN SCREECH-OWL

Megascops asio

The diminutive Eastern Screech-Owl is Florida's smallest owl. It is resident from the extreme southern region of Canada, throughout the eastern U.S. and into Mexico. In Florida, the Eastern Screech-Owl is found in all wooded areas of the mainland and the Upper Keys. It survives in even our largest cities, hunting in backyards and city parks at night and roosting quietly during the day in dense foliage or bird boxes. • Small land birds routinely mob Eastern Screech-Owls, and may be attracted when birders play tapes of the screech-owl's calls. • Unique among the owls found in Florida, Eastern Screech-Owls are polychromatic, showing two color morphs, "red" (really rufous) and gray. An intermediate brown plumage is sometimes considered a third morph, but the "brown morph" represents a continuum between the red and gray morphs. Red-morph owls can better tolerate higher temperatures and so are the more prevalent morph in Florida.

gray morph

red morph

ID: small, nocturnal owl with short "ear" tufts; rufous, brownish or gray upperparts with white spotting; white underparts densely marked with rufous, brown or gray; yellow eyes; pale bill.
Size: *L* 8–9 in; *W* 20–22 in.
Status: fairly common permanent resident of the mainland and the Upper Keys, wherever large trees remain.
Habitat: any wooded habitat with large trees or nest boxes available for nesting.

Nesting: in a natural cavity or artificial nest box; no lining is added; female incubates 4–5 white eggs for about 26 days; male brings food to the female.
Feeding: forages from dusk to dawn; takes mice and other small mammals, insects and small birds up to the size of the American Robin.
Voice: does not actually screech; calls are a horselike "whinny" and a "bounce call" consisting of a long, multi-trilled note.
Similar Species: *Northern Saw-whet Owl:* very rare and restricted to northeastern peninsula; no "ear" tufts; dark bill; bold rufous streaking on white breast.
Burrowing Owl (p. 204): no "ear" tufts; lives in the ground; diurnal.
Best Sites: widespread.

GREAT HORNED OWL

Bubo virginianus

The familiar low *hoo hoo-hoooo-hoo, hoo* that resounds through Florida's pinewoods, farmland and suburban areas is the call of the Great Horned Owl. This owl is one of the most widespread New World birds, ranging from northwestern Alaska through most of Canada, the entire continental U.S. and all of Central and South America! In Florida, the Great Horned Owl is found virtually statewide. • It is a formidable predator, using its acute hearing and powerful vision to hunt an amazingly wide variety of prey, from insects and mammals such as skunks and domestic cats to birds as large as American Coots and Red-tailed Hawks. • Great Horned Owls breed during winter so their young become independent when fledglings of avian prey are common. • An owl's large eyes are fixed in place, requiring the bird to move its entire head to look up, down, or side to side. As compensation, an owl can rotate its head 270 degrees to either side, as well as 90 degrees up and down!

ID: very large, stocky owl with prominent "horns"; heavily mottled brown upperparts; rufous facial disc, outlined in black; yellow eyes; densely barred underparts; feathered feet; powerful talons.

Size: *L* 18–25 in; *W* 3–5 ft.

Status: fairly common permanent resident of open and semi-open woodlands throughout the mainland; absent from the Keys.

Habitat: pine flatwoods, mixed oak-pine forests, agricultural land with scattered tall trees, riparian woodlands and wooded suburban areas.

Nesting: primarily during winter; usually uses an existing large nest, sometimes after evicting its rightful owners, often Bald Eagles; adds little or no material to the nest; chiefly the female incubates 2 whitish eggs for 28–35 days.

Feeding: mostly nocturnal; usually swoops from a perch; eats a wide variety of usually vertebrate prey, chiefly birds and mammals but also fish.

Voice: song usually consists of 5 low, deep hoots. *Juvenile:* begging call is an often-repeated high, wheezy, scratchy note.

Similar Species: none; no other large owl in Florida has prominent "horns."

Best Sites: widespread.

BURROWING OWL

Athene cunicularia

The Burrowing Owl is a delightful bird that, true to its name, nests and roosts underground in burrows. It is primarily a western species, breeding from extreme south-central Canada through the western U.S. to Mexico, but it is also found in Florida, the West Indies and South America. In Florida, the Burrowing Owl has greatly expanded its range as humans have drained wetlands and cleared forests. Originally restricted to the prairie region north and west of Lake Okeechobee, this owl is now found in the northern peninsula and the Keys. There is even a small population in the far western Panhandle. • A recent statewide survey from public roads found 946 active Burrowing Owl burrows, and not a single one was built in native habitats! Despite its expanding range, the Burrowing Owl's population is declining. This species suffers in human-modified habitats where it can fall victim to cats or continuing development. Its chances of surviving among Florida's ever-growing urban and suburban areas in the long-term are probably poor.

Nesting: often loosely colonial; uses talons to dig a burrow that extends 4–8 ft underground; sometimes uses an abandoned gopher tortoise burrow; may add grass, sticks or other debris, such as dried cow dung, to the nest site; female incubates 3–8 white eggs for 28–30 days; male feeds the incubating female.

Feeding: hunts from dusk to dawn; pounces on prey from the ground or swoops down in flight or from a fence post; eats mostly terrestrial insects; also takes crayfish, small vertebrates and even carrion.

Voice: harsh *chuk* or *QUEE! kuk-kuk-kuk-kuk-kuk* call. *Male:* mournful, whistled *coo-coo* courtship call.

Similar Species: none; unique.

Best Sites: Brian Piccolo Park (Cooper City); Cape Coral; Tamiami Executive Airport (Miami).

ID: unique, ground-dwelling owl, often visible during the day; brownish black body with white spotting; no "ear" tufts; large, yellow eyes; dark brown barring on white underparts; long legs.

Size: *L* 8–9 in; *W* 20–24 in.

Status: species of special concern (FWC); the endemic race, *A. c. floridana,* is a rare to somewhat common, very local and declining permanent resident of the peninsula and the Keys.

Habitat: pastures, ballparks, road shoulders and airports; previously and perhaps still in native dry prairies.

BARRED OWL
Strix varia

Memorable *Who cooks for you? Who cooks for you-all* calls of Barred Owls echo through Florida's swamps, bayheads and hammocks. The escalating, monkeylike laughs, hoots and caterwauling are proof that pairs of owls actively defend their territories year-round. • The Barred Owl is resident from southern Canada through the entire eastern U.S. In Florida, it is found in wooded areas throughout the mainland, but it is curiously absent from the Keys despite seemingly suitable habitat; perhaps there is insufficient prey to support the owls. • Barred Owls are the most diurnal of our owls and can usually be lured into view by imitating or playing recordings of their calls. Despite their large size, Barred Owls have relatively weak talons, so they are limited to taking much smaller prey than do Great Horned Owls.

ID: large, compact owl; brown upperparts with white speckling; dark eyes; no "ear" tufts; inconspicuously barred upper breast; brown-streaked white lower breast and belly.

Size: *L* 17–24 in; *W* 3½–4 ft.

Status: fairly common permanent resident of wooded areas throughout the mainland but only casual in the Keys.

Habitat: oak hammocks, cypress and tupelo swamps, bayheads and riparian areas.

Nesting: in a natural cavity or old nest of another species (1 record of a ground nest); adds very little material; female incubates

2–3 white eggs for 28–33 days; male feeds the female during incubation.

Feeding: diurnal and nocturnal; swoops down on prey from a perch; feeds mostly on rodents, but also takes fish, crayfish and birds such as Eastern Screech-Owls and Red-winged Blackbirds.

Voice: often calls by day; popular *Who cooks for you? Who cooks for you all?* plus a variety of other amazing non-owl-like sounds.

Similar Species: *Great Horned Owl* (p. 203): conspicuous "horns"; yellow eyes; barred underparts. *Short-eared Owl* (p. 206): rare winter resident, mostly nocturnal; no habitat overlap; yellow eyes; short "horns"; lacks bold streaking on underparts.

Best Sites: widespread.

SHORT-EARED OWL

Asio flammeus

Short-eared Owls have a cosmopolitan distribution; in North America, they breed throughout Alaska and northern Canada and in much of the U.S., mostly in the western half. They also breed in the West Indies and South America. Unlike most owls, which are birds of the forest, Short-eared Owls are found in open habitats such as fields, prairies and marshes, where they are often seen on the ground. • Two different populations of Short-eared Owls visit Florida, and they differ seasonally and regionally. Until recently, Short-eared Owls visited Florida only during winter, when breeders from farther north migrated south. But, beginning in 1978, Short-eared Owls from the poorly studied and expanding West Indian populations have strayed to the Florida Keys and the southern half of the mainland with increasing frequency. The taxonomic status of these West Indian owls, which differ from northerly populations, needs additional research. West Indian Short-eared Owls may represent one or more separate species.

ID: medium-sized terrestrial owl of open country; brown upperparts heavily marked with dark brown and white; short, inconspicuous "ear" tufts; yellow eyes surrounded by black; streaking on buff belly (heavy in northern owls, faint in West Indian owls). *In flight:* deep wingbeats; long wings; dark "wrist" crescents.
Size: *L* 13–17 in; *W* 3–4 ft.
Status: *Northern owl:* rare, very local and somewhat unpredictable resident of the mainland from October to March. *West*

Indian owl: rare but increasing postbreeding wanderers to the Keys and southern mainland, presumably from Cuba, from April to August.
Habitat: open areas, including pastures, prairies, marshes and agricultural fields.
Nesting: does not yet breed in Florida, but nesting by West Indian owls is anticipated.
Feeding: from dusk to dawn; flies low over fields and marshes; pounces on prey from the air; eats insects such as crickets, small rodents and small birds.
Voice: typically silent in Florida.
Similar Species: *Barred Owl* (p. 205): dark eyes; bold streaking on underparts; no habitat overlap.
Best Sites: *West Indian race:* Dry Tortugas NP; Key West. *Northern race:* Lake Apopka NSRA.

LESSER NIGHTHAWK

Chordeiles acutipennis

Nighthawks are members of the Caprimulgidae, a family of largely nocturnal, insectivorous species. Three nighthawks are found in North America, and all of them occur regularly in Florida. The Lesser Nighthawk breeds from the southwestern U.S. to central South America, and it winters from Florida to South America. • In Florida, the Lesser Nighthawk's status has either become clear only very recently, or it has changed. First documented in 1980, it was initially thought to be a spring migrant and very rare winter resident and fall migrant along the Gulf Coast. But observations since the late 1990s suggest that the Lesser Nighthawk is a regular winter resident in the southeastern mainland, with flocks of up to 75 birds being reported! • Lesser Nighthawks are very similar to Common Nighthawks, but there is only one documented record of the latter species in our state during the winter months. Unlike other nighthawks, the male Lesser Nighthawk does not incorporate courtship dives into its display.

ID: medium-sized aerial bird; long, narrow, pointed wings; tiny bill; mottled brown body; white (male) or buffy (female) forecollar; large, dark eyes; pale spots on outer primary feathers visible at rest. *In flight:* white (male) or buffy (female) patch near tips of outer primary feathers; male has white patches on undertail; butterfly-like flight.
Size: *L* 8–9 in; *W* 22 in.
Status: apparently regular, perhaps very locally common winter resident in the southeastern peninsula; very rare along the Gulf Coast during spring and fall.

Habitat: forages over open habitats such as agricultural fields, expanses of mowed grass and small ponds.
Nesting: does not breed in Florida.
Feeding: forages from dusk to dawn; scoops up flying insects with wide, gaping mouth during flight; usually forages within 10 ft of the ground.
Voice: silent in Florida.
Similar Species: *Common Nighthawk* (p. 208) and *Antillean Nighthawk* (p. 209): not regularly present during winter; no pale spots on outer primaries; forage higher above ground; frequent calls.
Best Sites: Everglades NP; Frog Pond WMA; Loxahatchee NWR.

COMMON NIGHTHAWK

Chordeiles minor

Many Floridians know the Common Nighthawk from the male's dramatic aerial courtship display. He flies perhaps 100–150 feet up in the air, uttering nasal *peent* notes and then dives with wings extended. At the bottom of the dive, wind rushing through the primary feathers produces a loud "booming" sound. • The Common Nighthawk breeds over the southern half of Canada and the entire continental U.S. through Central America, and it winters in the northern half of South America. In Florida, it breeds statewide but may be somewhat local in the Keys, where its range overlaps with that of the Antillean Nighthawk. • Nighthawks are often seen quietly perched during the day. They perch along the branches when in trees but at angles to the wires when on power lines.

ID: medium-sized, aerial bird; long, narrow, pointed wings; tiny bill; mottled dark brown body; heavily barred underparts; white (male) or buffy (female) forecollar. *In flight:* white patch near tips of primaries; bounding, erratic flight; male has white patches on undertail.

Size: *L* 8½–10 in; *W* 24 in.

Status: fairly common and widespread breeding resident statewide, although possibly only local in the Keys; locally common fall migrant, sometimes in flocks of dozens or hundreds of individuals, 1 winter record.

Habitat: over most natural habitats; suburban areas.

Nesting: on the ground; in an open field, prairie or sandy pond margin; may use a gravel rooftop; no nest is built; female incubates 2 heavily marked, creamy white eggs for about 19 days; both adults feed the well-camouflaged young.

Feeding: often by day, especially on cloudy days or after storms; feeds exclusively on insects captured in flight.

Voice: *Male:* frequently repeated, nasal *peent* and a rarely uttered *pit-pit;* nonvocal "booming" sound during courtship dives.

Similar Species: *Antillean Nighthawk* (p. 209): plumage often indistinguishable; different courtship calls; mostly restricted to the Keys. *Lesser Nighthawk* (p. 207): little seasonal overlap, occurring mostly during winter; shows pale spotting in primaries; flies lower to ground.

Best Sites: widespread.

ANTILLEAN NIGHTHAWK
Chordeiles gundlachii

The Antillean Nighthawk is a relative newcomer to Florida, having been discovered here in 1941, at Key West. Since then, it has expanded its range up the Keys as the forests have been cleared and wetlands have been filled in for development. As a breeding species, it was previously restricted to the West Indies; its wintering grounds are unknown but are presumed to be in South America. • The Common Nighthawk also breeds in the Keys, and it cannot be distinguished from the Antillean Nighthawk in the field except by voice. The males of each species call frequently during their residence in Florida. The male Common Nighthawk typically gives a nasal *peent* call, although it sometimes utters a *pit-pit* call. The male Antillean Nighthawk utters a series of two to six rapid notes that are often written as *pitty-pit-pit.*

ID: medium-sized, aerial bird; long, narrow, pointed wings; tiny bill; mottled dark brown body; white (male) or buffy (female) fore-collar; heavily barred underparts. *In flight*: white patch near tips of primaries; bounding, erratic flight; male has white patches on undertail.

Size: *L* 8 in; *W* 20–22 in.

Status: uncommon breeding resident of the Keys from April to September; rare in the extreme southeastern mainland.

Habitat: forages over hammocks and mangroves.

Nesting: on the ground; in a vacant lot or other dry, rocky sites; no nest is built;

female incubates 1–2 lightly speckled, creamy white eggs for about 20 days.

Feeding: mainly at dawn and dusk; feeds exclusively on flying insects.

Voice: *Male:* series of 2–6 short notes rapidly run together: *pitty-pit-pit,* resembling the rarely uttered *pit-pit* call of the Common Nighthawk; nonvocal courtship "boom" of wings is said to be higher pitched and quieter than that of Common Nighthawk.

Similar Species: *Common Nighthawk* (p. 208): distinguishable only by voice. *Lesser Nighthawk* (p. 207): little overlap (not reported from the Keys, except at Dry Tortugas NP); buffy spots on outer primaries; silent in Florida.

Best Sites: Marathon Airport; Stock I.; other Keys.

CHUCK-WILL'S-WIDOW

Caprimulgus carolinensis

The Chuck-will's-widow and the Whip-poor-will are in the same family as the nighthawks, but they differ in several respects: they are strictly nocturnal, they are not seen in flocks, they lack dramatic courtship displays and they sing for hours on end. • The Chuck-will's-widow breeds exclusively in the southeastern U.S. and winters from Florida and the West Indies to northern South America. In Florida, it breeds throughout the mainland and on the Upper Keys, and it winters mostly south of Lake Okeechobee. • At night during spring and summer, Chuck-will's-widows incessantly sing their name in open woodlands, even in suburban areas. • Like other members of its genus, Chuck-will's-widows forage at night for flying insects, which are funneled into their huge mouths by stiff bristles. At times, Chuck-will's-widows have even captured small birds such as White-eyed Vireos!

ID: large, nocturnal land bird; tiny bill; huge mouth; mottled brown and rufous body; large head and eyes. *In flight:* strong and direct, not bounding like nighthawks; long wings, somewhat rounded at tips. *Male:* white in outer tail feathers.

Size: *L* 12 in; *W* 26 in.

Status: fairly common breeding resident of the mainland and the Upper Keys but seldom seen during migration; apparently rare during winter south of Lake Okeechobee and perhaps very rare farther north.

Habitat: open pinewoods, sandhills and oak hammocks; lightly developed suburban areas.

Nesting: on bare ground; no nest is built; female incubates 2 heavily blotched, creamy white eggs for about 21 days and raises the young alone.

Feeding: strictly nocturnal; catches flying insects and very rarely small birds by aerial pursuit or hawking from a perch.

Voice: characteristic of Florida's open woodlands; 4-note *chuck-will's-widow*, with the first note much lower than the rest.

Similar Species: *Whip-poor-will* (p. 211): little seasonal overlap in most of the state; smaller; mottled gray-brown plumage, including tail; much more white on male's tail. *Common Nighthawk* (p. 208): slimmer; smaller; plumage usually darker; white patch on primary feathers; male has white forecollar.

Best Sites: widespread.

WHIP-POOR-WILL

Caprimulgus vociferus

Unlike the Chuck-will's-widow, the Whip-poor-will does not breed in Florida, so few birders get to hear its distinctive song. However, some "Whips" sing in March, just before migrating out of our state, and during this time, one may hear the songs of both species simultaneously. • The Whip-poor-will breeds over most of the eastern U.S. and extreme southeastern Canada, as well as from the Desert Southwest through Central America, and it winters from the Southeast through Central America. In Florida, it is a rare to locally uncommon winter residents statewide. • Caprimulgids are called "nightjars" because of their loud, "jarring" nocturnal songs; they are also known as "goatsuckers," a name that dates from Aristotle's time, when it was widely believed that these birds drank milk from the teats of goats and other livestock!

ID: medium-sized, nocturnal land bird seen on or near the ground; mottled gray-brown body with black markings; rufous tinge to rounded wings; black throat. *Male:* white forecollar and outer tail feathers. *Female:* buffy forecollar and outer tail feathers.
Size: *L* 9–10 in; *W* 16–20 in.
Status: rare to locally uncommon resident statewide from September to March; several recent summer observations, perhaps indicating attempts to breed.
Habitat: open woodlands; less-developed suburban areas.

Nesting: does not breed in Florida, but there have been several recent summer observations.
Feeding: strictly nocturnal; feeds exclusively on flying insects.
Voice: easily imitated single *whip!* call; song is a loud, whistled *whip-poor-WILL*.
Similar Species: *Chuck-will's-widow* (p. 210): larger; mottled brown and rufous plumage; less white on male's tail; completely different vocalizations. *Common Nighthawk* (p. 208): much slimmer; slender, pointed wings; white wing patches; male has white throat; female has buff throat; different behavior.
Best Sites: widespread.

CHIMNEY SWIFT

Chaetura pelagica

Swifts are an interesting family of birds, perhaps the most aerial land birds. They perform virtually every activity—even mating—on the wing. Only when nesting or roosting do they land. • The Chimney Swift is one of four species of swifts that have been observed in Florida, but is the only one that is widely distributed and that breeds in the state. This swift breeds over the entire eastern U.S. and extreme southeastern Canada, and it winters in central South America. Any swift seen in Florida during winter is apt to be a Vaux's Swift (*C. vauxi*). • Florida's Chimney Swifts have been expanding their breeding range for the past 70 years, probably as a result of increased development. In the 1930s, they did not occur south of Orlando, but they now breed south to the Miami area. • Although they originally nested in tree cavities, nearly all Chimney Swifts now nest in chimneys, often communally.

ID: small, long-winged aerial bird; sooty brown overall; squared tail. *In flight:* batlike flight on shallow rapid wingbeats; boomerang-shaped profile.
Size: *L* 4½–5½ in; *W* 12–13 in.

Status: fairly common to locally abundant breeding resident throughout the mainland; migrant statewide from March to October.

Habitat: forages over various habitats; roosts and nests in chimneys; may nest in tree cavities in natural habitats.
Nesting: often colonial; in a tree or on a vertical wall, such as a chimney or smokestack; pair uses saliva to attach a half-saucer nest of short twigs; pair incubates 4–5 white eggs for 19–21 days.
Feeding: feeds nearly exclusively on flying insects captured in flight.
Voice: utters *chip* notes a few at a time or several rapidly strung together.
Similar Species: *Vaux's Swift*: rare; virtually identical plumage, but with slightly paler throat; higher pitched *chip* notes.
Best Sites: widespread.

RUBY-THROATED HUMMINGBIRD

Archilochus colubris

Hummingbirds are the tiniest birds, with many weighing less than a penny. They are also the only birds capable of flying backward, and they have heart rates of over 1000 beats per minute at times! Their wings beat up to 60 times per second. • Ten species have been recorded in Florida, but only the Ruby-throated Hummingbird breeds here. Its breeding range extends across much of southern Canada and across the eastern U.S., and it winters along the Gulf Coast to Central America. In Florida, it breeds widely south to the central peninsula but is rare and local farther south on the mainland, and it winters throughout the peninsula and in the Keys. • Hummingbirds are specifically attracted to the color red. However, if you put out a hummingbird feeder, do not add red food coloring to the sugar water, because it may harm the birds.

ID: tiny bird with long, slender bill; iridescent green back, nape and crown; pale under-parts; mostly green tail. *Male:* red gorget (often looks black out of the light). *Female:* fine streaking on throat.
Size: L 3½–4 in; W 4½ in.
Status: fairly common breeder in the north but rare and local in the south; does not breed in the Keys; rare to uncommon statewide migrant and winter resident throughout the peninsula and the Keys, north at least to Tallahassee.
Habitat: suburban yards with flowers or hummingbird feeders; open mixed woodlands or plantations.

Nesting: on a horizontal limb; tiny, deep cup nest of plant down and fibers is held together with spider silk; lichens and leaves are attached to the outside; female incubates 2 white eggs for 13–16 days; only the female feeds the nestlings.
Feeding: uses long bill and tongue to probe flowers for nectar and feeders for sugar-sweetened water; also captures small insects and spiders.
Voice: high-pitched squeaky notes; non-vocal "hum" from rapidly beating wings.
Similar Species: *Black-chinned Hummingbird* (p. 214): extremely similar; crown usually grayish; slightly downcurved bill; bobs hind end frequently; male has black patch above purple gorget.
Best Sites: widespread.

213

BLACK-CHINNED HUMMINGBIRD

Archilochus alexandri

The Black-chinned Hummingbird is the western counterpart of the Ruby-throated Hummingbird. It breeds in the western third of the continental U.S. and in northern Mexico, and it winters primarily in Mexico. In Florida, recent banding studies have proven that it winters in the Panhandle and south to at least the central peninsula. • The Black-chinned Hummingbird was thought to be virtually indistinguishable from the Ruby-throated Hummingbird. Between the two species, the plumages of females, immatures and males in poor light are nearly identical, but in-hand measurements are diagnostic. Additionally, there is a behavioral trait that aids in identification, but it should not be considered conclusive on its own: when feeding, Ruby-throated Hummingbirds flick their tails occasionally, whereas Black-chinned Hummingbirds bob their hind ends frequently. • Ruby-throated Hummingbirds most commonly winter in the southern peninsula, where Black-chinned Hummingbirds are unknown, probably because they are overlooked.

ID: tiny bird with long, slender, slightly down-curved bill; iridescent green back; pale underparts; grayish green nape and crown. *Male:* black throat; purple gorget. *Female* and *juvenile:* duller crown and nape; plain or finely streaked throat.

Size: *L* 3–3½ in; *W* 4½ in.

Status: rare to locally uncommon but regular winter resident of the Panhandle and northern half of the peninsula and probably overlooked farther south; very rare spring migrant at Dry Tortugas NP.

Habitat: suburban yards with flowers or hummingbird feeders.

Nesting: does not breed in Florida.

Feeding: uses long bill and tongue to probe flowers for nectar and feeders for sugar-sweetened water; also captures small insects and spiders.

Voice: high-pitched squeaky notes.

Similar Species: *Ruby-throated Hummingbird* (p. 213): nearly identical; green crown and nape; slightly straighter bill; flicks tail only occasionally.

Best Sites: yards in the Panhandle with sugarwater feeders.

RUFOUS HUMMINGBIRD
Selasphorus rufus

Winter reports of this western species are increasingly common in Florida, possibly because the number of people providing hummingbird feeders during the winter is increasing. The Rufous Hummingbird is the northernmost representative of a family with mostly tropical affiliations. This hummingbird's breeding range extends from southern Alaska throughout most of the Pacific Northwest, and it overwinters in the southernmost states and Mexico. • The tiny Rufous Hummingbird is a delicate avian jewel, but its beauty hides a relentless "mean streak." Male hummers of most species are aggressively territorial. This behavior underlies the remarkable feistiness so evident wherever hummingbirds gather about a concentrated food source. • To attract pollinators such as hummingbirds, plants produce colorful flowers with sweet, energy-rich nectar. As the hummingbirds visit the flowers to drink the nectar, they spread pollen from one flower to another, ensuring fertilization of the plants' seeds.

ID: tiny bird with rusty or buffy underparts; long, slender bill. *Male:* orange-brown back, tail and flanks; iridescent, orange-red throat; green crown; white breast and belly; rufous tail. *Female:* red-spotted throat; green back; rufous sides and flanks contrast with white underparts; rufous base to most tail feathers. *Juvenile:* like female, but with plain whitish throat.
Size: *L* 3¼–3½ in; *W* 4½ in.
Status: rare but regular winter resident of suburban yards and gardens, primarily in the Panhandle and northern peninsula, but occurring south to the Miami area.

Habitat: suburban yards with hummingbird feeders; parks or gardens with an abundance of flowering plants, such as hibiscus and salvia.
Nesting: does not breed in Florida.
Feeding: uses long bill and tongue to probe flowers for nectar and feeders for sugar-sweetened water; also captures small insects and spiders.
Voice: low *chewp chewp* call.
Similar Species: *Ruby-throated Hummingbird* (p. 213) and *Black-chinned Hummingbird* (p. 214): body and tail lack rufous or orange color. *Allen's, Broad-tailed* and *Calliope hummingbirds:* orange or buffy flanks, but much rarer; Rufous and Allen's hummingbirds cannot be reliably distinguished in the field.
Best Sites: Gainesville; Pensacola; Tallahassee.

BELTED KINGFISHER

Ceryle alcyon

The boisterous Belted Kingfisher is an inhabitant of our lakes, rivers, streams, marshes and estuaries. Never far from water, it is often seen perched on a power line or tree, or heard uttering its distinctive, rattling call. With a precise head-first dive, the kingfisher can catch fish at depths of up to two feet. This bird has also been observed diving into water to elude avian predators. • Most Floridians know the kingfisher as a winter resident, with birds arriving as early as July and remaining into April. But the Belted Kingfisher breeds in the Panhandle and sparsely in the central peninsula along waterways and in rock quarries, where earthen banks provide nest sites. • During the breeding season, a pair of kingfishers typically takes turns excavating the nest burrow. The birds use their bills to chip away at an exposed sand or clay bank and then kick loose material out of the tunnel. The burrow is about the diameter of a grapefruit. • The female kingfisher is more colorful than her mate—she has a rusty band across her breast and along her flanks.

ID: large-headed bird with shaggy crest; bluish upperparts; blue-gray breast band; white collar; long, straight bill; short legs; white underwings; small white patch near eye.
Female: rusty breast band.
Size: *L* 11–14 in; *W* 20 in.
Status: uncommon and local breeder in the north; fairly common winter resident statewide.
Habitat: estuaries, lakes, rivers, marshes and quarries, especially near exposed soil banks, gravel pits or bluffs.

Nesting: in a sand or clay bank; pair excavates a cavity at the end of an earth burrow that is often up to 6 ft long; pair incubates 4–5 white eggs for 22–24 days; both adults feed the young.
Feeding: dives headfirst into water, either from a perch or from hovering flight; eats mostly small fish, aquatic invertebrates and tadpoles.
Voice: fast, repetitive, cackling rattle, like a machine-gun.
Similar Species: *Blue Jay* (p. 244): more intense blue color; smaller bill and head; behaves in a completely different fashion.
Best Sites: widespread.

RED-HEADED WOODPECKER

Melanerpes erythrocephalus

The spectacular Red-headed Woodpecker breeds in the eastern half of the U.S. and is resident over most of this range. In Florida, it is resident widely through the central peninsula but is absent from most of the area south of Lake Okeechobee. • The Red-headed Woodpecker was once common throughout its range, but its numbers have declined dramatically over the past century. Competition for nest sites from European Starlings, loss of habitat to extensive development and collisions with vehicles have all taken their toll. • During the breeding season, the Red-headed Woodpecker feeds primarily on insects, including flying insects that are hawked from the air. During fall, this woodpecker caches acorns and stores them in cracks and crevices in tree bark. It is one of only four woodpecker species that regularly caches food.

juvenile

ID: medium-sized woodpecker; red head; white underparts; bluish black upperparts; large, conspicuous, white wing patches. *Juvenile:* brown head, back, wings and tail; brown streaking on white underparts.
Size: *L* 9–9½ in; *W* 17 in.
Status: uncommon and somewhat local permanent resident throughout the central peninsula; rare and very local farther south; rare migrant in the Keys.
Habitat: open woodlands, especially sandhills; fields with snags or groves of scattered trees.
Nesting: in a dead tree or limb; male excavates a nest cavity; pair incubates 4–5 white eggs for 12–13 days.
Feeding: flycatches for insects; hammers dead and decaying wood for grubs; eats mostly insects, earthworms, spiders, nuts,

berries, seeds and fruit; may also eat some young birds and eggs.
Voice: loud series of *kweer* or *kwrring* notes; occasionally a chattering *kerr-r-ruck;* also drums softly in short bursts.
Similar Species: adult is distinctive. *Red-bellied Woodpecker* (p. 218): red on head is confined to crown and nape; whitish face and underparts; black-and-white-barred back. *Yellow-bellied Sapsucker* (p. 219): smaller; barred upperparts; yellow belly; found only during winter.
Best Sites: widespread.

RED-BELLIED WOODPECKER

Melanerpes carolinus

The familiar Red-bellied Woodpecker is the most common, widespread wood-pecker in Florida, occurring in all upland habitats, even suburban yards. It is resident throughout the eastern U.S. and is a statewide resident in Florida. • The Red-bellied Woodpecker often utters noisy, rolling *churr* calls as it forages; unlike most woodpeckers, it consumes large amounts of plant material, seldom excavating wood for insects. • Occasionally, a Red-bellied Woodpecker in Florida will exhibit xanthochroism—a condition in which red coloration appears yellowish because of a lack of some pigments. These yellow-crowned Red-bellied Woodpeckers often are misidentified as Golden-fronted Woodpeckers, which are resident from Texas to Central America. • The reddish belly patch that gives the Red-bellied Woodpecker its name is often either absent or very faint.

Nesting: in a cavity; female selects one of several sites excavated by the male, or may use a natural cavity, the abandoned cavity of another woodpecker or a bird house; pair incubates 4–5 white eggs for 12–14 days; both adults feed the young.

Feeding: forages in trees, on the ground or occasionally on the wing; eats mostly insects, seeds, nuts and fruit; may also eat small vertebrates such as tree frogs; often visits bird feeders.

ID: medium-sized woodpecker; white rump; black-and-white-barred back and wings; orange-red nape; gray-ish brown face; black tail; pale underparts; pinkish tinge on belly not always present. *Female:* grayish brown crown; orange-red forehead. *Male:* orange-red nape extends to forehead. *Juvenile:* grayish brown crown.

Size: *L* 9–10½ in; *W* 16 in.

Status: common permanent resident statewide.

Habitat: all wooded habitats, including city parks and suburban yards.

Voice: soft, rolling *churr-churr* call.

Similar Species: *Northern Flicker* (p. 223): brown back with dark barring; gray crown; black bib; large dark spots on underparts; yellow underwings; uncommon in residential areas. *Red-headed Woodpecker* (p. 217): red head; blue-black back and wings; white patch on trailing wing edge.

Best Sites: widespread.

YELLOW-BELLIED SAPSUCKER

Sphyrapicus varius

Sapsuckers are woodpeckers that drill resin wells in pines and other trees. Four species are found in North America, but only one occurs in the East. The Yellow-bellied Sapsucker breeds in southern Canada and the eastern U.S., and it winters from Missouri and Massachusetts through the West Indies to Central America. In Florida, it is a rare to uncommon migrant and winter resident statewide. • Lines of parallel, freshly drilled "wells" in pines, maples or other trees are a sure sign that a sapsucker is nearby. The wells fill with sweet, sticky sap that attracts insects; the sapsucker then makes its rounds, eating both the trapped bugs and the pooled sap. Several other animals, from hummingbirds and warblers to squirrels, also feed on the sap or the insects attracted to it. • During its residence in Florida, the Yellow-bellied Sapsucker is quiet and inconspicuous, which may make it seem rarer than it really is.

ID: medium-sized, inconspicuous woodpecker; black-and-white-mottled back and belly; bold white wing stripe; red crown; black-and-white-streaked face; red (male) or white (female) throat; black bib; yellow wash on lower breast and belly. *Juvenile:* brownish overall, with buffy facial stripes.
Size: *L* 7–9 in; *W* 16 in.
Status: rare to uncommon migrant and resident statewide from October to April.
Habitat: deciduous and mixed forests, especially swamps and moist riparian areas; upland forests, city parks and suburban yards.
Nesting: does not breed in Florida.

Feeding: flycatches and hammers dead trees for insects; drills wells in live trees to collect sap and trap insects.
Voice: nasal, catlike *keer*.
Similar Species: yellow belly of adult is distinctive. *Red-bellied Woodpecker* (p. 218): no white wing patch; gray or buffy throat; more extensive red on crown and nape. *Downy Woodpecker* (p. 220) and *Hairy Woodpecker* (p. 221): white back; heavy white spotting on black upperwing; black crown. *Red-cockaded Woodpecker* (p. 222): large white cheek patch; black crown; heavily spotted upperwing lacks wing stripe.
Best Sites: widespread.

WOODPECKERS

DOWNY WOODPECKER

Picoides pubescens

The Downy Woodpecker is the smallest woodpecker in North America. It is resident throughout the continent outside tundra or desert areas. In Florida, it is resident throughout the mainland but is surprisingly absent from the Keys. The Downy Woodpecker is found in all wooded habitats, even suburban backyards and city parks. • Downy and Hairy Woodpeckers are virtually identical in plumage, but several field marks can be used to distinguish the two. Downies have very short, thin bills, so they forage mostly on smaller branches and twigs of trees. Hairies have bills that are a typical size and shape, and they forage mostly on the trunks and largest branches of trees. The white outer tail feathers of Downy Woodpeckers typically have small black bars or spots, whereas those of Hairy Woodpeckers are all white. Vocalizations differ between the two species, as well. Finally, Downies are common and widespread, whereas Hairies are rare and very local.

ID: small, sparrow-sized woodpecker; short, stubby bill; white back; black wings with bold, white spots or bars; black-spotted white outer tail feathers; white head with black crown, eye stripe and "mustache." *Male:* red nape patch.
Size: *L* 6 in; *W* 10 in.

Status: common and widespread resident of the mainland; extremely rare in the Keys.
Habitat: all wooded habitats, even suburban backyards.
Nesting: in a dying or decaying trunk or limb; pair excavates a cavity and lines it with wood chips; pair incubates 4–5 white eggs for 11–13 days.
Feeding: forages mostly on smaller branches, twigs, trunks of saplings and shrubs; chips and probes for insects or spiders; also eats nuts and seeds.
Voice: call is a quiet *pik* or "whinny" series of notes lasting 2 seconds; drums shorter but more frequently than the Hairy Woodpecker.
Similar Species: *Hairy Woodpecker* (p. 221): rare; larger; longer, stouter bill; all-white outer tail feathers; louder, sharper call. *Yellow-bellied Sapsucker* (p. 219): larger; mostly on tree trunks; lacks white back but has large white wing patch; red crown.
Best Sites: widespread.

220

HAIRY WOODPECKER

Picoides villosus

The Hairy Woodpecker is resident across much of North America south through Central America. In Florida, it is fairly widespread on the mainland but is local in occurrence. • In our state, the Hairy Woodpecker seems to be dependent on fire-maintained pinewoods, where it feeds on the larvae of wood-boring beetles that become abundant shortly after a pine is killed. Seeing tree trunks or branches stripped of all bark after a recent fire is a sign that a *Picoides* woodpecker—probably a Hairy in Florida—is in the area. • The Hairy Woodpecker is nearly identical in appearance to its smaller relative, the Downy Woodpecker.

ID: medium-sized woodpecker; white back; black wings with bold white spots or bars; white head with black crown, eye stripe and "mustache"; white outer tail feathers.
Male: red nape patch.
Size: *L* 8–9½ in; *W* 15 in.
Status: rare to uncommon, local permanent resident of the mainland, becoming rare to very rare south of Lake Okeechobee; virtually unknown in the Keys.
Habitat: pine flatwoods or plantations; mixed pine and cypress forests; riparian forests; favors recently burned areas; absent from extensive suburban or urban areas.
Nesting: in a live or dead tree trunk or limb; pair excavates nest site and lines it with wood chips; pair incubates 4–5 white eggs for 12–14 days.
Feeding: forages on tree trunks and larger branches; chips, drills or debarks trees for insects; also eats nuts or fruit; sometimes flycatches.

Voice: loud, sharp *peek* or "whinny" series of notes lasting about 2 seconds, lower pitched but louder than the Downy Woodpecker's call; drums longer but less frequently than the Downy.
Similar Species: *Downy Woodpecker* (p. 220): usually found on smaller branches and twigs; smaller; tiny bill; black spots on white outer tail feathers. *Yellow-bellied Sapsucker* (p. 219): lacks white back but has large, white wing patch; red crown.
Best Sites: state and national forests; sites with large areas of fire-maintained pinewoods.

RED-COCKADED WOODPECKER

Picoides borealis

Unless the Ivory-billed Woodpecker persists in our state, the Red-cockaded Woodpecker is the rarest woodpecker in Florida. It is endemic to the Southeast, and Florida contains more of these birds than any other state. • The Red-cockaded Woodpecker was once common, but wholesale clear-cutting of old-growth pine forests drastically reduced its populations—1226 pairs were recorded on the mainland in 1999. • These woodpeckers build their nests in live pines, excavating cavities that can take two or more years to complete. Because these cavities represent a major effort for each pair of Red-cockaded Woodpeckers, they are used for several years. The birds remove bark around the cavity and drill "resin wells" around it to encourage sap to flow. Eventually much of the trunk of an active cavity is coated with sap, which helps to repel tree-climbing snakes that otherwise could eat the eggs or chicks. • Because cavities are limited, most pairs of Red-cockaded Woodpeckers have one or more helpers, usually sons from earlier broods.

Status: federally endangered (USFWS); species of special concern (FWC); rare to uncommon, extremely local resident of the mainland; unreported in the Keys.

Habitat: stands of open, old-growth pine flatwoods or sandhills with little understory; habitat maintained by frequent fires.

Nesting: in a living pine; cavity is used for several years; both parents incubate 2–5 white eggs for 10–15 days.

Feeding: flakes off bark to expose insects and spiders; sometimes eats seeds and berries.

Voice: syrupy *chew* call.

Similar Species: *Downy Woodpecker* (p. 220) and *Hairy Woodpecker* (p. 221) no white cheek patch; white back; different vocalizations.

Best Sites: Apalachicola NF; Eglin AFB; Osceola NF; Three Lakes WMA.

ID: medium-sized woodpecker with bold white cheek patch; black and white pattern on back and wings; white face with black crown and "mustache"; black-spotted white underparts. *Male:* red "cockade" (a few feathers behind and above the eye) is nearly invisible in the field.

Size: *L* 8½ in; *W* 14 in.

NORTHERN FLICKER
Colaptes auratus

Flickers are woodpeckers that spend much of their time on the ground, feeding on ants. They are named for their calls, which sound like *wicka-wicka-wicka*. The Northern Flicker is resident from southern Alaska to Mexico, with some northern withdrawal during fall. In Florida, it is resident throughout the mainland to the Upper Keys. • The two races of the Northern Flicker, the "Red-shafted Flicker" and the "Yellow-shafted Flicker," were once considered separate species. The "Yellow-shafted" is the eastern race, and it is the only one that has been documented in our state. A few flickers with salmon-colored underwings have been observed in Florida—possibly "Red-shafted" birds from the Desert Southwest—but no verifiable evidence exists. • Unlike some woodpeckers, the Northern Flicker fares poorly in suburban and urban areas, even where large trees or wooded areas remain. One possible explanation is that its ground-feeding behavior may make it especially susceptible to predation by domestic cats.

"Yellow-shafted Flicker"

ID: medium-sized woodpecker often seen on the ground; brown back and wings barred with black; brown face; gray nape and crown; red crescent on nape; black bib; pale buffy underparts with bold black spots. *Male:* black "mustache." *In flight:* white rump; yellow underwings and undertail.
Size: *L* 12½–13 in; *W* 20 in.
Status: uncommon and declining permanent resident of the mainland and the Upper Keys.
Habitat: open woodlands and forest edges; survives poorly in suburban areas.
Nesting: in a dead or dying tree, palmetto trunk, telephone pole or fence post; may also use a nest box; pair excavates cavity and lines it with wood chips; pair incubates 5–8 white eggs for 11–16 days.
Feeding: forages on the ground for ants and other terrestrial insects; probes bark; eats berries and nuts; occasionally fly-catches.
Voice: primary calls are *wicka-wicka-wicka* and a loud series of rapid notes very similar to a Pileated Woodpecker call.
Similar Species: *Red-bellied Woodpecker* (p. 218): black and white back; red crown and nape; lacks "bib"; pale underparts, often with reddish patch.
Best Sites: widespread.

PILEATED WOODPECKER

Dryocopus pileatus

B y far our largest common woodpecker, the Pileated is about the size of a crow. It is resident across southern Canada, along the Pacific Coast to California and throughout the eastern U.S. In Florida, it is a widespread and fairly common permanent resident throughout the mainland and on Key Largo. Despite its size, the Pileated Woodpecker remains surprisingly numerous in Florida, even occurring in suburban areas where large trees or palms remain. • With the potential rediscovery of the Ivory-billed Woodpecker in Arkansas in 2004, and the possibility that a few may persist in Florida, it is important for observers to study the field marks that distinguish these two large, mostly black woodpeckers. An Ivory-billed Woodpecker can only be confused with a Pileated, and misidentifications happen frequently in Florida.

Size: *L* 16–19 in; *W* 29 in.
Status: widespread permanent resident on the mainland and Key Largo.
Habitat: all wooded habitats, even many suburban neighborhoods and city parks.
Nesting: in a dead tree, palm or telephone pole; pair excavates a cavity and lines it with wood chips; pair incubates 3–5 white eggs for 15–18 days.
Feeding: chisels or flakes rotting wood in search of ants and beetle larvae; also eats fruit and seeds.
Voice: similar to the rapid call of the Northern Flicker, but much louder and more strident.
Similar Species: *Ivory-billed Woodpecker* (p. 364): very rare in Florida, if it exists at all; limited to remote areas; extensive white patch on wing; mostly black face with single white stripe; gleaming, whitish bill; shows much more white in wings in flight; female has black crest.
Best Sites: widespread.

ID: large woodpecker with bold red crest; blackish bill; predominantly black upperparts; white head with black eye-stripe and "mustache"; black underparts. *Male:* red patch on "mustache." *Female:* dark forecrest. *In flight:* strong and direct; black upperwing with white patch at base of primaries; mostly white underwing with black trailing edge and primary tips.

PASSERINES

Flycatchers

Shrikes & Vireos

Jays & Crows

Larks & Swallows

Chickadees,
Nuthatches & Wrens

Kinglets, Bluebirds
& Thrushes

Mimics, Starlings
& Waxwings

Wood-warblers
& Tanagers

Sparrows, Grosbeaks
& Buntings

Blackbirds
& Orioles

Finchlike Birds

Passerines are also commonly known as "songbirds" or "perching birds." Although these terms may be easier to comprehend, they are not as strictly accurate, because some passerines neither sing nor perch, and a number of nonpasserines do both. In a general sense, however, these terms represent passerines adequately: they are among the best singers, and they are typically seen perched on a branch or wire.

It is believed that passerines, which all belong to the order Passeriformes, make up the most recent evolutionary group of birds. Theirs is the most numerous of all orders, representing about 41 percent of the bird species in Florida and nearly three-fifths of all living birds worldwide.

Passerines are grouped together based on the sum of many similarities in form, structure and molecular details, including such things as the number of tail and flight feathers and reproductive characteristics. All passerines share the same foot shape, with three toes facing forward and one facing backward, and none have webbed toes. Also, all passerines have a tendon that runs along the back side of the ankle; tightening it gives the bird a firm grip when perching.

Some of our most common and easily identified birds, such as the Carolina Chickadee, American Robin and House Sparrow, are passerines. However, some of our most challenging and frustrating birds to identify—at least until their distinctive songs and calls are learned—are passerines as well.

225

EASTERN WOOD-PEWEE

Contopus virens

The Eastern Wood-Pewee introduces the largest order of birds—the Passeriformes—which are usually known as "passerines," songbirds or perching birds. The first passerine family found in Florida is the flycatchers, itself a large family. There are 26 species of flycatchers in our state, including three species of pewees. • The Eastern Wood-Pewee breeds throughout the eastern U.S. and extreme southeastern Canada, and it winters in South America. In Florida, it breeds in the Panhandle and northern third of the peninsula, and it migrates throughout our state. Observations of this bird are often mistakenly reported during winter, but there is no documented record. • The Eastern Wood-Pewee gets its name from its song, a plaintive *pee-a-wee, pee-ooh* during the breeding season and *pee-wee* during fall migration. • Like other flycatchers, the Eastern Wood-Pewee sallies from exposed perches to snatch flying insects in midair. This foraging technique is known as flycatching or hawking.

ID: sparrow-sized flycatcher; brownish olive upperparts; inconspicuous eye ring; short, yellow-based bill; dingy underparts with partial "vest"; black wings with 2 white (adult) or buffy (juvenile) wing bars.
Size: *L* 6–6½ in; *W* 10 in.
Status: fairly common migrant statewide; uncommon to fairly common breeder of the Panhandle and northern third of the peninsula; reports during winter presumably refer to misidentified Eastern Phoebes.
Habitat: *Breeding:* open pine or pine-oak woodlands. *In migration:* may be found in any wooded habitat.
Nesting: on the fork of a horizontal branch, well away from the trunk; open cup of grass, plant fibers and lichen is bound with spider silk; female incubates 3 whitish eggs with dark blotches concentrated at the larger end for 12–13 days.
Feeding: sallies from a perch for flying insects, returning to the same perch many times; may also glean insects from foliage when hovering.
Voice: ascending *pee-wee* call; clear, slow, plaintive *pee-a-wee, pee-ooh* song.
Similar Species: *Eastern Phoebe* (p. 229); lacks conspicuous wing bars; all-dark bill; often pumps its tail; little seasonal overlap. *Empidonax flycatchers* (pp. 227–28): smaller; more conspicuous wing bars; some have conspicuous eye rings.
Best Sites: widespread.

ACADIAN FLYCATCHER

Empidonax virescens

The Acadian Flycatcher is one of five species of *Empidonax* that are found in Florida. It breeds throughout the eastern U.S., and it winters in south Central America and northern South America. This flycatcher is the *Empidonax* most familiar to Florida birders because it both breeds in the state and vocalizes frequently during fall. Acadian Flycatchers migrate throughout Florida, and they breed south through the northern third of the peninsula. • The empids are among the most challenging birds to identify, and many individuals cannot be specifically identified; readers of this book are advised to use "*Empidonax* species" or "Acadian-type flycatcher" for most individuals seen in Florida. Empids are small flycatchers that often flip up their tails. Vocalizations are key to identifying these species—identification of most nonsinging *Empidonax* is not possible.

ID: small flycatcher; olive upperparts; black wings with 2 white (adult) or buffy (juvenile) wing bars; pale yellow eye ring; yellow lower mandible; whitish throat and underparts; long primary feathers.
Size: *L* 5½–6 in; *W* 9 in.
Status: fairly common to somewhat rare breeding resident of the Panhandle and northern third of the peninsula; fairly common fall migrant; less numerous in spring; occurs from April to October.

Habitat: *Breeding:* deciduous woodlands, riparian woodlands and swamps. *In migration:* any wooded habitat.
Nesting: low in a deciduous tree, usually 6–13 ft above the ground and near water; female builds a sloppy-looking cup nest of Spanish moss, twigs and grasses held together with spider silk; female incubates 3 lightly spotted, creamy white eggs for 13–15 days.
Feeding: feeds nearly exclusively on insects and spiders captured by leaping or gleaned from foliage.
Voice: *peet* call; song is an emphatic *peet-suh.*
Similar Species: *Yellow-bellied, Alder, Willow* and *Least* (p. 228) *flycatchers:* do not routinely sing in Florida.
Best Sites: widespread.

227

LEAST FLYCATCHER

Empidonax minimus

After the Acadian Flycatcher, the Least Flycatcher is the most frequently seen *Empidonax* in Florida. It breeds in much of Canada and the northern third of the continental U.S., and it winters from Florida and Mexico south through Central America. • In Florida, Least Flycatchers are generally rare migrants statewide and are rare to locally uncommon winter residents in the southern third of the peninsula and the Keys. Regular wintering in our state is apparently a fairly recent occurrence. • The Least Flycatcher is the only *Empidonax* that can often be identified based on plumage.

ID: small flycatcher; olive brown upperparts; proportionately large, olive head with bold white eye ring; whitish throat; black wing with 2 white bars; subtle olive brown "vest"; pale underparts with no obvious yellow wash.
Size: *L* 5–5½ in; *W* 7½ in.
Status: rare to uncommon migrant statewide; rare to locally uncommon resident of the southern half of the peninsula from September to April.

Habitat: various brushy or wooded habitats.
Nesting: does not breed in Florida.
Feeding: flycatches for flying insects or gleans insects from foliage.
Voice: clear, sharp *whit* call.
Similar Species: *Eastern Wood-Pewee* (p. 226): larger; lacks eye ring and conspicuous wing bars. *Acadian Flycatcher* (p. 227): greenish plumage with yellowish wash.
Best Sites: Lake Apopka NSRA.

EASTERN PHOEBE

Sayornis phoebe

Phoebes are flycatchers that lack wing bars and that habitually pump their tails downward. All three species in North America are found in Florida, but only the Eastern Phoebe occurs regularly. It breeds over much of Canada and in central Mississippi, Alabama and Georgia, and it winters in the southern U.S. and Mexico. In Florida, the Eastern Phoebe is a fairly common and conspicuous winter resident on the mainland. There are two breeding observations from the northwestern Panhandle, one from 1988 and the other from 1990. • The Eastern Phoebe is named after its song, a clear whistled *fee-bee*, which is seldom heard in Florida. • During winter, it is apparently often misidentified as an *Empidonax* flycatcher or an Eastern Kingbird. Listen for the phoebe's frequently uttered *chip* notes, and note its tail-wagging behavior, lack of wing bars or eye rings and solidly dark tail.

ID: small, tail-wagging flycatcher of open country; gray-brown upperparts; blackish head; white throat; short, black bill; solidly dark gray wings, sometimes with faint wing bars; blackish tail; white underparts often faintly washed with pale yellow.

Size: L 6½–7 in; W 10½ in.

Status: fairly common migrant and winter resident of the mainland from October to April; rare in the Keys; very rare breeder in the extreme northwest.

Habitat: *Breeding:* under bridges near water. *In migration* and *winter:* open country, such as pastures, fields or open woodlands.

Nesting: under a bridge or similar structure; cup-shaped mud nest is lined with plant material or feathers; female incubates 4–5 sparsely spotted, white eggs for about 16 days.

Feeding: sallies for flying insects or gleans insects and spiders from foliage.

Voice: sharp *chip* call.

Similar Species: *Eastern Wood-Pewee* (p. 226): olive-brown above; head and back are same color; yellow-orange lower mandible; does not pump tail. Empidonax *flycatchers* (pp. 227–28): smaller; most have wing bars and eye rings; rare or absent during winter. *Eastern Kingbird* (p. 234): larger; white-tipped tail; black upperparts; absent during winter.

Best Sites: widespread.

VERMILION FLYCATCHER

Pyrocephalus rubinus

The Vermilion Flycatcher is resident from the Desert Southwest through central South America. Most breeders in the U.S. winter farther south. In Florida, this bird is a rare fall migrant and winter resident; there is no noticeable northward movement in spring. • The adult male Vermilion Flycatcher is one of the most brilliantly plumaged birds of Florida. When seen in direct sunlight, his plumage is a vivid red touched with orange, hence this bird's name. *Pyrocephalus*, which means "fire head," also accurately describes the adult male. • In Florida, the Vermilion Flycatcher is found in open areas such as marshes, pastures, fields and golf courses, invariably close to a pond or lake. It often perches on fences or trees, from which it watches for prey.

ID: small, open-country flycatcher. *Male:* brownish black back and wings; shockingly bright red head and underparts; brownish black ear patch and nape; short, black bill. *Female:* grayish brown upperparts and head; white eyebrow; dark mask; white throat; white breast narrowly streaked with brown; dark pinkish lower belly and undertail coverts. *Juvenile:* variably patchy red head and upperparts; yellowish lower belly and undertail coverts.
Size: *L* 6 in; *W* 10 in.

Status: rare winter resident and migrant of the mainland from September to April; not yet reported in the Keys.
Habitat: open habitats with scattered trees and near open water.
Nesting: does not breed in Florida.
Feeding: sallies for insects on or near the ground.
Voice: generally silent in Florida.
Similar Species: none. *Say's Phoebe:* very rare; superficially similar to adult female Vermilion Flycatcher, but larger, with gray throat and unstreaked gray breast.
Best Sites: St. Marks NWR usually supports 1 or more birds each year.

GREAT CRESTED FLYCATCHER
Myiarchus crinitus

One of the most conspicuous sounds of Florida's woodlands is the loud emphatic *wheep!* of a Great Crested Flycatcher. This species breeds across the eastern U.S. and extreme southern Canada, and it winters from Florida to northern South America. In Florida, the Great Crested Flycatcher breeds throughout the wooded areas of the state, and it winters in the southern half of the peninsula and in the Keys. • The Great Crested Flycatcher has unusual nesting habits. Instead of building a traditional cup nest, as do other flycatchers, it lays its eggs in a natural or artificial cavity such as a nest box, mailbox or other structure. Most nests incorporate shed snake skins into the lining. • The Great Crested Flycatcher sallies from perches to capture prey.

Habitat: virtually any wooded habitat.
Nesting: in a cavity, nest box or other structure; cavity is lined with grass, bark strips, feathers and shed snake skin; female incubates 4–5 variably marked, creamy white to pale buff eggs for 13–15 days.
Feeding: usually forages high in foliage; sallies for flying insects; also eats some fruit.
Voice: loud, burry, whistled *wheep!* and rolling notes.
Similar Species: *Western Kingbird* (p. 233): typically perches on wires in the open; light gray head with black mask; black tail with white outer feathers. *Brown-crested Flycatcher:* rare; paler underparts; black lower mandible; clear *whit* call. *Ash-throated Flycatcher* (p. 364): rare; paler underparts with whitish throat; dark tail tip; rough *prrrt* call.
Best Sites: widespread.

ID: large flycatcher that rarely perches in the open on power lines; olive back; slightly crested head; gray face and throat; large bill with yellow base on lower mandible; dark wings with rufous primaries; bright yellow belly and undertail coverts; rufous tail.
Size: *L* 8–9 in; *W* 13 in.
Status: fairly common and widespread breeding resident statewide from March to September; rare to fairly common during winter in the southern half of the peninsula and in the Keys.

231

LA SAGRA'S FLYCATCHER

Myiarchus sagrae

The La Sagra's Flycatcher is resident in the Bahamas, Cuba and Grand Cayman. First recorded in Florida in 1982, it now is found annually along the southern Atlantic Coast and in the Keys. Most sightings are in winter, when the birds are silent and difficult to identify. At least one of the individuals observed in Florida was of the Bahaman race *M. s. lucaysiensis*, but some of the birds that visit the Keys may originate from Cuba. • Of the four species of *Myiarchus* that may be seen in southeastern Florida, the La Sagra's is perhaps the easiest to identify. Its underparts are very pale, with almost no yellow wash and it perches with its body leaning forward, unlike the more vertical posture of the other species. Its call notes are also distinctive.

ID: medium-sized flycatcher found in tropical foliage; olive brown back and head; pale face and throat; fairly stout, all-black bill; dark wings with pale rufous primaries; dingy breast; pale belly; faintly rufous tail.
Size: *L* 7½ in; *W* 10½ in.
Status: rare but annual visitor to the southeastern mainland and the Keys from October to May.
Habitat: tropical hardwood hammocks.

Nesting: does not breed in Florida.
Feeding: generally forages in the understory; plucks insects from foliage while hovering; also eats fruit.
Voice: high *wink* call, often doubled.
Similar Species: *Great Crested Flycatcher* (p. 231): bright yellow underparts; rufous in primaries and tail; lower mandible with yellow base; loud, burry *wheep!* call. *Ash-throated Flycatcher* (p. 364) and *Brown-crested Flycatcher*: underparts have faint but noticeable yellow wash; different call notes; Ash-throated Flycatcher unknown in the Keys.
Best Sites: unpredictable.

WESTERN KINGBIRD

Tyrannus verticalis

Kingbirds are a group of flycatchers that perch on wires in the open and fearlessly chase larger birds out of their breeding territories. Western Kingbirds breed across the western continental U.S. and southwestern Canada. They winter in Florida and from Mexico through Central America. In Florida, Western Kingbirds are rare to uncommon migrants and winter residents statewide. They are more numerous southward, where flocks of 20 or more individuals may be seen at favored areas. • Western Kingbirds and other yellow-bellied kingbirds are often mistaken for *Myiarchus* flycatchers because their plumages are superficially similar. However, behavior and habitat differ considerably between the two groups: kingbirds are birds of open habitats and usually perch in the open on power lines and fences, whereas *Myiarchus* flycatchers are birds of wooded areas that do not regularly perch in the open.

to April; may be locally common at favored winter roosts.

Habitat: fields, pastures and other open areas.

Nesting: does not breed in Florida.

Feeding: sallies for insects captured in flight or on the ground; also eats fruit.

Voice: generally silent in Florida; sharp *whit* call.

ID: large, open-country flycatcher; greenish gray back and wings; short, black bill; gray head with small, black mask and white throat; gray breast; yellow belly and undertail coverts; black tail with white outer feathers.

Size: *L* 8–9 in; *W* 15½ in.

Status: rare to uncommon migrant and winter resident statewide from September

Similar Species: *Great Crested Flycatcher* (p. 231): slight crest; brownish upperparts; rufous in wings and tail; lacks white edges to outer tail feathers; seldom found in open habitats or perched on power lines. *Tropical Kingbird:* very rare; large bill; lacks white outer tail feathers. *Cassin's Kingbird:* very rare; dark gray throat emphasizes narrow, white "mustache" patch; lacks white outer tail feathers.

Best Sites: large winter roost at Lake Apopka NSRA.

EASTERN KINGBIRD

Tyrannus tyrannus

The Eastern Kingbird breeds over much of southern Canada and most of the continental U.S., and it winters in central South America. In Florida, it breeds throughout the mainland and is a characteristic breeding resident of the state's open pine flatwoods and prairies, often placing its nests in pines. This bird is surprisingly absent from the Keys, although it occurs there in migration. Despite annual reports on Christmas bird counts, the Eastern Kingbird is not regularly found in our state during winter; in fact, there is only one documented record. Most of these reports are undoubtedly misidentified Eastern Phoebes—or perhaps Loggerhead Shrikes. • The Eastern Kingbird lives up to its reputation as an avian tyrant. It is often seen vigorously pursuing and pecking hawks, crows or even humans to drive them out of its territory. • The Eastern Kingbird hunts from a conspicuous perch and sallies after prey.

ID: medium-sized flycatcher; white underparts; blackish upperparts; black tail with conspicuous white tip.
Size: *L* 8½ in; *W* 15 in.
Status: fairly common breeding resident of the mainland but absent from the Keys; fairly common to common migrant statewide.
Habitat: *Breeding:* open pinewoods or fields with scattered trees. *In migration:* any wooded habitat.
Nesting: in a tree or shrub, usually a pine; pair builds a cup nest of twigs and grass and lines it with root fibers, grass and fur;

female incubates 3–4 darkly blotched, white to pinkish white eggs for 14–18 days.
Feeding: sallies for insects in the air or on the ground; feeds on fruit during migration.
Voice: buzzy *dzee* call, often in a series.
Similar Species: *Gray Kingbird* (p. 235): dark gray upperparts; dark mask; huge bill; notched tail lacks white band; mostly coastal. *Eastern Phoebe* (p. 229): little seasonal overlap; smaller; darker head than back; tail lacks white band.
Best Sites: widespread.

GRAY KINGBIRD

Tyrannus dominicensis

The Gray Kingbird is another Florida "specialty" that draws birders to our state. It breeds from Georgia to Mississippi, in the West Indies and in northern South America, and it winters from the southern West Indies to northern South America. In Florida, the Gray Kingbird breeds along both coasts but is most common in Florida Bay and the Keys, where mangrove keys are numerous. • Like other kingbirds, the Gray Kingbird hunts from a conspicuous perch, often a power line. • Most flycatchers have large bills to aid in capturing flying insects, but the bill of a Gray Kingbird is especially large. Taken together, its bill size, dark mask and *pe-cheery* calls make this bird easy to distinguish from other flycatchers. • The word *dominicensis* translates to "of Hispaniola," referring to the location where the first specimen was collected in the late 1700s.

ID: medium-sized flycatcher with huge, dark bill; gray upperparts; dark mask; white cheek and throat; white underparts; notched, gray tail.
Size: *L* 9 in; *W* 14 in.
Status: fairly common breeding resident of most coastal areas from April to September, most numerous in the Keys; rare inland and during winter.

Habitat: primarily coastal, in mangrove forests, dune vegetation and hardwood hammocks.
Nesting: in a mangrove or tree near or over salt water; loose cup nest of twigs and grasses is lined with fine grass and rootlets; female incubates 2–4 brown-blotched, pinkish or creamy white eggs for 12–13 days.
Feeding: primarily sallies for flying insects; also eats fruit and small fish or reptiles.
Voice: twittering *pe-cheery* call.
Similar Species: none; coastal habitats, dark mask, huge bill and plain gray plumage are unique.
Best Sites: widespread.

235

SCISSOR-TAILED FLYCATCHER

Tyrannus forficatus

One of Florida's most spectacular birds, the adult male Scissor-tailed Flycatcher has pinkish underparts and wing linings and a tail that exceeds his body length. • The Scissor-tailed Flycatcher breeds in south central U.S. and extreme northeastern Mexico. It winters in Florida and from Mexico through Central America. In Florida, this flycatcher is a rare to fairly common migrant mostly along the Gulf Coast and a rare to fairly common winter resident of the southern half of the peninsula and the Keys. • In favored winter roosts in the state, as many as 15 or more Scissor-tailed Flycatchers may be seen, invariably with Western Kingbirds and perhaps other species. • In recent decades, Scissor-tailed Flycatchers have been expanding their breeding range eastward, and eventually they will likely begin breeding in Florida, at least occasionally. • This bird sallies for insects in flight or on the ground.

ID: slender flycatcher; long, black tail with white outer feathers; pale gray upperparts; mostly white head and underparts. *Male:* extremely long tail; bright pink underwings and paler undertail coverts. *Female* and *juvenile:* shorter tail; pale pink or yellowish underparts.
Size: *L* 10 in (up to 15 in for male); *W* 15 in.
Status: rare migrant; rare to locally uncommon resident in the southern half of the peninsula and the Keys from September to April.
Habitat: perches on power lines over pastures, fields and other open habitats.
Nesting: does not breed in Florida.
Feeding: sallies in the air or forages on the ground for insects, especially grasshoppers; also eats fruit.
Voice: short *kip* call.

Similar Species:
Fork-tailed Flycatcher (p. 365): very rare; dark gray upperparts; black head with white throat. *Northern Mockingbird* (p. 278): much shorter tail; 2 white wing bars; light gray underparts.
Best Sites: Lake Apopka NSRA; Key West.

LOGGERHEAD SHRIKE

Lanius ludovicianus

Shrikes are small, predatory songbirds that impale their prey on barbed wire fences or thorny vegetation. Two species occur in North America, but only one of them is found in Florida. The Loggerhead Shrike is largely resident in much of the western and southern U.S. and Mexico. In Florida, it breeds throughout the mainland but is absent from the Keys. • Because it lacks the talons and strong feet of hawks and owls, the shrike must impale its prey. This behavior has earned it the colloquial name "butcher bird." Impaling prey also serves another purpose for the male; it demonstrates his hunting prowess, which helps him attract a mate. • Loggerhead Shrikes are found in a variety of open habitats but seem unable to survive in developed areas, probably because many birds are struck by vehicles as they swoop down to capture prey. Throughout the continent, populations are declining about 7% per year; as a result, some populations are now endangered.

ID: medium-sized songbird; large head; hooked bill; gray back and crown; wide, black mask; white throat; black wings with white primary patch; long, black tail with white corners; white underparts. *Juvenile:* brownish gray-barred underparts. *In flight:* fast wingbeats; white patches in wings and tail.
Size: *L* 9 in; *W* 12 in.
Status: fairly common permanent resident throughout the mainland; rare or uncommon in the extreme southern peninsula and the Keys during winter.
Habitat: open habitats, such as pastures, fields, prairies, ball fields and cemeteries.

Nesting: in the crotch of a shrub or tree; bulky cup nest of twigs and grass is lined with animal hair, feathers and rootlets; female incubates 5–6 darkly spotted, pale buff to grayish white eggs for 15–17 days; 2 broods per year.
Feeding: swoops down on prey from a perch or attacks in pursuit; takes mostly large insects; regularly eats small birds and other vertebrates.
Voice: harsh *shack-shack* call; song is a series of warbles, trills and other notes.
Similar Species: *Northern Mockingbird* (p. 278): much thinner bill; lacks black mask; paler wings; slower, more buoyant wingbeats.
Best Sites: widespread.

WHITE-EYED VIREO
Vireo griseus

Vireos are small land birds with large bills, "spectacles" and slow, deliberate movements. Ten species have been found in Florida, but only a few are common, and only the White-eyed Vireo is resident. • White-eyed Vireos breed throughout the eastern U.S. and Mexico, and they winter from the extreme southern states and Cuba through Central America. In Florida, they are resident throughout the state, being one of our most widespread land birds. • White-eyed Vireos can be a challenge to spot but are readily identified by their variable songs, which start and end with an emphatic *chick* note. Expert mimics, White-eyed Vireos often incorporate into their songs the songs or calls of other birds, such as the Downy Woodpecker, Florida Scrub-Jay, Summer Tanager or Eastern Towhee. • Vireos construct intricate hanging nests, usually low in foliage.

ID: small, elusive land bird with bold yellow "spectacles"; greenish back and crown; gray face; white throat; 2 white wing bars; mostly yellow underparts; white eyes.
Juvenile: dark eyes.
Size: *L* 5 in; *W* 7½ in.
Status: fairly common and widespread permanent resident statewide; common coastal migrant at times.
Habitat: dense, shrubby undergrowth, scrub and woodland edges.

Nesting: in a shrub or small tree; cup nest hangs from a horizontal fork; pair incubates 4 lightly speckled, white eggs for 13–15 days.
Feeding: gleans insects from the ground or foliage; rarely eats fruits or seeds.
Voice: loud, snappy song with 4–7 notes, usually beginning and ending with *chick* notes; often mimics other birds.
Similar Species: bold white eyes and yellow "spectacles" of adults are diagnostic. *Bell's Vireo* (p. 365): resembles juvenile White-eyed Vireo but is very rare in Florida and always has brown eyes and white "spectacles."
Best Sites: widespread.

PHILADELPHIA VIREO
Vireo philadelphicus

Although it occurs in Florida annually, finding a Philadelphia Vireo requires good timing and a bit of luck. This vireo breeds in southern Canada and the extreme northern U.S. from North Dakota to New England and winters from Mexico to Panama. In Florida, it is regularly seen in migration during the first half of October, but it is rare; typically only one or two are seen, even during the peak periods. It may be equally numerous during spring, but it seems to be less reliable. • The Philadelphia Vireo often forages high in foliage, and its plumage is very similar to that of the Tennessee Warbler, which is much more numerous in our state during fall. The Philadelphia Vireo is also nearly identical to the Warbling Vireo, which is even rarer and less predictable in occurrence. • The Philadelphia Vireo is named after the city where, in 1851, the first specimen was collected.

ID: small, nondescript songbird with short, rather thick bill; greenish gray upperparts, including crown; white eyebrow; dark eye line; dark lores; pale yellow throat; pale yellowish underparts.
Size: *L* 4½–5 in; *W* 8 in.
Status: rare but regular migrant statewide from March to May and from September to October, when sightings are more likely.

Habitat: virtually any wooded habitat.
Nesting: does not breed in Florida.
Feeding: gleans insects, especially caterpillars and moths, from foliage.
Voice: usually silent in Florida.
Similar Species: *Warbling Vireo:* very rare in Florida; virtually identical plumage, except with somewhat duller upperparts, paler underparts and pale lores. *Tennessee Warbler* (p. 287): gray cap often contrasts with greenish back; white underparts; thinner bill; more active movements.
Best Sites: widespread but rare.

RED-EYED VIREO

Vireo olivaceus

The Red-eyed Vireo is one of the most common songbirds in eastern North America. It breeds over southern Canada and all but the southwestern U.S., and it winters in central South America. In Florida, the Red-eyed Vireo breeds fairly commonly throughout the Panhandle and peninsula south to Big Cypress Swamp, its southernmost breeding site anywhere. This species also migrates throughout the state, and it is more numerous during fall. • Red-eyed Vireos breed in swamps and moist deciduous or mixed forests. The birds are hard to see, because they forage high in the canopy, where their dull colors offer camouflage. However, the vocal endurance of males is well known. During spring and summer, males sing more or less continuously through the day. One particularly vigorous Red-eyed Vireo male holds the record for the most songs—about 22,000!—delivered by a single bird in a single day.

ID: smallish arboreal songbird, but large for a vireo; olive green upperparts; gray crown; white eyebrow; black eye line; red eyes (difficult to see); white throat and underparts, with yellow wash on flanks and undertail coverts, especially during fall.
Size: *L* 6 in; *W* 10 in.
Status: fairly common breeding resident of the Panhandle and northern half of the peninsula; rare and local south to Big Cypress Swamp; uncommon to common migrant statewide.
Habitat: *Breeding:* swamps, riparian areas and other wet deciduous woodlands. *In migration:* any wooded habitat.

Nesting: in a deciduous tree; in a horizontal fork; pair builds a hanging basketlike cup nest of grass and rootlets, bound with spider silk; female incubates 4 darkly spotted, white eggs for 11–14 days.
Feeding: gleans foliage for prey; feeds mostly on insects and spiders but eats fruit during migration.
Voice: descending nasal *sherr* call; song is a variable series of short phrases with distinct pauses in between, uttered for long periods.
Similar Species: *Black-whiskered Vireo* (p. 243): virtually identical plumage, except for dark "whisker," which may be faint on some birds; restricted to coastal habitats in southern Florida.
Best Sites: widespread.

BLACK-WHISKERED VIREO
Vireo altiloquus

Found in North America only in southern Florida, the Black-whiskered Vireo is believed to have expanded its range to include our state in the mid-1800s. It breeds in Florida and the West Indies and winters in South America. In Florida, the breeding range of the Black-whiskered Vireo has contracted in the past 20 years. Previously occurring north to Tampa Bay and Merritt Island, the species is now restricted to the southern peninsula and the Keys. Brood parasitism by Brown-headed Cowbirds has been identified as a possible cause of the population decline. • Black-whiskered Vireos are inhabitants of Florida's mangrove forests, keys and adjacent hardwood hammocks on the mainland. They are seldom seen except by the most dedicated birders, although their short songs, sung throughout the day, are one of the most conspicuous sounds of coastal habitats.

ID: small land bird of coastal forests; olive brown upperparts; dull gray crown; pale eyebrow; dark eye line; pale face with black "whisker" stripe; red eyes; pale underparts with yellowish flanks.
Size: *L* 6–6½ in; *W* 10 in.
Status: fairly common breeding resident of the southern third of the peninsula and the Keys from March to September.
Habitat: mangrove forests and hardwood hammocks.

Nesting: among mangroves, 5–8 ft above the water; female builds a hanging cup of woven vegetation suspended in the fork of a horizontal branch; female incubates 2–3 darkly spotted, white eggs for about 14 days.
Feeding: gleans insects and spiders from foliage; also eats some fruit.
Voice: song is a repeated series of short, paired phrases.
Similar Species: *Red-eyed Vireo* (p. 242): nearly identical in plumage but lacks dark "whisker" mark; very different song and habitat.
Best Sites: Everglades NP; "Ding" Darling NWR; the Keys.

BLUE JAY
Cyanocitta cristata

One of the most ubiquitous birds in Florida, the Blue Jay is found in virtually any wooded habitat, even in urban areas. This jay breeds from southern Canada throughout the central and eastern U.S. In Florida, it is resident throughout the mainland and the Upper Keys. The race that breeds in Florida is *C. c. cristata*, but flocks of the northern-breeding *C. c. bromia* race migrate to Florida during fall, often in large flocks. • Blue Jays embody all the admirable traits and aggressive qualities of the corvids: they are attractively plumaged, intelligent, resourceful and vocally diverse. They also serve as excellent sentinels for spotting predators, uttering their loud *jay* calls to warn other Blue Jays and other birds. They readily mob and attack hawks and owls; no predator, not even the Great Horned Owl, is too formidable for this bird to harass. • Blue Jays are predators of a variety of small vertebrates, and they steal eggs or nestlings from other birds' nests.

ID: medium-sized land bird; mostly blue upperparts; conspicuous crest; white face and upper breast boldly outlined with black; 1 white wing bar; white secondary edges on wing; pale gray and white underparts; long tail with black bars and white corners.

Size: *L* 11–12½ in; *W* 16 in.

Status: common permanent resident throughout the mainland and less common in the Upper Keys; absent from the Middle and Lower Keys.

Habitat: virtually any wooded habitat.

Nesting: in any of various trees; pair builds a bulky stick nest; pair incubates 4–5 variably marked, greenish, buff or pale blue eggs for 16–18 days.

Feeding: forages on the ground and among vegetation for a wide range of food, from small vertebrates to insects and fruit; caches acorns in the sand; visits bird feeders.

Voice: calls include *jay-jay-jay* and *queedle queedle queedle-queedle;* expert mimic of Red-shouldered Hawk and Osprey calls.

Similar Species: *Florida Scrub-Jay* (p. 245): local and mostly terrestrial; lacks crest; lacks white in wings or tail.

Best Sites: widespread.

244

FLORIDA SCRUB-JAY

Aphelocoma coerulescens

The Florida Scrub-Jay is the only bird species restricted entirely to our state. It is limited to xeric oak scrub, an endemic and rapidly disappearing habitat. • Florida Scrub-Jays feed mostly on insects, especially grasshoppers and caterpillars, and other invertebrates during spring and summer. During fall, each scrub-jay caches between 6500 and 8000 acorns, to be dug up and eaten throughout the winter, when animal prey is scarce. On rare occasions, scrub-jays have been known to prey on larger vertebrates, such as snakes or even birds. • This jay is one of few cooperative-breeding birds in North America: young from previous broods often remain with their parents for one or more years to help defend the territory and to raise subsequent broods. • Where they are not persecuted, Florida Scrub-Jays become extremely tame, often perching on the hands, shoulders or heads of people.

Voice: harsh scolds or high-pitched *shreep* calls. *Female:* exclusive mechanical "hiccup" call that varies regionally.

Habitat: limited to xeric oak scrub or sandhills that burn every 8–15 years.

Nesting: in an oak shrub 3–6 feet above the ground; pair builds a sturdy basket of oak twigs and lines it with palmetto fibers or rootlets; female incubates 3–4 bluish eggs, blotched with reddish brown, for 17–18 days.

Similar Species: *Blue Jay* (p. 244): conspicuous blue crest; pure white underparts with black breast band; white in wings and tail; found in forested habitats.

Best Sites: along the Lake Wales Ridge (e.g., Archbold Biological Station, Lake Wales Ridge SF); Merritt Island NWR; Ocala NF; Oscar Scherer SP.

ID: medium-sized, mostly terrestrial bird; blue upperparts with grayish brown back; blue wings and tail; rounded head with whitish forehead; grayish underparts with blue breast band. *Juvenile:* fluffy, brown head; acquires adult plumage by September.

Size: *L* 11 in; *W* 16 in.

Status: federally threatened (USFWS); locally common permanent resident of the peninsula, primarily the central portion.

AMERICAN CROW

Corvus brachyrhynchos

Crows are large, all-black birds that are often seen on the ground. Five species of crows are found in North America, with two of them occurring in Florida. The familiar American Crow is resident over much of southern Canada and the continental U.S.; Canadian breeders move south during fall. In Florida, this crow is resident throughout the mainland, but it is absent from the region southeast of Lake Okeechobee and from the Keys. • American Crows are found in open country with scattered trees for nesting. They do not occur in developed areas and are strictly inland in occurrence, except for a population along Florida Bay in Everglades National Park. • Wary and intelligent, American Crows are often seen feeding on roadkill, calmly walking toward the shoulder of the road when oncoming traffic approaches too closely. • These birds use a variety of calls to communicate and can expertly mimic human speech and other sounds. • The American Crow's cumbersome-sounding scientific name is Latin for "raven with the small nose." • Crows are closely related to ravens, which are not found in Florida.

ID: large, black, often terrestrial bird; large, black bill; black legs; broad wings; square-shaped tail.
Size: *L* 17–21 in; *W* 3 ft.
Status: fairly common permanent resident throughout the mainland, although curiously absent from Palm Beach and Broward counties; absent from the Keys.
Habitat: pastures, agricultural fields and oak and mixed oak-pine woodlands; absent from developed areas.

Nesting: in a tree; pair builds a large stick nest lined with fur and soft plant materials; female incubates 4–6 gray-green to blue-green eggs, blotched with brown and gray, for about 18 days.
Feeding: very opportunistic; feeds on carrion and animal prey as diverse as insects, bird eggs, nestlings and other small vertebrates; also eats acorns and berries.
Voice: distinctive *caw-caw-caw* call.
Similar Species: *Fish Crow* (p. 247): slightly smaller; usually readily distinguished by voice; nasal *uh-uh* call is typical, but also gives nasal *car-car-car-car-car* like that of the American Crow.
Best Sites: widespread.

FISH CROW

Corvus ossifragus

The Fish Crown is a coastal species found only in the eastern U.S., from Massachusetts to Texas. In Florida, it is a permanent resident nearly statewide, being absent from only the Big Cypress Swamp–Everglades region and most of the Keys. • Fish Crows have readily adapted to developed areas and are found in our most densely urbanized cities. Flocks of Fish Crows, known as "murders," roost on islands around St. Petersburg and Tampa and contain thousands of individuals. This behavior makes them easy to distinguish from American Crows, which are found in small family groups inland, away from developed areas. • The Fish Crow can also be distinguished from the American Crow by its call notes. The common call of a Fish Crow is an *uh* or *uh-uh*, whereas the common call of an American Crow is a raucous *caw!* It is not known whether competition or habitat preferences segregate Florida's two species of crows, but it is rare to find them occurring together.

ID: large, black land bird; virtually identical to the American Crow, except with smaller head and bill and more pointed, swept-back wing tips; relatively long, square-shaped tail; best identified by voice.
Size: *L* 15½ in; *W* 3 ft.
Status: fairly common to abundant permanent resident throughout the mainland, even occurring in large flocks in cities; rare and possibly increasing permanent resident of the Keys, primarily Key West.
Habitat: urban and suburban areas, coastlines and along lakes and rivers inland.

Nesting: often in a small, loose colony; in a tree; pair builds a bulky nest of sticks; female incubates 4–5 heavily marked, greenish eggs for 16–18 days.
Feeding: opportunistic; walks on the ground looking for prey; flies into wading bird rookeries; often scavenges; feeds on a wide variety of foods, including bird eggs, carrion, fish, marine crustaceans and insects.
Voice: common call is a nasal *uh* or *uh-uh;* less frequent nasal *car-car-car-car-car,* reminiscent of the American Crow.
Similar Species: *American Crow* (p. 246): slightly larger; not found in flocks or near the coast; well-known boisterous *caw!* call, often doubled.
Best Sites: widespread.

PURPLE MARTIN

Progne subis

The Purple Martin is the largest swallow in North America, and it is a popular yard bird. • Purple Martins breed in southern Canada, throughout the eastern U.S., and locally in the West. They are believed to winter in South America. In Florida, martins breed throughout the mainland but are surprisingly absent as breeders from the Keys. During fall, they roost in huge flocks that may contain thousands of individuals. • Purple Martins historically bred in tree cavities and cliff crevices, but Native Americans encouraged martins to nest in hollowed-out gourds hung on poles. Later, North Americans introduced wood or metal multi-room "apartment houses." Today, most Purple Martins in the East nest in birdhouses or gourds. Residents who wish to attract martins should set out, or open up, their martin houses in early February, and they should routinely remove any House Sparrow nests that are built—the sparrows are a nonnative species, so it is legal to remove their nests without a permit. • Despite a wide reputation as superb "mosquito hawks," Purple Martins virtually never feed on mosquitoes.

ID: large, vocal swallow with glossy dark blue upperparts; small, dark bill. *Male:* dark blue overall. *Female* and *juvenile:* gray forehead; "scaly," dark and whitish underparts. *In flight:* shallowly forked tail.
Size: *L* 7–8 in; *W* 18 in.
Status: rare to locally common breeding resident throughout the mainland; uncommon to locally abundant migrant from February to September.
Habitat: much more common in suburban areas than in large natural areas; forages over any habitat.

Nesting: communal; usually in an apartment-style birdhouse or hollowed-out gourd, rarely in a natural palm cavity; nest materials include feathers, grass, mud and vegetation; female incubates 4–5 white eggs for 15–18 days.
Feeding: aerial forager; feeds on flying insects such as ants, wasps and flies.
Voice: rich, pleasant chirping notes, often in flight.
Similar Species: *European Starling* (p. 280): juvenile resembles juvenile Purple Martin, but with square-tipped tail and long, pointed bill. *Northern Rough-winged Swallow* (p. 250): resembles juvenile Purple Martin, but smaller, with square-tipped tail
Best Sites: widespread.

TREE SWALLOW
Tachycineta bicolor

The Tree Swallow breeds across Alaska, Canada and most of the continental U.S., and it winters in the extreme southern U.S. and the West Indies to northern South America. In Florida, the Tree Swallow is a winter resident statewide, especially in the southern peninsula. It winters in huge flocks—at times estimated to exceed one million birds—that appear like clouds of smoke over marshes or fields. • The Tree Swallow is more cold hardy than other swallows, which explains its presence in Florida in such huge numbers during winter. It readily switches to a diet of berries when low temperatures cause insects to become scarce, and large flocks of Tree Swallows gleaning the abundant berries from wax myrtle bushes is a common sight in our state. • In bright spring sunshine, the iridescent back of a Tree Swallow appears dark blue, but during fall it appears green. Unlike other North American swallows, a female Tree Swallow does not acquire her full adult plumage until her second or third year. • The word *bicolor,* Latin for "two colors," refers to the contrast between the bird's dark upperparts and white underparts.

ID: white-bellied swallow often seen in large flocks; iridescent dark blue or green upperparts; dark rump; white underparts; shallowly forked tail.
Size: *L* 5½ in; *W* 14½ in.
Status: rare to abundant resident statewide from October to April.
Habitat: over any habitat.

Nesting: does not breed in Florida.
Feeding: plucks flying insects from the air; gleans berries, especially those of wax myrtle, from foliage.
Voice: call is a soft twitter.
Similar Species: *Barn Swallow* (p. 254): may appear all white below, but has shallowly forked tail.
Best Sites: widespread.

249

NORTHERN ROUGH-WINGED SWALLOW
Stelgidopteryx serripennis

The Northern Rough-winged Swallow breeds from extreme southern Canada to Costa Rica and winters from the extreme southern U.S. to Panama. In Florida, it breeds widely in the Panhandle and locally in the peninsula south to the Miami area. It is also a fairly common migrant statewide, appearing more numerous during fall, and flocks of dozens of swallows winter south of Lake Okeechobee. • Unlike other swallows, male Northern Rough-wings have curved barbs along the outer edge of their primary wing feathers. The purpose of this saw-toothed edge remains a mystery, but it may be used to produce sound during courtship displays. This bird's common and scientific names both relate to this structure; *stelgidopteryx* means "scraper wing," and *serripennis* means "saw feather."

ID: small swallow with dull brown upperparts, including the head; whitish underparts with indistinct brown wash on breast. *Juvenile:* wide, rufous wing bars. *In flight:* short, notched tail.

Size: *L* 5½ in; *W* 14 in.

Status: fairly common breeding resident in the Panhandle and rare to uncommon throughout the peninsula; fairly common migrant statewide, at times abundant during fall; rare to locally common during winter in the southern peninsula.

Habitat: nests in riverbanks, drain pipes, exhaust pipes or other artificial cavities; forages over most habitats, especially near water.

Nesting: sometimes in small colonies but usually solitary; in an earthen bank; pair excavates a burrow and lines the nesting chamber with leaves and dry grass; mostly the female incubates 4–8 white eggs for 12–16 days.

Feeding: catches flying insects on the wing.

Voice: short, squeaky call note.

Similar Species: *Bank Swallow* (p. 251): brown breast band; white underparts. *Tree Swallow* (p. 249): drab birds appear brown above, but with pure white underparts.

Best Sites: widespread.

BANK SWALLOW

Riparia riparia

One of the most broadly distributed members of the swallow family, the Bank Swallow occurs in both the New World and Old World. It breeds over most of Alaska, Canada, the continental U.S. and a tiny bit of northeastern Mexico, and it winters in South America. • In Florida, this swallow is strictly a migrant, occurring more numerously during fall, usually among flocks that include other swallows. • On its breeding grounds, the Bank Swallow excavates its own nest burrow in an earthen river or stream bank, initially using its small bill and later digging with its feet. • *Riparia* is Latin for "riverbank." In the Old World, this swallow is known as "Sand Martin." • In medieval Europe, when swallows vanished each fall, they were believed to have gone into the mud at the bottom of swamps. In those days, it was beyond imagination that the birds might fly south.

ID: small swallow with brown upperparts; white forehead, throat and ear patch; brown crown and cheek; white underparts except for well-defined brown breast band.
Size: *L* 5½ in; *W* 13 in.
Status: rare to fairly common migrant statewide from April to May and from August to October, when they are more numerous.
Habitat: over most habitats.
Nesting: does not breed in Florida.
Feeding: catches flying insects on the wing.
Voice: call is a series of buzzy twitters.
Similar Species: *Northern Rough-winged Swallow* (p. 250): lacks well-defined breast band. *Tree Swallow* (p. 249): drab birds appear brown above, but with pure white underparts.
Best Sites: fairly widespread.

CLIFF SWALLOW

Petrochelidon pyrrhonota

The two species of *Petrochelidon* swallows found in North America—Cliff and Cave Swallows—are very similar in plumage, with orange rumps and short, square tails. Both occur in Florida, and each seems to be colonizing the state as a breeding species. The Cliff Swallow breeds over most of North America except for northeastern Canada and the Deep South, and it winters in the southern half of South America. In Florida, it is a rare statewide migrant. • There are two breeding records for Cliff Swallows in our state: under a bridge near Lake Okeechobee in 1974 and on a boathouse near Apalachicola in 1998. Cliff Swallows build their nests out of pellets of mud, which are pressed together to form their characteristic gourd-shaped nests. Because of this nest material requirement, breeding in Florida likely will be limited to areas with muddy soil—the Apalachicola nests were made mostly of sand and quickly collapsed.

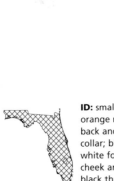

Habitat: forages over most habitats; nests over water.

Nesting: 2 isolated records in Florida; colonial; under a bridge over water or on a building built in water; pair builds a gourd-shaped mud (or sand, in Florida) nest with a small opening near the bottom; pair incubates 4–5 brown-spotted, white to pinkish eggs for 14–16 days.

Feeding: catches flying insects on the wing.

Voice: twittering *churrr-churrr* call.

Similar Species: *Cave Swallow* (p. 253): usually dark rufous forehead is pale in Mexican race; usually pale throat.

Best Sites: fairly widespread migrant.

ID: small swallow with orange rump; blackish back and wings; pale collar; blackish crown; white forehead; orange cheek and ear patches; black throat; pale underparts; black tail.

Size: *L* 5½ in; *W* 13½ in.

Status: generally rare migrant statewide from April to May and from August to October; has bred on 2 occasions.

CAVE SWALLOW

Petrochelidon fulva

As its name suggests, the Cave Swallow originally nested solely in caves, and some populations continue to do so. But, like the Cliff Swallow, the Cave Swallow has adapted to the human landscape, and many colonies now nest under bridges or on buildings. The Cave Swallow is largely resident from southern Arizona and Texas to Mexico and from southern Florida to the West Indies. • The western or Mexican Cave Swallow *(P. f. pelodoma)* and the eastern or West Indian race *(P. f. fulva)* have been found in Florida. *P. f. fulva* has bred under bridges or highway overpasses in the south Miami area since 1987 or earlier. This population is now largely resident in the area, and it may expand into other areas in the southeastern peninsula. • Because the Cliff Swallow is virtually unknown in our state during winter, any square-tailed, orange-rumped swallow observed during that season is most likely a Cave Swallow.

ID: small swallow with orange rump; blackish back, wings and tail. *P. f. fulva:* dusky nape; orange head with blackish crown and eye line that join behind the eye; pale or buffy orange underparts. *P. f. pelodoma:* pale head; buffy throat; pale underparts.
Size: *L* 5½ in; *W* 13½ in.
Status: locally uncommon near-permanent resident of southern Miami–Dade County;

rare to very rare migrant statewide, usually along the coasts.
Habitat: nests under bridges over water; forages over most habitats.
Nesting: colonial; under a bridge over water; pair builds an open cup nest or a gourd-shaped nest of mud and lines it with feathers and plant down; nest may be reused from year to year; pair incubates 3–4 brown-speckled, white eggs for 15–18 days.
Feeding: catches flying insects on the wing.
Voice: soft *chu, chu* call.
Similar Species: *Cliff Swallow* (p. 252): no breeding range overlap at present; white forehead; dark throat.
Best Sites: breeds at Cutler Ridge (Miami); becoming regular south to Homestead.

BARN SWALLOW
Hirundo rustica

The Barn Swallow is the most widely distributed swallow in the world, as well as in North America and Florida. It breeds from southern Alaska through northern South America, and it winters from Mexico and the West Indies south through South America. It also occurs in the Old World, where it is known as simply "Swallow." • Barn Swallows first bred in Florida in 1946 at Pensacola. They now breed in most of the Panhandle and northern peninsula and sparingly all the way to Key West. They are also common migrants statewide, especially during fall, when they are conspicuous migrants from late July through early September. One or a few Barn Swallows are reported during most winters, and any such sightings should be documented with photographs.

ID: large swallow with long, deeply forked tail; blue upperparts; blue crown, nape and ear patch; orange forehead, cheek and throat; orange underparts that may appear very pale in some birds. *Juvenile:* pale underparts; short tail.
Size: *L* 7 in; *W* 15 in.
Status: uncommon to abundant migrant statewide from August to May; rare to locally common breeding resident of the peninsula; rare during winter.
Habitat: nests over water, under an artificial structure; forages over any habitat.
Nesting: usually in colonies; under a roadway or bridge, rarely inside a building; pair builds a half or full cup nest of mud and grass; pair incubates 3–5 brown-spotted, white eggs for about 15 days.
Feeding: forages exclusively on the wing, catching flying insects.
Voice: continuous, twittering chatter; *wit* call, often doubled.
Similar Species: none; orange underparts and long, forked tail are diagnostic.
Best Sites: widespread.

CAROLINA CHICKADEE
Poecile carolinensis

Chickadees are tiny, charming songbirds with black bibs, and they are named for their calls. Seven species are native to North America, but only the Carolina Chickadee is found in Florida. It is endemic to the southeastern U.S. In Florida, the Carolina Chickadee is resident in the Panhandle and northern half of the peninsula, where it is fairly common, but it is rare or absent south of Tampa Bay, Kissimmee and New Smyrna Beach. • This bird is a cavity nester, so it cannot survive in developed areas where snags are removed for aesthetics and safety. In rural areas, it will nest in birdhouses. • Outside the breeding season, chickadees join the company of mixed-species foraging flocks that also contain Downy Woodpeckers, Tufted Titmice, Blue-headed Vireos, White-eyed Vireos, Ruby-crowned Kinglets (and Golden-crowned Kinglets in northern Florida) and several species of warblers.

ID: small songbird with black cap and bib separated by white cheeks; gray back; tiny, dark bill; gray wings with pale edging on secondary feathers; whitish underparts with pale peach flanks.
Size: L 4½ in; W 7½ in.
Status: fairly common permanent resident of the Panhandle and northern half of the peninsula and virtually absent farther south in the peninsula.

Habitat: most wooded habitats, including urban and suburban areas.
Nesting: usually in a snag or fence post; pair excavates a cavity or may use a nest box; cavity is lined with soft plant material and animal hair; female incubates 5–8 finely speckled, white eggs for 11–14 days.
Feeding: gleans insects, spiders and some fruit from vegetation, often hanging upside down; also visits bird feeders.
Voice: rapid *chick-a-dee-dee* call; song is a whistled 4-note *fee-bee fee-bay*.
Similar Species: none; black head with large white cheek area is unique.
Best Sites: widespread.

255

TUFTED TITMOUSE

Baeolophus bicolor

Titmice are small, "friendly" songbirds that belong to the same family as chickadees. They are known in the Old World simply as "tits," and their curious name refers to their small size. • Tufted Titmice are resident throughout the eastern U.S. and Mexico. In Florida, they are resident throughout the Panhandle and northern half of the peninsula, but they are local farther south. • When not breeding, Tufted Titmice join flocks composed of other small songbirds, such as Carolina Chickadees, White-eyed Vireos, Blue-headed Vireos, Blue-gray Gnatcatchers and various species of warblers. Often the first to detect danger, they scold with loud, harsh notes that attract other birds to help mob an intruder. • Tufted Titmice forage actively as they move from branch to branch, and they often hang upside down as they search for prey. Their call, a clear whistle usually written as *peter peter peter*, is a common avian sound of our pinewoods and oak hammocks.

ID: small, lively songbird with prominent crest; gray upperparts; white face with bold black eye; white underparts with orange flanks. **Size:** *L* 6–6½ in; *W* 10 in.

Status: generally common permanent resident of the Panhandle and northern half of the peninsula; rarer and local farther south; absent from the Keys.
Habitat: most wooded habitats.

Nesting: in a natural cavity or birdhouse lined with soft vegetation and animal hair; female incubates 5–6 finely dotted, white eggs for 12–14 days; female may be fed by the male from courtship to time of hatching.
Feeding: forages on branches and occasionally on the ground for insects, spiders and seeds; also visits bird feeders.
Voice: call is a series of harsh scolds; song is a whistled *peter peter peter*.
Similar Species: none; gray plumage and crest are unique.
Best Sites: widespread.

RED-BREASTED NUTHATCH
Sitta canadensis

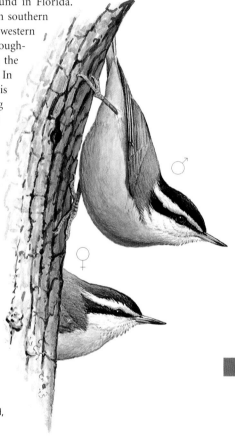

Nuthatches are curious little birds that have unique foraging styles. Like woodpeckers and a few other species, they forage mostly on the trunks and larger branches of pines or other trees. But, unlike other species, they often are seen moving down a trunk headfirst! • Four nuthatch species occur in North America, and three of them are found in Florida. The Red-breasted Nuthatch breeds in southern Canada and the northeastern and western regions of the U.S., and it winters throughout its breeding range as well as in the remainder of the continental U.S. In Florida, the Red-breasted Nuthatch is an irruptive winter resident, appearing during some years and remaining absent during others. Even during irruptions, it is usually restricted to the Panhandle and is generally rare. • *Sitta* means "nuthatch" in Greek; *canadensis* refers to this bird's partially Canadian distribution.

ID: small, short-tailed, tree-climbing bird; short, straight bill; blue-gray upperparts; white head with black crown and thick eye line. *Male:* rich peach underparts. *Female:* pale peach underparts.
Size: *L* 4½ in; *W* 8½ in.
Status: irruptive resident of the Panhandle and, rarely, the northern half of the peninsula from October to April; otherwise usually rare or absent.
Habitat: pinewoods and mixed pine-oak woodlands.

Nesting: does not breed in Florida.
Feeding: forages on tree trunks and branches for insects, spiders and pine seeds.
Voice: weak, nasal *yenk* call.
Similar Species: *Carolina Wren* (p. 261): also forages on trunks; remarkably similar plumage pattern, but with rich rufous upperparts, including head, and rich buffy underparts; bolder eyebrow; very vocal. *White-breasted Nuthatch* (p. 258): larger; lacks black eye line; white underparts.
Best Sites: none; irruptive.

WHITE-BREASTED NUTHATCH

Sitta carolinensis

The disappearance of the White-breasted Nuthatch from most of its Florida range since the 1930s is a mystery that has never been satisfactorily solved. Although the extensive clear-cut logging of the pinewoods through the early 1900s undoubtedly affected nuthatch numbers, populations of other species affected by the same widespread deforestation never became extirpated and in many cases are again fairly common. In any event, the White-breasted Nuthatch is now one of Florida's most range-restricted birds.

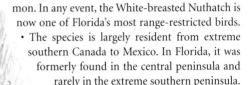

• The species is largely resident from extreme southern Canada to Mexico. In Florida, it was formerly found in the central peninsula and rarely in the extreme southern peninsula. Today, the White-breasted Nuthatch is restricted to the Red Hills physiographic region around Tallahassee.

• White-breasted Nuthatches forage on trunks and branches of pines and other trees.

ID: small, short-tailed, tree-climbing bird; gray back and wings; white face; bold black (male) or grayish (female) crown and nape; white underparts with rusty undertail coverts.

Size: *L* 5½–6 in; *W* 11 in.

Status: fairly common permanent resident of the Red Hills region around Tallahassee; virtually unknown elsewhere in Florida.

Habitat: pinewoods and mixed pine-oak woods.

Nesting: in a natural cavity in a tree or snag; female lines the cavity with bark, grass, fur and feathers; female incubates 4–7 brown-spotted, white eggs for 12–14 days.

Feeding: forages on tree trunks and branches for insects, spiders and pine seeds; also visits bird feeders.

Voice: nasal *yank* call, often as a series.

Similar Species: *Brown-headed Nuthatch* (p. 259): smaller; brown cap with white spot on nape. *Red-breasted Nuthatch* (p. 257): irruptive; smaller; white eyebrow and black eye line; rusty underparts.

Best Sites: sites around Tallahassee, including Tall Timbers Research Station.

BROWN-HEADED NUTHATCH

Sitta pusilla

The Brown-headed Nuthatch is the only nuthatch seen over most of the state. It is endemic to the pine forests of the Deep South, making it one of very few bird species found exclusively in the U.S. In Florida, it is fairly widespread in the Panhandle but is local in the peninsula, especially the southern half. • The Brown-headed Nuthatch is one of very few North American birds to use tools. It will use a flake of bark or a cone bract to pry off other bark flakes in search of prey hiding underneath, sometimes carrying the tool from tree to tree and sometimes discarding it once prey is found. • Like other nuthatches, the Brown-headed is commonly seen foraging during winter in larger, multi-species flocks that usually include Eastern Bluebirds, Carolina Chickadees, Tufted Titmice and Pine Warblers along with other species.

ID: small, short-tailed, tree-climbing bird; short, straight bill; dull blue-gray back and wings; brownish gray nape and crown; white cheek and throat; white nape patch; whitish underparts.
Size: *L* 4½ in; *W* 7½ in.
Status: fairly common permanent resident of the Panhandle and northern half of the peninsula; less numerous and local farther south; unknown in the Keys.
Habitat: open and mixed pine woodlands.
Nesting: in a pine snag or fence post; pair excavates a nest cavity and lines it with

wood chips and grass; male feeds the female as she incubates 4–7 profusely speckled, white eggs for 13–15 days.
Feeding: forages on tree trunks and branches for insects, spiders and pine seeds; also uses pine flakes as tools to pry off other bark flakes.
Voice: squeaky 2-note "rubber ducky" calls.
Similar Species: *Red-breasted Nuthatch* (p. 257): rare winter resident; blue-gray upperparts; black-and-white-striped head; pale or bright orange underparts. *White-breasted Nuthatch* (p. 258): Tallahassee area only; larger; black crown; white face.
Best Sites: widespread.

BROWN CREEPER

Certhia americana

Although many species of creepers inhabit Europe and Asia, the Brown Creeper is the only member of its family that is found in North America. It breeds in scattered regions from southern Alaska to Central America, and it winters throughout its breeding range and across the continental U.S. In Florida, it is a rare and inconspicuous winter resident, primarily of the Panhandle. Like some other northern-wintering songbirds, the Brown Creeper is somewhat irruptive in our state, appearing uncommonly in our northern regions—or moving into the central or southern peninsula—at intervals of several years. • The Brown Creeper feeds by slowly spiraling up a tree trunk, searching for spiders and insects. When it reaches the upper branches, the creeper flies down to the base of a neighboring tree to begin another foraging ascent. Its long, stiff tail feathers prop it up against vertical tree trunks as it hitches its way skyward.

Status: somewhat irruptive; normally rare resident of the Panhandle from October to March, but occasionally irrupts to the southern peninsula.

Habitat: most wooded habitats.

Nesting: does not breed in Florida.

Feeding: spirals up tree trunks and large limbs using its tail as a prop; probes bark for insects and spiders.

Voice: high *tseee* call.

Similar Species: unique plumage. *Carolina Wren* (p. 261) and *Nuthatches* (pp. 257–59): forage on trunks but do not ascend them in spiral fashion.

Best Sites: fairly widespread in the Panhandle.

ID: small, brown land bird; mottled brown and white upperparts; brown head with pale eyebrow; white throat; short, downcurved bill; white underparts with buffy undertail coverts.

Size: *L* 5–5½ in; *W* 7½ in.

CAROLINA WREN
Thryothorus ludovicianus

The song of the Carolina Wren—amazingly loud for such a small bird—is one of the most distinctive sounds of Florida's woodlands. Pairs perform lively "duets" at any time of the day and in any season. • The Carolina Wren is resident throughout the eastern U.S. to Central America. In Florida, it is found in most open wooded habitats throughout the mainland, but, because it forages and nests close to the ground, it cannot persist in heavily developed areas, where cats and other human-introduced dangers lurk. In less developed areas, the Carolina Wren often nests in garages, on ledges or in birdhouses. This versatile bird will even build its nest against a car radiator or in clothes hanging on the line!

ID: small, active bird often seen around rural residences; rich brown upperparts, including nape and crown; longish, slightly downcurved bill; bold white eyebrow; rusty cheek; white throat; rich buffy underparts; rather long tail for a wren.
Size: *L* 5½ in; *W* 7½ in.
Status: generally common permanent resident throughout the mainland; absent from the Keys, except rare on Key Largo.
Habitat: thickets and dense forest undergrowth; rural areas that retain palmettos and other native groundcover.
Nesting: in a cavity, birdhouse or other artificial object; pair builds a dome nest; female incubates 3–5 brown-flecked, creamy white eggs for 12–14 days; 2–3 broods per year.
Feeding: usually forages in pairs on the ground and among vegetation; eats mostly insects and other invertebrates; also takes berries, fruits and seeds; eats peanuts and suet at bird feeders.
Voice: loud song; usually written as *tea-kettle-tea-kettle-tea-kettle,* but most 2- or 3-syllable words would work (e.g., *cheese-burger-cheeseburger-cheeseburger-cheese*); also, a loud, ringing *churt* call.
Similar Species: *Red-breasted Nuthatch* (p. 257): similar tree-climbing habit and plumage pattern, but with blue-gray upperparts and black crown; rare in Florida, found solely during winter; lacks loud ringing calls; partial to pines.
Best Sites: widespread.

HOUSE WREN

Troglodytes aedon

Wrens are small songbirds with very short tails, often held up at an angle, and loud, "bubbly" songs. There are 74 species in the New World, seven of which occur in Florida. The House Wren breeds across southern Canada, the entire continental U.S., except for the Deep South, and throughout Central and South America. Northern-breeding populations winter in the southern U.S. In Florida, the House Wren is a winter resident statewide. • Unlike most birds that only winter in Florida, House Wrens often sing their rollicking, bubbly song while in our state. When alarmed, they give a series of harsh scolds, which is often the only indication of their presence. • These birds skulk about among tangled bushes and brush piles; a glimpse is all you get before they move to another location. *Troglodytes* is Greek for "creeping in holes" or "cave dweller," referring to the wren's skulking behavior.

ID: small wren; brown tail, back and wings mottled with black; gray nape and crown; faint pale eyebrow; dusky cheek; grayish buff underparts; barred undertail coverts.
Size: *L* 4½ –5 in; *W* 6 in.
Status: fairly common resident statewide from October to April but rare in the extreme southern peninsula and the Keys.
Habitat: shrubby fields, thickets or woodland edges.
Nesting: does not breed in Florida.

Feeding: gleans the ground, vegetation or human dwellings for insects, spiders and snails.
Voice: call is a series of harsh scolding notes; song is a rapid warbling of rolling trills and rattles lasting 2–3 seconds.
Similar Species: *Winter Wren* (p. 263): rare; only in northern Florida; smaller; darker overall; shorter, stubby tail; prominent black barring on belly and flanks. *Sedge Wren* (p. 264): paler upperparts; streaked back and crown; bold eyebrow; buffy breast.
Best Sites: widespread.

WINTER WREN
Troglodytes troglodytes

A rare winter resident of northern Florida, the Winter Wren breeds in coastal Alaska, across southern Canada and in the northeastern and western continental U.S. It winters along the entire Pacific Coast and in much of the eastern U.S. In Florida, it winters in the Panhandle and northern peninsula, where it is found in dense undergrowth near water. • Because of its small size, secretive behavior and preference for relatively inaccessible habitats, our knowledge of the Winter Wren in Florida may be incomplete. In the past, this wren seems to have been more widely distributed in our state than it is at present. Today, any report south of Gainesville should be documented thoroughly because of this bird's similarity to the House Wren. Like the House Wren, the Winter Wren may be heard singing in our state before it migrates northward to breed. • The Winter Wren is the only wren that is also found in the Old World, where it is known simply as "Wren."

ID: very tiny wren with very short tail; dark brown upperparts, including wings; distinct pale eyebrow; pale brown throat and breast, with rest of underparts heavily barred with black.
Size: *L* 4 in; *W* 5½ in.
Status: rare winter resident of the Panhandle from October to April and perhaps irregular in the northern third of the peninsula; absent farther south.
Habitat: tangled brush piles and woodland thickets, usually along lakes, streams or rivers.

Nesting: does not breed in Florida.
Feeding: gleans the ground or vegetation for insects, spiders and snails.
Voice: sharp *chip-chip* call; song is a melodious series of quick trills and twitters, often lasting for more than 8 seconds.
Similar Species: *House Wren* (p. 262): paler overall; weak or absent pale eyebrow; lacks barring on flanks and undertail coverts. *Sedge Wren* (p. 264): paler overall; boldly streaked back, wings and crown; lacks barring on flanks and undertail coverts; found in grassy fields.
Best Sites: Florida Caverns SP; Torreya SP.

SEDGE WREN

Cistothorus platensis

The North American race of the Sedge Wren breeds in southeastern Canada and the northeastern U.S., and it winters in the southeastern U.S. and northern Mexico. Other subspecies are resident in Central and South America. In Florida, the Sedge Wren is a fairly common winter resident throughout the mainland but very rare in the Keys. • Sedge Wrens are small and secretive inhabitants of grassy habitats, and birders not familiar with their double-chip calls will consider the birds much less numerous than they really are. These birds usually do not flush until they are nearly stepped on. • Although Sedge Wrens often remain in our state until late May and have been heard singing in spring and in August, no breeding has been observed in Florida.

Habitat: grassy fields, dry prairie, pond or lake edges and salt marshes.

Nesting: does not breed in Florida.

Feeding: forages in dense vegetation, often near the ground; feeds on insects and spiders.

Voice: clear *chip-chip* call; song is a few short chips followed by a rattling trill.

Similar Species: *Marsh Wren* (p. 265): black back with white streaking; unstreaked crown and rusty shoulders; bold eyebrow. *House Wren* (p. 262): not found in grassy fields; unstreaked, brown upperparts; pale eye ring; lacks pale eyebrow. *Winter Wren* (p. 263): rare in north Florida; not found in grassy fields; much darker above, with an unstreaked crown and heavily barred underparts.

Best Sites: widespread.

ID: tiny wren of grassy habitats; streaked back and wings; dusky nape; streaked crown; pale eyebrow; blackish eye line; white throat; buffy underparts; short, narrow tail.

Size: L 4–4½ in; W 5½ in.

Status: fairly common resident of the Panhandle and northern half of the peninsula from October to April; less numerous in the southern peninsula; very rare in the Keys.

MARSH WREN
Cistothorus palustris

The Marsh Wren breeds in southern Canada and in various regions of the continental U.S. It winters in the southern U.S. and Mexico. In Florida, two races breed in different coastal regions: "Worthington's Marsh Wren" *(C. p. griseus)* is found around Jacksonville, and "Marian's Marsh Wren" *(C. p. marianae)* breeds along the eastern Panhandle and northern peninsular Gulf Coast. Individuals of five other races winter in the state, occurring throughout the mainland. • The male Marsh Wren is polygynous and may mate with two or more females at one time. For each female he is courting, he typically builds at least six "dummy" nests and takes his potential mate on a tour to inspect them. The female March Wren often rejects all of his nests, preferring to build her own, but if she does find one suitable, she lines it with feathers, cattail down and grass before laying her eggs.

ID: small wren; variable plumage; black back with white streaks; brown nape; dark crown; bold white eyebrow; dark eye line; pale throat; brown or rusty wings; grayish brown or rusty underparts; brown tail with black bands.
Size: *L* 5 in; *W* 6 in.
Status: fairly common permanent resident of coastal marshes around Jacksonville and along the Gulf Coast from St. Marks to New Port Richey; uncommon resident throughout the mainland from October to April; very rare in the Keys.
Habitat: salt, brackish or freshwater marshes; flooded brushy or weedy fields.
Nesting: in a brackish or salt marsh; attached to a reed, shrub or mangrove; large, domed nest of marsh vegetation is lined with finer materials; female incubates 4–6 darkly marked, white to pale brown eggs for 12–16 days; 2–3 broods per year.

Feeding: gleans vegetation for insects and spiders; sometimes eats small crustaceans and mollusks.
Voice: harsh *chek* call, often doubled or tripled; song is a rapid, weak series of gurgling notes followed by a trill.
Similar Species: *Sedge Wren* (p. 264): brown-streaked back; streaked crown; less distinct buffy eyebrow; streaked wings. *House Wren* (p. 262): unstreaked, gray-brown upperparts; lacks bold eyebrow; pale buffy underparts.
Best Sites: widespread.

265

RED-WHISKERED BULBUL

Pycnonotus jocosus

The bulbuls are a family of small, active songbirds native to the Old World tropics. There are more than 100 species of bulbuls, but only the Red-whiskered Bulbul has established populations in California and Florida. Bulbuls were once popular as pets, but importation is now banned. • In Florida, a small number of Red-whiskered Bulbuls escaped at Kendall, a suburban area south of Miami, in 1960. The birds quickly began breeding. By 1970, the population was estimated at 250 individuals occupying about 2 square miles. There have been no subsequent censuses, but Red-whiskered Bulbuls persist at Kendall and appear to have expanded their range slightly. • Red-whiskered Bulbuls feed on a variety of fruit and seem to favor the berries of Brazilian pepper. Although bulbuls are considered agricultural pests in some parts of the world, their presence in Florida is benign, at least partially because the birds have never moved out of the heavily suburbanized area where they escaped more than 40 years ago.

ID: smallish, dark songbird with conspicuous crest; blackish brown upperparts; blackish head; narrow red ear patch or "whisker"; white cheek outlined in black; white throat; dingy underparts with blackish "spur" on upper breast; red undertail coverts; longish, black tail with mostly white tip.
Size: *L* 7–8 in; *W* 11 in.
Status: uncommon permanent resident of suburban areas of Kendall south of Miami.
Habitat: residential areas with a variety of native and exotic fruiting and flowering plants.

Nesting: in a shrub or tree; in the fork of a branch; cup nest of grass and other plant material is decorated with debris, such as paper, plastic or bark; pair incubates 3 grayish or pinkish eggs, mottled with red or purple, for 12–14 days.
Feeding: plucks small fruits from vegetation; also sallies or gleans insects and eats nectar.
Voice: calls include chattering notes; song is a loud, clear musical whistle that rises and falls.
Similar Species: none.
Best Sites: various sites in Kendall.

GOLDEN-CROWNED KINGLET

Regulus satrapa

Kinglets are small, active songbirds that frequently flick their wings as they forage. Both of North America's two species are found in Florida. The Golden-crowned Kinglet is our smallest songbird, and, except for hummingbirds, it is Florida's smallest bird. It breeds in parts of southern Alaska, Canada and the northeastern and western continental U.S., and winters from southern Alaska and Canada through the U.S. to Mexico and Guatemala. • In Florida, this bird is an irruptive winter resident, although it is usually present in the Panhandle and northern peninsula. It is usually absent farther south in the peninsula, and it is unreported from the Keys. • In the northern parts of their wintering range, Golden-crowned Kinglets survive frigid winter temperatures by roosting together in groups on tree limbs or by using vacant squirrel nests. Like chickadees, kinglets can lower their body temperature at night to conserve energy.

ID: tiny, active songbird; boldly marked head; tiny bill; grayish green upperparts; orange and yellow (male) or yellow (female) crown patch bordered with black; white eyebrow; black eye line; white face with faint black "mustache"; gray underparts; black wing with 1 white bar.

Size: *L* 4 in; *W* 7 in.

Status: rare to uncommon irruptive resident from October to April in most years in the Panhandle and northern third of the peninsula; less predictable south to L. Okeechobee.

Habitat: virtually any wooded habitat, including suburban yards and city parks.

Nesting: does not breed in Florida.

Feeding: gleans or hover-gleans from vegetation; feeds on insects and spiders.

Voice: very high-pitched *see-see-see* call.

Similar Species: *Ruby-crowned Kinglet* (p. 268): bold, broken white eye ring; crown and face lack bold stripes.

Best Sites: fairly widespread.

267

RUBY-CROWNED KINGLET

Regulus calendula

In contrast to the Golden-crowned Kinglet, which is an irruptive winter resident primarily of the Panhandle, the Ruby-crowned Kinglet is found throughout Florida. It breeds across Alaska and Canada and in the northeastern and western continental U.S., and it winters in the U.S. and south to Mexico and Guatemala. In Florida, the Ruby-crowned Kinglet occurs throughout the Keys but is most numerous north of Lake Okeechobee. It is found among mixed flocks that contain species such as the Downy Woodpecker, Carolina Chickadee, Tufted Titmouse, Blue-gray Gnatcatcher, White-eyed Vireo, Blue-headed Vireo and several species of warbler. • Throughout most of the year, the male's colorful crown is impossible to see, hidden among the dull feathers on his head. It is only visible during courtship or when he is agitated, such as when he is mobbing a predator. • The Ruby-crowned Kinglet's frequent hovering and energetic wing-flicking set this tiny bird apart from look-alikes. The purpose of the constant wing-flicking behavior is not known.

ID: tiny, active songbird; broken eye ring; tiny bill; grayish green upperparts, including head; black wings with 2 white wing bars; pale greenish gray underparts. *Male:* red crown patch, usually concealed.
Size: L 4 in; W 7½ in.
Status: fairly common resident south to about Lake Okeechobee from October to April and rare farther south.
Habitat: any wooded habitat, including suburban yards and city parks.

Nesting: does not breed in Florida.
Feeding: gleans and hover-gleans vegetation; feeds on insects and spiders; sometimes eats fruit.
Voice: short *je-dit* call.
Similar Species: *Golden-crowned Kinglet* (p. 267): boldly striped crown and face; orange and yellow or yellow crown; lacks broken eye ring. Empidonax *flycatchers* (p. 227–28): eye ring complete in some species, absent in others; larger bill; very different foraging behavior.
Best Sites: widespread.

BLUE-GRAY GNATCATCHER

Polioptila caerulea

Gnatcatchers are small, long-tailed songbirds that are constantly in movement. North America's five species are all similar in plumage, shape and behavior, but only the Blue-gray Gnatcatcher is found in Florida. It breeds across the southern U.S. to Mexico and Belize and winters in the extreme southern U.S., the West Indies and Central America. In Florida, it breeds over most of the mainland, and it migrates and winters statewide. • The Blue-gray Gnatcatcher may forage high in the canopy, often holding its tail upward like a wren while uttering its high-pitched calls. • During winter, Blue-gray Gnatcatchers join roving flocks of other small land birds, such as Downy Woodpeckers, Tufted Titmice, Carolina Chickadees, White-eyed Vireos, Blue-headed Vireos and several species of warblers such as Yellow-rumped Warblers and Black-and-white Warblers. • Although the Blue-gray Gnatcatcher undoubtedly eats gnats, this food item is only a small part of its diet.

nonbreeding

ID: small, active songbird with long tail and tiny bill; blue-gray upperparts; white eye ring; pale throat and underparts; black tail with white outer feathers. *Breeding male:* black forehead.

Size: *L* 4½ in; *W* 6 in.

Status: fairly common to locally abundant permanent resident over most of the mainland, although generally rare in the north; more numerous during winter, especially in the south.

Habitat: most wooded habitats.

Nesting: on a branch; in a tree, often quite high; pair builds a compact cup of plant fibers and spider webs, decorates it with lichens and lines it with fine materials; female incubates 3–6 (usually 4 in Florida) brown-dotted, pale bluish white eggs for 11–15 days.

Feeding: gleans or hover-gleans vegetation for insects and spiders; also sallies for flying insects.

Voice: high-pitched *speee* call; song is a series of quiet, high-pitched *mew* and other notes

Similar Species: none.

Best Sites: widespread.

269

EASTERN BLUEBIRD

Sialia sialis

Bluebirds are thrushes that are named for the males' brilliant blue plumage. Only one of North America's three species is found regularly in Florida. The Eastern Bluebird breeds from southeastern Canada to El Salvador and Nicaragua, and it winters from the southeastern U.S. to Central America. In Florida, the Eastern Bluebird is a fairly common permanent resident throughout the Panhandle and the northern half of the peninsula. It was extirpated from the Long Pine Key area of Everglades NP in the 1960s, but populations have recently reestablished there. • In earlier decades, nesting competition with European Starlings and House Sparrows, both exotic species, reduced some bluebird populations. The establishment of "trails" of bluebird nest boxes mounted on fence posts along lightly traveled roadways in rural areas has aided in the recovery of this species.

Habitat: open pine flatwoods or sandhills, dry prairie and pastures with scattered trees or nest boxes.

Nesting: in a tree; in a natural cavity or nest box; female builds a cup nest of pine needles and grass stems and lines it with finer materials; mostly the female incubates 3–6 (usually 4–5) pale blue eggs for 13–15 days; 2–3 broods per year.

Feeding: swoops from a perch to capture prey on the ground; feeds on insects, spiders and berries.

Voice: common call is a pleasant *chur-lee*, often given in flight; song is a short series of rich musical notes.

Similar Species: *Blue Grosbeak* (p. 337) and *Indigo Bunting* (p. 338): thick bills; males are entirely blue or blue with orange wing bars; females are brown overall, with very little blue.

Best Sites: widespread.

ID: medium-sized songbird; blue wings; orange breast; white belly; upright posture; often perches on power lines. *Male:* bright blue upperparts; bright orange breast. *Female:* muted colors; brownish gray back and head. *Juvenile:* blue restricted to wings and tail; brown-spotted back, breast and belly.

Size: *L* 7 in; *W* 13 in.

Status: fairly common resident of the Panhandle and northern half of the peninsula; mostly restricted to the western half of the peninsula south of Lake Okeechobee; irruptive during winter, when it may reach the Keys.

VEERY

Catharus fuscescens

Thrushes are medium-sized songbirds with generally muted plumage, and they usually have spotted breasts. Although most nest in trees, thrushes spend much time foraging on the ground. In addition to the American Robin, five species of spotted thrushes are found in Florida, with three of them occurring solely during migration. The Veery is one of these three; it breeds across southern Canada and the northern continental U.S., and it winters in Brazil. • In Florida, the Veery occurs statewide during migration, and it is about equally numerous during spring and fall, although generally more coastal during spring. • Three races of the Veery have been found in Florida—*C. f. fuliginosus, C. f. fuscescens* and *C. f. subpallidus*—but they cannot be distinguished in the field. • The Veery is named after a note in its song. The scientific name *fuscescens*—Latin for "dusky"—is a strange choice for such a richly colored bird. • It is the most terrestrial of the spotted thrushes, foraging and nesting on the ground among tangled vegetation. Unlike the American Robin, which walks or runs, the Veery travels across the ground in short, springy hops.

ID: medium-sized thrush; rich rufous upperparts, including head; pale eye ring; white underparts except for buffy breast and throat with limited rufous markings.
Size: *L* 6½–7½ in; *W* 12 in.
Status: rare to uncommon migrant statewide; no winter records.
Habitat: any wooded habitat, especially where dense cover is provided.

Nesting: does not breed in Florida.
Feeding: gleans insects, spiders, worms and snails from the ground or leaf litter; also plucks fruit from trees or shrubs.
Voice: high, down slurred call note.
Similar Species: *Swainson's Thrush* (p. 273): duller, olive upperparts; buffy eye ring; bold blackish spotting on upper breast. *Hermit Thrush* (p. 274): little or no seasonal overlap; bold black spotting on breast; rusty tail.
Best Sites: widespread.

271

GRAY-CHEEKED THRUSH

Catharus minimus

The Gray-cheeked Thrush is an inconspicuous and skulking species that few birders in Florida regularly observe. A champion migrant, it breeds in subarctic Alaska and Canada and winters in Panama and South America. • In Florida, Gray-cheeked Thrushes are generally rare migrants statewide, roughly equally scarce during spring and fall. Most sightings involve a few birds, often among loose flocks of other thrushes, but there have been several counts of 40 or more Gray-cheeked Thrushes found at one site during a single day. The bulk of the spring migration takes place in late April and early May, and most fall migrants move through in early October. • The Gray-cheeked Thrush is well named; its face and breast are "cold" gray. By contrast the Veery, the Swainson's Thrush and the Hermit Thrush have "warm" buffy tones.

ID: medium-sized thrush; olive brown upperparts, including tail; grayish face with indistinct gray eye ring; pale throat; dense black spotting on breast; grayish flanks.

Size: *L* 7–8 in; *W* 13 in.

Status: rare migrant statewide from April to May and from August to October.

Habitat: any wooded habitat, especially where dense cover is provided.

Nesting: does not breed in Florida.

Feeding: gleans insects, spiders, worms and snails from the ground or leaf litter; also plucks fruit from trees or shrubs.

Voice: downslurred *queep* daytime call and descending *spee-a* nocturnal flight call.

Similar Species: *Swainson's Thrush* (p. 273): buffy eye ring and breast. *Hermit Thrush* (p. 274): little or no seasonal overlap; brighter upperparts; buffy breast and flanks; rusty tail.

Best Sites: fairly widespread.

SWAINSON'S THRUSH

Catharus ustulatus

The Swainson's Thrush breeds across most of Alaska, Canada and the Rocky Mountains, and it winters from Mexico to Brazil and Argentina. In Florida, it is a fairly common migrant statewide. It is found mostly coastally during spring but statewide during fall. • Among the spotted thrushes, the Swainson's Thrush may be the most numerous species in our state; only the Veery approaches it in abundance. Skilled observers who know its distinctive nocturnal flight call may identify dozens of individuals during especially heavy flights, but few birders ever see more than a few individuals on any day. • The Swainson's Thrush was named in honor of the English naturalist William Swainson (1789–1855), as were the Swainson's Hawk and the Swainson's Warbler. • Veeries and Swainson's Thrushes are reported on Christmas Bird Counts in Florida nearly annually, but no verified winter record exists for either species, or for Gray-cheeked Thrushes. Any suspected observation of these three species in our state from December to February should be photographed or videotaped.

ID: medium-sized thrush; olive brown upperparts, including tail; buffy face, "spectacles" and throat; white belly and undertail covert; olive flanks and dense black spotting on buffy breast.
Size: *L* 7 in; *W* 12 in.
Status: fairly common migrant statewide from April to May and from September to October, when it is more numerous and widespread.
Habitat: any wooded habitat, especially where dense cover is provided.
Nesting: does not breed in Florida.
Feeding: gleans insects, spiders, worms and snails from the ground or leaf litter; also plucks fruit from trees or shrubs.

Voice: sharp *whit* call; nocturnal flight call is a distinct *eep*.
Similar Species: *Gray-cheeked Thrush* (p. 272): very similar, but with gray eye ring and cheek; less buffy breast. *Hermit Thrush* (p. 274): little or no seasonal overlap; rusty tinge on upperparts, especially on tail and primaries. *Veery* (p. 271): noticeably rusty upperparts; faint rusty eye ring; more buffy breast with no bold spots.
Best Sites: widespread.

HERMIT THRUSH

Catharus guttatus

The Hermit Thrush is unique among the spotted thrushes in being the only species that winters in North America. It breeds in Alaska, southern Canada and the northeastern and western continental U.S., and it winters from British Columbia and Ontario south to Guatemala and El Salvador. In Florida, it winters statewide, but it is most numerous in the Panhandle and the northern peninsula and is least numerous in the Keys. • Hermit Thrushes migrate later in fall and earlier in spring than do the other spotted thrushes. • On its breeding grounds, this thrush is considered to be one of the finest singers of all of North America's birds, but the song is rarely heard in Florida. When alarmed, the Hermit Thrush flicks its wings, raises its tail and utters harsh *chuck* notes. • True to its common name, the Hermit Thrush is always encountered singly, never in groups.

ID: medium-sized thrush; brown upperparts, including head; white eye ring; white underparts with buffy flanks and black spotting on throat and breast; rusty wings and tail.

Size: *L* 7 in; *W* 11½ in.

Status: fairly common resident south through the central peninsula from October to April, uncommon farther south in the peninsula and rare in the Keys.

Habitat: most brushy or wooded habitats with leaf litter, especially near water.

Nesting: does not breed in Florida.

Feeding: gleans insects, spiders, worms and snails from the ground or leaf litter; also plucks fruit from trees or shrubs.

Voice: dry *chuck* call.

Similar Species: *Swainson's Thrush* (p. 273): little or no seasonal overlap; olive brown upperparts, including tail, have no rusty tone; warm buff face. *Veery* (p. 271): little or no seasonal overlap; rich rufous upperparts; buffy breast lightly marked with brown. *Gray-cheeked Thrush* (p. 272): little or no seasonal overlap; olive brown upperparts, including tail, have no rusty tone; gray cheek; lacks conspicuous eye ring. *Fox Sparrow:* rare; found only in northern Florida; stockier build; conical bill; rusty streaking on breast.

Best Sites: widespread.

WOOD THRUSH

Hylocichla mustelina

O f the six species of spotted thrushes that are found in Florida, only the Wood Thrush remains to nest here. It breeds in the eastern U.S. and extreme southeastern Canada, and it winters from Mexico to Panama and Colombia. In Florida, it breeds in the north, migrates statewide and winters on very rare occasions throughout the state. • Wood Thrushes are found in moist deciduous woodlands and suburban areas that provide extensive cover. • The song of the Wood Thrush is a rich series of flutelike and bubbly notes that may be heard from April to August. The structure of the male's syrinx (its "voice box"; the avian equivalent of the mammal's larynx) allows it to sing different notes simultaneously, a trait shared by some other birds, including other thrushes.

ID: medium-sized thrush with bright rusty nape and crown; white underparts boldly spotted with black; rufous back and wings; white eye ring; dusky cheek; rufous tail.

Size: *L* 8 in; *W* 13 in.

Status: fairly common breeding resident of the Panhandle and less numerous south to Gainesville; rare migrant statewide, more frequently observed during fall; rare and probably irregular statewide during winter.

Habitat: *Breeding:* moist, deciduous woodlands or mixed forests, including treed neighborhoods. *In migration:* any wooded habitat.

Nesting: low in a deciduous tree; in a fork; female builds a bulky cup nest of grass and twigs held together with mud and lines it with finer materials; female incubates 3–4 pale greenish blue eggs for 13–14 days; 2 broods per year.

Feeding: forages on the ground or gleans foliage; feeds on insects, spiders, worms and snails; also eats fruit during fall and winter.

Voice: calls include *pit-pit* and a buzzy *jeeen* nocturnal flight call; beautiful song is a series of haunting, flutelike phrases of 3–5 notes, each at a different pitch and followed by a trill.

Similar Species: *Other thrushes* (p. 271–276): olive brown or brown upperparts; no contrast between back and nape; smaller, less distinct spots on underparts. *Brown Thrasher* (p. 279): larger; larger bill; rufous upperparts; underparts heavily streaked with black; long tail.

Best Sites: fairly widespread.

275

AMERICAN ROBIN
Turdus migratorius

Despite its name, the American Robin is actually a thrush. English colonists named it after the Robin (*Erithacus rubecula*) of their native land, because both species have bright orange breasts, but the similarity ends there. The two species are only distantly related. • The American Robin is one of North America's most familiar birds. It breeds throughout North America, from Alaska to Mexico, and it winters from the continental U.S. to Mexico and Guatemala. In Florida, it breeds sparingly in the Panhandle and northern peninsula, but it occurs statewide during winter. • Although it is a well-known habit farther north, American Robins are seldom seen feeding on earthworms in Florida, probably because worms are scarce in sandy soil. Instead, robins feed heavily on berries, especially those of holly and Brazilian pepper.

ID: rather large song-bird with orange underparts; slate upperparts, darker on the head; white spots around eyes; yellow bill; slate tail with white tips to outer feathers. *Juvenile:* paler upperparts, with pale tips to feathers on back and wing coverts; darkly spotted, pale orange breast.
Size: *L* 10 in; *W* 17 in.
Status: rare and local breeding resident of the Panhandle, even rarer in the northern half of the peninsula; irruptive resident statewide from October to March, with abundance varying considerably from year to year.

Habitat: *Breeding:* open woodlands, including suburban yards and city parks. *Winter:* any wooded habitat; roosting is often on or near the ground in dense saw palmetto clumps.
Nesting: in a tree; sturdy cup nest of twigs and grass is cemented with mud; female incubates 3–5 (usually 4) light blue eggs for 12–14 days; 2–3 broods each year.
Feeding: forages on the ground for earth-worms and insects; also gleans berries from trees and shrubs, especially during winter.
Voice: rapid *tut-tut-tut* call; song is an evenly spaced warble often written as *cheerily cheer-up cheerio*.
Similar Species: none; dark upperparts and orange underparts are distinctive.
Best Sites: widespread.

276

GRAY CATBIRD

Dumetella carolinensis

The Gray Catbird is a member of the Mimidae, a family of medium-sized, long-tailed, ground-loving birds that can mimic sounds. The Gray Catbird breeds in southern Canada and across most of the continental U.S., and it winters from the Southeast and the West Indies south to Panama. In Florida, it breeds sparingly in the Panhandle and northern third of the peninsula, but it occurs statewide during migration and winter. • Gray Catbirds are often hidden by the dense vegetation that they inhabit, but their presence is revealed by their frequent *mew* notes, which are reminiscent of a cat. These birds can sing two notes at once because both sides of the syrinx can operate independently. • Although they now breed rather widely in northern Florida, Gray Catbirds were not documented as breeding birds in our state until 1973. The reasons for this recent colonization of Florida are not known.

ID: medium-sized songbird of dense thickets; dark sooty gray overall, except for black cap and rusty undertail coverts; black eyes, bill, legs and feet.

Size: *L* 8½–9 in; *W* 11 in.

Status: fairly common to abundant migrant statewide from September to April; uncommon local breeding resident of the Panhandle and northern third of the peninsula; occasional south to Lake Okeechobee.

Habitat: dense thickets and shrubby or brushy fields or hedgerows, often near water.

Nesting: in a dense shrub; bulky cup nest is loosely built with twigs, leaves and grass and lined with finer material; female incubates 3–4 greenish blue eggs for 12–13 days.

Feeding: forages on or near the ground; feeds on a wide variety of insects, spiders and fruit.

Voice: common call is a catlike *mew;* song is a variety of warbles, squeaks and mimicked phrases repeated only once.

Similar Species: none; plumage coloration is unique.

Best Sites: widespread.

277

NORTHERN MOCKINGBIRD

Mimus polyglottos

The Northern Mockingbird is the state bird of Florida. Although it is not showy, its vocal repertoire and ability to survive—even thrive—in urban areas justifies such a title. The Northern Mockingbird is largely resident across much of the continental U.S. and the West Indies and south to Central America. In Florida, it is among the most conspicuous and wide-ranging of our birds, occurring commonly even in the most urban regions. • The Northern Mockingbird is renowned for its mimicry abilities; its scientific name translates to "many-tongued mimic." More than 400 different song types have been attributed to this bird. It can imitate almost any sound, from the songs or calls of other birds and animals to musical instruments. • Northern Mockingbirds have the trait of curiously lifting their wings in a display known as "wing flashing"; this behavior's purpose is not clear.

ID: medium-sized, conspicuous songbird; gray back, nape and crown; pale face; yellow eyes; white throat; whitish underparts; black wing with 2 narrow white wing bars; long, blackish tail with white outer feathers. *Juvenile:* paler overall; lightly spotted breast. *In flight:* large white patch at base of primaries.
Size: *L* 10 in; *W* 14 in.
Status: common to abundant permanent resident of urban and suburban areas; far less common in natural habitats; avoids deep forests and extensively open habitats.

Habitat: any area with at least a scattering of trees or shrubs.
Nesting: in a shrub or small tree; cup nest of twigs is lined with finer materials; female incubates 3–4 brown-blotched, bluish gray to greenish eggs for 12–13 days; multiple broods per year.
Feeding: forages on or near the ground; feeds on a variety of berries and other fruit plus insects and other invertebrates.
Voice: calls include a harsh *check*; song is a medley of an amazing variety of mimicked phrases that are often repeated 3 or more times.
Similar Species: *Loggerhead Shrike* (p. 237): smaller; black wings; black mask; thick, hooked bill.
Best Sites: widespread.

BROWN THRASHER

Toxostoma rufum

Thrashers are large songbirds that spend most of their time on or near the ground. Of North America's eight species, three are found in Florida but two are rare. The Brown Thrasher breeds in extreme southern Canada and the eastern half of the U.S., and it winters in the Southeast. In Florida, it is a fairly common permanent resident throughout the peninsula but is rare and local in the Keys. • Unlike the Northern Mockingbird, the Brown Thrasher does not survive in developed areas, perhaps because its ground-dwelling habits put it at greater risk from cats and cars. • The Brown Thrasher is an expert mimic, with the most extensive repertoire of any North American bird. It is estimated to produce up to 3000 distinctive song combinations! Unlike mockingbirds, which tend to repeat phrases three times each, the Brown Thrasher repeats each phrase only once.

ID: large, terrestrial songbird; long tail; rich rufous upperparts; grayish cheek; yellow eyes; dark "mustache"; downcurved bill; rufous wing with 2 white bars; pale underparts with blackish streaking.

Size: *L* 11½ in; *W* 13 in.

Status: fairly common to common permanent resident throughout the mainland; rare in the Keys; most numerous during winter, with the arrival of northern breeders.

Habitat: dense thickets, citrus groves and woodland edges; generally away from suburbia.

Nesting: usually in a low shrub or tree; pair builds a cup nest of twigs and leaves and lines it with fine vegetation; pair incubates 4 bluish white to pale blue eggs, dotted with reddish brown, for 11–14 days.

Feeding: gleans the ground and vegetation or uses bill to toss aside leaf litter; feeds on insects, spiders, small reptiles or amphibians, fruit and seeds.

Voice: common call is a harsh *chuck;* song is a variety of phrases, with each phrase usually repeated once.

Similar Species: *Thrushes* (pp. 271–76): seasonal; dark eyes; shorter tails; all lack wing bars, rich rufous upperparts and bold black streaking on underparts.

Best Sites: widespread.

279

EUROPEAN STARLING

Sturnus vulgaris

Native to the Old World, the European Starling was intentionally introduced to our shores. In 1890 and 1891, 100 starlings were released into New York City as part of a plan to release into the U.S. all of the birds mentioned in William Shakespeare's works. The introduction succeeded dramatically, and more than 200 million starlings are believed to currently occupy the continent from southern Alaska to northern Mexico! • In Florida, European Starlings were first recorded at Amelia Island in 1918; they now are found throughout our state except for expansive natural areas such as Apalachicola National Forest–Tates Hell Swamp and Big Cypress Swamp–Everglades. • As cavity nesters, European Starlings have affected local populations of many species, such as woodpeckers, Great Crested Flycatchers and Eastern Bluebirds.

breeding

ID: medium-sized songbird with particularly short tail; pointed bill. *Breeding:* black body with purple iridescence on head and green iridescence on back and body; yellow bill; brown-spotted undertail coverts; pink legs. *Nonbreeding:* black body heavily spotted with white; black bill; rufous edges on wing feathers; black head heavily streaked with white. *Juvenile:* drab gray-brown overall with pale throat; dark bill.
Size: *L* 8½ in; *W* 16 in.
Status: fairly common permanent resident mostly of developed areas statewide; locally abundant during winter with the addition of northern breeders.

Habitat: generally in urban and suburban areas; found in virtually any wooded habitat except deep forests.
Nesting: in a natural or artificial cavity or nest box; cavity filled with a variety of natural or artificial materials, such as plastic; mostly the female incubates 4–6 bluish to greenish white eggs for 12–14 days.
Feeding: forages mostly on the ground; gleans insects, other invertebrates, berries, seeds and discarded human food.
Voice: variety of whistles, squeaks and gurgles; imitates other birds.
Similar Species: yellow-billed breeding adult is distinctive, as is white-spotted winter plumage. *Brown-headed Cowbird* (p. 350): female resembles juvenile starling but with more conical bill and longer tail.
Best Sites: widespread.

COMMON MYNA

Acridotheres tristis

Mynas belong to the same family as the starlings. Two species native to Asia are found in North America, and both are restricted to Florida. The Common Myna is native from the Middle East to China and Southeast Asia. It is also found in Florida, Hawaii, Africa, Australia, New Zealand and Oceania, as a consequence of intentional or accidental releases. • In Florida, Common Mynas were first found at Miami in 1983. Since that time, they have colonized much of the urban strip between West Palm Beach and Homestead and have established "outposts" at Clewiston and Sanford. The population in Florida has never been studied, but it is thought to number in the thousands of individuals. • Common Mynas are found mostly in shopping centers, where they often nest in the lettering on buildings and stroll the parking lots searching for food.

ID: medium-sized, terrestrial songbird found in urban areas; brown back; blackish head; yellow eyes and bill; bare, yellow wattles; black wings with white primary patches; brown underparts with white undertail coverts; black tail with white tips. *In flight:* strong but floppy flight; mostly white underwings.
Size: *L* 9½ in; *W* 18 in; male is larger than female.
Status: locally fairly common permanent resident from West Palm Beach to Homestead; range expanding and numbers increasing.

Habitat: urban and suburban areas, predominantly shopping centers.
Nesting: in signs, streetlights and other artificial cavities; pair lines a cavity with grass, wood, feathers, plastic and hair; pair incubate 3–5 glossy, turquoise to blue-green eggs for 14–16 days.
Feeding: walks on the ground searching for insects, seeds and fruit; also takes human handouts—loves french fries!
Voice: song is a pleasant warbling.
Similar Species: *Hill Myna* (p. 282): arboreal; nests in natural cavities; more limited range; entirely black body, including underwings and tail.
Best Sites: West Palm Beach to Homestead.

281

HILL MYNA

Gracula religiosa

The Hill Myna, popularly known as "Talking Myna," was very popular as a pet in the 1960s. Like the Common Myna, it is native to the Old World. Its natural range is India, China and the East Indies, but exotic populations are found in Florida and Puerto Rico. • In Florida, Hill Mynas were discovered around West Palm Beach in 1968, presumably as a result of escaped pets. In less than 10 years, they were found sparingly from West Palm Beach to Miami, and it appeared that they were becoming established. However, by the late 1980s, Hill Mynas were restricted to parts of the Miami metropolitan area, and they still persist in the region. There has been no study of Hill Mynas, but the population probably numbers in the low hundreds. • Unlike Common Mynas, which forage primarily on the ground, Hill Mynas are exclusively arboreal.

ID: medium-sized, arboreal songbird found in urban areas; black body; large white patch at base of primaries; black eyes; yellow wattles; orange bill; yellow legs and feet.
Size: *L* 10½ in; *W* 20 in.
Status: uncommon and local permanent resident of parts of the Miami metropolitan area, including Cutler and Kendall.
Habitat: urban and suburban areas with extensive foliage, especially fruiting trees and palms.

Nesting: in a palm snag; in a natural cavity; pair lines the cavity with grass, wood and other items; pair incubate 3–5 glossy, turquoise to blue-green eggs for 14–16 days.
Feeding: exclusively arboreal; feeds primarily on fruit.
Voice: wide repertoire of whistled tunes and twitters; mimics a variety of sounds, including human speech.
Similar Species: *Common Myna* (p. 281): often terrestrial; nests in artificial cavities; brown body with black head; yellow eyes; white tail tip.
Best Sites: Kendall Baptist Hospital; Matheson Hammock Park.

AMERICAN PIPIT

Anthus rubescens

Pipits are sparrowlike, terrestrial songbirds with long, slender bills and white outer tail feathers. They walk on the ground and wag their tails almost constantly. Of the six species in North America, two are found in Florida. • The American Pipit breeds in Alaska, northern and western Canada and locally in the western U.S., and it winters coastally from British Columbia and New York through the West Indies to Mexico and Guatemala. In Florida, the American Pipit is a winter resident throughout the mainland. • These birds are fond of muddy freshwater areas such as lakeshores and dairies but are usually not found on coastal mudflats. They are often located by their distinctive *pip-it, pip-it* calls, which they usually utter in flight. • Until recently the American Pipit was combined with an Old World species, the Water Pipit *(A. spinoletta)*, but the two forms differ strongly genetically.

ID: sparrowlike songbird found in muddy habitats; usually found in flocks; grayish brown, faintly streaked upperparts; white eyebrow; white throat with black "mustache"; grayish brown wing with 2 faint white bars; pale buff underparts heavily streaked with black; blackish tail with white outer feathers; dark legs and feet.
Size: L 6–7 in; W 10½ in.
Status: fairly common resident throughout the peninsula from October to April, although less numerous in the south; very rare in the Keys.
Habitat: favors freshwater muddy habitats, such as lake or pond shores, dairy farms and cattle feedlots, wastewater treatment facilities and agricultural fields.
Nesting: does not breed in Florida.
Feeding: gleans the ground or very shallow water; feeds on insects, spiders and seeds.
Voice: *pip-it, pip-it* flight call.
Similar Species: *Vesper Sparrow* (p. 323): hops rather than walks; does not wag tail; found in brushy fields.
Best Sites: widespread.

CEDAR WAXWING
Bombycilla cedrorum

Waxwings are sleek-plumaged songbirds with distinct crests and yellow-tipped tails. The tips of their secondary flight feathers appear as if they are coated in red wax. Two species are found in North America, with one of them occurring in Florida. • The Cedar Waxwing breeds across southern Canada and the northern continental U.S., and it winters from extreme southern Canada to Panama. In Florida, it is an irruptive winter resident throughout the mainland, with annual numbers varying considerably. • Cedar Waxwings often do not arrive in numbers until December or even later, in spring, when they are found in tight flocks of dozens or hundreds of individuals. Their high-pitched trilling calls are distinctive. While in Florida, Cedar Waxwings feed mostly on fruit, so they are frequently observed in suburban neighborhoods that contain hollies and other fruit-bearing trees and shrubs.

ID: smallish, slender-crested songbird usually found in tight flocks; gray rump; rich brown upperparts, including head and crest; black mask and throat separated by white streak; gray wings with brown upperwing coverts; rich brown breast shades to pale yellow belly; white undertail coverts; black tail with gray base and black and yellow tip. *Juvenile:* dull grayish brown above; pale throat; white underparts streaked with grayish brown.
Size: *L* 7 in; *W* 12 in.
Status: irruptive winter resident statewide from October to May; most numerous during late winter or spring; usually common in the Panhandle and less numerous in the peninsula; very rare in the Keys.
Habitat: virtually any wooded habitat, especially those with abundant fruiting trees or shrubs.
Nesting: does not breed in Florida.
Feeding: gleans berries and other fruit from foliage; also gleans insects and sallies for flying insects.
Voice: faint, high-pitched, trilled whistle, often given in flight.
Similar Species: none.
Best Sites: widespread.

BLUE-WINGED WARBLER

Vermivora pinus

This species introduces the wood-warblers, a family of 115 species of small, active insectivorous birds, mostly with bright plumages. The Blue-winged Warbler breeds from the northeastern U.S. to northern Alabama and Georgia. It winters in Mexico and Central America. In Florida, it is a rare migrant statewide and a rare, but perhaps regular, winter resident in the extreme south. • Blue-winged Warblers hybridize with Golden-winged Warblers and produce two types of fertile young. "Brewster's Warblers" resemble Blue-winged Warblers, and "Lawrence's Warblers" look more like Golden-winged Warblers. "Brewster's Warblers" are produced directly from a pairing of "purer" individuals of each species, whereas "Lawrence's Warblers" are the result of a pairing between a "pure" adult and a "Brewster's Warbler."

ID: small songbird with bright yellow under-parts. *Male:* grayish green back and nape; yellow head; black eye line extending to bill; blue-gray wing with 2 broad, white wing bars; white undertail coverts. *Female* and *juvenile:* duller overall; less conspicuous wing bars.
Size: *L* 4½–5 in; *W* 7½ in.
Status: rare migrant statewide from April to May and from August to October; rare but possibly regular winter resident of the extreme southern peninsula and the Keys.
Habitat: *In migration:* any wooded habitat. *Winter:* favors tropical hardwood hammocks.

Nesting: does not breed in Florida.
Feeding: gleans insects and spiders from foliage.
Voice: sharp *chick* call.
Similar Species: *"Brewster's Warbler"* (hybrid): variable; may have pale or white underparts or yellow wing bars. *"Lawrence's Warbler"* (hybrid): usually shows black throat; often has yellow wing bars. *Cerulean Warbler* (p. 304): juvenile has bluish green upperparts, bold, yellowish eyebrow and pale buff underparts with some grayish streaking on flanks. *Pine Warbler* (p. 299): larger; much larger bill; lacks black eye line; "dirty" yellow underparts; olive streaking on breast and flanks.
Best Sites: widespread.

GOLDEN-WINGED WARBLER

Vermivora chrysoptera

The Golden-winged Warbler, the other parent (along with the Blue-winged Warbler) of "Brewster's" and "Lawrence's" warbler hybrids, is a declining species. The causes of its decline include habitat loss, interbreeding with Blue-winged Warblers and brood parasitism by Brown-headed Cowbirds. • Golden-winged Warblers breed in extreme southeastern Canada and the northeastern continental U.S., and they winter from Mexico and Guatemala to Colombia and Venezuela. In Florida, they are rare migrants statewide and are perhaps a bit more numerous along the Gulf Coast during spring than elsewhere in our state. An indication of their rarity is that the highest one-day count from any location is six individuals; most observations are of singles. • Golden-winged Warblers are active foragers, often hanging upside down to investigate clumps of dead leaves.

ID: small arboreal songbird; yellow wing bars joined to form single patch. *Male:* gray back and nape; yellow crown; white eyebrow and "mustache"; black cheek, throat and breast; otherwise pale gray underparts; gray wing with yellow panel. *Female* and *juvenile:* gray replaces black on head and breast.
Size: *L* 4½–5 in; *W* 7½ in.

Status: rare migrant statewide from April to May and from August to October; no winter reports.
Habitat: any wooded habitat.
Nesting: does not breed in Florida.
Feeding: actively gleans insects and spiders from foliage.
Voice: sharp *chick* call.
Similar Species: *"Lawrence's Warbler"* (hybrid): usually shows yellow underparts and 2 white wing bars. *Carolina Chickadee* (p. 255): black crown; lacks white eyebrow and yellow wing patch.
Best Sites: fairly widespread.

TENNESSEE WARBLER

Vermivora peregrina

The Tennessee Warbler breeds in boreal forests across Canada and in the extreme northern continental U.S., and it winters from Mexico and the West Indies to northern South America. In Florida, it is a statewide migrant and a very rare winter resident. • During migration, the Tennessee Warbler is more numerous during fall than spring. This rather late fall migrant is most numerous in Florida during the first half of October, with a few birds often still moving through in early November. • Fall-plumaged Tennessee Warblers are very similar to nonbreeding Philadelphia Vireos, which also migrate through Florida primarily during the first half of October, but the warblers are much more numerous. • Although they nest on the ground, Tennessee Warblers are strictly arboreal while in Florida, often feeding in the outer canopy of trees. • Tennessee Warbler populations fluctuate according to the availability of spruce budworms, their primary prey on their breeding grounds.

breeding

ID: small arboreal songbird with relatively nondescript plumage. *Breeding male:* yellow-green upperparts; gray nape and crown, white eyebrow; black eye line; dusky ear patch; white throat; short, thin bill; white underparts. *Breeding female:* resembles male, but with duller upperparts; yellow wash on breast and eyebrow. *Nonbreeding:* olive brown upperparts; buffy eyebrow, breast and belly; white undertail coverts.
Size: *L* 4½–5 in; *W* 8 in.
Status: uncommon to fairly common statewide migrant from September to November; rare statewide migrant from March to May; 2 verifiable winter records.

Habitat: any wooded habitat, especially oak woodlands.
Nesting: does not breed in Florida.
Feeding: gleans foliage for insects and spiders; feeds on fruit and nectar during winter.
Voice: high, sharp *chip* call.
Similar Species: *Philadelphia Vireo* (p. 241): nonbreeding is very similar, but with slower, more deliberate movements, thicker bill, blackish forehead and yellow throat. *Orange-crowned Warbler* (p. 288): tends to forage low to the ground; dull streaking on breast and flanks; yellow undertail coverts.
Best Sites: widespread.

287

ORANGE-CROWNED WARBLER
Vermivora celata

A nondescript bird, the Orange-crowned Warbler causes identification problems for many birders. • This species breeds in Alaska, Canada and the western U.S., and it winters along the coast from British Columbia and Virginia through the southern U.S. to Mexico and Guatemala. • In Florida, it is an uncommon migrant and winter resident statewide. • Most individuals seen in our state are dull olive, but sometimes a rather bright yellow individual is found. • In other states, Orange-crowned Warblers routinely feed on sap or insects attracted to the sap wells drilled by Yellow-bellied Sapsuckers, but this behavior has not been reported in Florida. • The word *celata* is derived from the Latin word for "hidden," a reference to this bird's inconspicuous crown patch.

ID: small warbler with variable, drab plumage; rather deliberate foraging movements; greenish gray upperparts; faint pale eyebrow; dark eye line divides pale eye ring; grayish green underparts with yellowish throat and undertail coverts; faint streaking on breast and flanks; seldom-seen orange crown patch. *First-winter:* grayish green upperparts; grayish head; whitish throat; grayish underparts with faint streaking on breast and flanks.
Size: L 5 in; W 7 in.
Status: uncommon migrant and resident statewide from October to April.

Habitat: any wooded habitat, especially oak woodlands.
Nesting: does not breed in Florida.
Feeding: gleans foliage for insects and spiders, fruit and sap; may hover-glean or probe clumps of dead leaves.
Voice: clear, sharp *chip* call.
Similar Species: *Tennessee Warbler* (p. 287): juvenile often has more distinct eyebrow and no split eye ring, narrow, pale wing bars, with undertail coverts always paler than rest of underparts. *Yellow Warbler* (p. 290): juvenile is very drab, without eyebrow or eye line, and has complete eye ring. *Common Yellowthroat* (p. 314): juvenile has no eyebrow, eye line or breast streaking and has complete eye ring.
Best Sites: widespread.

NORTHERN PARULA

Parula americana

The rising, buzzy song of the Northern Parula is one of the most characteristic avian sounds of Florida's woodlands. • This species breeds in extreme southeastern Canada and over much of the eastern U.S., and it winters from Florida and Mexico to Guatemala and Belize. In Florida, the status of the Northern Parulas varies by region. It migrates statewide, breeds south to Big Cypress Swamp and winters in the southern half of the peninsula and in the Keys. • The parula is a common resident of habitats that contains an abundance of Spanish moss, in which it nests. • Parulas are small birds, even by wood-warbler standards. Their name is a form of *Parus*—which, until a few years ago was the genus of chickadees and titmice—and means "little *Parus*" or "little chickadee." "Parula" has two correct pronunciations, *PAIR-yuh-luh* and *PAIR-uh-luh*. The pronunciation *puh-ROO-luh*, although popular, is incorrect.

ID: small arboreal warbler; yellowish green back; blue-gray head; conspicuous white eye crescents; yellow lower mandible, throat and breast; bold, white wing bars on blue-gray wings; white belly and undertail coverts. *Male:* narrow, dusky blue and rufous breast band.
Size: *L* 4½ in; *W* 7 in.
Status: fairly common migrant statewide; fairly common breeding resident of the Panhandle and the northern half of the peninsula but rare in the southern half; rare winter resident in the southern half of the peninsula and the Keys.

Habitat: *Breeding:* oak hammocks, riparian woodlands, cypress swamps or other woodlands festooned with Spanish moss. *In migration* and *winter:* any wooded habitat, especially oak woodlands.
Nesting: pair builds a cup nest within hanging clumps of Spanish moss; pair incubates 4–5 brown-marked, whitish eggs for 12–14 days.
Feeding: forages for insects, spiders and other invertebrates by hovering, gleaning or hawking; occasionally eats fruit.
Voice: clear *chip* call; song is a rising, buzzy trill ending with a lower-pitched *zip*.
Similar Species: none; small size, bluish gray head, yellow-green back, white eye crescents and yellow breast are diagnostic.
Best Sites: widespread.

YELLOW WARBLER

Dendroica petechia

The Yellow Warbler breeds across North America, except the extreme south, and into Mexico and the West Indies. It winters from the southernmost regions of the U.S. to Peru and Venezuela. • In Florida, two separate Yellow Warbler populations are found. More northerly breeding races, primarily the eastern-breeding *D. p. aestiva*, migrate statewide, whereas the West Indian race, *D. p. gundlachi*, is a permanent resident in the extreme south. Except for some *D. p. gundlachi* males that have chestnut on the crown, the Yellow Warbler races cannot be conclusively distinguished by plumage.

breeding

ID: small arboreal songbird. *Male:* yellow overall, darker on upperparts, including nape and crown (*D. p. gundlachi* males may have chestnut crown); black eyes; bold, orange streaking on breast and flanks; darker wing with 2 yellow wing bars. *Female:* less orange streaking, if any. *Juvenile:* plain buffy (*D. p. aestiva*) or gray (*D. p. gundlachi*) overall.
Size: *L* 5 in; *W* 8 in.
Status: *D. p. aestiva:* rare to uncommon migrant statewide from April to May and uncommon to fairly common, especially near water, from July to October.
D. p. gundlachi: uncommon permanent resident of mangrove forests in the extreme southern peninsula and the Keys, perhaps with some withdrawal during fall.

Habitat: *D. p. aestiva:* shrubby or wooded areas, especially near water. *D. p. gundlachi:* mangrove forests.
Nesting: *D. p. gundlachi:* in a mangrove; female builds a compact cup nest of seaweed and other plant material and lines it with feathers; female incubates 4–5 speckled or spotted, greenish white eggs for 11–12 days.
Feeding: gleans vegetation for insects and spiders; occasionally takes fruit.
Voice: clear, loud *chip* call; song is a series of 6–8 high, sweet notes with a rapid ending.
Similar Species: *Orange-crowned Warbler* (p. 288): little seasonal overlap; darker olive plumage overall; pale eyebrow; dark eye line; dusky, not orange, streaking on breast and flanks. *Common Yellowthroat* (p. 314): skulky female stays close to ground and has olive upperparts, including nape and crown.
Best Sites: widespread.

CHESTNUT-SIDED WARBLER

Dendroica pensylvanica

Most wood-warblers molt into a duller but still recognizable "winter" plumage after breeding, but the Chestnut-sided Warbler undergoes a dramatic transformation that causes its plumage in fall to bear little resemblance to its appearance in spring and summer. • In Florida, we seldom see the Chestnut-sided Warbler in its distinctive breeding plumage because its northern migration route is west of our state. We are much more likely to see it in fall, when it may have rusty colored flanks and resemble a fall-plumaged Bay-breasted Warbler. Good views of the head and underparts are necessary for correct identification, but body posture is also a helpful clue. A Chestnut-sided Warbler often feeds with its tail slightly raised and its wings held slightly away from its body, a posture not characteristic of the Bay-breasted Warbler. • This bird breeds in southeastern Canada and from the northeastern U.S. southward through the Appalachian Mountains. It winters from Mexico to Guatemala.

breeding

ID: small, arboreal songbird with 2 pale yellow wingbars. *Breeding:* rarely seen in Florida; yellow upperparts, with black streaking; yellow crown; white cheek partially framed by black; white underparts with chestnut flanks. *Nonbreeding:* yellow-green upperparts, usually with black streaking; yellow-green nape and crown; gray face with white eye ring; white throat; plain white underparts (female and juvenile) or with some chestnut on flanks (male).
Size: *L* 5 in; *W* 8 in.
Status: rare to very rare migrant statewide from April to May and uncommon from September to October; 1 verified winter record.
Habitat: any wooded habitat, especially oak woodlands.
Nesting: does not breed in Florida.
Feeding: gleans foliage or flycatches; feeds on insects and spiders.
Voice: clear *chip* call; song, rarely heard in Florida, is *I'm so pleased to meetcha.*
Similar Species: yellow-green upperparts, gray face with white eye ring and yellow wing bars are generally diagnostic. *Bay-breasted Warbler* (p. 302): nonbreeding plumage can be very similar during fall, but with duller upperparts, faint buffy eyebrow, buffy underparts, including undertail coverts and no eye ring.
Best Sites: widespread.

291

MAGNOLIA WARBLER

Dendroica magnolia

This species was originally called the Black-and-Yellow Warbler by its discoverer, Alexander Wilson, but the name "Magnolia Warbler" was eventually chosen because the first specimen was collected from a magnolia. It is a striking warbler during spring but molts into a much duller nonbreeding plumage. The Magnolia Warbler breeds across southern Canada and the extreme northern continental U.S. It winters from Florida, Mexico and the West Indies to Panama. In Florida, it is a statewide migrant and winters in small numbers in the extreme south. • This warbler's southbound migration route is west of the northbound route, so we see more Magnolia Warblers during fall than during spring. • It is an active feeder, often fanning its tail to reveal the distinctive white band on the uppertail and the equally characteristic two-tone undertail.

breeding

ID: small, arboreal songbird with unique tail pattern: yellow rump; diagnostic black uppertail with white spots and white undertail with black tip. *Breeding male:* black upperparts; gray crown; black mask; white eyebrow and lower eye arc; yellow throat; dark wing with white patch; yellow underparts with heavy black streaking. *Breeding female:* duller plumage. *Nonbreeding and juvenile:* gray upperparts may have black streaking; gray head; white eye ring; yellow throat; gray wing with 2 white wing bars; yellow underparts may have black streaking.
Size: *L* 4½–5 in; *W* 7½ in.

Status: rare migrant statewide from April to May and uncommon from September to October; rare winter resident in the southern third of the peninsula and the Keys.
Habitat: any wooded habitat, especially oak woodlands.
Nesting: does not breed in Florida.
Feeding: gleans vegetation and flycatches; feeds on insects and spiders; may also eat fruit.
Voice: hoarse *vink* call.
Similar Species: unique uppertail and undertail patterns. *Cape May Warbler* (p. 293): nonbreeding bird has no eye ring but has pale eyebrow and often-pale underparts. *Prairie Warbler* (p. 300): bobs tail; lacks eyering and yellow rump; yellow lower eye arc.
Best Sites: widespread.

CAPE MAY WARBLER

Dendroica tigrina

The Cape May Warbler's scientific name translates to "little tiger of the trees," referring to the stripes on the underparts of the adults. • This warbler breeds across much of Canada and the extreme northern fringe of the eastern U.S. It winters in Florida and the West Indies and throughout Central America. In Florida, the Cape May Warblers is a fairly common spring migrant and is generally uncommon during fall. It winters in small numbers in the extreme south. • This bird's semitubular tongue is unique among wood-warblers and allows it to feed on nectar and fruit juices. • On its breeding grounds, the Cape May Warbler requires mature forests that support an abundance of canopy-dwelling insects, especially the larvae of spruce budworm. This warbler fledges more young during years of budworm outbreaks.

ID: very active warbler; yellow rump. *Male:* grayish yellow back with bold, black streaks; yellow nape; blackish crown; rusty cheek; yellow "mustache"; yellow throat and underparts heavily streaked with black; large white wing patch. *Female:* much duller; 2 indistinct wing bars; gray nape, crown and cheek. *Juvenile:* grayish overall; pale yellow rump and ear patch; indistinct streaking on underparts.
Size: *L* 4½–5½ in; *W* 8 in.
Status: fairly common spring migrant except in the Panhandle; generally rare fall migrant except common along the southern Atlantic Coast; generally rare resident of Everglades NP and the Keys from September to April.
Habitat: *Winter:* mostly in mangroves and hardwood hammocks. *In migration:* any wooded habitat.
Nesting: does not breed in Florida.
Feeding: gleans foliage for insects and spiders; eats figs and other fruit during winter.
Voice: high-pitched *tsee* call.
Similar Species: *Prairie Warbler* (p. 300): female wags tail and has olive rump, with black streaking on underparts limited to flanks. *Yellow-rumped Warbler* (p. 295): nonbreeding bird is very similar to Cape May juvenile, but with browner plumage, more distinct yellow rump, partial white eye ring and yellow flanks.
Best Sites: widespread.

BLACK-THROATED BLUE WARBLER

Dendroica caerulescens

A striking example of sexual dimorphism, Black-throated Blue Warbler males and females are so different in appearance that early ornithologists thought that they were separate species! Whereas the males are boldly marked in blue, black and white, the females resemble drab vireos. However, most females share the small white wing patch displayed by the males—a diagnostic mark of this species. • Black-throated Blue Warblers breed in southeastern Canada and the northeastern U.S. south through the Appalachian Mountains, and they winter from southern Florida and the West Indies to Mexico and Belize.• In Florida, they migrate statewide but are decidedly more numerous during fall than spring, and they winter rarely in the extreme south. • Both races of Black-throated Blue Warbler are found in our state. The northernmost is *D. c. caerulescens*, which has a plain blue back and crown. The Appalachian-breeding *D. c. cairnsi* has black mottling on its crown and back.

ID: small, arboreal songbird, usually with small white wing patch. *Male:* dark blue upperparts, including nape and crown, may have black mottling; black face; black upper breast and flanks; white underparts. *Female:* olive brown upperparts, including head; white or pale eyebrow and lower eye arc; pale yellow or buff underparts; white wing patch may be absent.
Size: L 5–5½ in; W 7½ in.
Status: uncommon to fairly common migrant statewide from April to May and from September to October, although less numerous in the Panhandle; very rare to rare during winter in the extreme southern peninsula and the Keys.
Habitat: any wooded habitat, especially oak woodlands.
Nesting: does not breed in Florida.
Feeding: gleans foliage or flycatches for insects and spiders; also takes fruit, such as mulberry and beautyberry.
Voice: short *chip* call; song, rarely heard in Florida, is a series of 4–5 ascending wheezy notes.
Similar Species: white wing patch is distinctive, as is male's plumage. *American Redstart* (p. 306): female is very active and has yellow wing patch, white underparts and yellow tail patches. *Tennessee Warbler* (p. 287): darker eyeline; lacks lower eye arc; lacks white wing patch.
Best Sites: widespread.

YELLOW-RUMPED WARBLER

Dendroica coronata

The Yellow-rumped Warbler is the most abundant and widespread wood-warbler in North America. The four races of Yellow-rumped Warbler were once considered two species: the two white-throated eastern races were known as the "Myrtle Warbler," and the two yellow-throated western races were called "Audubon's Warbler." • "Myrtle Warblers" breed across most of Alaska, Canada and New England, and they winter coastally from Washington and New England through the West Indies to Panama. "Audubon's Warblers" breed in the West, from southern Alaska to Mexico and Guatemala, and they winter from British Columbia and Idaho to Guatemala and Honduras. • In Florida, the Myrtle Warbler is a common and widespread winter resident, while Audubon's Warbler is a very rare visitor, with few verifiable records. • The scientific name *coronata* is Latin for "crowned." It refers to the yellow crown of the male in breeding plumage, which is seldom seen in Florida.

breeding ♂

"Myrtle Warbler"

♀

ID: small arboreal songbird with yellow rump; partial white eye ring. *Breeding male:* rarely seen in Florida; bluish gray upperparts with black streaking; blue-gray nape; yellow crown; white eyebrow; black cheek patch; white throat; white underparts with bold, black streaking on breast and flanks. *Breeding female:* rarely seen in Florida; like male but duller; no yellow crown. *Nonbreeding:* brown upperparts with faint black streaking; brown head with pale eyebrow; pale throat; dark wing with 2 narrow, white wing bars; dingy underparts with brown streaking on breast and flanks; yellow flank patch.

Size: *L* 5–6 in; *W* 9 in.
Status: *"Myrtle Warbler":* common to abundant resident statewide from November to April. *"Audubon's Warbler":* very rare visitor, usually at Dry Tortugas in spring.
Habitat: any shrubby or wooded habitat, especially where wax myrtles are present.
Nesting: does not breed in Florida.
Feeding: gleans fruit, particularly berries from wax myrtles; also gleans or hawks flying insects or spiders.
Voice: loud, clear *chip* call.
Similar Species: diagnostic dull brown upperparts, yellow rump and yellow flank patch; little seasonal overlap with other warblers that have yellow rumps.
Best Sites: widespread.

295

BLACK-THROATED GREEN WARBLER

Dendroica virens

The male Black-throated Green Warbler is accurately named, having a green, black and white plumage that is unique among eastern wood-warblers. The female and juvenile are very similar but have mottled black or pale yellow throats. A diagnostic field mark of all plumages is a yellow wash to the undertail coverts. • The Black-throated Green Warbler breeds across southern Canada and the eastern U.S., and it winters from Florida and Mexico through the West Indies and Central America to Panama. In Florida, it is a generally rare or uncommon migrant statewide and a rare winter resident of the southern peninsula and Keys. • This bird is rarely observed in large numbers, even during "fallouts" of migrants following strong winds. Rather, one or two Black-throated Green Warblers are normally observed among flocks of other warblers and other small land birds. • Both races, the southern-breeding *D. v. waynei* and the widespread *D. v. virens,* have been found in Florida, but they cannot be distinguished in the field.

ID: small arboreal songbird; plain olive upperparts including nape and crown; yellow face with faint olive eye line extending to cheek; blackish wing with 2 white wing bars; black breast and flanks; white underparts with pale yellow undertail coverts. *Male:* black throat. *Female:* yellow throat.
Size: L 4½–5 in; W 7½ in.
Status: rare to uncommon migrant statewide from April to May and from September to October, when it is decidedly more numerous; generally rare winter resident of the southern half of the peninsula and the Keys.
Habitat: any wooded habitat, especially oak woodlands.
Nesting: does not breed in Florida.
Feeding: gleans vegetation or flycatches for insects and spiders; also eats fruit.
Voice: clear *chip* call; song, rarely heard in Florida, is a series of 5 notes with a lower-pitched 4th note.
Similar Species: *Blackburnian Warbler* (p. 297): female and juvenile have streaked backs and orange or butterscotch on heads and throats.
Best Sites: widespread.

BLACKBURNIAN WARBLER

Dendroica fusca

A breeding-plumaged male Blackburnian Warbler is one of the most dazzling of North American birds. Unfortunately, Florida birders do not often see this plumage, because the northbound migration route takes the birds over the western Gulf of Mexico. • The Blackburnian Warbler breeds in southern Canada and the northeastern U.S. southward through the Appalachian Mountains. It winters from Panama to Peru. In Florida, it occurs solely as a migrant. • Blackburnian Warblers are often found in our state in small flocks, which typically forage high in the tree canopy. The white or pale "braces" on the back, when present, are diagnostic of this species. • The Blackburnian Warbler was named after Anna Blackburne (1726–93), an English botanist and museum curator whose brother collected birds in the U.S. The Latin word *fusca*, which means "dusky," is a strange name to be given to a species typically so brightly colored.

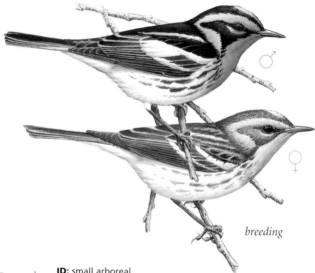

breeding

ID: small arboreal songbird; distinctive face pattern of dark cheek patch and pale lower eye arc; white undertail coverts. *Breeding male:* black upperparts with pale "braces"; black nape and hindcrown; orange forecrown, face, lower eye arc and throat; black cheek; black wing with white panel; orange breast; black streaking on flanks. *Breeding female:* duller upperparts with brown crown; duller orange; 2 white wing bars. *Juvenile:* like female, but butterscotch instead of orange; streaking on flanks may be brownish.
Size: *L* 4½–5½ in; *W* 8½ in.

Status: uncommon migrant statewide from April to May and from August to October, more numerous during fall; no verified winter records.
Habitat: any wooded habitat, especially oak woodlands.
Nesting: does not breed in Florida.
Feeding: gleans vegetation or flycatches for insects and spiders; also eats fruit.
Voice: rich *chip* call; song, rarely heard in Florida, is a series of very high-pitched notes.
Similar Species: orange on adults is diagnostic. *Yellow-throated Warbler* (p. 298): tree-creeping behavior; blue-gray upperparts; white eyebrow and ear patch; bright yellow throat.
Best Sites: widespread.

YELLOW-THROATED WARBLER

Dendroica dominica

The Yellow-throated Warbler is characteristic of Florida's mixed pine and cypress woodlands that are festooned with Spanish moss. This species breeds throughout the eastern U.S. and winters from the Gulf Coast through the West Indies to Costa Rica.• In Florida, it migrates statewide but its seasonal status varies by region; it is largely resident in the north and winters in the south. • This warbler forages by creeping along the trunks and branches of trees. • The Yellow-throated Warbler has three races, and all occur in Florida. The *D. d. dominica* and *D. d. stoddardi* subspecies, with yellow lores, breed in Florida. The *D. d. albilora* race, with white lores, is found here during migration and winter.

♂

Yellow-lored morph

ID: small arboreal songbird; creeps around tree trunks and branches; plain gray upperparts, including nape and hindcrown; black forehead and forecrown; bold, white eyebrow; black cheek patch reaches to flanks; bright yellow throat and breast; dark wing with 2 white wing bars; white underparts; black streaking on flanks.

Size: *L* 5–5½ in; *W* 8 in.

Status: fairly common migrant statewide; fairly common permanent resident of the Panhandle and northern half of the peninsula, withdrawing from the western Panhandle during fall; fairly common winter resident of the southern half of the peninsula and the Keys.

Habitat: *Breeding:* mixed pine-cypress woodlands or hardwood swamps. *In migration* and *winter:* any wooded habitat, especially oak woodlands.

Nesting: high in a tree with hanging clumps of Spanish moss; mostly the female builds a cup nest in Spanish moss and lines it with plant down and feathers; female incubates 3–4 variably marked, greenish or grayish white eggs for 12–13 days; probably raises 2 broods per year.

Feeding: gleans insects, spiders and other small prey from trunks or branches; also sallies for flying insects.

Voice: soft clear *chip* call; song is a beautiful series of downslurred whistles.

Similar Species: *Black-and-white Warbler* (p. 305): similar foraging style and plumage pattern but lacks yellow throat. *Blackburnian Warbler* (p. 297): bright orange or butterscotch throat and eyebrow; streaked back; different foraging style.

Best Sites: widespread.

PINE WARBLER

Dendroica pinus

The Pine Warbler is one of the few wood-warblers whose range is almost entirely limited to North America. It breeds in extreme southeastern Canada, the eastern U.S. and the Bahamas. It winters in the southeastern U.S. and the Bahamas. In Florida, it is a common resident of pinewoods throughout the mainland. Except in the Keys, where it is absent, the Pine Warbler's breeding range closely mirrors the distribution of pines. During winter, however, Pine Warblers are regularly encountered away from pines—in some cases, miles from the nearest pinewoods. • In winter, bright Pine Warbler males are frequently misidentified as Yellow-throated Vireos, which are very rare during this season away from the extreme southeastern peninsula or the Keys. Wintering Pine Warblers typically flock with Eastern Bluebirds and Chipping Sparrows, often feeding on the ground.

ID: small arboreal songbird; plain upperparts, including tail and 2 white wing bars. *Male:* olive upperparts, including nape and crown; narrow, yellow eyebrow; olive cheek; yellow throat, breast and belly; olive streaking on flanks; white undertail coverts. *Female:* duller than male; reduced streaking on flanks, if any. *Juvenile:* may be particularly dull; olive brown or brown upperparts; dingy underparts may lack yellow.

Size: L 5–5½ in; W 8½ in.

Status: common permanent resident of the mainland; very rare in the Keys, seen mainly during winter.

Habitat: *Breeding:* pine woodlands and plantations. *In migration:* may be found far from pines, often occurring in mixed winter flocks.

Nesting: invariably on a pine branch; female builds a deep cup nest of twigs, needles and stems and lines it with feathers and plant down; pair incubates 3–5 brown-speckled, whitish eggs for about 10 days; probably raises 2 broods per year.

Feeding: gleans foliage for insects, spiders and sometimes fruit or seeds; often feeds on the ground during winter.

Voice: sweet *chip* call; year-round song is a musical trill lasting 2–4 seconds.

Similar Species: *Yellow-throated Vireo* (p. 239): bright yellow "spectacles"; gray rump; no dingy streaking on breast and flanks.

Best Sites: widespread.

299

PRAIRIE WARBLER

Dendroica discolor

The inappropriately named Prairie Warbler is a denizen of shrubby or wooded habitats and is not found in prairies or other open habitats. It breeds in the eastern U.S. and in a few spots in southeasternmost Canada. It winters in Florida, the West Indies and islands off Central America. • In Florida, two Prairie Warbler races occur, with different regional and seasonal distributions. The eastern race *(D. d. discolor)* migrates statewide, breeds in the north and winters in the south. The Florida race *(D. d. paludicola)* is an endemic resident of mangrove forests in the southern peninsula and the Keys. The two races cannot accurately be distinguished in the field by plumage characteristics.

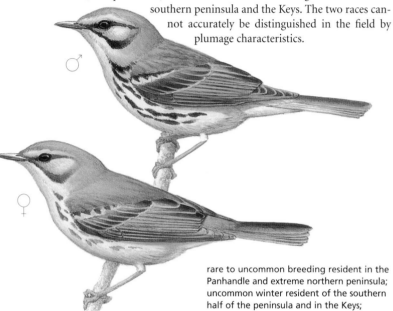

ID: small arboreal tail-wagging songbird; olive upperparts including nape and crown; yellow eyebrow and lower eye arc; olive cheek patch; yellow throat; olive wing with 2 whitish wing bars; yellow underparts with pale undertail coverts. *Male:* chestnut streaks on back; black eye line, "mustache" and streaking on flanks. *Female* and *juvenile:* duller; olive replaces black on face; reduced streaking on flanks.
Size: *L* 4½–5 in; *W* 7 in.
Status: *D. d. paludicola:* fairly common coastal resident in the southern half of the peninsula and in the Keys. *D. d. discolor:*
rare to uncommon breeding resident in the Panhandle and extreme northern peninsula; uncommon winter resident of the southern half of the peninsula and in the Keys; uncommon migrant statewide.
Habitat: *D. d. paludicola:* mangrove forests. *D. d. discolor: Breeding:* stands of young pines, often mixed with young oaks. *Nonbreeding:* any wooded habitat, especially oak woodlands.
Nesting: low in a mangrove or coastal oak (*D. d. paludicola*) or a pine (*D. d. discolor*); female builds an open cup of soft vegetation and lines it with feathers, hair or plant down; female incubates 2–4 brown-spotted, whitish eggs for 11–14 days.
Feeding: gleans or hover-gleans for insects and spiders; may also eat fruit.
Voice: sweet *chip* call; song is an ascending series of buzzy *zee* notes.
Similar Species: none; tail-wagging behavior, facial pattern, yellow underparts with bold, black streaking and dark rump are diagnostic.
Best Sites: widespread.

PALM WARBLER

Dendroica palmarum

The Palm Warbler is one of the easiest wood-warblers to identify thanks to its flocking behavior, terrestrial habits and constant tail-wagging. It breeds across southern Canada and the extreme north-central and northeastern U.S. It winters in the southeastern U.S., the West Indies and the Yucatan Peninsula, with small numbers along the Pacific Coast from Washington to Nicaragua. In Florida, the Palm Warbler is a common winter resident statewide, found in fields and open woodlands even in the Keys. • Both races are regularly found in our state, although the drab brown western-breeding race *(D. p. palmarum)* is much more numerous than is the yellow-breasted eastern race *(D. p. hypochrysea)*. • Despite their name, Palm Warblers are found on or near the ground, usually in small to moderate-sized flocks; in their breeding area, they favor bogs. • The ground-dwelling, flocking behavior and drab plumage of most Palm Warblers may cause confusion with sparrows, but the yellow undertail coverts and tail-wagging behavior are both unsparrow-like.

nonbreeding

ID: small, conspicuous, tail-wagging, terrestrial songbird; found in loose flocks; yellow undertail coverts; dark eye line; dull brown upperparts; brownish cheek; bold, pale eyebrow. *Breeding:* chestnut crown. *Nonbreeding:* dull brown crown; pale throat; indistinct, brownish streaking on pale, grayish brown *(D. p. palmarum)* or yellow *(D. p. hypochrysea)* underparts.
Size: *L* 4–5½ in; *W* 8 in.
Status: common resident statewide from October to April, more numerous in the southern part of the state.
Habitat: fields, dunes and other open areas; rarely seen in woodlands.

Nesting: does not breed in Florida.
Feeding: gleans the ground, low vegetation and, rarely, trees, for insects and spiders; also takes fruit and seeds.
Voice: weak *tsip* call; song, rarely heard in Florida, is a weak, buzzy trill with a quick finish.
Similar Species: ground-dwelling habit (usually in flocks), yellow undertail coverts, rusty cap and dull, faintly streaked underparts are diagnostic among warblers. *American Pipit* (p. 283): gray rump and crown; entirely white outer tail feathers; distinctive *pip-it* call.
Best Sites: widespread.

301

BAY-BREASTED WARBLER

Dendroica castanea

The Bay-breasted Warbler is another species with a great degree of sexual dimorphism. However, because its northward migratory route takes it far west of our state, few Florida birders see this species in its resplendent breeding state. The male's distinctive breeding plumage is largely lost during the molt into nonbreeding plumage. • The Bay-breasted Warbler breeds across southern Canada and in New England, and it winters from Costa Rica and Panama to Venezuela. In Florida, it occurs solely as a migrant, with its numbers greatly increasing during fall. • On their breeding grounds, Bay-breasted Warblers are spruce budworm specialists, and their populations fluctuate along with the cyclical pattern of budworm numbers. In an outbreak year, a single Bay-breasted Warbler may consume more than 5000 budworms.

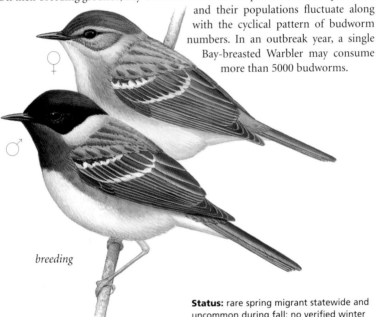

breeding

ID: small arboreal songbird; streaked back; 2 white wing bars on dark wings. *Breeding male:* dusky upperparts; rufous crown and throat separated by black mask; buff patch on side of neck; rufous upper breast and flanks; pale buff underparts. *Breeding female:* like male, but with dusky mask and duller rufous areas. *Nonbreeding and juvenile:* olive upperparts, including nape and crown; pale eyebrow and throat; pale yellow or buff underparts, possibly with some rufous on lower flanks.
Size: *L* 5–6 in; *W* 9 in.

Status: rare spring migrant statewide and uncommon during fall; no verified winter records.
Habitat: any wooded habitat, especially oak woodlands.
Nesting: does not breed in Florida.
Feeding: gleans vegetation for insects and spiders; may also eat fruit.
Voice: loud *chip* call; song, rarely heard in Florida, is a series of 3–10 high-pitched *see* or *see-see* notes.
Similar Species: breeding adults are unmistakable. *Chestnut-sided Warbler* (p. 291): nonbreeding has greener upperparts, plain gray face, narrow, white eye ring, yellowish wing bars and white underparts. *Blackpoll Warbler* (p. 303): nonbreeding has white or pale yellow underparts, faint streaking on sides of neck and flanks, white undertail coverts and, usually, yellow legs and feet.
Best Sites: widespread.

BLACKPOLL WARBLER

Dendroica striata

Of the 115 or so species of wood-warblers found in the Americas, none migrates farther than the Blackpoll Warbler. It breeds from Alaska to New England and winters in northern South America. Spring migration is mostly through Florida, but fall migrants fly a much greater distance over water. Taking off from the coast of the northeastern states or eastern Canada, Blackpoll Warblers head out over the Atlantic Ocean for a nonstop flight to Venezuela, a trip that may take up to 88 hours to complete! • In Florida this species is a statewide migrant, and it appears much more widely, and usually numerously, during spring than fall, although strong east winds can push large numbers of southbound migrants to our eastern coast.

breeding

ID: small arboreal songbird; distinctive yellow legs and feet; streaked back; dark wing with 2 white bars. *Breeding male:* dark upperparts; black cap extends to eyes; white cheek and throat; black "mustache" merges with streaking on flanks. *Breeding female:* streaked head with faint eyebrow. *Nonbreeding* and *juvenile:* like breeding female, but with olive upperparts; pale yellow eyebrow, throat, breast and belly; no "mustache"; much reduced streaking on flanks, if any; may have dark legs and feet.
Size: *L* 5–5½ in; *W* 9 in.
Status: common migrant statewide from April to May and from September to October, although least numerous in the Panhandle; no verified winter records.

Habitat: any wooded habitat, especially oak woodlands.
Nesting: does not breed in Florida.
Feeding: gleans vegetation or flycatches for insects and spiders; may also take fruit.
Voice: loud *chip* call; song, rarely heard in Florida, is a very high-pitched trill.
Similar Species: *Black-and-white Warbler* (p. 305): tree-creeping behavior; black and white back; bold, white eyebrow; boldly streaked flanks; dark legs and feet. *Bay-breasted Warbler* (p. 302): nonbreeding bird has bolder eye line, yellower underparts with faint streaking on flanks, white undertail coverts and dark legs and feet.
Best Sites: widespread.

303

CERULEAN WARBLER

Dendroica cerulea

The Cerulean Warbler is one of the least-known of Florida's regularly occurring warblers. It breeds in much of the eastern U.S. except the Deep South, and it winters in northern South America. Throughout Florida, this warbler is a rare spring migrant and a rare to uncommon early fall migrant, with most individuals passing through in August and early September. • The Cerulean Warbler often feeds quietly in the canopy, and this behavior, together with its small size, means that it is often overlooked. The highest number ever seen in our state at one spot in one day is 13. • On its breeding grounds, this bird has very specific habitat requirements, and overall populations have declined severely in recent decades. As a result, the Cerulean Warbler may soon be listed as a threatened species.

ID: tiny, short-tailed canopy warbler; 2 white wing bars. *Male:* blue upperparts with pale streaking on back; blue head; white throat; white underparts with black breast band and black-streaked flanks. *Female:* unique blue-green upperparts; pale yellow eyebrow and throat; pale underparts with dark streaking on breast and flanks. *Juvenile:* like female, but with bold yellow eyebrow and unstreaked, yellow underparts. **Size:** *L* 4½–5 in; *W* 7 in.
Status: rare migrant statewide from April to May and rare to uncommon from July to October, with most individuals passing through in August and early September.
Habitat: any mature wooded habitat.

Nesting: does not breed in Florida.
Feeding: gleans insects from foliage, primarily the upper canopy.
Voice: clear *chip* call.
Similar Species: *Northern Parula* (p. 289): male resembles male Cerulean, but with yellow back and throat and orange breast. *Black-throated Blue Warbler* (p. 294): no wing bars; male has black face and throat; female has small white wing patch. *Blackburnian Warbler* (p. 297): juvenile resembles female Cerulean, but with pale or white "braces" on back, white belly with pale streaking and dark cheek patch surrounded by yellow.
Best Sites: fairly widespread.

BLACK-AND-WHITE WARBLER

Mniotilta varia

The foraging behavior of the Black-and-white Warbler stands in sharp contrast to that of most of its kin. Rather than flitting quickly between twigs, the Black-and-white Warbler behaves like a creeper or nuthatch, which are only distantly related species, and creeps along the trunks and larger branches of trees as it searches for prey. It shares this tree-creeping foraging behavior with the Yellow-throated Warbler, which it strongly resembles if the latter's bright yellow throat is not visible. • This species breeds across much of southern Canada and the eastern U.S., and it winters from Florida and the West Indies to northern South America. • In Florida, Black-and-white Warblers are fairly common migrants and winter residents statewide. They are one of the first warblers to return during "fall," with the first arrivals—usually females or juveniles—moving through in the latter half of July.

ID: small tree-creeping songbird; mostly black upperparts with white streaks; black crown with white median stripe; white eyebrow; black wing with 2 white bars. *Male:* black cheek patch and throat separated by white "mustache"; white underparts heavily streaked with black. *Female* and *juvenile:* white throat; less boldly streaked underparts washed with pale buff.
Size: *L* 4½–5½ in; *W* 8 in.
Status: generally fairly common migrant and resident statewide from July to May; rare during winter in the western Panhandle.

Habitat: any wooded habitat.
Nesting: does not breed in Florida.
Feeding: creeps along tree trunks and larger branches; gleans insects and spiders.
Voice: soft, high *seet* call; song, rarely heard in Florida, is a series of high, thin 2-syllable notes.
Similar Species: *Yellow-throated Warbler* (p. 298): generally similar tree-climbing behavior and plumage but with distinct yellow throat. *Blackpoll Warbler* (p. 303): spring male has solid black cap, all-white undertail coverts and yellow legs and feet.
Best Sites: widespread.

AMERICAN REDSTART

Setophaga ruticilla

Because of its similar plumage, the American Redstart was named after the Old World redstarts, which are in the flycatcher family. "Start" comes from the Old English *steort*, which means tail. • The American Redstart breeds over most of Canada and the continental U.S. It winters from Florida and the West Indies to northern South America. In Florida, it is a fairly common statewide migrant, more common along the Atlantic coast during spring and the Gulf Coast during fall. This warbler winters in small numbers in the southern part of our state, and it may nest regularly in the extreme northwestern Panhandle. • American Redstarts are consistent favorites among birders because of their bright colors and their active foraging behavior, during which they habitually flash their orange or yellow wing and tail patches.

ID: active warbler with conspicuous wing and tail patches. *Male:* black upperparts; orange wing patch; black breast; orange flanks; white belly and undertail coverts; orange tail patches. *Female* and *juvenile:* olive brown upperparts; gray head; pale underparts; yellow shoulder, wing and tail patches.
Size: *L* 5 in; *W* 8 in.
Status: fairly common migrant statewide; rare, perhaps irregular breeder in the northwestern Panhandle; small numbers are regular winter residents in the southern third of the peninsula and in the Keys.

Habitat: *Breeding:* open deciduous or mixed forests with a thick understory, often near water. *In migration* and *winter:* any wooded habitat.
Nesting: in the fork of a shrub or sapling, usually in a wet area; female builds a cup nest of twigs, plant down and lichen and lines it with feathers; female incubates 4 variably marked, whitish eggs for 11–12 days.
Feeding: actively gleans foliage for insects and spiders, often hover-gleans; also sallies for flying insects.
Voice: sharp *chip* call; song, rarely heard in Florida, is a highly variable series of high, thin notes with a downslurred ending.
Similar Species: none; active foraging behavior while flashing wing and tail patches is unique.
Best Sites: widespread.

PROTHONOTARY WARBLER

Protonotaria citrea

The stunning Prothonotary Warbler is the only eastern wood-warbler that nests in cavities. It breeds in swamps and along rivers and creeks in snags that stand in or near stagnant water. This bird remains partial to forested wetlands even during migration. • The Prothonotary Warbler breeds throughout the eastern U.S. and winters from Mexico to northern South America. In Florida, it migrates statewide and breeds widely in the Panhandle but is less numerous and local in the peninsula. • This bird acquired its unusual name because its plumage was thought to resemble the yellow hoods worn by prothonotaries, who are high-ranking clerics in the Roman Catholic Church. • It is usually found close to the ground and is often located by its sharp *chink* call.

ID: big-headed warbler; yellow head and breast; shortish gray tail with white patches in outer feathers; conspicuous, large black eyes. *Male:* olive back; gray wings; yellow underparts with white undertail coverts. *Female* and *juvenile:* duller head and underparts.
Size: *L* 5½ in; *W* 8½ in.
Status: uncommon migrant statewide from March to October; fairly common and widespread breeding resident in the Panhandle but local and uncommon in the northern half of the peninsula; rare and very local in Big Cypress National Preserve.
Habitat: swamps and riparian forests.

Nesting: in a natural cavity or birdhouse; mostly the male builds a cup nest of twigs and leaves and lines it with finer materials; female incubates 4–6 brown-spotted, pale eggs for 12–14 days; 2 broods per year.
Feeding: gleans vegetation near the ground or creeps along trunks; feeds mostly on insects and spiders.
Voice: sharp, metallic *chink* call; song is a series of loud, ringing *sweet* notes issued on a single pitch.
Similar Species: *Blue-winged Warbler* (p. 285): usually high up in trees; bold, white wing bars; black eye line. *Yellow Warbler* (p. 290): entirely yellow body; dark wing with yellow wing bars; male has reddish streaks on breast. *Hooded Warbler* (p. 315): female has olive upperparts, all-yellow underparts and, often, blackish crown.
Best Sites: widespread.

307

WORM-EATING WARBLER

Helmitheros vermivora

A subtly attractive species, the Worm-eating Warbler is eagerly sought by birders during its migration. • This warbler breeds in the eastern U.S., with just a few breeding reports for Florida, from steep ravines in the western Panhandle along the border with Alabama. It winters from southern Florida and the West Indies southward through Central America. • The Worm-eating Warbler nests on the ground, the only Florida-breeding warbler to do so. • Most Florida birders know this species as a migrant that quietly forages high in foliage, where it can be easily overlooked. Worm-eating Warblers often hang upside-down while carefully searching clumps of dead leaves for prey.

ID: largish warbler that probes clumps of dead leaves; large head and bill; grayish buff tail, back and wings; grayish buff head; bold, black stripes on crown; buffy underparts; pale legs and feet.

Size: *L* 5 in; *W* 8½ in.

Status: uncommon migrant statewide; rare winter resident in the extreme southern peninsula and the Keys; rare, perhaps irregular breeding resident along the Alabama border.

Habitat: *Breeding:* steep, deciduous woodland slopes, swampy woodlands with shrubby understory cover and ravines. *In migration:* any deciduous habitat.

Nesting: on a hillside or ravine bank, often near water; on the ground, hidden under leaf litter; female builds a cup nest of decaying leaves and lines it with fine materials; female incubates 3–5 brown-speckled, white eggs for about 13 days.

Feeding: gleans prey from the ground or foliage or probes clumps of dead leaves; feeds mostly on caterpillars and other insects and spiders.

Voice: loud *chip* call; song is a rapid, dry trill.

Similar Species: *Swainson's Warbler* (p. 309): similar plumage pattern and ground-dwelling habits; unstriped, rusty crown.

Best Sites: widespread.

SWAINSON'S WARBLER

Limnothlypis swainsonii

The Swainson's Warbler is a little-known inhabitant of dense thickets in swamps of the Southeast. It breeds from West Virginia to Texas, and it winters in the West Indies and Central America. In Florida, it is a rare migrant statewide and an uncommon breeding resident of the Panhandle. • The Swainson's Warbler breeds in canebrakes and rhododendron thickets farther north, but it uses saw palmetto and other thick underbrush in wet areas and along streams in our state. It remains on or near the ground, relying on its nonshowy plumage and unassuming manner for concealment. • Except for the presumably extinct Bachman's Warbler *(Vermivora bachmanii),* the Swainson's Warbler is the only wood-warbler that lays unmarked, white eggs. • Like the Swainson's Hawk and Swainson's Thrush, this species is named for William Swainson (1789–1855), a noted British writer and naturalist.

ID: inconspicuous ground-dwelling warbler; fairly large bill; brown upperparts; rusty cap; pale face; whitish eyebrow; dark eye line; pale throat and underparts; pinkish legs.

Size: *L* 5½ in; *W* 9 in.

Status: generally rare migrant statewide; uncommon and local breeding resident of the Panhandle and extreme northwestern peninsula.

Habitat: *Breeding:* stands of saw palmetto and other dense thickets in wet areas and the edges of swamps. *In migration:* variety of dense habitats.

Nesting: near the ground, often among palmetto fronds; female builds a bulky cup nest of leaves, pine needles and other vegetation; female incubates 3–5 sparsely spotted, white eggs for 13–15 days.

Feeding: gleans prey from the ground or foliage or flips over leaves; feeds primarily on insects, spiders and millipedes.

Voice: loud *chip* call; song is a short series of slurred, whistled notes, often ending with a rising *tea-o.*

Similar Species: *Worm-eating Warbler* (p. 308): similar plumage pattern but often forages high in foliage; buffy crown, boldly striped with black.

Best Sites: fairly widespread.

OVENBIRD

Seiurus aurocapilla

The Ovenbird's plain olive upperparts and spotted breast make it appear thrushlike, but its small size, striped crown, and ground-nesting habits place it among the wood-warblers. • This songbird breeds in much of Canada and the north-central U.S. It winters from Florida and Mexico through Central America and the West Indies to Panama and Venezuela. In Florida, the Ovenbird is a rather common statewide migrant, and although regional differences do exist, it appears to be equally numerous during spring and fall. It also winters regularly from the central peninsula south through the Keys. • The Ovenbird is almost exclusively terrestrial while in Florida, walking with deliberate steps around hammocks and other open woodlands like a windup toy, often while bobbing its head. It can be quite tame during migration, allowing birders to approach to within a few feet. At other times, it shows agitation by slightly raising its crests and uttering loud *chip*s. • Ovenbird plumage varies little with age or gender.

ID: small, thrushlike songbird usually seen on or close to ground; olive upperparts; rufous crown bordered by black stripes; olive face; white eye ring and throat; white underparts with black spots forming stripes to lower belly; pink legs and feet.
Size: *L* 6 in; *W* 9½ in.
Status: fairly common migrant statewide from March to May and from August to October; rare to uncommon winter resident in the southern half of the peninsula and the Keys.

Habitat: any wooded habitat, especially oak woodlands.
Nesting: does not breed in Florida.
Feeding: gleans the ground for worms, snails and insects; also gleans vegetation for fruit.
Voice: loud *chip* call; song, rarely heard in Florida, is a series of doubled notes increasing in volume.
Similar Species: *Thrushes* (pp. 271–76): larger; no rufous crown outlined with black; most have buffy or dusky breasts with little or no streaking on lower belly. *Northern Waterthrush* (p. 311) and *Louisiana Waterthrush* (p. 312): entirely dark crowns; bold, white or yellowish eyebrows; no white eye rings; bob hind ends constantly.
Best Sites: widespread.

NORTHERN WATERTHRUSH

Seiurus noveboracensis

Despite their names, North America's two species of waterthrushes are wood-warblers and are only distantly related to thrushes. But they are closely associated with water, even during migration. Both species are ground-dwellers that continuously bob their entire hind ends, not just their tails like Palm Warblers do. • The Northern Waterthrush breeds in most of Alaska, Canada and the northern continental U.S. It winters from Florida and Mexico through Central America and the West Indies to Ecuador. In Florida, it migrates fairly commonly statewide and is a less numerous winter resident in the southern peninsula and the Keys. • The Northern Waterthrush is more numerous in our state than its close relative the Louisiana Waterthrush, and it is more likely to be found in winter. Field marks to distinguish the two species include the presence of streaking on the throat (Northern) or buff on the flanks (Louisiana).

ID: small, terrestrial songbird; bobs its hind end constantly; typically seen near water; dark brown upperparts, including nape and crown; white or pale buff eyebrow; dusky face; dark "mustache"; whitish throat and underparts, streaked with black to lower belly; pale pink legs and feet.
Size: *L* 5–6 in; *W* 9½ in.
Status: uncommon to fairly common migrant statewide from April to May and from September to October; rare to uncommon winter resident in the southern half of the peninsula and in the Keys.

Habitat: always around water; bayheads, swamps and riparian forests.
Nesting: does not breed in Florida.
Feeding: gleans the ground, leaf litter or low vegetation; feeds on insects, spiders, worms, snails and small crustaceans; often tosses aside leaf litter with its bill; may even take small fish from shallow water.
Voice: loud, sharp *chink* call.
Similar Species: *Louisiana Waterthrush* (p. 312): broader white eyebrow that widens behind the eye; plain white throat; buffy wash on flanks. *Ovenbird* (p. 310): does not bob tail; rufous crown bordered by black stripes; white eye ring; no eyebrow.
Best Sites: widespread.

LOUISIANA WATERTHRUSH

Seiurus motacilla

The Louisiana Waterthrush is the first wood-warbler to migrate north through Florida in spring, and the first to return south in fall. The earliest "spring" migrants are seen in late February, and the first "fall" migrants move through in late June. • This wood-warbler breeds across the eastern U.S. and winters from Mexico and the West Indies to Panama and Venezuela. In Florida, the Louisiana Waterthrush is a rare breeder in the Panhandle and is an uncommon migrant statewide. • This bird is a scarcer migrant than the Northern Waterthrush. In addition to small plumage differences, the Louisiana Waterthrush has a few habits that make it easily distinguishable from its close cousin. It bobs its hind end at a slower rate than the Northern Waterthrush, and it also sways its tail from side to side.

ID: small, terrestrial songbird; constantly bobs hind end; usually seen near water; dark brown upperparts, including nape and crown; white eyebrow broadens behind the eye; dark eyeline; white throat; white underparts and buffy flanks, streaked with black to lower belly.

Size: *L* 6 in; *W* 10 in.

Status: uncommon migrant statewide from March to April and from July to September; rare breeding resident in the Panhandle; very rare to rare winter resident in the southern half of the peninsula and the Keys.

Habitat: wooded areas around water.

Nesting: concealed within a tangle of tree roots; pair builds a cup nest of twigs, leaves and moss and lines it with hair and plant down; female incubates 3–6 speckled, creamy white eggs for about 14 days.

Feeding: gleans the ground, leaf litter or low vegetation; feeds on insects, spiders, worms, snails and small crustaceans; often tosses aside leaf litter with its bill; may even take small fish from shallow water.

Voice: loud, sharp *chink* call; song is a series of 3–4 distinctive slurred whistles followed by a descending twitter.

Similar Species: *Northern Waterthrush* (p. 311): yellowish to buff eyebrow narrows behind eye; streaked throat; no buffy wash on flanks. *Ovenbird* (p. 310): does not bob tail; rufous crown bordered by black stripes; white eye ring; no eyebrow.

Best Sites: widespread.

KENTUCKY WARBLER

Oporornis formosus

As is typical of its genus, the Kentucky Warbler exhibits wary, skulking behavior as it feeds on or close to the ground among dense thickets, where it is usually difficult to find. • This bird breeds across the eastern half of the continental U.S. It winters from Mexico through Central America to Panama. In Florida, it breeds uncommonly in the north, and it migrates statewide. • Dead birds collected at the bases of tall towers confirm that many more Kentucky Warblers migrate through our state during fall than spring, but few of these migrants are seen because of their secretive behavior and preference for woodlands with dense understories. Most Florida birders never hear the song of the Kentucky Warbler, but on the breeding grounds confusion with the Carolina Wren's song is possible. However, the warbler sings the same pattern repeatedly, whereas the wren often varies its songs.

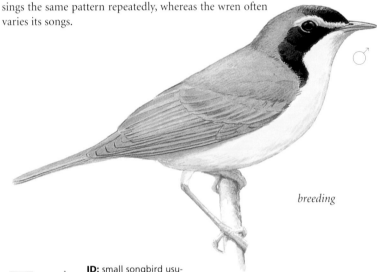

breeding

ID: small songbird usually seen on or near ground; olive upperparts, including nape; yellow "spectacles"; entirely yellow underparts; pink legs and feet. *Breeding male:* black crown; black patch below eye. *Female:* nearly identical to male, but with less distinct facial pattern. *Nonbreeding* and *juvenile:* olive crown; little or no black on face.

Size: *L* 5–5½ in; *W* 8½ in.

Status: rare to uncommon breeding resident of the Panhandle and extreme northwestern peninsula from April to October; rare migrant statewide.

Habitat: moist deciduous or mixed woodlands and riparian areas with dense understory.

Nesting: on or close to the ground; pair builds a cup nest of plant material and lines it with rootlets and hair; female incubates 4–5 cream-colored eggs, spotted or blotched with reddish brown, for 12–13 days; occasionally 2 broods per year.

Feeding: flips over leaves or gleans the ground or low vegetation; feeds on insects and spiders; also takes fruit.

Voice: low *chuck* call; song is a rich and loud rolling series of 2- or 3-syllable notes, similar to the song of the Carolina Wren.

Similar Species: *Common Yellowthroat* (p. 314): no yellow "spectacles"; adult male's black mask includes forehead and eyes; other plumages have dingier bellies and undertail coverts.

Best Sites: fairly widespread.

COMMON YELLOWTHROAT

Geothlypis trichas

The Common Yellowthroat is one of the most numerous and widespread wood-warblers in North America. It breeds from southern Alaska through most of Canada and the continental U.S. to Mexico, and it winters coastally from California and Maryland through Central America and the West Indies to Panama. In Florida, this warbler is largely resident statewide but does not breed in the Keys. • The Common Yellowthroat has more races than all other warblers but the Yellow Warbler. As many as seven of these races have been recorded in our state, but only *G. t. ignota* breeds here; the other races are found only during migration and winter. • Yellowthroats are very curious, and readily respond to "pishing," often flying to within a few feet of a birder.

ID: small songbird seen near ground in dense vegetation; olive upperparts, including nape and hindcrown; pale to dusky belly and undertail coverts; pink legs and feet. *Male:* black mask, including forehead and forecrown, bordered by pale line on upper edge; yellow throat and breast. *Female:* no mask; olive face; narrow, pale eye ring. *Juvenile:* similar to female; male shows hint of mask.

Size: *L* 5 in; *W* 6½ in.

Status: fairly common to common permanent resident throughout the mainland; does not breed in the Keys; uncommon to abundant migrant statewide.

Habitat: palmetto thickets and other dense understory, often near water.

Nesting: on or near the ground; female builds a bulky cup of grass and sedges and lines it with finer grass; female incubates 3–4 darkly spotted, creamy white eggs for 12 days; 2 broods per year.

Feeding: on or near the ground; gleans vegetation for insects and spiders; occasionally eats seeds.

Voice: distinctive loud *check* call; song is a series of rolling notes: *witchity-witchity-witchity.*

Similar Species: male's black mask is diagnostic. *Kentucky Warbler* (p. 313): yellow "spectacles"; yellow underparts. *Yellow Warbler* (p. 290): arboreal; yellow upperparts and underparts; distinct black eye. *Wilson's Warbler* (p. 366): rare; yellow face and eye ring; dark tail.

Best Sites: widespread.

HOODED WARBLER

Wilsonia citrina

With his black hood that contrasts with his bright yellow face and underparts, the male Hooded Warbler is one of the most striking and distinctive birds in Florida. • This species breeds in southern Ontario and across most of the eastern U.S. It winters from Mexico to Panama. In Florida, it breeds in moist woodlands in the Panhandle and the northern peninsula, and it migrates statewide. • Females often show some black hood, but even those without the hood can be identified by their unique tail-flicking behavior. • Hooded Warblers segregate by habitat on their wintering grounds. The males use humid mature forests and the females use drier, open woodlands or shrubby fields.

ID: small songbird seen near ground; frequently flicks open tail, showing white patches; olive upperparts; large, black eyes; yellow underparts. *Male:* yellow face; black crown and throat, connected along hindneck. *Female* and *juvenile:* olive crown and neck; may show hint of male's face pattern; yellow throat.
Size: *L* 5½ in; *W* 7 in.
Status: uncommon to fairly common breeding resident from April to October in the Panhandle and northern third of the peninsula; fairly common migrant statewide, perhaps a bit more numerous during spring; one winter record.
Habitat: *Breeding:* hardwood forests near water or in swamps. *In migration:* any wooded habitat with a dense understory.

Nesting: low in a shrub; mostly the female builds a cup of dead leaves and lines it with spiderwebs and plant fibers; female incubates 3–4 brown-spotted, creamy white eggs for about 12 days; 2 broods per year.
Feeding: gleans foliage or the ground for insects and spiders.
Voice: metallic *tink* call; song is a series of whistled phrases with the final note lower in pitch.
Similar Species: male's head pattern is diagnostic. *Common Yellowthroat,* (p. 314): female has pale eye ring, olive tail and yellow breast that contrasts with pale or buffy belly and undertail coverts. *Kentucky Warbler* (p. 313): bold, yellow "spectacles." *Wilson's Warbler* (p. 366): rare; dark tail.
Best Sites: widespread.

YELLOW-BREASTED CHAT

Icteria virens

The Yellow-breasted Chat is our most unusual wood-warbler, and at 7½ inches, it is also by far our largest. Its bill is thick and stocky, more like a tropical tanager's, and its song and courtship displays are reminiscent of a thrasher or mockingbird. • The Yellow-breasted Chat breeds in extreme southern Canada, most of the continental U.S. and Mexico, and it winters from the extreme southern U.S. to Panama. In Florida, it breeds in the Panhandle and the northwestern peninsula, and it is a rare migrant and winter resident statewide. • Because of its skulking habits and preference for thick vegetation, the Yellow-breasted Chat may often be overlooked. Certainly, most birders in the peninsula encounter this species no more frequently than once or twice every few years. However, the chat may be more numerous than observations suggest • The male Yellow-breasted Chat performs an impressive courtship ritual. He sings a most unwarblerlike series of caws, squeaks, grunts, whistles and other sounds while flying up in the air and briefly hovering before dropping back down with his tail pumping, feet dangling and wings arched above his body.

ID: medium-sized songbird; favors dense shrubbery; olive brown upperparts; white "spectacles"; short, stocky bill; yellow throat and breast; whitish belly. *Female:* black lores. *Male:* gray lores.

Size: *L* 7½ in; *W* 9½.

Status: fairly common breeding resident of the Panhandle, Lake Apopka and northwestern peninsula; very rare to rare migrant and winter resident statewide.

Habitat: dense thickets and woodland edges.

Nesting: in a dense tangle, often among thorny bushes; female builds a well-concealed cup nest of stems, vines and leaves and lines it with fine grass; female incubates 3–6 (usually 5) darkly spotted, white eggs for 11 days.

Feeding: gleans insects, spiders, small crustaceans and fruit from low vegetation.

Voice: calls include *whoit, chack* and *kook;* song is a series of whistles, squawks, grunts, squeals and various other sounds, uttered during an aerial display and sometimes at night.

Similar Species: none.

Best Sites: widespread breeder in the Panhandle; generally unpredictable in the peninsula.

SUMMER TANAGER
Piranga rubra

Tanagers are a large family of mostly tropical birds that are restricted to the New World. Most species, including the five species that occur in North America, have brightly colored plumages. Three of these species are found in Florida, but only the Summer Tanager breeds here. Its overall breeding range covers the eastern and southwestern U.S. and Mexico. It winters from Florida and Mexico to Bolivia and Brazil. In Florida, the Summer Tanager breeds widely south to the central peninsula, and it is a regular migrant and rare winter resident statewide. • The song of the Summer Tanager is one of the more characteristic avian sounds of Florida's open pine or mixed pine-oak woodlands.

ID: medium-sized arboreal songbird; longish pale yellow bill. *Male:* dull red overall. *Female* and *juvenile:* dull yellow-orange overall, sometimes with dull reddish wash; juvenile male acquires red plumage gradually.
Size: *L* 7–8 in; *W* 12 in.
Status: fairly common breeding resident of the Panhandle and northern half of the peninsula from March to October but rare farther south in the peninsula; fairly common statewide migrant, more numerous during spring; rare during winter virtually statewide.
Habitat: *Breeding:* open pinewoods or mixed oak-pine hammocks. *In migration* and *winter:* any wooded habitat.
Nesting: on a high, horizontal tree limb; female builds a flimsy, shallow cup of weed stems and Spanish moss and lines it with fine grass; female incubates 3–4 pale, blue-green eggs, spotted with reddish brown, for 11–12 days.
Feeding: gleans insects from foliage or sallies for flying insects; especially fond of bees and wasps; migrants also feed on fruit.
Voice: rolling *pitty-tucky-tuck* or *pit-tuck* call; song is a series of 3–5 sweet, clear, whistled phrases.
Similar Species: *Scarlet Tanager* (p. 318): smaller, darker bill; male has black tail and black wings; female and juvenile are yellow-green overall. *Northern Cardinal* (p. 335): male has red crest, black face and thick, red-orange bill. *Orchard Oriole* (p. 351) and *Baltimore Oriole* (p. 353): females have 2 white wing bars and much more pointed bills.
Best Sites: widespread.

317

SCARLET TANAGER
Piranga olivacea

A brilliantly colored songbird, the Scarlet Tanager breeds in extreme southeastern Canada and across the eastern U.S., except in the Deep South. It winters from Panama to Bolivia. In Florida, it is a generally uncommon migrant statewide. • Scarlet Tanagers are often are seen here in small flocks during spring, when west winds blow trans-Gulf migrants east to our Gulf Coast. • Unlike the male Summer Tanager, which remains red year-round, the male Scarlet Tanager molts into a female-like plumage after breeding. Also unlike the Summer Tanager, there are no documented records of a Scarlet Tanager occurring in our state during winter.

breeding

ID: medium-sized arboreal songbird. *Breeding male:* bright red body with black wings and tail; grayish bill. *Nonbreeding male:* yellowish green replaces red; paler bill. *Female:* like nonbreeding male, but with dusky wings and tail.
Size: *L* 7 in; *W* 11½ in.
Status: generally uncommon migrant statewide from April to May and from September to October, when it may be less numerous.

Habitat: any wooded habitat.
Nesting: does not breed in Florida.
Feeding: gleans insects or fruit from the tree canopy and sometimes from the ground; may hover-glean insects in midair.
Voice: hard *chip-burrr* call.
Similar Species: *Summer Tanager* (p. 317): larger, yellow bill; male has entirely red plumage; female and juvenile are orange-red. *Northern Cardinal* (p. 335): male has black face, red crest and thick, red-orange bill. *Orchard Oriole* (p. 351) and *Baltimore Oriole* (p. 353): females have 2 white wing bars and much more pointed bills.
Best Sites: widespread migrant.

EASTERN TOWHEE

Pipilo erythrophthalmus

Towhees are large, chunky sparrows with long tails. Of Florida's three species, two are extremely rare, but the Eastern Towhee is common. It breeds across the eastern United States and extreme southern Canada, and it winters in the southern half of its breeding range. In Florida, Eastern Towhees are found throughout the mainland, where their sweet *tweee* call is often heard from dense cover. • Three races of the Eastern Towhee breed in Florida. The two in the Panhandle have red eyes, and a peninsula race has white eyes. Northern-breeding races that also have red eyes winter in the peninsula. • Until recently, the Eastern Towhee and its close relative, the Spotted Towhee (*P. maculatus*) were grouped together as the "Rufous-sided Towhee."

ID: medium-sized sparrow; inhabits dense cover. *Male:* black upperparts; white, yellow, orange or red eyes; black wing with small white patch at base of the primaries; white underparts except for black breast and rufous flanks; long, black tail with limited white on tips. *Female:* resembles male, but brown replaces black. *Juvenile:* mostly brown overall; dark eyes; paler underparts heavily streaked with brown.
Size: *L* 7–8½ in; *W* 10½ in.
Status: fairly common to abundant permanent resident of the mainland; rare in the Keys during winter.
Habitat: any shrubby or wooded habitat with abundant leaf litter.

Nesting: on the ground or low in a saw palmetto or other dense shrub; female builds a cup nest of twigs and leaves and lines it with grass; mostly the female incubates 3–4 brown-spotted, creamy white to pale gray eggs for 12–13 days; 2–3 broods per year.
Feeding: noisy; scratches leaf litter on the ground with both feet simultaneously; feeds mostly on seeds and fruit; also takes insects and spiders.
Voice: quite variable; white-eyed birds have loud, rich *tweee* calls; song of 1–2 notes, followed by trill, often buzzy.
Similar Species: adult is distinctive; juvenile is much larger than other sparrows with white-tipped outer tail feathers.
Best Sites: widespread.

319

BACHMAN'S SPARROW

Aimophila aestivalis

The sparrows are a large family of small, mostly ground-dwelling birds, usually with drab plumage. Of Florida's 28 species, only four, including the Bachman's Sparrow, breed in our state. The Bachman's is endemic to the southeastern U.S. In Florida, it is a permanent resident of the Panhandle and peninsula south to Lake Okeechobee. • The Bachman's Sparrow is commonly associated with pine flatwoods, but it occurs perhaps equally commonly in native dry prairies. It is extremely secretive and difficult to observe except for males in song from March through July. Although drab in plumage and inconspicuous, the Bachman's has one of the most beautiful songs of any of Florida's birds. • When disturbed, Bachman's Sparrows often take refuge in burrows! • This species is named after John Bachman (1790–1874), a South Carolina ornithologist whose two daughters married the two sons of John James Audubon.

ID: small, non-flocking sparrow; long tail; grayish brown upper-parts streaked with brown and rufous; dark crown; gray eyebrow; brown eye line; grayish cheek and throat; gray underparts with buffy breast. *Juvenile:* conspicuous eye ring; finely dark-streaked breast.

Size: *L* 5–6 in; *W* 7 in.

Status: fairly common permanent resident of the Panhandle and the northern two-thirds of the peninsula; virtually absent south of Lake Okeechobee; unreported in the Keys.

Habitat: pine flatwoods, dry prairie; may winter in shrubby fields.

Nesting: on the ground, usually in a saw palmetto clump; female builds a domed nest of grass; female incubates 2–5 white eggs for 12–14 days; may have 2–3 broods per year.

Feeding: on or close to the ground; feeds mainly on insects, especially grasshoppers and crickets, and on spiders; eats mostly seeds during winter.

Voice: high, thin call note; beautiful song is a variable, long, clear whistled note followed by 1 or more trills: *Heeeeere-kittty-kitty-kitty-kitty*.

Similar Species: few other sparrows breed within same range. *Grasshopper Sparrow* (p. 325): juveniles resemble and flock with Bachman's juveniles.

Best Sites: widespread.

CHIPPING SPARROW

Spizella passerina

The Chipping Sparrow has one of the most extensive breeding ranges of any sparrow in North America and is well known over most of the continent. It breeds from Alaska through most of Canada and the continental U.S. to Honduras and Nicaragua, and it winters in the southern U.S. and Mexico. In Florida, Chipping Sparrows are fairly common winter residents in the Panhandle and peninsula but are very rare in the Keys. There are several breeding reports from the Panhandle; the most recent is from 1959. • Unlike most sparrows, which occur in mixed flocks in brushy or weedy fields, Chipping Sparrows usually occur in single species flocks, often in trees or tall shrubs. They often visit bird feeders during winter.

breeding

ID: small sparrow often observed in flocks in trees; short tail; brown upperparts and crown streaked with black; gray nape; pale eyebrow; black eye line; gray face; white throat; pinkish bill; brown wing with 2 white bars; grayish underparts. *Breeding:* bright rusty cap bordered with black; dark bill.

Size: *L* 5–6 in; *W* 8½ in.

Status: fairly common to common winter resident in the Panhandle and northern third of the peninsula; rare to fairly common during winter farther south in the peninsula; irregular and very rare in the Keys during winter; several breeding reports from the Panhandle.

Habitat: open pine woodlands, scrub and shrubby fields; also yards with dense shrubbery.

Nesting: very rare in Florida; in a tree or shrub; male and female build a compact cup nest of grass and weed stems and line it with rootlets and hair; female incubates 4 pale blue eggs for 11–12 days.

Feeding: gleans the ground for insects, spiders and seeds; visits bird feeders during winter.

Voice: high-pitched *chip* call; the song, rarely heard in Florida, is a rapid, dry trill.

Similar Species: *Clay-colored Sparrow* (p. 366): very similar; buffy eyebrow; dark "mustache"; buffy breast. *American Tree Sparrow:* very rare in Florida; larger; rufous crown; blackish spot on breast.

Best Sites: widespread.

FIELD SPARROW

Spizella pusilla

A familiar winter resident in the northern parts of Florida, the Field Sparrow is rarely seen by birders farther south. • This sparrow breeds in extreme southeastern Canada and across most of the eastern U.S. It winters in much of the breeding range and southward to Mexico.• In Florida, Field Sparrows are regular winter residents south into the central peninsula but are rare farther south. Small numbers breed in the Panhandle and northwestern peninsula, where they are found in young pine plantations or fields overgrown with small pines or other trees. • North of Florida, and perhaps also in our state, Field Sparrows abandon nests that have been parasitized by Brown-headed Cowbirds. One female in Michigan built seven nests in one season but failed to raise a single brood. • The Field Sparrow is one of Florida's easiest sparrows to identify—only it and the much larger White-crowned Sparrow have pinkish bills.

NP; small numbers breed in the Panhandle and northwestern peninsula.
Habitat: *Breeding:* young pine plantations. *Winter:* shrubby fields and abandoned citrus groves.
Nesting: on or near the ground; male and female build a cup nest of grass and line it with soft material; female incubates 3–5 brown-spotted, whitish to bluish white eggs for 10–12 days.
Feeding: gleans the ground for insects, spiders and seeds.
Voice: *chip* call; song is a series of musical, downslurred whistles accelerating into a trill.
Similar Species: few other sparrows have pink bills. *White-crowned Sparrow* (p. 333): juvenile is larger, with no eye ring or rufous coloration on head, and has dark eye line.
Best Sites: widespread.

ID: small terrestrial sparrow; white eye ring; pink bill; rufous upperparts streaked with black; rufous crown and ear patch; gray face; rusty wing with 2 white bars; buffy breast washed with rufous; pinkish legs and feet.
Size: *L* 5–6 in; *W* 8 in.
Status: rare to common resident of the mainland from October to March; less common in the south; unreported in winter from the Keys except for 1 at Dry Tortugas

VESPER SPARROW

Pooecetes gramineus

The Vesper Sparrow is one of several species of sparrows that may be found in Florida's shrubby fields or overgrown citrus groves during winter. It breeds across the southern half of Canada and the northern half of the continental U.S., and it winters in the southern U.S. and Mexico. In Florida, the Vesper Sparrow winters statewide, but it is most numerous in the Panhandle and northern peninsula and rarest in the Keys. • This species prefers fields that are somewhat brushy but not overgrown with shrubs or trees. • The white outer tail feathers of the Vesper Sparrow can be hard to see but are diagnostic. Among the sparrows regularly found in our state, only the boldly marked Lark Sparrow and Dark-eyed Junco share this feature. If the tail feathers are not visible, the Vesper Sparrow may be confused with the common Savannah Sparrow. • The Vesper Sparrows gets its name from its habit of singing in the evening, although other sparrows—and many other songbirds—share this behavior. *Pooecetes* is Greek for "grass dweller."

ID: terrestrial sparrow; white outer tail feathers; pale brown upperparts with dark streaking; white eye ring; dark-bordered, grayish brown cheek; dark "mustache"; white throat; 2 faint white wing bars; buffy breast and flanks with brown streaking; pinkish legs and feet.
Size: *L* 6 in; *W* 10 in.
Status: rare to fairly common resident statewide from November to March, less numerous southward; rare in the Keys.

Habitat: densely weedy or shrubby fields.
Nesting: does not breed in Florida.
Feeding: forages on the ground for seeds, insects and spiders.
Voice: sharp *chip* call.
Similar Species: no other sparrow has both streaked breast and white outer tail feathers. *American Pipit* (p. 283): favors open muddy areas away from cover; often in large flocks; wags tail; has white outer tail feathers and streaked plumage, but with thinner bill, unstreaked back and dark legs.
Best Sites: widespread.

SAVANNAH SPARROW

Passerculus sandwichensis

The Savannah Sparrow is arguably Florida's most common and widespread nonbreeding sparrow. This highly variable species breeds throughout Alaska and Canada into the northern half of the continental U.S. and in Mexico. It winters in the southern United States, the West Indies and Mexico. In Florida, the Savannah Sparrow is a statewide winter resident, occurring even along the grassy top of Fort Jefferson at Dry Tortugas NP. • Birders confused by the assortment of Florida's wintering sparrows should study the Savannah Sparrow, which is commonly found in flocks that often perch conspicuously on weed stalks or fences. This bird's boldly streaked breast (usually with no central spot), yellow lores and plain tail are diagnostic field marks. When other sparrows are compared to the Savannah, identification of this confusing group is much easier. • The English and scientific names of this bird reflect its broad North American distribution: "Savannah" refers to the city in Georgia in which it was first noted, and *sandwichensis* is derived from Sandwich Bay, Alaska.

ID: streaked breast; yellow lores; variable plumage; grayish brown upperparts with dark streaks; strongly patterned head; gray eyebrow; black eye line; dark cheek and "mustache"; white throat; pale underparts with heavy, dark streaking (may show a central breast spot); white belly and undertail coverts.
Size: *L* 5–6 in; *W* 6½ in.

Status: fairly common to common winter resident statewide from October to April.
Habitat: grassy fields; abandoned citrus groves; dry prairie.
Nesting: does not breed in Florida.
Feeding: forages on the ground or low in vegetation; feeds on insects, spiders and seeds.
Voice: high, thin *tsit* call.
Similar Species: *Vesper Sparrow* (p. 323): white outer tail feathers. *Song Sparrow* (p. 330): rarer in south; gray eyebrow; lacks yellow lores; bold central breast spot; longer rounded tail.
Best Sites: widespread.

GRASSHOPPER SPARROW

Ammodramus savannarum

The Grasshopper Sparrow is an inconspicuous bird of the New World. From March through July, the male sings two completely different breeding songs, one to defend his territory and the other to attract a mate. • Grasshopper Sparrows found in Florida fall into two races. The Eastern Grasshopper Sparrow (*A. s. pratensis*) is a fairly common winter resident of grassy areas statewide, whereas the Florida Grasshopper Sparrow (*A. s. floridanus*) is an endangered subspecies endemic to the dry prairie ecosystem lying north and west of Lake Okeechobee. Loss of habitat for cattle pastures and agricultural fields has dramatically reduced *A. s. floridanus* numbers. As of this writing, perhaps 1000 individuals remain.

ID: short-tailed sparrow with large, flat head; white median stripe; yellow lores; pale eye ring; relatively large conical bill; pale upperparts heavily streaked with brown; white underparts with unstreaked, buffy breast; yellow patch at bend of wing. *Juvenile:* white underparts with bold, dark streaking.

Size: *L* 5–5½ in; *W* 7½ in.

Status: *A. s. pratensis:* fairly common resident from October to April. *A. s. floridanus:* endangered permanent resident (FWC).

Habitat: *A. s. pratensis:* any type of open, grassy habitat. *A. s. floridanus:* endemic to remaining patches of native dry prairie.

Nesting: in a shallow depression on the ground, usually concealed by saw palmetto, dwarf live oak, grass or shrubs; female builds a small, domed nest of grass and lines it with fine plant material; female incubates 3–5 creamy white eggs, spotted with gray and reddish brown, for 11–13 days; probably 2–3 broods per year.

Feeding: gleans insects, spiders and other invertebrates from the ground; switches to seeds during winter.

Voice: high, thin *tip* call; "short song" is high and faint: *tik-tok-zeeeeeeee;* "long song" is a jumble of notes lasting 5–15 seconds.

Similar Species: *Savannah Sparrow* (p. 324): white underparts with bold, brownish streaking. *Henslow's Sparrow* (p. 326): generally rare; dull olive head; chestnut wings; narrow, black streaking on breast and flanks.

Best Sites: *A. s. pratensis:* widespread. *A. s. floridanus:* Kissimmee Prairie Preserve SP; Three Lakes WMA.

HENSLOW'S SPARROW

Ammodramus henslowii

Actively sought by Florida birders, the Henslow's Sparrow is a secretive bird of wet grassy areas. It breeds in the midwestern U.S. and extreme southeastern Canada and winters in the Southeast. In Florida, Henslow's Sparrow is a rare to locally uncommon winter resident of the Panhandle and northern half of the peninsula. This bird's secretive behavior masks its southern limits in our state, but it is a regular at least as far south as Kissimmee Prairie, where banding efforts have documented fair numbers wintering in native dry prairies. In the Panhandle, Henslow's Sparrow is found mostly in recently burned pine savannas, such as at Apalachicola National Forest, where it may be fairly common. • Because of loss of habitat on its breeding and wintering grounds, the Henslow's Sparrow is a declining species. • John James Audubon named this sparrow after his friend John Stevens Henslow (1796–1861), an English naturalist and teacher of Charles Darwin.

ID: secretive, ground-dwelling sparrow; short tail; brown back with white streaks; olive head and nape; white eye ring; dark crown with pale median stripe; dark "mustache"; rufous wings; white underparts with blackish streaking on buffy breast and flanks.

Size: *L* 5–5½ in; *W* 6½ in.

Status: rare to locally common resident from October to April, most numerous in the Panhandle, irregular south of L. Okeechobee and not known from the Keys; declining.

Habitat: wet grassy or brushy fields, dry prairie and brushy lakeshores.

Nesting: does not breed in Florida.

Feeding: gleans insects and seeds from the ground.

Voice: generally silent in Florida; high, sharp *tsik* call; weak, liquidy, cricketlike *tse-lick* song may be heard in spring prior to migrating northward.

Similar Species: *Grasshopper Sparrow* (p. 325): head and nape not olive; no dark "mustache"; no prominent streaking on breast and flanks. *Savannah Sparrow* (p. 324): numerous and conspicuous; often perches up; lacks olive head and nape; no buffy breast. *Le Conte's Sparrow:* buffy median stripe on black crown; bold, orange triangle surrounds gray cheek.

Best Sites: Apalachicola NF; Kissimmee Prairie Preserve SP; St. Marks NWR.

NELSON'S SHARP-TAILED SPARROW

Ammodramus nelsoni

Previously considered to be a single species, the five races of the Sharp-tailed Sparrow were divided into two separate species—the Nelson's Sharp-tailed Sparrow and the Saltmarsh Sharp-tailed Sparrow—by the American Ornithologists' Union in 1995. Both species occur in Florida, but their abundance and distribution are unclear. The Nelson's Sharp-tailed Sparrow is known to be numerous along the Gulf Coast, but its status along the Atlantic Coast is uncertain. • All three Nelson's races have been recorded in Florida. Based on specimen evidence, *A. n. alterus* seems restricted to our Gulf Coast, *A. n. nelsoni* occurs on both coasts but is probably more numerous along the Gulf, and *A. n. subvirgatus* is known only from the Atlantic Coast. • This species is named after Edward William Nelson (1878–1934), chief of the U.S. Biological Survey (the present-day U.S. Fish and Wildlife Service), who in 1916 wrote the Migratory Bird Treaty Act.

ID: small songbird restricted to coastal marshes; distinctive orange triangle on face; black and white streaks on back; unstreaked, gray nape and ear patch; dark crown with gray stripe; pale throat; orange breast and flanks with faint streaking; white belly.
Size: *L* 5 in; *W* 7 in.
Status: fairly common resident of the Gulf Coast south to Port Richey from October to April and perhaps less numerous along the Atlantic Coast south to about Merritt Island NWR.

Habitat: salt or brackish coastal marshes.
Nesting: does not breed in Florida.
Feeding gleans vegetation or mud for insects or seeds.
Voice: low *check* call.
Similar Species: *Saltmarsh Sharp-tailed Sparrow* (p. 328): primarily along Atlantic Coast; orange on face brighter than on breast; streaking on breast generally bolder; breast less buffy. *Le Conte's Sparrow:* found in noncoastal fields; streaked nape; white crown stripe.
Best Sites: widespread, mostly along the Gulf Coast.

SALTMARSH SHARP-TAILED SPARROW

Ammodramus caudacutus

As explained in the previous account, the Saltmarsh Sharp-tailed Sparrow and the Nelson's Sharp-tailed Sparrow were formerly considered to be a single species. • The Saltmarsh Sharp-tailed Sparrow has two races. *A. c. caudacutus* breeds from Maine to New Jersey, and *A. c. diversus* breeds from New Jersey to North Carolina. Our knowledge of the status and distribution of the Saltmarsh Sharp-tailed Sparrow in Florida is incomplete. Specimen evidence indicates that both races winter here; however they cannot be distinguished in the field. Interestingly, both races have been found along the Gulf Coast as well as along the Atlantic, despite their breeding ranges being restricted to the Atlantic. The Saltmarsh Sharp-tailed Sparrow migrates across the peninsula to winter along the Gulf Coast, but few migrants have been found inland, where they might be confused with Le Conte's Sparrow *(A. leconteii)*. Along the coasts, great care is necessary to distinguish the Saltmarsh Sharp-tailed Sparrow from Nelson's Sharp-tailed Sparrow.

ID: small songbird restricted to coastal marshes; distinctive orange triangle on face; black and white streaks on back; unstreaked, gray nape and ear patch; dark crown with gray stripe; pale throat; orange on flanks paler than on head; bold streaking on breast and flanks; white belly.
Size: *L* 5½ in; *W* 7 in.
Status: fairly common resident of Atlantic coastal marshes south to about Merritt Island NWR. from October to April; rare along the Gulf Coast south to Port Richey and apparently at Everglades NP.
Habitat: salt or brackish coastal marshes.
Nesting: does not breed in Florida.
Feeding gleans vegetation or mud for insects or seeds.
Voice: low *check* call.
Similar Species: *Nelson's Sharp-tailed Sparrow* (p. 327): primarily along Gulf Coast; no contrast between orange on face and breast; generally fainter streaking on breast; buffier breast. *Le Conte's Sparrow:* uses noncoastal fields, not coastal marshes; streaked nape; white crown stripe.
Best Sites: widespread, mostly along the Atlantic Coast.

SEASIDE SPARROW

Ammodramus maritimus

One of the most variable species in Florida, the Seaside Sparrow is represented by six or seven races. A few of these races were previously considered separate species, and some splitting of Seaside Sparrow races is likely over the next several years. • The Seaside Sparrow is a uniquely American species that is a permanent coastal resident most of the way from New Hampshire to Texas, with only casual records for extreme southeastern Canada. • In Florida, one race, the Dusky Seaside Sparrow *(A. m. nigrescens)*, which was endemic to Brevard County, is now extinct. Four or five other races continue to breed discontinuously along the coast (or inland for the Cape Sable race, *A. m. mirabilis*), and at least one other race winters in our state. All are found in marshes, where they can be difficult to study.

ID: small songbird restricted to coastal marshes; dark, variable plumage; dusky upperparts, including nape and crown, with blackish stripes; dusky head with yellow lores and white "mustache"; white throat; dusky underparts with indistinct streaking. *A. m. mirabilis:* olive upperparts; white underparts with bold, black streaking.
Size: *L* 6 in; *W* 7½ in.
Status: fairly common permanent resident of coastal marshes south to Port Richey and Jacksonville; during winter, northern-breeding races may occur farther south in the peninsula; *A. m. mirabilis* is fairly common resident endemic to Everglades NP and Big Cypress National Preserve; several races are endangered or of special concern (FWC), and one is extinct.

Habitat: coastal marshes. *A. m. mirabilis:* inland marshes.
Nesting: in marsh vegetation, 8–10 in above the ground; female builds a cup nest of grass and rushes and lines it with finer materials; female incubates 3–4 brown-speckled, pale greenish white eggs for 11–12 days; *A. m. mirabilis* produces 3 broods per year.
Feeding: gleans the ground or vegetation for insects, spiders and small crabs.
Voice: low *chup* call; song resembles that of a distant Red-winged Blackbird.
Similar Species: *Swamp Sparrow* (p. 331): rusty wings and tail; gray eyebrow, face and lores. *Saltmarsh Sharp-tailed Sparrow* (p. 328) and *Nelson's Sharp-tailed Sparrow* (p. 327): orange facial triangle; buffy breast and flanks.
Best Sites: widespread.

SONG SPARROW

Melospiza melodia

The Song Sparrow is one of the most widely distributed sparrows in North America, breeding from the Aleutian Islands and Canada's Maritime Provinces to Baja California and Georgia and wintering in much of the continental U.S. • It is also one of the most variable sparrows, with perhaps 30 races described. Some of these races may be good candidates for elevation to species status over the next few years, as their relationships become better understood using DNA analysis. • In Florida, Song Sparrows are winter residents throughout much of the mainland, and are represented by at least three races—*M. m. euphonia, M. m. juddi* and *M. m. melodia*—that may not be distinguishable in the field. • Despite its abundance elsewhere in North America, the Song Sparrow is rather rare in most of the peninsula, where it is greatly outnumbered by the similar Savannah Sparrow. In addition to its larger size and bold central breast spot, the Song Sparrow can be recognized by its long, rounded tail, which is conspicuous as the bird flies away.

ID: white underparts with bold, dark streaking on flanks and breast; central breast spot; brown upperparts with dark streaks; dark nape and crown; broad, gray eyebrow; dusky cheek; dark "mustache"; white throat; long, rounded tail.

Size: *L* 6–7 in; *W* 8½ in.

Status: fairly common resident of the Panhandle and northern third of the peninsula from October to March; rare farther south in the peninsula; very rare in the Keys.

Habitat: shrubby fields or other brushy areas.

Nesting: does not breed in Florida.

Feeding: scratches leaf litter with both feet or gleans food from the ground; feeds on insects, spiders, millipedes and other invertebrates; may also feed on seeds and fruit.

Voice: sharp *tsip* call.

Similar Species: *Fox Sparrow:* rare and restricted to the Panhandle and northern third of the peninsula; larger; rusty upperparts and cheek; no dark "mustache." *Savannah Sparrow* (p. 324): usually in flocks; paler upperparts; yellow lores; narrow, white eyebrow; lightly streaked breast usually with no central spot; short, notched tail.

Best Sites: widespread.

SWAMP SPARROW

Melospiza georgiana

The Swamp Sparrow is a relative rarity for a wintering sparrow: it prefers shrubby marshes, flooded thickets and other similar habitats over dry grassy or weedy fields. Despite its name, it is not found in densely wooded swamps. • This sparrow breeds in much of southern Canada and the northeastern U.S. It winters along the Pacific Coast and in much of the eastern U.S. and Mexico. In Florida, it is a statewide migrant and winter resident but is most numerous on the mainland. This sparrow is fairly common in Florida's central peninsula, where most of our other wintering sparrows are rare. • Swamp Sparrows readily respond to pishing, and a marsh or shrubby wetland that seemed to lack birds moments earlier may suddenly become alive with these sparrows and a few other responsive species, such as Common Yellowthroats. • The call notes of Swamp Sparrows are distinctive, even if the birds remain hidden by dense thickets.

ID: small sparrow found in wet, shrubby habitats; rusty upperparts and tail; dark streaking on back; gray head with rusty crown and dark eye line; faint "mustache"; white throat; gray breast may have faint streaking; white belly; pale flanks.
Size: *L* 5–6 in; *W* 7½ in.
Status: fairly common migrant and resident in the Panhandle and northern half of the peninsula from October to April, becoming less numerous farther south; rare in the Keys.
Habitat: salt, brackish or freshwater marshes; weedy pond edges; wet fields or thickets.

Nesting: does not breed in Florida.
Feeding: gleans the ground or shallow water for insects, spiders and seeds.
Voice: metallic *chip* and nasal *zeeee* calls.
Similar Species: *Lincoln's Sparrow* (p. 367): rare; brown upperparts; dark crown; broad, gray eyebrow; narrow eye ring; buffy breast with fine streaking. *White-throated Sparrow* (p. 332): rare; larger; brown upperparts; dark crown; yellow lores; may have white eyebrow; 2 white wing bars.
Best Sites: widespread.

331

WHITE-THROATED SPARROW

Zonotrichia albicollis

The White-throated Sparrow breeds across Canada and in the northeastern U.S. It winters along the Pacific Coast from British Columbia to California and on the Atlantic Coast from Canada's Maritime Provinces to Florida and extreme northern Mexico. In Florida, it is a migrant and winter resident throughout the mainland, ranging from common in the north to rare in the south. • Two color morphs of the White-throated Sparrow occur in Florida. One morph has black and white stripes on its head, and the other has brown and tan stripes. White-striped males are more aggressive than their tan-striped counterparts, whereas tan-striped females are more nurturing than are white-striped birds. The two morphs are perpetuated because most pairings are of birds of opposing morphs. • *Zonotrichia* means "hairlike," an apparent reference to the striped heads of the birds in this genus; *albicollis* is Latin for "white neck"—an inaccuracy, because, although the throat is white, the neck is gray.

white-striped morph

tan-striped morph

ID: large terrestrial sparrow; brown back with dark streaking; dark nape; pale crown stripe; broad, white or buffy eyebrow; black eye line; gray cheek; yellow lores; gray bill; white throat outlined by blackish stripes; rich brown wing with 2 white bars; gray breast with rest of underparts paler.
Size: L 6½–7½ in; W 9 in.
Status: fairly common migrant and resident of the Panhandle and northern third of the peninsula from October to April;

less numerous farther south in the peninsula; very rare in the Keys.
Habitat: shrubby fields or other brushy areas; open woodlands; pond edges.
Nesting: does not breed in Florida.
Feeding: scratches leaf litter with both feet simultaneously for insects, spiders, millipedes, snails and seeds; may visit bird feeders.
Voice: loud *chink* call; song consists of 2 clear, whistled notes followed by 3 triplets, often written as *Old Sam Peabody, Peabody, Peabody.*
Similar Species: *White-crowned Sparrow* (p. 333): gray nape; lacks yellow lores; pink bill; gray throat. *Swamp Sparrow* (p. 331): smaller; rusty tail, wings and crown; lacks white wing bars and yellow lores.
Best Sites: widespread.

WHITE-CROWNED SPARROW

Zonotrichia leucophrys

Although the White-crowned Sparrow is one of the most studied birds in North America, it has never been formally studied in Florida. This species breeds in Alaska, northern and western Canada and the western U.S. It winters from British Columbia and Ontario to Mexico and the West Indies. In Florida, it is a generally rare migrant and winter resident statewide, sometimes found in small flocks. • The eastern-breeding race, *Z. l. leucophrys,* is the race expected in our state, but the *Z. l. gambelii* race, which breeds in Alaska and western Canada, has occurred occasionally. Although variation exists within the various races of the White-crowned Sparrow—and intergrades between races are known—the two races that occur in Florida should be distinguishable in the field. *Z. l. gambelii* has a white eyebrow that extends to its bill, whereas *Z. l. leucophrys* has black lores. Adults of both races are very distinctive. • With their head and crown boldly alternating in black and white stripes, adult White-crowned Sparrows are easy to recognize, but many of the birds seen in Florida are juveniles and have much less striking head patterns. However, even these birds can still be correctly identified by their pinkish bills, upright posture and rounded heads.

ID: large terrestrial sparrow; distinctive pink bill; gray or brown back with dark streaking; gray nape; crown boldly marked with black and white; black eye line; gray throat and breast, with rest of underparts paler. *Juvenile:* head subtly marked with tan and gray; brown eye line.
Size: *L* 5½–7 in; *W* 9½ in.
Status: rare migrant and resident statewide from October to April.

Habitat: shrubby fields, fencerows or other brushy areas.
Nesting: does not breed in Florida.
Feeding: scratches the ground or leaf litter with both feet simultaneously to expose insects, spiders, millipedes and seeds; may also eat fruit or visit bird feeders.
Voice: loud *chink* call.
Similar Species: *White-throated Sparrow* (p. 332): yellow lores; grayish bill; bold, white throat; rich brown wings.
Best Sites: widespread.

DARK-EYED JUNCO

Junco hyemalis

Juncos are sparrows with typically uniform, unstreaked plumage as adults. Of the four species of juncos, two occur in North America. The Dark-eyed Junco, formerly considered five separate species, is the only species that occurs in the east. It breeds over most of Alaska, Canada and the western and northeastern continental U.S. It winters from southern Canada through northern Mexico. In Florida, the Dark-eyed Junco is generally a rare winter resident of the Panhandle, and it is rare to very rare in the northern peninsula. • The "Slate-colored" race *(J. h. hyemalis)* is the expected form in our state, but at least two "Oregon Juncos" *(J. h. cismontanus)* have been recorded. • The name "junco" originates with a genus of rushes *(Juncus)* that a particular Old World bird frequented, and this term was somehow later associated with certain New World sparrows—even though they do not have any connection with *Juncus* marshes. • Dark-eyed Juncos are typically found feeding on the ground, often in the company of other sparrows.

"Slate-colored Junco"

ID: small ground-dwelling sparrow with distinctive plumage. *"Slate-colored" male:* entirely dark gray upperparts; pink bill; white belly; white outer tail feathers. *"Slate-colored" female:* duller plumage, with some brown in wings. *"Oregon" male:* rusty upperparts and flanks contrast strongly with black head. *"Oregon" female:* muted colors; dark gray head. **Size:** *L* 5½–7 in; *W* 9½ in.

Status: rare to uncommon, perhaps somewhat irruptive resident of the Panhandle from November to March; rare in the northern third of the peninsula; very rare farther south; only 1 report from the Keys. **Habitat:** woodland edges; brushy fields, rural or suburban yards. **Nesting:** does not breed in Florida. **Feeding:** forages on the ground; scratches for seeds and invertebrates; also visits bird feeders. **Voice:** generally silent in Florida. **Similar Species:** none; plumage pattern, small size and ground-dwelling habits are distinctive. **Best Sites:** fairly widespread in the north of our state.

NORTHERN CARDINAL

Cardinalis cardinalis

Resident from the eastern half of the U.S. to Guatemala and Belize, the Northern Cardinal is one of the most recognizable and loved birds in North America. The male's bright plumage often decorates calendars or Christmas cards. The Northern Cardinal is one of the few birds that occurs truly throughout our state, being found in all mainland regions, including densely developed urban areas, and all of the Mainline Keys. • Male Northern Cardinals are highly territorial and often attack their own reflections in mirrors or shiny objects. • The Northern Cardinal owes its name to the vivid red plumage of the male, which resembles the red robes of Roman Catholic cardinals.

ID: medium-sized songbird with crest; thick red-orange bill; rather long tail. *Male:* bright red overall; black face and eyes. *Female:* warm brown back and head; reddish crest; less distinct black face; pale red wings; reddish brown breast; white belly; reddish tail. *Juvenile:* like female, but with duller plumage; brown face; blackish bill.
Size: *L* 7½–9 in; *W* 12 in.
Status: generally common permanent resident throughout the mainland; less numerous on some of the Keys.
Habitat: any shrubby or open wooded habitat; shuns dense woodlands.

Nesting: in a dense shrub or vine tangle or low in a tree (especially citrus); female builds a cup nest of twigs, leaves and grass and lines it with finer materials; female incubates 2–5 (usually 3) profusely marked, whitish to greenish white eggs for 12–13 days; 2–3 broods per year.
Feeding: gleans seeds, fruit and insects from the ground or low vegetation; visits bird feeders; fond of sunflower seeds.
Voice: loud, metallic *tick* call; song is a variable series of clear, whistled notes.
Similar Species: *Tufted Titmouse* (p. 256): resembles juvenile Northern Cardinal but much smaller, with gray upperparts and buff-washed, pale underparts. *Summer Tanager* (p. 317): mostly arboreal; male has no crest or black on face and has longer, paler bill.
Best Sites: widespread.

ROSE-BREASTED GROSBEAK
Pheucticus ludovicianus

True to their name, grosbeaks are songbirds with large, conical bills. Six species (in two separate families) are found in North America, and four of them occur in Florida. • The Rose-breasted Grosbeak breeds across southern Canada and the northeastern continental U.S. It winters from Mexico through northern South America. In Florida, it is a regular statewide migrant, perhaps somewhat more numerous during fall. • Flocks of several Rose-breasted Grosbeaks—at times even dozens of individuals—may be seen after storms. • Although breeding males are distinctive, other plumages of the Rose-breasted Grosbeak are very similar to those of the Black-headed Grosbeak, a very rare visitor from western North America.

breeding

ID: medium-sized arboreal songbird; large, conical bill. *Breeding male:* white rump; black back and head; pale bill; black wing with bold, white markings; white underparts with red breast and pale tan wash on flanks; black tail with white outer feathers; shows red underwings and white patch at base of outer flight feathers in flight. *Female, nonbreeding male* and *juvenile:* sparrowlike, with black-streaked, brown upperparts and dark-streaked, white underparts; boldly striped head with wide, white eyebrow; may have buffy or pinkish breast and flanks; shows buffy or pink underwings and no white patch in flight.
Size: *L* 7–8½ in; *W* 12½ in.

Status: rare to uncommon migrant statewide from April to May and from September to October; very rare winter resident in the extreme south.
Habitat: any wooded habitat, especially with oaks.
Nesting: does not breed in Florida.
Feeding: gleans vegetation or occasionally hover-gleans or sallies; feeds on insects, spiders and some seeds and fruit.
Voice: distinctive loud *eek!* call.
Similar Species: adult male is distinctive. *Black-headed Grosbeak:* very rare; non-breeding male has richer buff underparts with little or no streaking and shows yellow underwings and no white patch in flight. *Purple Finch* (p. 367) or *House Finch* (p. 354): little seasonal overlap; females are much smaller and have more boldly streaked underparts with no buff on breast.
Best Sites: widespread.

BLUE GROSBEAK

Passerina caerulea

Despite its name, the Blue Grosbeak is more closely related to the Indigo Bunting than to other grosbeaks. • It breeds from the southern two-thirds of the continental U.S. to southern Central America, and it winters from northern Mexico to Panama. In Florida, the Blue Grosbeak breeds north to the central peninsula, and it migrates statewide. Small numbers are being seen more frequently during winter. • Although solitary when nesting, flocks of Blue Grosbeaks are often seen during spring migration. Wintering birds may be seen in fields with Indigo Buntings and other species. • The bright plumage of males results not from molt but from wear. As the brown tips of the nonbreeding plumage feathers wear away, they reveal the deep blue of the breeding plumage.

ID: smallish songbird of brushy habitats; large conical bill; orange wingbars; characteristically flicks tail. *Male:* blue body, becoming mottled with brown after breeding; black face; dark wing with wide wing bars. *Female* and *juvenile:* rich brown overall; plain face; paler underparts; rump and shoulders washed with blue; juvenile male acquires adult plumage gradually.
Size: *L* 6–7½ in; *W* 11 in.
Status: fairly common breeding resident of the Panhandle and northern third of the peninsula from April to October; rare to absent farther south; fairly common migrant statewide; recently detected during winter, mostly in the southern half of the peninsula.

Habitat: woodland edges, abandoned citrus groves and other brushy habitats.
Nesting: in a shrub or small tree; pair builds a cup nest of twigs and weed stems and lines it with finer materials; female incubates 3–5 (usually 4) pale blue eggs for 11–12 days.
Feeding: gleans insects from the ground or foliage; also eats seeds or fruit.
Voice: loud *chink* call; song is a sweet series of melodious, warbling phrases that rise and fall.
Similar Species: *Indigo Bunting* (p. 338): smaller body; smaller bill; no orange wing bars; male has all-blue face. *Brown-headed Cowbird* (p. 350): female has similar plumage but is mostly terrestrial, and longer tail is often raised.
Best Sites: widespread.

337

INDIGO BUNTING

Passerina cyanea

The word "bunting" once referred to a chunky person or animal, and the term was originally applied to a European songbird. Since that time, several birds have been called buntings—even though not all of them are closely related. • The Indigo Bunting breeds in extreme southeastern Canada and from the eastern to southwestern U.S., and it winters from Florida, Texas and the West Indies to Panama and Colombia. In Florida, it has a variable distribution, breeding in the north, wintering in the south and migrating statewide. Indigo Buntings are often seen in flocks during migration, especially during spring, and at bird feeders during winter. Unlike Blue Grosbeaks and Painted Buntings, adult male Indigo Buntings do not retain the same plumage year-round.

breeding

winter resident, mostly in the southern half of the peninsula.

Habitat: brushy fields, abandoned citrus groves and other shrubby areas.

Nesting: in a shrub, small tree or vine tangle; female builds a cup nest of grass, leaves and bark strips and lines it with finer materials; female incubates 3–4 white to bluish white eggs for 12–13 days.

Feeding: forages on or near the ground; gleans insects, spiders, seeds and fruit; visits bird feeders, especially during winter.

Voice: quick *spit* call; song consists of melodious paired, warbled whistles.

Similar Species: *Blue Grosbeak* (p. 337): larger overall; much larger bill; 2 orange wing bars; male has black face. *Brown-headed Cowbird* (p. 350): female is similar in plumage but lacks blue in wings and tail, is mostly terrestrial and longer tail is often raised.

Best Sites: widespread.

ID: small songbird of brushy habitats; conical bill. *Male:* brilliant blue plumage, becoming mottled with brown after breeding. *Female* and *juvenile:* rich brown overall; pale throat; faint buffy wing bars; may show bluish wash on wings and tail; juvenile male acquires adult plumage gradually.

Size: *L* 5½ in; *W* 8 in.

Status: fairly common breeding resident of the Panhandle and northern third of the peninsula from March to October; fairly common migrant statewide, more numerous during spring; rare to locally uncommon

PAINTED BUNTING

Passerina ciris

The Painted Bunting is unquestionably one of Florida's most colorful birds. • This species has two separate breeding ranges: one is along the Atlantic Coast from North Carolina to Florida, and the other is mostly inland, from Alabama to Mexico. It winters from Florida and the West Indies to Panama. In Florida, the Painted Bunting breeds south to about Merritt Island, with a few isolated pairs at Apalachicola along the Panhandle coast. It winters south of Lake Okeechobee, and it can be found anywhere during migration. • Although not nearly as unmistakable—gaudy even—as that of the male, the plumage of the female is nonetheless attractive: a rich greenish above and pale yellow below. Unlike some other finches, including the Indigo Bunting, the adult male Painted Bunting retains his bright colors during winter, brightening up any yard where he is found. • In recent years, numbers of Painted Buntings have declined along the Atlantic Coast; this has been attributed mostly to increased brood parasitism by the Brown-headed Cowbird.

ID: small finch of brushy habitats. *Male:* stunning plumage; greenish yellow back and wings; brilliant blue head with red orbital ring; red underparts, including throat. *Female:* brilliant yellow-green above and pale yellow below; yellow orbital ring. *Juvenile:* similar to female but duller and more grayish green.
Size: L 5½ in; W 8½ in.
Status: rare to uncommon breeding resident along the northern Atlantic Coast; generally rare migrant statewide; rare to uncommon winter resident primarily south of Lake Okeechobee.

Habitat: *Breeding:* shrubby fields, hammock edges and citrus groves. *Winter:* variety of habitats, including backyards with plenty of cover.
Nesting: in a shrub or low tree; female weaves an open cup from grass, weed stems and leaves and lines it with fine plant materials and animal hair; female incubates 3–4 finely speckled, white eggs for 11–12 days; usually 2 broods per year.
Feeding: forages mostly on the ground; feeds primarily on seeds but also eats insects; commonly visits bird feeders, especially during winter.
Voice: sharp *chip* call; song is a sweet, clear series of warbling notes.
Similar Species: male is unmistakable; plumage of female is also distinct.
Best Sites: *Breeding*: Talbot Islands SP. *Wintering*: Everglades NP; Corkscrew Swamp Sanctuary; Castellow Hammock P. (Miami).

DICKCISSEL
Spiza americana

Until recently, Dickcissels were rare migrants and winter residents in Florida. But, in 1999, a few pairs of Dickcissels nested along the north shore of Lake Apopka, establishing the first breeding record for our state. In spring 2005, Dickcissels again bred at Lake Apopka, and more than 130 singing males were found! Dickcissels are opportunistic breeders, often colonizing sites far from their core range, depending on local habitat conditions. Indeed, other observations from Florida have suggested that Dickcissels may also have bred recently in the western Panhandle and the southern peninsula. Their primary breeding range covers much of the central U.S. • Dickcissels winter from the southern U.S. to northern South America, gathering in immense flocks in Venezuela—some flocks contain one million or more birds! Sadly, Venezuelan farmers often poison thousands of birds at a time to protect their crops, but recent conservation initiatives may be reversing this trend.

ID: small land bird of grasslands. *Male:* grayish back with blackish streaks; gray head with dark crown; yellow eyebrow and "mustache"; white throat; brown wing with rusty shoulder; gray underparts; yellow breast with black "V." *Female:* sparrowlike plumage; resembles male but with muted colors and no "V" on breast.

Size: *L* 6–7 in; *W* 9½ in.

Status: rare and unpredictable migrant and resident statewide from September to April; recent breeding at L. Apopka and perhaps elsewhere.

Habitat: *Breeding:* shrubby fields. *Winter:* any shrubby habitat.

Nesting: in a shrub among dense vegetation; female builds a bulky cup nest of grass and other plants and lines it with finer materials; female incubates 4 pale blue eggs for 12–13 days.

Feeding: gleans insects and seeds on or near the ground; also visits bird feeders.

Voice: buzzerlike *bzrrrrt* flight call; song consists of 2–3 single notes followed by a trill, paraphrased as *dick-dick-dick-cissel*.

Similar Species: *House Sparrow* (p. 357): female resembles Dickcissel female but without "mustache" or yellow in face or on breast.

Best Sites: unpredictable. *Spring* and *summer:* Lake Apopka NSRA.

BOBOLINK
Dolichonyx oryzivorus

The Bobolink breeds in southern Canada and the northern U.S. and winters in southern South America. Some individuals migrate an amazing 12,000 miles annually between their breeding and wintering areas, making the Bobolink the premiere long-distance land bird in the Western Hemisphere. One banded female made the round trip nine times during her lifetime, the equivalent to circling the Earth at the equator four times! • In Florida, Bobolinks are generally rare spring migrants, when the bulk of their migration is well to the west of us, and locally common fall migrants statewide. During fall, flocks of hundreds or even thousands of migrating Bobolinks may be seen in large, brushy fields, and their distinctive *ink* calls can be heard overhead shortly after dawn.

breeding

ID: medium-sized terrestrial songbird; pointed tail feathers. *Breeding male:* white rump; black back; pale yellow nape; black face; black wing has large white patch on shoulder; entirely black underparts; black tail feathers. *Breeding female:* sparrowlike; black cap; pale back streaked with black; pale eyebrow; black eye line; pale bill and underparts. *Nonbreeding:* resembles breeding female, but with rich buff wash overall. **Size:** *L* 6–8 in; *W* 11½ in.
Status: rare to fairly common spring migrant from April to May and uncommon to locally abundant from August to October; 1 winter record.

Habitat: grassy or brushy fields, dry prairie and agricultural fields.
Nesting: does not breed in Florida.
Feeding: forages on the ground and low vegetation for insects, spiders and seeds.
Voice: low *chuck* call; distinctive *ink* flight call; song (sometimes heard in spring) is a series of bubbly warbling notes.
Similar Species: breeding male is distinctive. *Sparrows* (pp. 319–34): generally smaller, without pointed tail feathers or entirely buffy underparts; often in smaller flocks.
Best Sites: widespread migrant.

341

RED-WINGED BLACKBIRD

Agelaius phoeniceus

Without question, the Red-winged Blackbird is one of our most common and widespread birds. It breeds from southern Alaska across most of Canada, the entire continental U.S., the northern Bahamas and as far south as Nicaragua and Costa Rica. In Florida and across most of the U.S., it is a year-round resident. • Given the abundance of Red-winged Blackbirds and their tolerance for a variety of habitats, Florida's population must be in the millions. After breeding, these blackbirds gather, along with other icterids—members of the blackbird, grackle and cowbird family— in immense flocks that can number in the hundreds of thousands of birds. • Experimental studies indicate the importance of the males' red shoulders: when their shoulders were painted black, the males quickly lost their territories to rival males with normal red shoulders.

ID: medium-sized songbird of marshy areas; dark bill, legs and feet. *Male:* black overall except for large red shoulder patch edged in yellow. *Female:* brown upperparts and pale underparts heavily streaked with dark brown; pale eyebrow and throat often pink-tinged.
Size: *L* 7–9½ in; *W* 13 in.
Status: common to abundant permanent resident; numbers increase from fall through spring with the addition of northern breeders.
Habitat: any shrubby or brushy wetland; dry prairie.
Nesting: usually loosely colonial; in a shrub or tree, usually near or over water; female weaves a deep cup of dried leaves and grass and lines it with fine grass; female incubates 3–4 darkly marked, pale, blue-green eggs for 10–12 days; 2 broods per year.
Feeding: on or near the ground; gleans grain, other seeds and invertebrates; visits bird feeders.
Voice: calls include a harsh *check* and a high *tseert;* song is *konk-a-ree.*
Similar Species: plumage of male is distinctive; female resembles sparrow or finch but is much larger, is found in flocks in open habitats and has pointed bill.
Best Sites: widespread.

EASTERN MEADOWLARK

Sturnella magna

Meadowlarks are terrestrial songbirds with chunky bodies, short tails and rather long, pointed bills. North America's two species—the Eastern Meadowlark and the Western Meadowlark—are nearly identical in plumage. Both occur in Florida, but the Western is very rare. • The Eastern Meadowlark is largely resident, with some northern withdrawal during fall, in the eastern U.S. and most of the southwestern U.S., Cuba, Central America and the northern half of South America. In Florida, it remains surprisingly widespread throughout the mainland but does not occur in the Keys. • Eastern Meadowlarks are found in native grasslands and open pinewoods, as well as in fields, in vacant lots, and on road shoulders. Two subspecies occur in our state, the northern-breeding *S. m. magna* and the Florida-breeding *S. m. argutula*; they cannot be distinguished in the field.

ID: medium-sized terrestrial songbird; short, mostly white tail; strongly streaked upperparts; dark crown; white eyebrow; black eye line; yellow throat, breast and upper belly marked with bold, black "V" and flank streaking.
Size: *L* 9–9½ in; *W* 14 in.
Status: fairly common to common permanent resident of the mainland, becoming more numerous in the north during winter; very rare in the Keys.
Habitat: open grassy habitats, with or without scattered trees, including suburban areas.
Nesting: on the ground, sometimes in a slight depression, concealed by dense grass; female builds a domed grass nest woven into surrounding vegetation; female incubates 3–7 brown-speckled, white eggs for 13–15 days; probably raises 2 broods per year.
Feeding: forages on the ground; gleans insects—especially grasshoppers and crickets—and spiders; also eats seeds.
Voice: calls include a rattle in flight and a high, buzzy *dzeart;* song is a rich series of 2–8 melodic, slurred whistles.
Similar Species: generally unmistakable. *Dickcissel* (p. 340): much smaller and less numerous; rarely seen on ground; yellow restricted to male's throat and upper breast; no streaking on flanks. *Bobolink* (p. 341): smaller; seen only during migration; buffy, not yellow, underparts; no black "V" on breast.
Best Sites: widespread.

YELLOW-HEADED BLACKBIRD

Xanthocephalus xanthocephalus

The spectacular Yellow-headed Blackbird breeds in southwestern Canada and the central and western thirds of the continental U.S. It winters from the extreme southern U.S. to central Mexico. Small numbers of this species move eastward along the Gulf of Mexico during fall. In Florida, the Yellow-headed Blackbird is a rare migrant and winter resident statewide, and it may be seen at any site where large numbers of blackbirds, grackles and cowbirds congregate. At times, a dozen or more individuals have been seen together in our state. • The bird's scientific name *xanthocephalus* means "yellow head."

ID: medium-sized songbird of open habitats. *Male:* black body; yellow head and breast; black mask; white patch on upperwing. *Female* and *juvenile:* brown replaces black; dusky nape and crown; duller yellow face and breast; wing patch faint or absent.
Size: *L* 8–11 in; *W* 15 in.
Status: rare migrant and resident statewide from September to April.
Habitat: agricultural fields, dairy farms and cattle feedlots.
Nesting: does not breed in Florida.

Feeding: forages on the ground for grain, other seeds and insects; may visit bird feeders.
Voice: deep *croak* call.
Similar Species: male is distinctive. *Boat-tailed Grackle* (p. 347): female and juvenile resemble female or juvenile Yellow-headed Blackbird but larger, buffy rather than yellow, with longer tail and without white wing patches.
Best Sites: dairy farms or feedlots.

BREWER'S BLACKBIRD

Euphagus cyanocephalus

A relatively new addition to our avifauna, the Brewer's Blackbird breeds in western Canada and the western United States, and it winters from British Columbia to Georgia and into Mexico. For the past century, it has been expanding its range eastward as forests have been cleared and cattle have been introduced. In Florida, the Brewer's Blackbird was first found at Panama City in 1939. It had spread to Key West by 1953, but populations have subsequently declined. Today, it is a winter resident, at times fairly common in the western Panhandle but generally rare elsewhere. • Although the Brewer's Blackbird can be seen among flocks of other icterids or European Starlings, it is usually found in small flocks or as a single individual in pastures, where it is often seen probing cow patties in search of seeds. • John James Audubon named this bird after Thomas Mayo Brewer (1814–80), a friend and prominent ornithologist.

nonbreeding

ID: medium-sized, mostly terrestrial blackbird. *Breeding male:* black body with purple gloss on head and green gloss on wings; pale eyes. *Female:* drab grayish brown above, paler on head and breast; dark eyes. *Nonbreeding male:* resembles breeding male, but with duller plumage.
Size: *L* 8–10 in; *W* 15½ in.
Status: irruptive winter resident, at times fairly common in the Panhandle but generally rare in the peninsula, especially the southern two-thirds; 1 report in the Keys.

Habitat: open habitats such as fields or pastures, with or without scattered trees.
Nesting: does not breed in Florida.
Feeding: gleans grain and other seeds from the ground or manure piles; also eats some insects.
Voice: metallic *chuck* call.
Similar Species: *Rusty Blackbird:* found in forested wetlands; nonbreeding male has rusty "scaling" on upperparts; female has yellow eyes. *Common Grackle* (p. 346): much larger; much longer, keel-shaped tail; larger bill. *Brown-headed Cowbird* (p. 350): female resembles female Brewer's, but with thicker bill and shorter tail; often raises tail when feeding.
Best Sites: dairy farms or feedlots in the Panhandle.

COMMON GRACKLE
Quiscalus quiscula

Grackles are large, mostly terrestrial blackbirds with heavy bills and long, keel-shaped tails. Of the three species found in North America, two are resident in Florida and the third (the Great-tailed Grackle, *Q. mexicanus*) is expected to eventually colonize our state. The Common Grackle breeds in southern Canada and the eastern U.S., and it winters in the eastern U.S. In Florida, it breeds throughout the state, but most of the breeders in the Keys fly north to winter on the mainland. • Grackles are one of several species that practice "anting." The grackle either allows ants to crawl over its body or it rubs squished ants through its feathers. The formic acid from the ants' bodies helps eliminate parasites. When ants are not available, grackles may substitute lemons or mothballs instead!

ID: large, mostly terrestrial blackbird; long, keel-shaped tail. *Male:* black with purple iridescence on head, green on back and blue on tail; eyes always yellow. *Female:* resembles male but duller, with less iridescence. *Juvenile:* resembles female, but with even less iridescence and dark eyes.
Size: *L* 11–13½ in; *W* 17 in.
Status: common to abundant permanent resident statewide, even in the Keys.
Habitat: most open or semi-wooded upland habitats; also in forested wetlands and suburban areas.
Nesting: singly or in a small colony; in a dense tree or shrub, often near water; female builds a bulky cup nest of twigs, plant fibers and mud and lines it with fine grass or feathers; female incubates 4–5 brown-blotched, pale blue eggs for 12–14 days.
Feeding: on or close to the ground; feeds mostly on vegetable matter such as seeds, berries and acorns, but also takes insects and other invertebrates and occasional small vertebrates.
Voice: call is a loud *chack*; song is a series of harsh, strained notes ending with a squeak.
Similar Species: *Boat-tailed Grackle* (p. 347): much larger, with larger tail; usually dark eyes; female has brown plumage and pale throat. *Rusty Blackbird* and *Brewer's Blackbird* (p. 345): much rarer; local and present only during winter; much smaller; smaller bill; no keel on tail.
Best Sites: widespread.

BOAT-TAILED GRACKLE

Quiscalus major

The Boat-tailed Grackle is our largest blackbird, larger even than the Fish Crow. It is resident along the coast from New York to Texas. In Florida, it is found throughout the peninsula, even inland, but is mostly coastal in the Panhandle, and it is absent from the Keys. • The Boat-tailed Grackle has adapted well to suburbia, occupying most shopping center parking lots, where it displays from planted trees and forages among cars and shoppers. It is also commonly seen nesting in stormwater retention ponds. • With fluffed feathers, spread tails, fluttering wings and bills held skyward, groups of male Boat-tailed Grackles display for females, uttering series of loud *cheep* notes and other sounds.

ID: large, mostly terrestrial blackbird; long, dark bill. *Male:* black plumage with greenish blue iridescence on body and purple on head; brown eyes (except yellow around Jacksonville); very long, keel-shaped tail. *Female* and *juvenile:* mostly dark brown above and paler brown on head and underparts; whitish throat; less keel-shaped tail.
Size: *Male:* L 16½ in; W 23 in. *Female:* L 14 in; W 17½ in.
Status: common to abundant permanent resident of most of the peninsula, rare to uncommon in the Panhandle; very rare in the Keys.
Habitat: usually near fresh, brackish, or salt water, including stormwater retention ponds in suburban and urban areas.

Nesting: colonial; in vegetation over or near water; female builds bulky cup nest of marsh vegetation and lines it with mud and grass; female incubates 2–3 darkly scrawled, pale blue eggs for 12–14 days and raises the young alone.
Feeding: forages on or near the ground or in shallow water, gleaning prey from the surface; normally takes insects, crustaceans and other invertebrates but may also eat small vertebrates and some seeds; sometimes gleans insects from radiator grills!
Voice: most frequent song is a series of loud *jeep* notes; also gives a variety of rattles, chatters, squeaks and a soft *chuck*.
Similar Species: *Common Grackle* (p. 346): much smaller, with shorter tail; eyes always yellow; never has pale brown in plumage.
Best Sites: widespread.

SHINY COWBIRD

Molothrus bonariensis

Cowbirds are the only brood parasites in North America that do not also raise their own young. Cowbird females lay their eggs in the nests of other birds, and the "foster parents" raise the nestling cowbirds. Three species of cowbirds occur in North America, and they are all now found in Florida. • The Shiny Cowbird was originally restricted to South America, but it has greatly expanded its range throughout the West Indies over the past 100 years, primarily because of deforestation and the introduction of cattle. It was first found in Florida in the Keys in 1985 and has now spread to other coastal areas. To date, there is still no documented record of breeding in our state, although breeding has probably occurred.

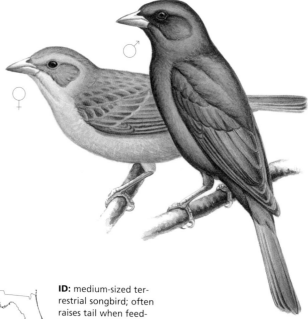

ID: medium-sized terrestrial songbird; often raises tail when feeding. *Male:* black body with bluish or purplish iridescence; black eyes, bill, legs and feet. *Female:* dull grayish brown overall; little contrast at throat; breast has very faint or no streaking; dark face; faint eyebrow, "beady" eyes; possible pale base to lower mandible. *Juvenile:* brown above with buffy highlights; buffy eyebrow; pale, unstreaked underparts; black bill.
Size: *L* 7½–8 in; *W* 12 in.
Status: rare permanent resident in the extreme south; generally rare spring coastal migrant; very rare inland.
Habitat: any wooded or shrubby habitat.

Nesting: brood parasite, 1 egg per nest in up to 5 nests; white, creamy, pale blue or gray eggs can be unmarked or darkly marked and hatch after 11-13 days.
Feeding: on ground; actively pursues insects and spiders; also eats seeds; visits bird feeders.
Voice: song is 3–5 bubbling notes followed by 2–3 high notes; also sings a canary-like "twitter song."
Similar Species: *Brown-headed Cowbird* (p. 350): chunkier; rounded head; short, thick bill; shorter tail; male has brown head; female is gray with white throat and faintly streaked breast.
Best Sites: Dry Tortugas NP; Everglades NP; Key West.

BRONZED COWBIRD

Molothrus aeneus

The opening of the Southwest to cattle grazing and agriculture in the early 20th century created new habitat for the Bronzed Cowbird. Previously found only from Mexico to Panama, this brood parasite was first recorded in North America in Arizona in 1909. It spread steadily eastward, arriving in Florida in 1962. Since then, the Bronzed Cowbird has been found in more than 20 counties in our state. As of 2004, it appears to have become a permanent resident, but breeding has yet to be confirmed. • Like other cowbirds, Bronzed Cowbirds favor open areas such as parks and golf courses, and they gather at dairy farms and cattle feedlots. As many as 42 of these birds have been seen at one time in one site! • A male Bronzed Cowbird courts a female with a display that includes fluffing out his ruff (the feathers on the nape), spreading his tail and walking toward her with his bright red eyes flared.

ID: medium-sized songbird; brownish black plumage; heavy, conical bill; red eyes. *Male:* thick ruff on neck; iridescent blue wings. *Female:* smaller than male; slightly duller overall; no blue on wings. *Juvenile:* resembles female, but with dark eyes.
Size: *L* 8½–9 in; *W* 14 in.
Status: rare to uncommon and increasing winter resident statewide from October to April; potentially a rare, possibly increasing breeding resident, perhaps statewide.

Habitat: open or lightly wooded habitats, especially around cattle or farmland; also suburban areas.
Nesting: brood parasite; 1 egg per nest in up to 5 nests; pale blue or greenish blue eggs hatch after 10-13 days.
Feeding: forages on or near the ground; feeds mostly on grain and other seeds; also takes snails, insects and spiders.
Voice: song consists of varied high, bubbling whistles.
Similar Species: red eyes of adult diagnostic. *Other cowbirds* (pp. 348, 350): identification of juveniles may be difficult.
Best Sites: unpredictable, but at times fairly reliable at sites such as Eagle Lakes Park in Naples.

349

BROWN-HEADED COWBIRD
Molothrus ater

The Brown-headed Cowbird is the most successful brood parasite in North America. It has been recorded depositing its eggs into the nests of 220 other bird species. While not all nest parasitism is successful—some birds eject the cowbird eggs or build new nests elsewhere, and others, such as doves, cannot properly feed the young cowbird, causing it to starve—nearly 150 of the species parasitized by the Brown-headed Cowbirds successfully raise the cowbird young. • This species has greatly expanded its range in the past 150 years, as people have cleared forests and established cattle feedlots and dairy farms. It now breeds from southern Alaska to northern Mexico, and it winters in much of the continental U.S. and Mexico. This cowbird first bred in Florida in 1956, at Pensacola. By 1991, it had colonized the entire peninsula and probably also the Keys. • Brown-headed Cowbirds have been implicated in the decline of Painted Buntings along the northern Atlantic Coast and of Black-whiskered Vireos and Florida Prairie Warblers along the southern Gulf Coast.

ID: small songbird with shortish tail; conical bill; raises tail when foraging on ground. *Male:* black body with green iridescence; brown head. *Female:* dull grayish brown overall; pale throat; faint streaking on breast. *Juvenile:* resembles female, but back and wings appear "scaly"; streaked underparts.
Size: *L* 6–8 in; *W* 12 in.
Status: common permanent resident of the Panhandle and northern third of the peninsula; less numerous and generally coastal farther south; at times abundant during winter.
Habitat: any habitat with at least scattered trees. *Winter:* large flocks at dairy farms and feedlots.
Nesting: brood parasite; 1 egg per nest in up to 30 nests; variably marked, whitish eggs hatch after 10–13 days.
Feeding: forages on the ground for seeds; rarely takes insects.
Voice: high-pitched *seep* call, often given in flight; song is a liquidy 3-syllable gurgle.
Similar Species: *Bronzed Cowbird* (p. 349): male has red eyes; female is uniformly dull black. *Shiny Cowbird* (p. 348): male is uniformly black; female closely resembles Brown-headed female but is darker overall, with faint eyebrow and darker, less contrasty throat.
Best Sites: widespread.

ORCHARD ORIOLE

Icterus spurius

Orioles are members of the blackbird family that have brilliant orange or yellow plumages. Of North America's nine oriole species, five have occurred in Florida, but two of them are rare. • The Orchard Oriole breeds throughout the eastern U.S. and northern Mexico, and it winters from Mexico to Colombia and Venezuela. • In Florida, it breeds widely in the Panhandle and northern third of the peninsula, but is rare farther south to about Orlando. It is also a fairly common spring migrant statewide but is less numerous during fall. The Orchard Oriole is smaller than Florida's other regularly occurring oriole species, and it may be mistaken for a large warbler.

ID: smallish arboreal songbird. *Male:* mostly dark rufous, with black tail, back and head; black wing with rufous shoulder patch and 1 white wing bar. *Female:* yellow overall, darker on crown and nape; greenish gray back; darkish wing with 2 white wing bars. *Juvenile male:* like female, but with black throat patch.

Size: L 6–7 in; W 9½ in.

Status: fairly common breeding resident of the Panhandle and northern third of the peninsula; fairly common spring migrant statewide; very rare during winter, mainly in the extreme south.

Habitat: *Breeding:* open woodlands, suburban parklands and fields with scattered trees. *In migration:* any wooded habitat.

Nesting: in the fork of a deciduous tree or shrub; female builds a hanging pouch nest woven from grass and other plant fibers; female incubates 4–5 pale, bluish white eggs, blotched with gray, brown and purple, for about 12–15 days.

Feeding: gleans insects, spiders and fruit from vegetation.

Voice: quick *chuck* call; song is a loud, rapid, varied series of whistled notes.

Similar Species: *Baltimore Oriole* (p. 353): male has bright orange plumage and orange in tail; female has orange wash to plumage and mostly gray underparts. *Spot-breasted Oriole* (p. 352): very restricted range; resembles Orchard juvenile male but with generally orange plumage. *Summer Tanager* (p. 317) and *Scarlet Tanager* (p. 318): females have thicker, pale bills and no wing bars.

Best Sites: widespread.

SPOT-BREASTED ORIOLE

Icterus pectoralis

The colorful Spot-breasted Oriole is native to Mexico and Central America. It was introduced to Miami, probably accidentally, in 1948, and it rapidly colonized the southern Atlantic Coast. By the late 1960s, stragglers occurred north to Cocoa Beach. In the mid-1970s, unknown causes resulted in a population crash, and the species has not recovered. The Spot-breasted Oriole is now restricted to well-vegetated urban and suburban areas from West Palm Beach south to Homestead. These areas provide a wide variety of nectar- and fruit-bearing trees and shrubs. Listen for males singing from utility wires or tree branches. • Birders from throughout North America visit the Fort Lauderdale, Miami and West Palm Beach areas searching for Spot-breasted Orioles. However, backyard bird-watchers in the region often misidentify this species as Hooded, Scott's or Altamira orioles, all of which are native species that occur in the southwestern U.S. and Mexico.

ID: large songbird. *Male:* yellow-orange overall; black throat, wings and back; black spots on sides of breast; white in primary feathers; yellow-orange shoulder patch. *Female:* slightly duller coloration than male. *Juvenile:* entirely pale yellow plumage without any spotting.
Size: *L* 8–9½ in; *W* 13 in.
Status: uncommon, perhaps declining permanent resident of residential areas; rare to fairly common permanent resident of coastal southeastern Florida.
Habitat: suburban neighborhoods with tall exotic trees and shrubs that bear flowers or fruit.

Nesting: near the end of a slender branch, often well above the ground; female builds a long, hanging pouch of woven grass and other plant fibers; female incubates 2–5 whitish to pale blue eggs, scrawled with black and lilac, for 12–14 days; 2 broods per year.
Feeding: eats insects, berries, small fruit and nectar; forages among tree foliage; visits feeders.
Voice: song is a long, loud series of liquid whistled notes.
Similar Species: *Baltimore Oriole* (p. 353): male has black hood; female has 2 white wing bars and no black on throat. *Orchard Oriole* (p. 351): female is olive yellow, and lacks colored shoulder patch, black throat and dark breast spots.
Best Sites: residential areas of Broward, Miami-Dade and Palm Beach counties.

BALTIMORE ORIOLE

Icterus galbula

The Baltimore Oriole breeds in southern Canada and the eastern United States, and it winters from the southeastern U.S. and West Indies through Central America. In Florida, it is a rare or uncommon migrant and winter resident statewide. Because it feeds heavily on fruit and nectar during winter, this species is often seen around honeysuckle hedges, citrus groves and yards with feeders that supply nectar or orange slices. • Baltimore Orioles and Bullock's Orioles (*Icterus bullockii*)—which are rare migrants and winter residents in Florida—hybridize where their ranges overlap in the Great Plains. For years, the two species were combined as the Northern Oriole, but in 1995, the American Ornithologists' Union reinstated the birds' status as separate species. • The Baltimore Oriole was named after the black and orange coat of arms of George Calvert, who established the colony of Baltimore, Maryland.

ID: large songbird with orange plumage. *Male:* black upperparts, including head; black wing with orange shoulder bar and white wing bar; entirely orange underparts; black tail with orange outer feathers. *Female:* resembles male, but with dusky back and head; 2 white wing bars. *Juvenile:* brownish gray above; plain face; variable underparts, ranging from mostly grayish or yellowish to mostly orange.
Size: *L* 7–8 in; *W* 11½ in.
Status: rare to uncommon migrant and resident statewide from September to April; 1 breeding report from Key West in 1972!

Habitat: found in any wooded habitat.
Nesting: does not normally breed in Florida.
Feeding: gleans vegetation for caterpillars and other insect; eats much fruit and nectar during winter; may visit hummingbird feeders.
Voice: rich *hu-lee* call.
Similar Species: *Bullock's Oriole:* female is very similar to female Baltimore, but with "jagged" edge to upper wing bar and grayish wings. *Orchard Oriole* (p. 351): male has darker chestnut plumage; female is olive yellow overall. *Spot-breasted Oriole* (p. 352): limited to southern Atlantic Coast; resembles female Baltimore but has black throat and spots on breast; white in primary feathers.
Best Sites: widespread.

HOUSE FINCH

Carpodacus mexicanus

Native to the western United States and Mexico, the House Finch was brought to eastern cities for the cage bird trade in the late 1930s. When, in 1940, it became known that the House Finch was a protected species, some pet shop owners in New York City released their birds to avoid prosecution. From these few dozen birds, the population grew to exceed 10 million birds by the late 1990s, as the species colonized the entire eastern U.S. and extreme southern Canada! • In Florida, the first House Finch was found in Hollywood in 1980, but it may have been a local escapee. The first accepted record was near Pensacola in 1983, and breeding began at Tallahassee in 1988 or 1989. This finch now breeds locally south to Tampa and Lakeland, with an isolated colony, perhaps local escapees, at Fort Lauderdale. • The color of male House Finches varies from yellow to red, but females prefer the reddest-plumaged males.

ID: small finch with streaked brown upperparts; 2 pale wing bars; whitish underparts with brown streaking. *Male:* brown crown; usually red (but may be orange or yellow) on forehead, throat and breast; reddish rump. *Female:* resembles male, but without red (or orange or yellow) areas.
Size: *L* 5–6 in; *W* 9½ in.
Status: rare to uncommon local permanent resident of the Panhandle and northern half of the peninsula; range expanding southward.
Habitat: urban and suburban areas.

Nesting: in a natural or artificial cavity or birdhouse; female builds a cup nest of twigs and lines it with finer materials; female incubates 4–5 sparsely marked, pale blue eggs for 12–14 days.
Feeding: gleans seeds from the ground or vegetation; also eats some fruit and insects; visits bird feeders.
Voice: *cheer* call, given singly or in series; song is a variable series of rambling warbling notes.
Similar Species: *Purple Finch* (p. 367): rarer; winter only; male has darker red plumage and indistinct streaking on underparts; female has bold, white eyebrow and distinct brown streaking on breast.
Best Sites: fairly widespread.

PINE SISKIN
Carduelis pinus

The Pine Siskin is a winter-irruptive species in Florida, occurring in some years and remaining absent in others. It breeds in southern Alaska, across western and southern Canada, the western U.S. and Mexico, and it winters from southern Canada to Mexico. In Florida, it is most frequent in the Panhandle and northern third of the peninsula, where it can be common but is typically rare. • In very rare cases, numbers of Pine Siskins have irrupted as far south as the Keys. They are often found in flocks of American Goldfinches and are frequent visitors to feeders that provide thistle seed. In Florida, they have also been observed feeding on the "cones" of Australian pines. • In contrast to the greatly dimorphic plumages of most finches, plumage differences between male and female siskins are difficult to detect.

ID: small, heavily streaked finch; 2 wing bars; yellow patches in wings and tail; brown upperparts with faint streaking; whitish underparts with bold streaking.
Size: *L* 4½–5½ in; *W* 9 in.
Status: irruptive winter visitor statewide from November to April, at times locally common but usually rare or absent; especially rare in the southern peninsula and the Keys.

Habitat: open coniferous or mixed forests, residential areas.
Nesting: does not breed in Florida.
Feeding: gleans the ground and vegetation; feeds on seeds; regularly visits bird feeders.
Voice: buzzy, rising *zzzreeeee* call.
Similar Species: *Yellow-rumped Warbler* (p. 295): superficially similar, but with thin bill, unstreaked head, pale throat and yellow rump. *House Finch* (p. 354): female has thicker bill and no yellow in wings or tail. *Sparrows* (pp. 319–34): all lack yellow in wings and tail.
Best Sites: none; irruptive.

355

AMERICAN GOLDFINCH

Carduelis tristis

The American Goldfinch is colloquially known as wild canary because of the male's bright plumage and musical song. • It breeds in southern Canada and the northern two-thirds of the continental U. S., and it winters throughout the U. S. and northern Mexico. In Florida, the goldfinch is irruptive but is found throughout the state during most winters, perhaps because it breeds in the Deep South. This species breeds as far south as central Alabama and central Georgia, but despite summer occurrences in Florida, there are no known breeding observations from our state. • American Goldfinches often remain in Florida until early May or later, by which time they have molted into their breeding plumage, and the males have begun singing. • Although they also occur in natural habitats, American Goldfinches are common visitors to bird feeders that supply thistle seed.

nonbreeding

Size: *L* 4½–5½ in; *W* 9 in.
Status: irruptive, generally uncommon to abundant resident statewide from October to April.
Habitat: any weedy, shrubby or open woodland habitat, including suburbs.
Nesting: does not breed in Florida.
Feeding: gleans ground and vegetation; feeds primarily on seeds but takes some fruit; commonly visits feeders.
Voice: rollicky *per-chick-or-ee* call, often delivered in flight; song (heard during spring) is a long, varied series of trills, twitters, warbles and hissing notes.
Similar Species: none; no other unstreaked bird with yellow in plumage visits feeders.
Best Sites: widespread.

ID: small, stocky, arboreal finch; bold wing bars; usually some yellow in plumage. *Breeding male:* bright yellow body; black wing with white wing bars; black forehead and tail. *Breeding female:* like male, but body duller, no black on head. *Nonbreeding:* brownish or grayish upperparts; gray underparts; often some pale yellow on head and breast.

HOUSE SPARROW

Passer domesticus

A well-known resident of grocery store signs, fast-food parking lots and gas stations, the House Sparrow is a native of Europe and northern Africa. • House Sparrows were introduced to North America in 1850 or 1851, around Brooklyn, New York. Since then, they have colonized most human-altered environments on the continent, first appearing in Florida in 1882, and they have benefited greatly from their close association with people. • House Sparrows have been blamed for the decline of native cavity-nesting species such as Eastern Bluebirds, but populations of sparrows have also been declining for decades. Today, House Sparrows in Florida appear to depend on parking lots and dairy farms, where there is little competition with native species. • House Sparrows belong to the large Old World family of sparrows (Passeridae), which are only distantly related to the family that contains the New World sparrows (Emberizidae).

ID: small stocky bird of urban habitats. *Male:* gray crown; black bill, chin, throat and breast form bib; chestnut nape; light gray cheek; white wing bar; dark, mottled upperparts; gray underparts. *Female:* plain gray-brown overall, with paler underparts and streaked upperparts; buffy eyebrow.
Size: *L* 5½–6½ in; *W* 9½ in.
Status: locally common permanent resident statewide around shopping centers and gas stations; generally absent elsewhere.
Habitat: restricted to areas around human habitation; does not flock with native sparrows.

Nesting: often communal; usually on a building or in a birdhouse or other artificial cavity; pair builds a dome-shaped nest of grass, plant fibers and litter and often lines it with feathers; pair incubates 4–6 whitish to greenish white eggs, dotted with gray and brown, for 10–13 days.
Feeding: gleans seeds and other grains from the ground; visits feeders for birdseed.
Voice: short *chill-up* call; song is a plain, familiar *cheep-cheep-cheep-cheep*.
Similar Species: unlikely to be confused with any other species; no native species shares nesting habitat.
Best Sites: widespread.

MORE FLORIDA BIRDS

The following is a selection of 39 of the less common or unpredictable species known to occur in Florida. For a full listing of these species, see the checklist (pp. 371–75).

GREATER WHITE-FRONTED GOOSE
Anser albifrons

Greater White-fronted Geese breed on the Arctic tundra and winter along the Pacific Coast, the Mississippi River Basin and the western Gulf Coast to Mexico. They rarely straggle to Florida, but they are occasionally seen from November to March, especially in the Panhandle. They occur mostly along the coast in marshes or wastewater treatment facilities, or in agricultural fields, where they feed on seeds and roots.

Greater White-fronted Goose

ID: brown body; white band on face; pink or orange bill; black speckling on breast and belly; black band on upper surface of white tail; orange feet.
Size: *L* 27–33 in; *W* 4½–5 ft.

TUNDRA SWAN
Cygnus columbianus

Tundra Swan

Tundra Swans breed in the Arctic and winter locally along the Atlantic and Pacific coasts. On the East Coast, most Tundra Swans remain north of South Carolina, but singles or small groups occasionally reach Florida, primarily the Panhandle or northern third of the peninsula. They are found in brackish or freshwater marshes along the coast or on lakes inland, where they feed on plant material.

ID: huge bird; long thin neck. *Adult:* all-white plumage; black bill with yellow loral spot. *Immature:* plumage grayish brown plumage; mostly pink bill.
Size: *L* 4–5 ft; *W* 6–7 ft.

EURASIAN WIGEON
Anas penelope

Eurasian Wigeon

Nearly every year, one or more Eurasian Wigeons are found in Florida between November and March, invariably among flocks of American Wigeons. All observations have been of drakes; the hens are probably overlooked. Eurasian Wigeons breed in Eurasia, and small numbers winter regularly along both coasts of North America, where they feed on plant material.

ID: medium-sized puddle duck; rounded head; black-tipped blue-gray bill. *Drake:* chestnut head; buffy forehead; rosy breast; gray sides; black hindquarters. *Hen:* rufous hints on mostly brown head and breast; buffy flanks. *In flight:* large, white wing patch; gray underwings distinctive in all plumages.
Size: *L* 20 in; *W* 32 in.

CINNAMON TEAL
Anas cyanoptera

Cinnamon Teal

A few Cinnamon Teals probably stray eastward to Florida from the western U.S. and Canada each year between September and March. The drakes' bright plumage makes them stand out, but the hens are seldom noticed. Cinnamon Teals have been found throughout the mainland but are not definitively known from the Keys. They feed on plant material and mollusks, crustaceans and aquatic insects.

ID: small duck. *Drake:* unmistakable; rich cinnamon body with streaked back and wings; red eyes. *Hen:* mottled brown overall; large, spatulate bill.
Size: *L* 16 in; *W* 22 in.

SURF SCOTER
Melanitta perspicillata

Surf Scoter

Surf Scoters are generally rare residents along the northern portions of Florida's coasts from November to March, but surprisingly large numbers have been seen along the Atlantic Coast on rare occasions. Scoters are found in bays or on the ocean, where they dive for mollusks, crustaceans and other aquatic invertebrates.

ID: large sea duck; bulky triangular-shaped bill accentuates sloped forehead. *Drake:* black overall with a white forehead and nape; gaudy orange bill with large black spot outlined in white. *Hen:* brown overall; 2 whitish patches on each side of face.
Size: *L* 16–20 in; *W* 30 in.

LONG-TAILED DUCK
Clangula hyemalis

Until very recently known as "Oldsquaw," the Long-tailed Duck is a rarity in Florida. Only a few individuals are found each year between November and April, usually along the Panhandle coast. This duck feeds on mollusks and other aquatic invertebrates, as well as some fish, which are obtained by diving.

Long-tailed Duck

ID: medium-sized sea duck. *Nonbreeding drake:* pale head with gray eye patch and dark cheek patch; pale neck and belly; dark breast; long white patches on back; pink bill with dark base; long, dark central tail feathers. *Nonbreeding hen:* short tail feathers; gray bill; dark crown, cheek patch, wings and back; white underparts.
Size: *L* 17–20 in; *W* 28 in.

EARED GREBE
Podiceps nigricollis

Eared Grebes breed in the western and central U.S. and Canada, and small numbers winter in Florida in the Panhandle and the peninsula from October to April. They are found along the coast, in sewage treatment facilities and on mine impoundments. Eared Grebes dive for small fish, crustaceans and other aquatic invertebrates.

Eared Grebe

ID: small diving bird; red eyes; short, thin bill. *Nonbreeding:* white throat; dark crown, cheek and upperparts; pale underparts; dusky upper foreneck and flanks.
Size: *L* 11½–14 in; *W* 16 in.

BLACK-CAPPED PETREL
Pterodroma hasitata

Black-capped Petrel

Only 2000 Black-capped Petrels are believed to exist worldwide. They breed in burrows on Cuba and Hispaniola and feed in Atlantic waters from spring to fall. Black-capped Petrels occur regularly in Florida waters, at times within 15 miles of shore. They feed on squid and small crustaceans plucked from the ocean's surface.

ID: well-marked black and white seabird; dark gray upperparts; white underparts; black cap accentuated by white forehead and collar; stubby black bill. *In flight:* triangular black bar on leading edge of white underwing; prominent white rump with black-tipped tail.
Size: *L* 16 in; *W* 3 ft.

BAND-RUMPED STORM-PETREL
Oceanodroma castro

Although perhaps the least common of Florida's three storm-petrels, the Band-rumped Storm-Petrel nonetheless may be the most numerous species off the northern Gulf Coast, primarily during spring and summer. It breeds on islands in tropical oceans; the colony nearest to Florida is in the Atlantic Ocean off Portugal. The Band-rumped Storm-Petrel is attracted to upwellings where zooplankton and other marine creatures are plentiful.

ID: small seabird; flies just above ocean's surface; blackish brown overall; well-defined white rump band; paler brown wing bar; tail appears square from distance. *In fight:* legs generally hidden underneath tail.
Size: *L* 9 in; *W* 19 in.

WHITE-TAILED TROPICBIRD
Phaethon lepturus

The White-tailed Tropicbird is a spectacular seabird. The adults have slender central tail feathers that form long streamers. This species visits Florida's offshore waters from April to September, primarily off the Keys or the southern Atlantic Coast. The White-tailed Tropicbird feeds primarily on flying fish and squid, which are captured during shallow dives. It nests on vertical cliffs on tropical or subtropical islands.

White-tailed Tropicbird

ID: ternlike aerial seabird; white body; long, white central tail feathers; black marking on upperwing; yellowish bill. *Immature:* delicate black barring on upperparts.
Size: *L* 11–15 in (body only), 32 in (including tail); *W* 3 ft.

RED-FOOTED BOOBY
Sula sula

This tropical booby breeds on islands in the Caribbean Sea and tropical oceans. It occurs almost annually at Dry Tortugas National Park from April to September; most observations are of single individuals, typically immatures. The Red-footed Booby has two color morphs, brown and white, and it is the brown morph that occurs in Florida. This pelagic species feeds on squid and fish.

ID: smallest booby; slender and long-winged; white tail; red to orange-red legs and feet; blue-gray bill; facial skin a combination of pink, red, and blue. *Juvenile:* brown tail.
Size: *L* 27–31 in; *W* 5 ft.

Red-footed Booby

SWAINSON'S HAWK
Buteo swainsoni

The Swainson's Hawk undertakes one of the longest migrations of any raptor, traveling between breeding grounds in Canada and wintering areas in South America. A few birds, mostly light-morph immatures, stray eastward to winter in extreme southern Florida, where they feed on grasshoppers and other invertebrates and small mammals.

ID: large hawk; long wings held in slight V-formation. *Light morph:* brown upperparts; white underparts; white face; maroon breast patch; white wing linings contrast with dark flight feathers; finely barred tail. *Juvenile:* brown upperparts; paler head; pale buff underparts with black splotches; black "mustache."
Size: *L* 18 in; *W* 4½ ft.

Swainson's Hawk

CURLEW SANDPIPER
Calidris ferruginea

The Curlew Sandpiper is an Old World species that breeds in northern Siberia and winters in much of the Old World. It is an extremely rare visitor to Florida between late summer and spring. The Curlew Sandpiper is found in fresh or brackish habitats, such as estuaries, impoundments and flooded agricultural fields. It feeds on small mollusks, crustaceans, worms and insects.

Curlew Sandpiper

ID: stocky shorebird; uniformly downcurved bill; black legs; gray upperparts: white underparts; distinct white rump. *Breeding adults:* rich cinnamon overall except white lower belly and undertail.
Size: *L* 8¹/₂ in; *W* 18 in.

RUFF
Philomachus pugnax

The Ruff is an Old World species that migrates regularly through North America. In Florida, it is chiefly seen during fall, mostly at flooded agricultural fields or in coastal estuaries in the southern half of the peninsula. The Ruff forages by picking aquatic prey off the mud's surface or by probing its bill into mud or sand.

Ruff

ID: medium-sized shorebird; plump body; small head; billowy back feathers often flutter in the wind; yellow-green or orange legs; short stocky blackish or yellowish bill. *In flight:* white U-shaped band on dark rump and tail.
Size: *L* 8¹/₂–11 in; *W* 18–21 in.

RED-NECKED PHALAROPE
Phalaropus lobatus

Red-necked Phalaropes migrate between their arctic breeding grounds and their tropical oceanic wintering areas via the Atlantic Coast, passing by Florida during spring and fall. They are usually rare in the state and are typically found offshore. They feed on crustaceans, insects and other invertebrates and small fish that they stir up with their feet. The plumage of the females is brighter than that of the males.

Red-necked Phalarope

ID: delicate shorebird; thin black bill; long, dark legs. *Nonbreeding:* white underparts; blue-gray upperparts with whitish back stripes; black cap; broad dark band from eye to ear.
Size: *L* 7 in; *W* 15 in.

RED PHALAROPE
Phalaropus fulicarius

Red Phalarope

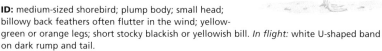

Red Phalaropes breed in the Arctic and winter in Florida, primarily off the Atlantic Coast, usually far offshore. Flocks of hundreds have been observed on occasion. Red Phalaropes feed on crustaceans, insects and other invertebrates and small fish.

ID: *Breeding female:* chestnut neck and underparts; white face; black on crown and around base of bill; stout yellow bill with black tip. *Breeding male:* colors muted. *Nonbreeding:* white head, neck and underparts; gray upperparts; black bill; black mark extending from eye to ear.
Size: *L* 8–9 in; *W* 14–16 in.

FRANKLIN'S GULL
Larus pipixcan

Franklin's Gull

The Franklin's Gull breeds in south-central Canada and the northwestern U.S., and it winters primarily along the Pacific Coast of South America. Most observations in Florida have been in the Panhandle between August and November. The Franklin's Gull feeds on insects and small fish.

ID: small gull; dark gray mantle; prominent, broken white eye-ring; white underparts; white tail. *Nonbreeding:* white head; dark patch on side of head; small, black bill. *Immature:* similar to winter adult but tail mostly black with diagnostic white outer feathers.
Size: *L* 13–15 in; *W* 3 ft.

GLAUCOUS GULL
Larus hyperboreus

Glaucous Gull

Glaucous Gulls breed in the Arctic and rarely range south to winter in Florida. In Florida, they are most frequent along the Atlantic Coast, especially the extreme northern portion. Nearly all Glaucous Gulls seen in the state have been immatures, typically in their first winter. These gulls feed or scavenge on a variety of marine life, such as fish or crustaceans.

ID: large, robust gull. *Immature:* almost entirely white; dark eyes; relatively large, pale, black-tipped bill; varying amounts of brown flecking on the body.
Size: *L* 27 in; *W* 5 ft.

SABINE'S GULL
Xema sabini

The Sabine's Gull (pronounced *SAB-inz*) is an exception among the gulls—it is easy to identify! This gull breeds in the Arctic and winters at sea south of the equator, flying off Florida's Atlantic Coast during late fall. Most observations in the state have been of juveniles. Sabine's Gull feeds on small fish, crustaceans and other marine animals.

ID: small, elegant gull; slightly forked tail; *Juvenile:* brown scalloped upperparts; white head with brown hood; white underparts; white tail with black tip; boldly marked black, brown, and white "M" pattern on upperwings.
Size: *L* 13–14 in; *W* 3 ft.

Sabine's Gull

KEY WEST QUAIL-DOVE
Geotrygon chrysia

According to John James Audubon, Key West Quail-Doves bred rather commonly on Key West in 1832. However, fewer than 25 observations have been made subsequently, mostly along the southern Atlantic Coast or in the Keys, and none of the birds seen has shown any evidence of breeding. Key West Quail-Doves are found throughout the Greater Antilles. They feed on fruit, seeds and snails.

ID: stocky, terrestrial dove; short legs; short tail; prominent white facial stripe; reddish brown upperparts glossed with purple and green sheen.
Size: *L* 12 in; *W* 19 in.

Key West Quail-Dove

BLUE-CROWNED PARAKEET
Aratinga acuticaudata

Blue-crowned Parakeets are native to South America. In Florida, they are found in several cities in the peninsula and the Keys. They are generally uncommon and seem to be most numerous in the Fort Lauderdale area. Like other exotic parrots and parakeets in Florida, Blue-crowned Parakeets nest in cavities in palms or trees. They feed on a variety of fruit, seeds and other plant material; they also visit bird feeders.

Blue-crowned Parakeet

ID: large parakeet; pale green overall; blue frontal portion of head; bold, white, teardrop-shaped orbital ring; pink upper mandible; blackish lower mandible; reddish undertail.
Size: *L* 14½ in; *W* 24 in.

CHESTNUT-FRONTED MACAW
Ara severus

The Chestnut-fronted Macaw is the largest parrot seen in any number in Florida. Perhaps 100 individuals are found at Fort Lauderdale and Miami. All nests discovered in Florida have been built in cavities in royal palm snags. The Chestnut-fronted Macaw feeds on a variety of fruits, nuts and other plant material. This bird is native from Panama to the Amazon River.

ID: very large parrot; long tail; mainly green upperparts; white, unfeathered face with narrow chestnut border; chestnut forehead; blue primaries. *In flight:* reddish underwing linings; long pointed, reddish tail.
Size: *L* 18 in; *W* 30 in.

Chestnut-fronted Macaw

BLACK-BILLED CUCKOO
Coccyzus erythropthalmus

The Black-billed Cuckoo is by far the rarest of Florida's three cuckoo species. It breeds from south-central Canada through northern Alabama, Georgia and South Carolina, and it winters in South America. The Black-billed Cuckoo is found throughout Florida, although strictly as a rare migrant from April to May and from September to October. It rarely if ever vocalizes in Florida, which increases the difficulty of finding it. This cuckoo feeds mostly on caterpillars.

Black-billed Cuckoo

ID: sleek, medium-sized landbird; long tail; gray-brown upperparts; grayish white underparts; reddish orbital ring; all dark, slightly downcurved bill; white-spotted undertail.
Size: *L* 11–13 in; *W* 18 in.

GROOVE-BILLED ANI
Crotophaga sulcirostris

The Groove-billed Ani ranges from southern Texas through northern South America. It is found in Florida annually from October to April, singly or even in small flocks, primarily along the Panhandle coast. The Groove-billed Ani is found in brushy fields or hedgerows, where it feeds on insects, spiders and fruit.

ID: fairly large, disheveled-looking bird; found on or near ground; entirely black with green and purple iridescence; scruffy looking head feathers; large black eyes; large "puffinlike" bill with grooves on upper mandible; short wings; long graduated tail.
Size: *L* 12–14 in; *W* 18½ in.

BUFF-BELLIED HUMMINGBIRD
Amazilia yucatanensis

The Buff-bellied Hummingbird is a newcomer to Florida, having been first observed in 1982. Its native range is from extreme southern Texas to Belize and Guatemala, but it wanders regularly along the Gulf Coast. Several birds are found in Florida in most years, usually in the Panhandle, but as far south as Naples on occasion. In addition to nectar, the Buff-bellied Hummingbird feeds on spiders and insects.

ID: small hummingbird; iridescent green head and breast; golden green back; rusty flanks and outer tail feathers; buffy belly; long, downcurved, red bill with black tip.
Size: *L* 4–4¹/₂ in; *W* 5¹/₂ in.

IVORY-BILLED WOODPECKER
Campephilus principalis

Ivory-billed Woodpecker

The possible discovery of a male Ivory-billed Woodpecker in eastern Arkansas in February 2004, and one or more birds in spring 2005, stunned ornithologists and birders worldwide. The last unequivocal record for this species dates back to 1948, in Louisiana! The Ivory-billed Woodpecker formerly occurred in much of the Southeast, inhabiting old-growth pinelands and cypress swamps. Wholesale logging dramatically reduced its populations. In Florida, the Ivory-billed Woodpecker was a widespread resident of the mainland. The last documented record dates from 1925, with credible reports made through 1955. Unverified sightings continue to be reported.

ID: very large woodpecker; extensive white patches in wings; pale white bill; black throat. *Male:* red crest. *Female:* black crest. *In flight:* fast and direct; upperwings have black leading half and white trailing half; underwings are white divided by widening black center.
Size: *L* 19 in; *W* 33 in.

ASH-THROATED FLYCATCHER
Myiarchus cinerascens

Sightings of Ash-throated Flycatchers have increased dramatically in Florida since the first observation in 1944. The birds breed in the western U.S. and Mexico and winter from the Desert Southwest to Central America. Each fall, several Ash-throated Flycatchers move eastward along the Gulf Coast to winter in Florida. They feed on flying insects and fruit.

ID: large flycatcher; slightly crested head; blackish bill; grayish throat and breast; pale yellow belly and undertail coverts; rufous tail has brown edging that wraps around the tip; *prrrt* call.
Size: *L* 7–8 in; *W* 12 in.

Ash-throated Flycatcher

FORK-TAILED FLYCATCHER
Tyrannus savana

This spectacular species is the only bird native to South America that often strays to North America. When a Fork-tailed Flycatcher shows up in the U.S. or Canada, it is as a result of "mirror migration," in which a bird that intends to fly south flies north instead. In Florida, there have been about 20 observations in the peninsula between April and January, all since 1952. The Fork-tailed Flycatcher feeds on flying insects and fruit.

ID: large flycatcher with extremely long, white-edged, black tail; dark gray upperparts; white underparts; black cap; white collar nearly circles neck.
Size: *L* 10 in (16 in including tail); *W* 14 in.

BELL'S VIREO
Vireo bellii

The Bell's Vireo is a little-known bird in Florida, with only a few reports per year between September and April. It is more active than most other vireos and appears warblerlike as it forages among vegetation. It feeds mostly on insects. Presumably, all Florida observations represent the eastern race *(V. b. bellii)*, which breeds in the Midwest and winters in Central America.

Bell's Vireo

ID: small, secretive bird; olive-green upperparts; dull yellow underparts; small, blunt bill; 1–2 dull white wing bars; narrow whitish eyebrow; whitish eye-ring and lores; dark legs.
Size: *L* 4¹/₂ in; *W* 7 in.

BAHAMA MOCKINGBIRD
Mimus gundlachii

Native to the Bahamas and Cuba, the Bahama Mockingbird behaves more like a thrasher than a mockingbird. It occurs nearly annually in Florida along the southern Atlantic Coast and in the Keys, from about West Palm Beach southward to the Dry Tortugas. All observations have been of single individuals; although two nests were built at Key West, they were never occupied. The Bahama Mockingbird feeds primarily on insects and fruit.

Bahama Mockingbird

ID: large, brown bird; long tail; no white in wings; prominent black streaks on sides and undertail coverts; gray throat with dark "mustache."
Size: *L* 11 in; *W* 14¹/₂ in.

NASHVILLE WARBLER
Vermivora ruficapilla

The Nashville Warbler breeds in much of southern Canada, the northeastern U.S. and along the Pacific Coast. It winters in Central America. In Florida, it is primarily a rare migrant in the Panhandle, but it winters in the peninsula and the Keys as well. The Nashville Warbler is found in forests or brushy fields and feeds primarily on insects.

ID: small, stubby warbler; bright yellow underparts, gray head; conspicuous white eye ring; yellow-green upperparts; inconspicuous white area surrounds base of legs. *Male:* blue-gray head; may show small chestnut crown. *Female:* duller overall.
Size: *L* 4¹/₂–5 in; *W* 7¹/₂ in.

Nashville Warbler

CONNECTICUT WARBLER
Oporornis agilis

The Connecticut Warbler is one of the most sought-after birds that regularly occurs in Florida. In spring, it may show up just about anywhere, usually between May 5 and May 15, but locating this bird takes patience and good fortune because of its secretive habits. The Connecticut Warbler feeds mostly on insects and spiders obtained on or near the ground.

Connecticut Warbler

ID: stocky warbler; dark head and upper breast create hooded appearance; wide-eyed facial expression caused by large eye and bold white eye ring; yellow underparts; olive green upperparts; long undertail coverts cause tail to appear short; pink legs.
Size: *L* 5–6 in; *W* 9 in.

WILSON'S WARBLER
Wilsonia pusilla

The Wilson's Warbler breeds in Alaska, Canada and the western U.S., and it winters throughout Central America. In Florida, it is normally a rare migrant and winter resident, although there was an "invasion" of birds a few winters ago. The Wilson's Warbler forages for insects and spiders and often darts after flying insects. The eastern race is *W. p. pusilla;* the western race, *W. p. pileolata,* may occur occasionally.

Wilson's Warbler

ID: small warbler; bright yellow underparts; yellow-green upperparts; beady black eyes; thin, pointed black bill; orange legs. *Male:* prominent black cap. *Female:* faint cap, if any. **Size:** *L* 4¹/₂–5 in; *W* 7 in.

BANANAQUIT
Coereba flaveola

The Bananaquit is a colorful resident of the West Indies and Central and South America. Every few years, a bird that probably came from the Bahamas is found in Florida, usually along the southern Atlantic Coast between January and May. The Bananaquit is an active little bird that probes flowers for insects and nectar; it also feeds on fruit.

Bananaquit

ID: small, active, colorful land bird; sharp downcurved bill; black back, nape, crown and cheek contrast with bold white eyebrow, white throat and pale yellow and white underparts; small orange patch near base of bill. *In flight:* yellow rump patch; square tail. **Size:** *L* 4¹/₂ in; *W* 7¹/₂ in.

WESTERN SPINDALIS
Spindalis zena

Until recently known as "Stripe-headed Tanager," the Western Spindalis is resident in the West Indies. It strays to Florida almost annually and is usually seen along the southern Atlantic Coast or in the Keys. Two races of the Western Spindalis have been seen in Florida, with most birds being the race from the northern and central Bahamas (*S. z. zena*). This species feeds on figs and other small fruits.

ID: small tanager. *Male:* strikingly patterned; distinctive black and white head stripes; black or greenish back; tawny nape, throat, chest and rump. *Female:* drab olive overall; distinctive white patch at base of primaries. **Size:** *L* 6¹/₂ in; *W* 9¹/₂ in.

CLAY-COLORED SPARROW
Spizella pallida

The Clay-colored Sparrow breeds in southern Canada and the northern U.S., and it winters primarily in Mexico. It is a rare but regular migrant and resident statewide from September to April. It sometimes flocks with Chipping Sparrows, which it closely resembles. This sparrow forages in grassy or brushy fields, where it feeds on seeds and insects; it may also visit bird feeders.

ID: small well-patterned sparrow; unstreaked white underparts; buffy breast; gray nape; light brown cheek edged with darker brown; white eyebrow and "mustache" bordered with brown. **Size:** *L* 5–6 in; *W* 7¹/₂ in.

Clay-colored Sparrow

LARK SPARROW
Chondestes grammacus

The distinctive Lark Sparrow is typically the first sparrow to return to Florida during fall, with the first individuals arriving in August. It is a rare migrant and winter resident statewide. The Lark Sparrow was formerly fairly common in Florida, but the population in the eastern U.S. has declined. This bird feeds on seeds and insects.

ID: robust sparrow; distinctive face pattern created by white throat, eyebrow and crown stripe edged with black on a chestnut head; unstreaked pale breast with dark central spot; rounded, black tail with flashy white corners.
Size: *L* 6 in; *W* 11 in.

Lark Sparrow

LINCOLN'S SPARROW
Melospiza lincolnii

The Lincoln's Sparrow breeds in Alaska, Canada, the New England states and the Rocky Mountains, and it winters primarily in Central America. In Florida, it is a rare migrant and resident statewide from October to April. The Lincoln's Sparrow is found in shrubby marshes or shallowly flooded fields, where it feeds on weed seeds and insects.

ID: small streaked sparrow; buff washed breast; gray face, contrasting with buffy "mustache" and dark cheek; reddish crown with gray central stripe; white throat and belly; streaked gray brown to reddish brown upperparts; narrow white eye ring.
Size: *L* 5½ in; *W* 7½ in.

Lincoln's Sparrow

PURPLE FINCH
Carpodacus purpureus

The Purple Finch breeds across Canada and the northeastern U.S., and it winters throughout the east. In Florida, it is an irruptive resident, primarily of the Panhandle, from November to April. In some years, the Purple Finch is not seen in the state. This bird feeds on weed seeds and some fruit, and it readily visits bird feeders.

ID: stocky finch. *Male:* rose red head and rump; brown back and wings, edged with red; reddish face with distinct brown cheek. *Female:* brown upperparts; heavily streaked overall; bold face pattern marked by prominent brown ear-patch, bold white eyebrow and "mustache."
Size: *L* 5–6 in; *W* 10 in.

Purple Finch

GLOSSARY

accipiter: a forest hawk (genus *Accipiter*), characterized by a long tail and short, rounded wings; feeds mostly on birds.

alcid: member of the family Alcidae, which includes auks, razorbills, guillemots, murres and puffins.

brood: *n.* a family of young from one hatching; *v.* to incubate the eggs.

brood parasite: a bird that lays its eggs in other birds' nests.

buteo: a high-soaring hawk (genus *Buteo*), characterized by broad wings and a short, wide tail; feeds mostly on small mammals and other land animals.

cere: a fleshy area at the base of the bill that contains the nostrils.

clutch: the number of eggs laid by the female at one time.

corvid: a member of the family Corvidae; includes crows, jays, magpies and ravens.

dabbling: a foraging technique used by some ducks, in which the head and neck are submerged but the body and tail remain on the water's surface; dabbling ducks can usually walk easily on land, can take off without running and have brightly colored speculums.

diurnal: most active during the day.

drake: a male duck, goose or swan.

eclipse plumage: a cryptic plumage, similar to that of females, worn by some male ducks in fall when they molt their flight feathers and consequently are unable to fly.

endangered: a species that is facing extirpation or extinction in all or part of its range.

extirpated: a species that no longer exists in the wild in a particular region but occurs elsewhere.

flatwoods: habitat characterized by poorly drained, sandy soils, often with standing water during the rainy season; typical vegetation includes pines, saw palmetto, wax myrtle and wiregrasses.

flushing: when frightened birds explode into flight in response to a disturbance.

flycatching: a feeding behavior in which the bird leaves a perch, snatches an insect in midair and returns to the same perch; also known as "sallying."

gorget: a conspicuous area of the chin, throat and upper breast; is often iridescent.

gular: the throat area under the "chin."

hawking: attempting to capture insects through aerial pursuit.

hen: a female duck, goose or swan; also a female domestic fowl.

irruption: a sporadic mass migration of birds into an unusual range.

kettle: a large concentration of hawks, usually seen during migration.

lek: a place where males (especially grouse and similar species) gather to display for females in spring.

mantle: the area that includes the back and uppersides of the wings.

molt: the periodic shedding and regrowth of worn feathers (often twice a year).

nocturnal: most active at night.

peep: a sandpiper of the *Calidris* genus.

pelagic: inhabiting or occurring on the open ocean.

pishing: a repeated sibilant sound made especially to attract birds.

polyandy: a mating strategy in which one female breeds with many males.

polygyny: a mating strategy in which one male breeds with many females.

precocial: a bird that is relatively well developed at hatching; precocial birds usually have open eyes, extensive down and are fairly mobile.

primaries: the outermost flight feathers of a bird's wing.

raft: a gathering of birds resting on the water.

raptor: a carnivorous bird; includes eagles, hawks, falcons and owls.

riparian: habitat along rivers or streams.

sallying: a feeding behavior in which the bird leaves a perch, snatches an insect in midair and returns to the same perch; also known as "flycatching."

sexual dimorphism: a difference in plumage, size, or other characteristics between males and females of the same species.

special concern: a species that has characteristics that make it particularly sensitive to human activities or disturbance, requires a very specific or unique habitat or whose status is such that it requires careful monitoring.

speculum: a brightly colored patch on the wings of many dabbling ducks.

stage: to gather in one place during migration, usually when birds are flightless or partly flightless during molting.

stoop: a steep dive through the air, usually performed by birds of prey while foraging or during courtship displays.

syrinx: a bird's voice organ.

taxonomy: the system of classification of animals and plants.

thistle feeder: a feeder that dispenses thistle (niger) seed; especially attractive to finches.

threatened: a species likely to become endangered in the near future in all or part of its range.

understory: the shrub or thicket layer beneath a canopy of trees.

vagrant: a bird that has wandered outside of its normal migration range.

vent: the single opening for excretion of uric acid and other wastes and for sexual reproduction; also known as the "cloaca."

wattle: bare folded skin hanging from the lower bill or "chin"; seen on turkeys and domestic fowl.

crown

"eyebrow"/
supercilium

eye line

lore

wing bars

"chin"

greater coverts

throat

rump

breast

tips of primary feathers

flank

tail feathers

belly

undertail coverts

secondary feathers

RECOMMENDED READING

American Birding Association. 2002. *ABA Checklist: Birds of the Continental United States and Canada.* 6th ed. American Birding Association, Colorado Springs, CO. (The 7th edition will be available in 2006).

American Ornithologists' Union. 1998. *Check-list of North American Birds.* 7th ed. American Ornithologists' Union, Washington, D.C. (Updates and a complete checklist are available online at http://www.aou.org/checklist/index.php3).

Choate, E.A. 1985. *The Dictionary of American Bird Names.* Rev. ed. Harvard Common Press, Cambridge, MA.

Clements, J.F. *Birds of the World: A Checklist.* Ibis Publishing, Vista, CA.

Duncan, R.A. 1994. *Bird Migration, Weather, and Fallout, Including the Migrant Traps of Alabama and Northwest Florida.* (Available from R.A. Duncan, 614 Fairpoint Dr., Gulf Breeze, FL 32561.)

Duncan, R.A., and L.R. Duncan. 2000. *The Birds of Escambia, Santa Rosa, and Okaloosa Counties, Florida.* (Available from R.A. Duncan, 614 Fairpoint Dr., Gulf Breeze, FL 32561.)

Ehrlich, P.R., D.S. Dobkin & D. Wheye. 1988. *The Birder's Handbook: A Field Guide to the Natural History of North American Birds.* Simon & Schuster Inc., New York.

Emslie, S.D. 1998. *Avian Community Change, Climate, and Sea-Level Changes in the Plio-Pleistocene of the Florida Peninsula.* Ornithological Monograph No. 50. American Ornithologists' Union, Washington, D.C.

Leahy, C.W. 2004. *The Birdwatcher's Companion to North American Birdlife.* Princeton University Press, Princeton.

National Geographic Society. 2002. *Field Guide to the Birds of North America.* 4th ed. National Geographic Society, Washington, DC. (The 5th edition is due in 2006 or 2007).

National Geographic Society. 2005. *Complete Birds of North America.* National Geographic Society, Washington, D.C.

Pranty, B. 2005. *A Birder's Guide to Florida.* American Birding Assn., Colorado Springs, CO.

Robertson, W.B., Jr., and G.E. Woolfenden. 1992. *Florida Bird Species: An Annotated List.* Special Publication No. 6, Florida Ornithological Society, Gainesville, FL.

Rowan, R., and M. Manetz. 1995. *A Birdwatcher's Guide to Alachua County, Florida.* Published by the authors, Gainesville, FL. (A revised edition is due in 2006).

Sibley, D.A. 2000. *National Audubon Society: The Sibley Guide to Birds.* Alfred A. Knopf, New York.

Sibley, D.A. 2001. *National Audubon Society: The Sibley Guide to Bird Life and Behavior.* Alfred A. Knopf, New York.

Stevenson, H.M., and B.H. Anderson. 1994. *The Birdlife of Florida.* University Press of Florida, Gainesville.

CHECKLIST

The following checklist contains 494 species of birds that have been officially recorded in Florida, plus eight introduced, exotic species. Species are grouped by family and listed in taxonomic order in accordance with the A.O.U. *Check-list of North American Birds* (7th ed.) and its supplements.

The following risk categories are noted: extinct or extirpated (ex), endangered (en), threatened (th) and species of special concern (sc).

We wish to thank the Florida Ornithological Society for providing the information for this checklist.

Waterfowl (Anatidae)
- ❏ Black-bellied Whistling-Duck
- ❏ Fulvous Whistling-Duck
- ❏ Greater White-fronted Goose
- ❏ Snow Goose
- ❏ Ross's Goose
- ❏ Brant
- ❏ Cackling Goose
- ❏ Canada Goose
- ❏ Tundra Swan
- ❏ Muscovy Duck
- ❏ Wood Duck
- ❏ Gadwall
- ❏ Eurasian Wigeon
- ❏ American Wigeon
- ❏ American Black Duck
- ❏ Mallard
- ❏ Mottled Duck
- ❏ Blue-winged Teal
- ❏ Cinnamon Teal
- ❏ Northern Shoveler
- ❏ White-cheeked Pintail
- ❏ Northern Pintail
- ❏ Green-winged Teal
- ❏ Canvasback
- ❏ Redhead
- ❏ Ring-necked Duck
- ❏ Greater Scaup
- ❏ Lesser Scaup
- ❏ King Eider
- ❏ Common Eider
- ❏ Harlequin Duck
- ❏ Surf Scoter
- ❏ White-winged Scoter
- ❏ Black Scoter
- ❏ Long-tailed Duck
- ❏ Bufflehead
- ❏ Common Goldeneye
- ❏ Hooded Merganser
- ❏ Common Merganser
- ❏ Red-breasted Merganser
- ❏ Masked Duck
- ❏ Ruddy Duck

Grouse & Allies (Phasianidae)
- ❏ Wild Turkey

Quails (Odontophoridae)
- ❏ Northern Bobwhite

Loons (Gaviidae)
- ❏ Red-throated Loon
- ❏ Pacific Loon
- ❏ Common Loon

Grebes (Podicipedidae)
- ❏ Least Grebe
- ❏ Pied-billed Grebe
- ❏ Horned Grebe
- ❏ Red-necked Grebe
- ❏ Eared Grebe
- ❏ Western Grebe

Albatrosses (Diomedeidae)
- ❏ Yellow-nosed Albatross

Petrels & Shearwaters (Procellariidae)
- ❏ Black-capped Petrel
- ❏ Cory's Shearwater
- ❏ Greater Shearwater
- ❏ Sooty Shearwater
- ❏ Short-tailed Shearwater
- ❏ Manx Shearwater
- ❏ Audubon's Shearwater

Storm-Petrels (Hydrobatidae)
- ❏ Wilson's Storm-Petrel
- ❏ Leach's Storm-Petrel
- ❏ Band-rumped Storm-Petrel

Tropicbirds (Phaethontidae)
- ❏ White-tailed Tropicbird
- ❏ Red-billed Tropicbird

Boobies & Gannets (Sulidae)
- ❏ Masked Booby
- ❏ Brown Booby
- ❏ Red-footed Booby
- ❏ Northern Gannet

Pelicans (Pelecanidae)
- ❏ American White Pelican
- ❏ Brown Pelican (sc)

Cormorants (Phalacrocoracidae)
- ❏ Double-crested Cormorant
- ❏ Great Cormorant

Darters (Anhingidae)
- ❏ Anhinga

Frigatebirds (Fregatidae)
- ❏ Magnificent Frigatebird

Herons (Ardeidae)
- ❏ American Bittern
- ❏ Least Bittern
- ❏ Great Blue Heron
- ❏ Great Egret
- ❏ Snowy Egret (sc)
- ❏ Little Blue Heron (sc)
- ❏ Tricolored Heron (sc)
- ❏ Reddish Egret (sc)
- ❏ Cattle Egret
- ❏ Green Heron
- ❏ Black-crowned Night-Heron
- ❏ Yellow-crowned Night-Heron

Ibises (Threskiornithidae)
- ❏ White Ibis (sc)
- ❏ Scarlet Ibis
- ❏ Glossy Ibis
- ❏ White-faced Ibis
- ❏ Roseate Spoonbill (sc)

Storks (Ciconiidae)
- ❏ Wood Stork (en)

Vultures (Cathartidae)
- ❏ Black Vulture
- ❏ Turkey Vulture

Flamingos (Phoenicopteridae)
- ❏ Greater Flamingo

Eagles, Kites & Hawks (Accipitridae)
- ❏ Osprey (sc, Keys only)
- ❏ Swallow-tailed Kite
- ❏ White-tailed Kite
- ❏ Snail Kite (en)
- ❏ Mississippi Kite
- ❏ Bald Eagle (th)
- ❏ Northern Harrier
- ❏ Sharp-shinned Hawk
- ❏ Cooper's Hawk
- ❏ Northern Goshawk
- ❏ Red-shouldered Hawk
- ❏ Broad-winged Hawk
- ❏ Short-tailed Hawk
- ❏ Swainson's Hawk
- ❏ Zone-tailed hawk
- ❏ Red-tailed Hawk
- ❏ Ferruginous Hawk
- ❏ Rough-legged Hawk
- ❏ Golden Eagle

Falcons (Falconidae)
- ❏ Crested Caracara (th)
- ❏ Eurasian Kestrel
- ❏ American Kestrel
- ❏ Merlin
- ❏ Peregrine Falcon (en, Arctic race)

Rails (Rallidae)
- ❏ Yellow Rail
- ❏ Black Rail
- ❏ Clapper Rail
- ❏ King Rail
- ❏ Virginia Rail
- ❏ Sora
- ❏ Purple Swamphen
- ❏ Purple Gallinule
- ❏ Common Moorhen
- ❏ American Coot

Limpkins (Aramidae)
- ❏ Limpkin (sc)

Cranes (Gruidae)
- ❏ Sandhill Crane (th, FL ssp. only)
- ❏ Whooping Crane (ex)

Plovers (Charadriidae)
- ❏ Northern Lapwing
- ❏ Black-bellied Plover
- ❏ American Golden-Plover
- ❏ Snowy Plover (th)
- ❏ Wilson's Plover
- ❏ Semipalmated Plover
- ❏ Piping Plover (th)
- ❏ Killdeer
- ❏ Mountain Plover

Oystercatchers (Haematopodidae)
- ❏ American Oystercatcher (sc)

Stilts & Avocets (Recurvirostridae)
- ❏ Black-necked Stilt
- ❏ American Avocet

Sandpipers (Scolopacidae)
- ❏ Greater Yellowlegs
- ❏ Lesser Yellowlegs
- ❏ Solitary Sandpiper
- ❏ Willet
- ❏ Spotted Sandpiper
- ❏ Upland Sandpiper
- ❏ Whimbrel
- ❏ Long-billed Curlew
- ❏ Black-tailed Godwit
- ❏ Hudsonian Godwit
- ❏ Bar-tailed Godwit
- ❏ Marbled Godwit
- ❏ Ruddy Turnstone
- ❏ Surfbird
- ❏ Red Knot
- ❏ Sanderling
- ❏ Semipalmated Sandpiper
- ❏ Western Sandpiper
- ❏ Least Sandpiper
- ❏ White-rumped Sandpiper
- ❏ Baird's Sandpiper
- ❏ Pectoral Sandpiper
- ❏ Sharp-tailed Sandpiper
- ❏ Purple Sandpiper
- ❏ Dunlin
- ❏ Curlew Sandpiper
- ❏ Stilt Sandpiper
- ❏ Buff-breasted Sandpiper
- ❏ Ruff
- ❏ Short-billed Dowitcher
- ❏ Long-billed Dowitcher
- ❏ Common Snipe
- ❏ American Woodcock
- ❏ Wilson's Phalarope
- ❏ Red-necked Phalarope
- ❏ Red Phalarope

Jaegers, Gulls & Terns (Laridae)
- ❏ South Polar Skua
- ❏ Pomarine Jaeger
- ❏ Parasitic Jaeger
- ❏ Long-tailed Jaeger
- ❏ Laughing Gull
- ❏ Franklin's Gull
- ❏ Little Gull
- ❏ Black-headed Gull
- ❏ Bonaparte's Gull
- ❏ Heermann's Gull
- ❏ Gray-hooded Gull
- ❏ Belcher's Gull
- ❏ Ring-billed Gull
- ❏ California Gull
- ❏ Herring Gull
- ❏ Thayer's Gull
- ❏ Iceland Gull
- ❏ Lesser Black-backed Gull
- ❏ Slaty-backed Gull
- ❏ Glaucous Gull
- ❏ Great Black-backed Gull
- ❏ Sabine's Gull
- ❏ Black-legged Kittiwake
- ❏ Gull-billed Tern
- ❏ Caspian Tern
- ❏ Royal Tern
- ❏ Elegant Tern
- ❏ Sandwich Tern
- ❏ Roseate Tern (sc)
- ❏ Common Tern
- ❏ Arctic Tern
- ❏ Forster's Tern
- ❏ Least Tern (th)
- ❏ Bridled Tern
- ❏ Sooty Tern
- ❏ Black Tern
- ❏ Brown Noddy
- ❏ Black Noddy
- ❏ Black Skimmer (sc)

Alcids (Alcidae)
- ❏ Dovekie
- ❏ Thick-billed Murre
- ❏ Razorbill
- ❏ Long-billed Murrelet
- ❏ Atlantic Puffin

Pigeons & Doves (Columbidae)
- ❏ Rock Pigeon
- ❏ Scaly-naped Pigeon
- ❏ White-crowned Pigeon
- ❏ Band-tailed Pigeon
- ❏ European Turtle-Dove
- ❏ Eurasian Collared-Dove
- ❏ White-winged Dove
- ❏ Zenaida Dove
- ❏ Mourning Dove
- ❏ Passenger Pigeon (ex)
- ❏ Common Ground-Dove
- ❏ White-tipped Dove
- ❏ Key West Quail-Dove
- ❏ Ruddy Quail-Dove

Parakeets (Psittacidae)
- ❏ Budgerigar
- ❏ Rose-ringed Parakeet
- ❏ Mitred Parakeet
- ❏ Red-masked Parakeet
- ❏ Black-hooded Parakeet
- ❏ Monk Parakeet
- ❏ White-winged Parakeet
- ❏ Yellow-chevroned Parakeet
- ❏ Red-crowned Parrot
- ❏ Orange-winged Parrot
- ❏ Carolina Parakeet (ex)

Cuckoos & Anis (Cuculidae)
- ❏ Black-billed Cuckoo
- ❏ Yellow-billed Cuckoo
- ❏ Mangrove Cuckoo
- ❏ Smooth-billed Ani
- ❏ Groove-billed Ani

Barn Owls (Tytonidae)
- ❏ Barn Owl

Owls (Strigidae)
- ❏ Flammulated Owl
- ❏ Eastern Screech-Owl
- ❏ Great Horned Owl
- ❏ Snowy Owl
- ❏ Burrowing Owl (sc)
- ❏ Barred Owl
- ❏ Long-eared Owl
- ❏ Short-eared Owl
- ❏ Northern Saw-whet Owl

Nightjars (Caprimulgidae)
- ❏ Lesser Nighthawk
- ❏ Common Nighthawk
- ❏ Antillean Nighthawk
- ❏ Chuck-will's-widow
- ❏ Whip-poor-will

Swifts (Apodidae)
- ❏ White-collared Swift
- ❏ Chimney Swift
- ❏ Vaux's Swift
- ❏ Antillean Palm-Swift

Hummingbirds (Trochilidae)
- ❏ Broad-billed Hummingbird
- ❏ Buff-bellied Hummingbird
- ❏ Bahama Woodstar
- ❏ Ruby-throated Hummingbird
- ❏ Black-chinned Hummingbird
- ❏ Anna's Hummingbird
- ❏ Calliope Hummingbird
- ❏ Broad-tailed Hummingbird
- ❏ Rufous Hummingbird
- ❏ Allen's Hummingbird

Kingfishers (Alcedinidae)
- ❏ Belted Kingfisher

Woodpeckers (Picidae)
- ❏ Red-headed Woodpecker
- ❏ Golden-fronted Woodpecker
- ❏ Red-bellied Woodpecker
- ❏ Yellow-bellied Sapsucker

- ❏ Downy Woodpecker
- ❏ Hairy Woodpecker
- ❏ Red-cockaded Woodpecker (sc)
- ❏ Northern Flicker
- ❏ Pileated Woodpecker
- ❏ Ivory-billed Woodpecker (ex)

Flycatchers (Tyrannidae)
- ❏ Olive-sided Flycatcher
- ❏ Western Wood-Pewee
- ❏ Eastern Wood-Pewee
- ❏ Cuban Pewee
- ❏ Yellow-bellied Flycatcher
- ❏ Acadian Flycatcher
- ❏ Alder Flycatcher
- ❏ Willow Flycatcher
- ❏ Least Flycatcher
- ❏ Black Phoebe
- ❏ Eastern Phoebe
- ❏ Say's Phoebe
- ❏ Vermilion Flycatcher
- ❏ Ash-throated Flycatcher
- ❏ Great Crested Flycatcher
- ❏ Brown-crested Flycatcher
- ❏ La Sagra's Flycatcher
- ❏ Sulphur-bellied Flycatcher
- ❏ Piratic Flycatcher
- ❏ Tropical Kingbird
- ❏ Cassin's Kingbird
- ❏ Western Kingbird
- ❏ Eastern Kingbird
- ❏ Gray Kingbird
- ❏ Scissor-tailed Flycatcher
- ❏ Fork-tailed Flycatcher

Shrikes (Laniidae)
- ❏ Loggerhead Shrike

Vireos (Vireonidae)
- ❏ White-eyed Vireo
- ❏ Thick-billed Vireo
- ❏ Bell's Vireo
- ❏ Yellow-throated Vireo

- ❏ Blue-headed Vireo
- ❏ Warbling Vireo
- ❏ Philadelphia Vireo
- ❏ Red-eyed Vireo
- ❏ Yellow-green Vireo
- ❏ Black-whiskered Vireo

Jays & Crows (Corvidae)
- ❏ Blue Jay
- ❏ Florida Scrub-Jay (th)
- ❏ American Crow
- ❏ Fish Crow

Larks (Alaudidae)
- ❏ Horned Lark

Swallows (Hirundinidae)
- ❏ Purple Martin
- ❏ Cuban Martin
- ❏ Southern Martin
- ❏ Tree Swallow
- ❏ Mangrove Swallow
- ❏ Bahama Swallow
- ❏ Northern Rough-winged Swallow
- ❏ Bank Swallow
- ❏ Cliff Swallow
- ❏ Cave Swallow
- ❏ Barn Swallow

Chickadees & Titmice (Paridae)
- ❏ Carolina Chickadee
- ❏ Tufted Titmouse

Nuthatches (Sittidae)
- ❏ Red-breasted Nuthatch
- ❏ White-breasted Nuthatch
- ❏ Brown-headed Nuthatch

Creepers (Certhiidae)
- ❏ Brown Creeper

Wrens (Troglodytidae)
- ❏ Rock Wren
- ❏ Carolina Wren
- ❏ Bewick's Wren
- ❏ House Wren

- ❏ Winter Wren
- ❏ Sedge Wren
- ❏ Marsh Wren

Bulbuls (Pycnonotidae)
- ❏ Red-whiskered Bulbul

Kinglets (Regulidae)
- ❏ Golden-crowned Kinglet
- ❏ Ruby-crowned Kinglet

Gnatcatchers (Sylviidae)
- ❏ Blue-gray Gnatcatcher

Thrushes (Turdidae)
- ❏ Northern Wheatear
- ❏ Eastern Bluebird
- ❏ Mountain Bluebird
- ❏ Veery
- ❏ Gray-cheeked Thrush
- ❏ Bicknell's Thrush
- ❏ Swainson's Thrush
- ❏ Hermit Thrush
- ❏ Wood Thrush
- ❏ American Robin
- ❏ Varied Thrush

Mockingbirds & Thrashers (Mimidae)
- ❏ Gray Catbird
- ❏ Northern Mockingbird
- ❏ Bahama Mockingbird
- ❏ Sage Thrasher
- ❏ Brown Thrasher
- ❏ Curve-billed Thrasher

Starlings (Sturnidae)
- ❏ European Starling

Pipits (Motacillidae)
- ❏ American Pipit
- ❏ Sprague's Pipit

Waxwings (Bombycillidae)
- ❏ Cedar Waxwing

Wood-Warblers (Parulidae)
- ❏ Bachman's Warbler (ex)

❏ Blue-winged Warbler
❏ Golden-winged Warbler
❏ Tennessee Warbler
❏ Orange-crowned Warbler
❏ Nashville Warbler
❏ Northern Parula
❏ Yellow Warbler
❏ Chestnut-sided Warbler
❏ Magnolia Warbler
❏ Cape May Warbler
❏ Black-throated Blue Warbler
❏ Yellow-rumped Warbler
❏ Black-throated Gray Warbler
❏ Golden-cheeked Warbler
❏ Black-throated Green Warbler
❏ Townsend's Warbler
❏ Blackburnian Warbler
❏ Yellow-throated Warbler
❏ Pine Warbler
❏ Kirtland's Warbler
❏ Prairie Warbler
❏ Palm Warbler
❏ Bay-breasted Warbler
❏ Blackpoll Warbler
❏ Cerulean Warbler
❏ Black-and-white Warbler
❏ American Redstart
❏ Prothonotary Warbler
❏ Worm-eating Warbler
❏ Swainson's Warbler
❏ Ovenbird
❏ Northern Waterthrush
❏ Louisiana Waterthrush
❏ Kentucky Warbler
❏ Connecticut Warbler
❏ Mourning Warbler
❏ MacGillivray's Warbler
❏ Common Yellowthroat
❏ Hooded Warbler
❏ Wilson's Warbler
❏ Canada Warbler
❏ Yellow-breasted Chat

Bananaquits (Coerebidae)
❏ Bananaquit

Tanagers (Thraupidae)
❏ Summer Tanager
❏ Scarlet Tanager
❏ Western Tanager
❏ Western Spindalis

Sparrows & Allies (Emberizidae)
❏ Yellow-faced Grassquit
❏ Black-faced Grassquit
❏ Green-tailed Towhee
❏ Spotted Towhee
❏ Eastern Towhee
❏ Bachman's Sparrow
❏ American Tree Sparrow
❏ Chipping Sparrow
❏ Clay-colored Sparrow
❏ Field Sparrow
❏ Vesper Sparrow
❏ Lark Sparrow
❏ Black-throated Sparrow
❏ Lark Bunting
❏ Savannah Sparrow
❏ Grasshopper Sparrow (en, FL ssp. only)
❏ Henslow's Sparrow
❏ Le Conte's Sparrow
❏ Nelson's Sharp-tailed Sparrow
❏ Saltmarsh Sharp-tailed Sparrow
❏ Seaside Sparrow (en, several ssp.)
❏ Fox Sparrow
❏ Song Sparrow
❏ Lincoln's Sparrow
❏ Swamp Sparrow
❏ White-throated Sparrow
❏ Harris's Sparrow
❏ White-crowned Sparrow
❏ Golden-crowned Sparrow
❏ Dark-eyed Junco
❏ Lapland Longspur

❏ Chestnut-collared Longspur
❏ Snow Bunting

Grosbeaks & Buntings (Cardinalidae)
❏ Northern Cardinal
❏ Rose-breasted Grosbeak
❏ Black-headed Grosbeak
❏ Blue Grosbeak
❏ Lazuli Bunting
❏ Indigo Bunting
❏ Painted Bunting
❏ Dickcissel

Blackbirds & Orioles (Icteridae)
❏ Bobolink
❏ Red-winged Blackbird
❏ Tawny-shouldered Blackbird
❏ Eastern Meadowlark
❏ Western Meadowlark
❏ Yellow-headed Blackbird
❏ Rusty Blackbird
❏ Brewer's Blackbird
❏ Common Grackle
❏ Boat-tailed Grackle
❏ Shiny Cowbird
❏ Bronzed Cowbird
❏ Brown-headed Cowbird
❏ Orchard Oriole
❏ Hooded Oriole
❏ Bullock's Oriole
❏ Spot-breasted Oriole
❏ Baltimore Oriole

Finches (Fringillidae)
❏ Purple Finch
❏ House Finch
❏ Red Crossbill
❏ Pine Siskin
❏ American Goldfinch
❏ Evening Grosbeak

Old World Sparrows (Passeridae)
❏ House Sparrow

INDEX OF SCIENTIFIC NAMES

This index references only primary species and those found in the appendix and does not include subspecies.

Columbina passerina, 190
Contopus virens, 226
Coragyps atratus, 95
Corvus
  brachyrhynchos, 246
  ossifragus, 247
Crotophaga
  ani, 200
  sulcirostris, 363
Cuculus canorus, 198
Cyanocitta cristata, 244
Cygnus columbianus, 358

D

Dendrocygna
  autumnalis, 36
  bicolor, 37
Dendroica
  caerulescens, 294
  castanea, 302
  cerulea, 304
  coronata, 295
  discolor, 300
  dominica, 298
  fusca, 297
  magnolia, 292
  palmarum, 301
  pensylvanica, 291
  petechia, 290
  pinus, 299
  striata, 303
  tigrina, 293
  virens, 296
Dolichonyx oryzivorus, 341
Dryocopus pileatus, 224
Dumetella carolinensis, 277

E

Egretta
  caerulea, 84
  rufescens, 86
  thula, 83
  tricolor, 85
Elanoides forficatus, 99
Elanus leucurus, 100
Empidonax
  minimus, 228
  virescens, 227
Erithacus rubecula, 276
Eudocimus albus, 91
Euphagus cyanocephalus, 345

F

Falco
  columbarius, 113
  peregrinus, 114
  sparverius, 112
Fregata magnificens, 78
Fulica americana, 123

G

Gallinago delicata, 160
Gallinula chloropus, 122
Gavia
  immer, 65
  stellata, 64
Geothlypis trichas, 314
Geotrygon chrysia, 362
Gracula religiosa, 282
Grus
  americana, 126
  canadensis, 125

H

Haematopus palliatus, 134
Haliaeetus leucocephalus, 103
Helmitheros vermivora, 308
Himantopus mexicanus, 135
Hirundo rustica, 254
Hylocichla mustelina, 275

I, J

Icteria virens, 316
Icterus
  bullockii, 353
  galbula, 353
  pectoralis, 352
  spurius, 351
Ictinia mississippiensis, 102
Ixobrychus exilis, 80
Junco hyemalis, 334

L

Lanius ludovicianus, 237
Larus
  argentatus, 168
  atricilla, 165
  delawarensis, 167
  fuscus, 169
  hyperboreus, 362
  marinus, 170
  philadelphia, 166
  pipixcan, 362
Laterallus jamaicensis, 115
Limnodromus
  griseus, 158
  scolopaceus, 159
Limnothlypis swainsonii, 309
Limosa fedoa, 145
Lophodytes cucullatus, 59

M

Megascops asio, 202
Melanerpes
  carolinus, 218
  erythrocephalus, 217
Melanitta
  nigra, 56
  perspicillata, 359
Meleagris gallopavo, 62
Melopsittacus undulatus, 191
Melospiza
  georgiana, 331
  lincolnii, 367
  melodia, 330
Mergus serrator, 60
Mimus
  gundlachii, 365
  polyglottos, 278
Mniotilta varia, 305
Molothrus
  aeneus, 349
  ater, 350
  bonariensis, 348
Morus bassanus, 73
Mycteria americana, 94
Myiarchus
  cinerascens, 364
  crinitus, 231
  sagrae, 232
Myiopsitta monachus, 192

N

Nandayus nenday, 193
Numenius
  americanus, 144
  phaeopus, 143
Nyctanassa violacea, 90
Nycticorax nycticorax, 89

O

Oceanites oceanicus, 70
Oceanodroma castro, 360
Oporornis
  agilis, 365
  formosus, 313
Oxyura jamaicensis, 61

P, Q

Pandion haliaetus, 98
Parula americana, 289
Passer domesticus, 357
Passerculus sandwichensis,
  324

INDEX OF COMMON NAMES

Page numbers in **boldface** type refer to the primary, illustrated species accounts.

ABOUT THE AUTHORS

Bill Pranty is a native of Pittsburgh, Pennsylvania, and has lived in Florida since 1978. He is extensively involved in documenting the status and distribution of Florida's birdlife, from writing peer-reviewed papers to compiling field observations for *Florida Field Naturalist* and *North American Birds* and editing all of the state's Christmas bird counts. Bill is a member and the current chairman of the American Birding Association Checklist Committee, which is responsible for compiling an official list of the birds that have occurred in Alaska, Canada and the Lower 48 states. He is the author of *A Birder's Guide to Florida*, published by the American Birding Association in 2005, and has contributed to the National Geographic Society *Complete Birds of North America* (2005). Bill is a technical reviewer for the magazine *Birding* and the journal *North American Birds*. During the preparation of this book, he studied a population of Florida Scrub-Jays at Lake Wales Ridge State Forest in central Florida for Archbold Biological Station, a private ecological research facility. Since 1976, Bill has participated in 132 Christmas bird counts, all but one of these in central Florida.

Kurt A. Radamaker has been interested in nature, and especially birds, his entire life. He grew up in Southern California, where he began birding at the age of eight. At 15, he completed the Cornell Laboratory of Ornithology's seminars in ornithology, and went on his first Audubon Christmas bird count at 16. His obsession with birding continued, and in the early 1990s, he taught ornithology for the University of La Verne in Southern California. While at the university, he founded *Euphonia*, a scientific journal of the birds of Mexico. As editor of *Euphonia*, Kurt became captivated with Mexico and its birds and has been traveling there regularly ever since. In the mid-1990s, he began regular research trips to Baja California, Mexico, and in the early part of the millennium, much of his Baja California field notes were published in the ABA monograph, *Birds of Baja California: Status, Distribution and Taxonomy*. In 1998, he moved to Florida, where he and author Bill Pranty met. Bill and Kurt have co-authored a couple of research papers and developed a lasting friendship. In 2001, Kurt returned west to Arizona, where he is a founding member of the Arizona Field Ornithologists' Society and member of the Arizona Bird Records Committee. Kurt and his wife, Cindy, regularly lead birding trips for Arizona State Parks and the Maricopa Audubon Society.

Gregory Kennedy has been an active naturalist since he was very young. He is the author of many books on natural history and has also produced film and television shows on environmental issues and indigenous concerns in Southeast Asia, New Guinea, South and Central America, the High Arctic and elsewhere. He has also been involved in numerous research projects around the world ranging from studies in the upper canopy of tropical and temperate rainforests to deepwater marine investigations.